The Origins of the Second World War Reconsidered

Second Edition

The Origins of the Second World War Reconsidered

Second Edition

A.J.P. Taylor and the Historians

Edited by Gordon Martel

Routledge
Taylor & Francis Group

LONDON AND NEW YORK

First published 1996
by Unwin Hyman Ltd

Fifth impression 1990

Sixth impression published in 1992
by Routledge
2 Park Square, Milton Park, Abingdon, Oxon, OX14 4RN

Second edition 1999
Simultaneously published in the USA and Canada
by Routledge
270 Madison Avenue, New York, NY 10016

Reprinted 2003, 2006 (twice)

Routledge is an imprint of the Taylor & Francis Group, an informa business

© 1986, 1999 in selection and editorial matter, Gordon Martel;
individual contributions, individual contributors

Typeset in Baskerville by Routledge
Printed and bound in Great Britain by
MPG Books Ltd, Bodmin, Cornwall

British Library Cataloguing in Publication Data
A catalogue record for this book is available from the British Library

Library of Congress Cataloging in Publication Data
The origins of the Second World War reconsidered/
edited by Gordon Martel–2nd ed.
Includes bibliographical references and index.
1. World War, 1939–1945–Causes. I. Martel, Gordon.
D741.0745   1999
940.53'11–dc21   99-18880
CIP

ISBN 10 0–415–16324–2 (hbk)
ISBN 10 0–415–16325–0 (pbk)
ISBN 13 978–0–415–16324–8 (hbk)
ISBN 13 978–0–415–16325–5 (pbk)

For Valerie and Jane

Contents

Contributors

Alan Cassels is Professor of History Emeritus at McMaster University. His books include: *Mussolini's Early Diplomacy; Fascism; Fascist Italy* and, most recently, *Ideology and International Relations in the Modern World.*

Sean Greenwood is Professor of Modern History and Head of Department at Canterbury Christ Church University College. He has published on various aspects of British foreign policy from the 1930s to the present day and has recently completed a book on Britain and the Cold War.

Mary Habeck is Assistant Professor of History at Yale University. Her earliest work was on Soviet and German military doctrines during the inter-war period. She is currently finishing a manuscript on Soviet participation in the Spanish Civil War.

Talbot Imlay is currently a postdoctoral fellow at the John M. Olin Institute for Strategic Studies at Harvard University, a position he assumed following the completion of his doctorate at Yale University.

Paul Kennedy is the Dilworth Professor of History and Director of International Security Studies at Yale University. He is the author and editor of numerous books on British, European and international history, most notably *The Rise and Fall of the Great Powers.*

Sally Marks is the author of *The Illusion of Peace: International Relations in Europe 1918–33; Innocent Abroad: Belgium at the Paris Peace Conference of 1919* and the forthcoming *The Ebbing of European Pre-eminence: An International History, 1914–45.*

Gordon Martel is Professor and Chair of History at the University of Northern British Columbia. His books include: *Imperial Diplomacy; The Origins of the First World War* and the forthcoming *Appeasement Diary: A.L. Kennedy, The Times and the Foreign Office.* He edits 'The New International History' series (Routledge) and 'Seminar Studies in History' (Longman).

Richard Overy is Professor of Modern History at King's College, London. He has written extensively on the Third Reich and the coming of war in 1939.

His books include: *Why the Allies Won; Russia's War and The Road to War*. He is currently preparing the *Oxford History of the Second World War* and a volume of pre-trial interrogations of Nazi leaders in 1945.

Stephen A. Schuker is William W. Corcoran Professor History at the University of Virginia. His books include: *The End of French Predominance in Europe* (1976) and *American Reparations to Germany, 1919–1933* (1988). He has edited *Die westeuropaeische Sicherheit und die deutsch–franzoesischen Beziehungen, 1914–1963* (1999) and is currently completing *Watch on the Rhine: The Rhineland and the Security of the West, 1914–50*.

Brian R. Sullivan has taught at Yale and the Naval War College, and done strategic analysis at National Defense University. He specializes in the history of Fascist Italy and U.S. national security affairs and has co-authored *Il Duce's Other Woman*, a biography of Margherita Sarfatti. His current projects include editing works by the naval theorist Romeo Bernotti and researching Mussolini's intelligence agencies.

Teddy J. Uldricks is Professor of History at the University of North Carolina at Asheville. He is the author of *Diplomacy and Ideology: The Origins of Soviet Foreign Relations*, and is currently completing *Russia and the World in the Twentieth Century*.

Louise Young is Assistant Professor of Japanese History at New York University. She is the author of *Japan's Total Empire: Manchuria and the Culture of Wartime Imperialism* (1998), which received the John K. Fairbank prize from the American Historical Association. She is currently engaged in research on urban modernism in Japan.

Robert J. Young is Professor of History at the University of Winnipeg. His books include: *Power and Pleasure: Louis Barthou and the Third French Republic*; *France and the origins of the Second World War*, and *Under Siege: Portraits of Civilian Life in France during World War I*.

Preface to the Second Edition

Books have their own histories: they have births (usually painful), lives (sometimes long, sometimes short), and deaths (often slow). When, in 1983, I first had the idea for this one, it proved difficult to bring to fruition. Publishers were wary of the project, suggesting that it did not seem "marketable." Fifteen years, thousands of copies and six printings have shown that the people who commission books may be no better at forecasting the future than are those who propose them. So I begin by paying homage once again to Jane Harris-Matthews, then of Allen & Unwin, who was willing to take a chance on the idea – and on its proponent who, at the time, was only beginning his editorial career.

During its life to date this book has passed from Allen & Unwin to Unwin Hyman, then to HarperCollins, and now, perhaps finally, to Routledge. Its editor at Routledge, Heather McCallum, believing that it has a future still, asked me in 1996 if I would be prepared to prolong its life by producing a new edition. Uncertain as to whether the book's life deserved to be thus extended – and also of my own willingness to revitalize it – I consulted colleagues who had been using the book in their teaching. Somewhat to my surprise, they were unanimous in their opinion that a new edition would be helpful, and they were forthcoming with suggestions about how it might be made more useful. In producing this new edition, I have, in so far as it was possible, been guided by their advice. Unfortunately, it has not been possible to include in the second edition revised versions of all of the essays that appeared in the first. The fact that the contributions of Norman Rich, Piotr Wandycz, Lloyd Gardner, Akira Iriye, and Edward Ingram do not appear in revised form here is certainly no reflection on the quality of their essays. Students and scholars who wish to consult these authors may do so via the internet (at: http:// quarles.unbc.ca/history/hist.html).

The first edition was produced without the use of computers (or e-mail) and, with almost everyone now using them, I thought it would be helpful to contributors to work on a computerized version of their original essay. This work was willingly undertaken by my wife Valerie, who, in spite of her qualms about the computer age (which, she argues, means mainly that I am now able to work *all* of the time, *anywhere*), did the job with her customary dedication and good humor. So the renascence of this book owes much to her. The first edition, decided upon during a splendid meal in San Francisco attended by Valerie and hosted by Jane, would not have seen the light of day without the support and the encouragement of these two wonderful women, and it is to them that I dedicate this new edition.

1   The revisionist as moralist

A. J. P. Taylor and the lessons of European history

Gordon Martel

Images of the 1930s continue to flash past us: Hitler's moustache and Chamberlain's umbrella are still instantly recognizable; Nazi war criminals still make the front pages; novels and films warning of a new menace emanating from Brazil or Bavaria can be almost assured of popular success. The Second World War, its symbols and personalities, continue to grip the modern imagination. Thus the war – and its origins – functions today as a mental and moral shorthand: anyone wishing to evoke an image of wickedness personified need only mention "Hitler"; for stupidity, blundering or cowardice, substitute "Chamberlain." But political rhetoric extends the boundary beyond personality. The systems we condemn are "totalitarian" or "dictatorships" (frequently both), and we must never be guilty of "appeasement" in our relations with their leaders. Politicians find these words useful because ordinary citizens agree that the Second World War was caused by Hitler and his totalitarian dictatorship, and that it might have been prevented had it not been for the policy of appeasement that served only to whet his appetite.

Anyone who doubts that these simple assumptions are widely, almost universally, subscribed to is invited to witness the effect of setting loose a class of undergraduates on A. J. P. Taylor's *The Origins of the Second World War*. There the effect is electric: they are stunned to read that Hitler neither planned nor caused the war, that appeasement was not necessarily a bad thing, that new ideologies such as fascism and communism were much less significant than the aims and ambitions of statesmen, typical of all regimes, at all times. If the student is converted to the Taylor view, war is almost certain to break out on the home front; the young may be prepared to embrace new ideas, even if only as a temporary fashion, but their parents are more likely to regard them as treasonable. Two generations after its publication *Origins* has not lost its power to provoke.

When the book first appeared in 1961 it created a storm. Professional historians attacked Taylor for almost every imaginable sin: his evidence was scanty and unreliable; he distorted documents by means of selective citation and dismissed those he disliked by claiming they did not count; his logic was faulty; he contradicted himself repeatedly and drew conclusions at variance with his own evidence. Nor was the storm confined to the citadels of academia – to scholarly journals, college corridors, senior common-rooms and faculty clubs. The debate was carried on in public – in newspapers, on television and radio. Questions were asked in Parliament. Lifelong friendships were dissolved. Careers were made and unmade. Taylor was soon the best-known historian in Britain: his autobiography was a best-seller; an entire issue of *The Journal of Modern History* was devoted to him; he has been honored with three *Festschriften*, and any book with his name on it has been assured of popular success. One eminent historian, when asked to contribute an essay to the first edition of this book, declined on the ground that Taylor had no right to hold the first-mortgage on the subject of the origins of the Second World War. He may not have the right, but hold the mortgage he does. What other 38-year-old book on the war's origins continues not only to be available in paperback but can be seen to be stacked high in university bookstores throughout the English-speaking world? Teachers wishing to shake students out of their lethargy do well to introduce them to A. J. P. Taylor.

But the great man is now dead and most of the furor that emanated from his book has gone with him. Nevertheless, interest in him remains strong, the debate on the war's origins continues and the book stimulates controversy still. Book-length studies have now appeared in the form of Robert Cole's *A. J. P. Taylor: The Traitor Within the Gates* and Adam Sisman's *A. J. P. Taylor: A Biography*, the scholarship and insights of both of which will be surpassed by Kathy Burk's in her forthcoming biography.[1] New surveys, especially Philip Bell's *Origins of the Second World War in Europe* and Akira Iriye's *The Origins of the Second World War in Asia and the Pacific*, but also Andrew Crozier's *The Causes of the Second World War* and Richard Overy's *The Origins of the Second World War*, have certainly replaced Taylor's as books in which teachers can have confidence when introducing students to the subject. But those very characteristics that make these newer works more reliable make them less exciting, less challenging and – ultimately – less enduring. Less careful, less balanced, more opinionated and more provocative, Taylor's book will remain in print long after his successors' have ceased publication. It may be, as some argue, that he will continue to be read largely as "an historical curiosity," or mainly by graduate students exploring the historiography of the subject, or by general readers looking for someone who can be read for amusement and entertainment. But read Taylor certainly will be.

The first question to be asked is why the book caused such a storm when it appeared. The answer is that Taylor challenged an interpretation of the war's origins that had until 1961 satisfied almost everyone in the postwar world, and because he conducted his challenge in flamboyant prose with such scathing wit. Before Taylor launched his attack, the only point being debated was whether the appeasers were foolish cowards who allowed themselves to be duped by Hitler, or cunning capitalists who hoped to use Hitler to crush communism in the Soviet Union. Blaming the war on Hitler certainly suited the Germans: with the Nazis either dead or in hiding, they could claim to be blameless and to have a claim to a respectable role in the new democratic alliance. This was equally satisfactory in the west, where one might have expected an Orwellian unease to emerge when the enemy was transformed into ally and the ally into enemy – but the west now claimed to be united against "totalitarianism" rather than against states or nations. The Second World War had been fought for a great and noble principle, and this principle endured into the era of the Cold War. The enemy had merely changed location: his ambitions and tactics remained the same.

Taylor would have none of this. The war had not been fought over great principles, nor had Hitler planned its outbreak from the start. Taylor thereby challenged two of the most confident assumptions of the 1950s. While others saw in Hitler a demonic genius who was able to pull the strings of European politics so masterfully because he had a carefully mapped out plan, Taylor saw only an ordinary politician who responded to events as they occurred, who asked only how he might benefit from them. Where others saw laid down in *Mein Kampf* a blueprint, Taylor heard the confused babble of beer-hall chatter. Where others saw a timetable for war in such documents as the "Hossbach memorandum," Taylor saw the petty intrigue and political machinations typical of the Nazi system of government. If Taylor was right – if Hitler had not in fact carefully plotted his route to world dominion well in advance and then followed the route step-by-step – this could only raise new, and possibly awkward, questions. Some believed that Taylor was whitewashing Hitler, absolving him of guilt.

But Taylor did not stop with Hitler. He took a contrary view of almost every significant figure of the interwar period: Chamberlain was neither a bungler nor a coward, but a highly skilled politician who enjoyed the overwhelming support of his party and his nation; Stresemann, the "good German" but for whose death Germany might have followed a peaceful path, turns out to have shared Hitler's dreams of dominating eastern Europe; Roosevelt's economic policies were difficult to distinguish from Hitler's; Stalin turns out to have been Europe's most conservative statesman, proposing to uphold the peace settlement of 1919 and wishing the League of Nations to be an effective international institution, rather than a monstrous ideologue plotting world revolution. If readers were not offended by Taylor's revisionist sketch of Hitler himself, they were almost certain to find offense elsewhere in his book.

If readers discovered heroes and villains being turned upside down in *Origins*, they also found states being turned inside-out. Anyone who believed in a wicked Russia, a noble Poland, a beleaguered France, an efficient Italy or a nationalistic Czechoslovakia would have their assumptions rudely challenged. Russia never did more than ask to be accepted as a legitimate sovereign state; Poland – corrupt and elitist as it was – was not a state such that one could be proud of having fought to save it; France had consistently aimed to draw in the new states of central and eastern Europe to fight on its behalf – while never intending to assist them in any way; Italy was not the powerful representative of a dynamic new political system, but the foolish plaything of a blustering and blundering egomaniac; Czechoslovakia, even though democratic, "had a canker at her heart," its large German minority alienated from the Czech-dominated centralized state.[2]

Throughout *Origins* Taylor demonstrated an uncanny ability to see parallels and ironies that were certain to make readers squirm in their chairs. The intervention of the League of Nations in the Abyssinian crisis resulted in Haile Selassie losing all of his country instead of only half. Was Ramsay MacDonald not fittingly described as a "renegade socialist"? Was it better to be an abandoned Czech or a saved Pole? Did Munich not represent much that was best in British public life? There is hardly a page in the book that fails to unsettle complacent beliefs or challenge conventional wisdom, and this is always done crisply, with verve and frequently with biting sarcasm. Taylor's wit could cut deep. Samuel Hoare, he said, was "as able intellectually as any British foreign secretary of the twentieth century – perhaps not a very high standard" (p. 122). What was the response of the Slovaks to Hitler's destruction of their independence? They were to provide him with a steady and reliable satellite throughout the war (p. 240). When Britain and France declared war on Germany in September 1939, they went to war "for that part of the peace settlement which they had long regarded as least defensible" (p. 335).

The embittered irony characteristic of his approach was certain to arouse an impassioned response because Taylor treated the subject in an old-fashioned way. Instead of treating statesmen and their policies as the products of deep-rooted impersonal forces, he placed them at the center of the story. Popular audiences always respond more enthusiastically to history that concentrates on people, and those who read *Origins* when it appeared still had vivid impressions of, and strong feelings toward, the people about whom Taylor was writing. Those who had fought Hitler's Germany, seen the newsreels of Chamberlain's triumphant return from Munich, and argued over Franco's crusade in Spain, were in their 40s and 50s when the book appeared. Such proximity would have counted for less had Taylor been more concerned with impersonal forces – had he, for instance, treated the diplomatic crises of the 1930s as reverberations of the economic collapse of 1929 – but this he steadfastly refused to do. "There was no reason why it should cause international tension. In most countries the Depression led to a turning away from international affairs" (p. 89). He put the actors of the interwar years back on the stage, and shone the spotlight on ambitions, schemes, and characteristics that many preferred to forget. It was depressing to be reminded that Churchill had admired Mussolini and favored Franco; that Chamberlain's desire to avoid intervention in Europe followed the liberal traditions established by Cobden, Bright, and Gladstone; that Roosevelt turned his back on Europe; and that no western statesman showed any real concern about the plight of the Jews in Germany prior to the outbreak of the war.

Taylor struck a blow against the complacency of the 1950s. In his account the origins of the war ceased to be a simple morality play in which the weak-kneed failed to face up to the evil. His account really was old-fashioned. The interests of states and the ambitions of statesmen were treated as if there had been no break with the nineteenth century, as if ideology and technology were of trivial importance compared to the basic principles of modern statecraft first enunciated by Machiavelli four centuries earlier. The lines of continuity to be found in Germany's ambitious designs to dominate central and eastern Europe, in Russia's fears of invasion from the west, in Italy's dream of a neo-Roman Mediterranean, and in the traditions of British foreign policy, were of vastly greater significance in Taylor's treatment than were swastikas and fasces, than Marx and Nietzsche. It is ironic that this traditionalism was, in the world of 1961, a form of rebellion.

Eschewing underlying forces and political philosophies, Taylor restored drama to the events leading up to the war. He told his story in narrative form, but readers who followed the story would not find themselves, in the Churchillian phrase, being led "step-by-step" into the abyss. No – the events were not neat and simple but complicated, ragged, contradictory, and ironic. Few things were what they seemed: the Reichstag fire should be attributed not to clever Nazi plotting but to a Dutch arsonist (and the Nazis genuinely believed it to have been the communist intrigue they proclaimed it); the result – "odd and unforeseen" – of the Locarno treaties was to prevent military co-operation between Britain and France; the *Anschluss* between Germany and Austria was not the result of a carefully planned invasion – 70 percent of German vehicles broke down on their journey to the frontier, while 99 percent of the people of united Germany and Austria voted in favor of the union, "a genuine reflection of German feeling"; when the war itself broke out it was not to be regarded as a conflict between totalitarian dictatorship and democracy but as "the war between the three Western Powers over the settlement of Versailles" (p. 336).

The events leading to war were not what they appeared to be, nor were they brought about by those who appeared to be in control. In Taylor's presentation, instead of Hitler and Mussolini cleverly pulling all the strings that made the others move, it was the weak, the second-rate, and the forgotten who made things happen. The puppets and their masters had changed places. Papen and Hindenburg "thrust" power on Hitler by imploring him to become chancellor; he did not have to "seize" control (p. 101). Schuschnigg brought about the collapse of Austria when his police raided the headquarters of the Austrian Nazis – there was no "planned aggression only hasty improvisation" – Hitler was taken by surprise and Papen "started the ball rolling" (p.181). Blum and Baldwin, not Hitler and Mussolini, decided the outcome of the Spanish Civil War; French radicals "objected to aiding an allegedly Communist cause abroad" (pp. 157–8). Benes chose "to screw up the tension" in Czechoslovakia, negotiating with the Sudeten Germans in order to force them openly into demanding Czechoslovakia's dissolution and thereby compelling the western powers to assert themselves against such an extreme and unfavorable solution (pp. 192–3). Throughout *Origins* readers are given the distinct impression that no one was in control, that Hitler and Mussolini did no more than respond to the movements of others – to the agitations of Sudeten Germans, to the outbreak of Civil War in Spain, to the Slovakian demands for autonomy. Meanwhile, "the statesmen of western Europe moved in a moral and intellectual fog" (p. 141).

Finally, when men do act, seize the initiative, and attempt to control events, the results they get are seldom what they bargained for. The Lytton Commission, which condemned Japan for resorting to force in Manchuria and provoked it into withdrawing from the League of Nations, had actually been set up through an initiative of the Japanese. Franco rewarded the assistance of Germany and Italy by declaring his neutrality during the Munich crisis and maintaining it throughout the Second World War. When Hitler, following Munich, denounced the "warmongers" – Churchill, Eden, and Duff Cooper – "in the belief that this would lead to an explosion against them," he produced the opposite effect. When Chamberlain signed the alliance with Poland in 1939 he had, "without design," made Danzig the decisive question and thereby took a stand "on peculiarly weak ground" (pp. 264–5). According to Taylor, even when men know what they want and believe they see their way clear to getting it, the consequences are rarely foreseen and often turn out to be the opposite of what was intended.

The reason why *The Origins of the Second World War* proved so explosive is that Taylor's revisionism went far beyond the usual boundaries erected by his profession. Had he been content to create a more "balanced" view – by pointing out those occasions on which Hitler followed no timetable, contradicted himself, or was pushed along by others – he may have caused a stir, but this would likely have been restricted to a few specialists arguing the merits of the case in scholarly journals. Instead, Taylor turned the interwar world upside down – and shook it hard. Leaders turned out to be followers; ideologues became realists; the weak were strong. Events followed no pattern. Accidents ruined plans. Readers who pick up *Origins* for the first time now, long after it was written, are likely to find it exciting and entertaining still: there is hardly a page that fails to provoke, that fails to challenge someone's assumptions about something. The reverberations wrought by Taylor's shaking can still be felt.

The most surprising feature of the controversy that erupted is that anyone familiar with Taylor's work should have been surprised by the approach he took when he turned to this subject. All of the principal features of *Origins* – the crisp prose, the jokes, the biting sarcasm, the ironies, the narrative structure – are evident in his earlier works. So, too, were the basic lines of interpretation: statesmen everywhere scheme for advantage; accidents always destroy plans; interests invariably take precedence over ideas; and, most significantly, the course of modern international history is the story in the main of Germany's attempt to dominate Europe and the efforts of others to prevent it from succeeding. The style, philosophy, and interpretation were clearly evident in *The Italian Problem in European Diplomacy, 1847–1849* (1934), *Germany's First Bid for Colonies, 1884–1885* (1938), *The Habsburg Monarchy, 1809–1918* (1941), *The Course of German History* (1945), *Rumours of Wars* (1952), *The Struggle for Mastery in Europe, 1848–1918* (1954), *Bismarck, the Man and the Statesman* (1955), *The Troublemakers* (1957), and in numerous essays and reviews. As the titles of these works suggest, three subjects formed the core of Taylor's interests: central Europe; diplomacy; and modern history. Of particular concern was the way in which states were made and unmade, and how nationalism and imperialism – the two driving forces of the modern era – are connected with the onset of total war.

It would be astonishing that someone who had reached maturity in the 1920s should not have shown interest in war, nationalism, and revolution. The consequences of 1914–18 were readily apparent: the physical destruction, the disabled veterans, and the long lists of war dead inscribed on memorials; the disappearance of the Habsburg, Ottoman, and Russian empires, and their replacement by new "national" states and the Soviet Union. The greatest historical controversy of the decade raged over the question of responsibility for the outbreak of war in 1914; and Taylor later explained how he was struck by the contrast between this stormy debate and the quiet complacency that surrounded the origins of the Second World War. Even historians whose training and work had been in other fields and earlier periods turned to recent diplomatic history. One of them, the Austrian A. F. Pribram, had turned from Cromwell and the Puritan revolution of the seventeenth century to recent Anglo-Austrian relations. Thus, in one of the many "accidents" that transformed his "personal history," Taylor – who had gone to Vienna to work with Pribram on Cromwell – was diverted from English domestic history to European diplomacy. His personal and professional life exemplified the connection between the profound forces of the age and the effect of chance and circumstance.

Taylor also explained that he followed the fashion of the 1920s in assuming that Germany had been unfairly burdened with the guilt of having initiated the First World War. But, as he set about investigating various aspects of modern European history, he discovered that he and the "revisionists" were wrong, that the peacemakers of Versailles were right: the responsibility for the war lay with Germany. By the time he came to write *Origins*, he regarded Germany as the dynamic element in European politics over the past century; it was Germany that was growing, expanding, looking forward to a future when it would be dominant in Europe and able to take up the position of a full-fledged world power.

One of the distinctive features of *Origins* is the connections that are constantly made between the interwar years and the nineteenth century; while most historians concentrated on Hitlerism and ideology – usually treating these as aberrations in statecraft – Taylor was keen to show the links between William II and Hitler, the parallels between Chamberlain and Gladstone, the continuity of Russian policies from the Romanovs to the Soviets. The great powers hoped the Spanish Civil War would burn itself out, he insisted, "as Metternich had hoped would happen with the Greek revolt in the 1820s" (p. 158). Schuschnigg suffered from the perpetual illusion, peculiar to the Austrians, that exposing nationalistic intrigue would stir the conscience of Europe into action – just as it had "seemed to them axiomatic in 1859 that Cavour would be deserted by Napoleon III" (p. 178). Stresemann shared Bismarck's belief that peace was in Germany's interest, although he was "no more inclined to peace from moral principle than Bismarck had been" (p. 79). These allusions to European politics of the nineteenth century warn the reader not to trust those who would treat the 1930s as if they had existed in a vacuum.

Taylor admired few statesmen. His favourite book, *The Troublemakers*, extolled the virtues of the dissenting tradition; his heroes were the critics and outsiders of

English history – the Cobbetts and the Cobdens, the Lloyd Georges and the Beaverbrooks. And he showed how unreliable are the public utterances of men in power. While Lamartine, foreign minister and romantic poet, was boldly announcing a revolutionary French foreign policy in his manifesto of 1848, he was also apologizing for it in private, pleading with the Duke of Wellington to "understand its real sense" – that it was a gesture in public relations.[3] When Taylor treated Hitler's speeches and *Mein Kampf* as meaningless or untrustworthy pieces of self-advertisement, readers recoiled from the shock. But Taylor treated all statesmen in this way. "Great men in public life love power," he explained; "they fight to get it and they use it ruthlessly when it is in their hands."[4] They make speeches, write books and strike poses in order to dupe an unsuspecting public; it is the job of the historian not to be duped, to look for the reality behind the facade.

The principal reality highlighted by Taylor is that statesmen seek to maintain or extend the interests of their respective states. Those who take their own rhetoric and ideals too seriously are likely to land themselves in trouble. Palmerston's greatness resided in his ability to recognize that, although he trumpeted liberal Whig ideas, the interest of peace sometimes meant co-operating with Austria in spite of the two countries' ideological incompatibility. Palmerston would do the right thing when opportunity and interest combined (as they did during the unification of Italy), but he would do nothing for Poland or Hungary, as "the one was beyond his reach, the liberation of the other he supposed would have been against British interests."[5] Crispi, the prime minister who wished to turn his country into a great colonial power, "lived in a world of illusions and was leading Italy to disaster."[6] In all of Taylor's work a motif is constructed in which it is the dreamers, the speculators, and the ambitious who allow their grand designs to overpower their appreciation of what is possible. Napoleon III, who attempted to destroy the balance of power, "substitute his own hegemony," and replace the Holy Alliance with the "revolutionary association" of his dreams, led the Second Empire to destruction.[7]

Dreamers who act out their dreams are not the only ones who are dangerous in Taylor's world – there are also those reactionaries whose nightmare visions of the future lead them to oppose all change – and often end with them flinging themselves headlong into disaster in an act of national suicide. Such was Metternich, who "dreaded action, sought always to postpone decisions and cared only for repose"; when he fell from power he "brought down old Austria with him."[8] Conservatives are especially likely to fall prey to the temptation of believing that one dramatic act against liberals, radicals, nationalists, or revolutionaries will destroy the enemy, restore the balance, and remove uncertainty. When Austria–Hungary went to war in 1914, war was an end in itself: "the countless problems which had dragged on so long could all be crossed off the agenda." Instead Austria–Hungary disappeared from the map.[9] This is a complicated world that Taylor describes, one in which it is as dangerous to try to stop the movement of the world as it is to speed it up, and whether one chooses to act or stand still the consequences can rarely be foreseen with any accuracy. In this, the world of Europe between the wars was little different from the Europe of the nineteenth century. Men continued to dance "the perpetual quadrille of the Balance of Power," as much as some of them might wish the music to stop so "that they could sit out a dance without maintaining the ceaseless watch on one another."[10]

Although the faces were different after 1919, the problem confronting European diplomacy remained the same: how to deal with the fact that Germany, still the greatest of the European powers, was more convinced than ever that the international system had been specially designed to thwart its designs. In fact, ringing it with small states, and forcing the Soviet Union out of the European equation, meant that when it recovered its cohesion and efficiency it would be stronger than ever. Taylor was certainly convinced, long before writing *The Origins of the Second World War*, that Germany had decided to exploit its potential for establishing hegemony in Europe. This was signified most dramatically when William II dismissed Bismarck and replaced him with advisers who favoured "world policy," who imagined that Germany was capable of realizing this ambition "before she had secured the mastery of Europe."[11] The differences between Bismarck, Bethmann-Hollweg, and Hitler were matters of temperament and tactics: when the heirs of Bismarck rose up in 1944 it was "Hitler's failure, not his *policy*," that drove them to resist.[12] In the 1930s the Germans sought to reduce Hungary to its true national size while incorporating the rest of the Habsburg monarchy into the German Reich; but before 1914 they had been restrained from this only by "dynastic scruples" and "twinges of Bismarck's caution."[13] The First World War sprang from Germany's world policy, from its decisions to challenge both Russia and Great Britain as world powers.[14] By the 1950s Taylor was repeatedly referring to the war of 1939–45 as "the second German war."

It must have seemed bizarre to Taylor when *Origins* was criticized by some as an apologia for Hitler, because the essence of his interpretation was the continuous line of development in modern European history whereby Germany sought to establish its domination of Europe by controlling the center and the east. Although he dismissed the notion that Hitler was a careful and meticulous planner, he clearly and unequivocally explained that Hitler "intended Germany to become the dominant power in Europe." But he also insisted that in this Hitler was "like every other German statesman" (p. 171). These were the two arguments that distinguished Taylor most clearly from other historians: Hitler ceased to be the mad genius who pulled all the strings and had the whole play worked out in advance; and he became just another German, struggling for mastery in Europe. Even Hitler's anti-Semitism had been "the Socialism of fools" for years: "everything which Hitler did against the Jews followed logically from the racial doctrines in which most Germans vaguely believed" (p. 100). If Taylor was right, Hitler could not be expunged from the historical map because of his uniqueness: he must be seen as a part of German, and even of European, history.

This simple revisionist perspective enabled Taylor to go far beyond a condemnation of Hitler and Nazism. If Hitler had a simple "blueprint for aggression," it ought to have been the task of western statesmen – and a fairly simple one at that – to divine the plan and to wreck it; the "Hitler-blueprint" interpretation made Chamberlain and the other "appeasers" culpable, and let everyone else off the hook. But if Hitler had no plan, just vague wishes and daydreams, it meant that the range of responsibility extended far beyond a few individuals: it would include, in various ways and at different stages, those who believed in collective security, in self-determination, in disarmament, in anticommunism. And responsibility is different from guilt: those who believed in alternatives to war and the balance of power were not necessarily weak or evil – most of them genuinely believed that new ways for reconciling differences and righting wrongs had to be found if the world was to avoid a repeat performance of the catastrophe of 1914–18. Taylor attempted to show, against the background of the German drive to domination, how the whole complex of ideas and interests in interwar Europe helped to propel the great powers along the path to war. And it is this complexity – the contingencies, the accidents, the ironies and the paradoxes – that enriches *The Origins of the Second World War* and elevates it to the status it now enjoys as a classic work of historical writing. A work that merely turned Hitler on his head, while it might have enjoyed a brief sensation, would never have inspired the continuing controversy achieved by *Origins*.

Almost overlooked in the furor that its appearance provoked was Taylor's wider condemnation of the very nature of international politics; but his embittered, disillusioned treatment of politics and statesmanship must surely be one of the clues to his continuing popularity, as disillusionment with the simplicity of Cold-War rhetoric grew throughout the 1960s and 1970s. Reduced to its simplest elements, *Origins* stands as a monumental attack on the way in which the international system works. And Taylor discovered, in Hitler, an ingenious medium through which to launch this attack. All those Taylorian references to affairs before 1919 are intended to demonstrate that matters changed little with the advent of fascism: "Hitler and Mussolini glorified war and the warlike virtues. They used the threat of war to promote their aims. But this was not new. Statesmen had always done it" (p. 136). The balance of power was an endless dance: states have always sought to extend their power, and statesmen everywhere grab every opportunity to aggrandize themselves. The only difference between the fascist dictators and other statesmen was "that their appetite was greater; and they fed it by more unscrupulous means" (p. 140).

Hitler, as Taylor sketches him, was about as evil a man as may be imagined. Even though he acted as a sounding-board for the German nation, he bore the responsibility for the destruction of German democracy, for the concentration camps, and for the extermination of peoples during the Second World War. "He gave orders, which Germans executed, of a wickedness without parallel in civilized history" (p. 27). But in foreign policy Hitler was not unusual: he aimed to make Germany dominant in Europe and, perhaps, in the world. "Other

Powers have pursued similar aims and still do. Other Powers treat smaller countries as their satellites. Other Powers seek to defend their vital interests by force of arms" (p. 27). What does it say about the way in which international affairs are conducted that this personification of wickedness, when regarded from the perspective of traditional European diplomacy, was simply an ordinary statesman going about his business in a time-honored fashion? "In international affairs there was nothing wrong with Hitler except that he was a German."

So, in the final analysis, Taylor also chose to turn the interwar years into a morality play. But unlike his predecessors, the play he has written bears the signs of genius: few things are as they appear to the naked eye; honorable intentions lead to tragic conclusions; wicked designs are facilitated by the well-intentioned. His work will surely endure, if only because he rescued this vital part of the human story from the vapid simplicities of good versus evil and returned it to its proper place of complexity and paradox. "Human blunders...usually do more to shape history than human wickedness" (pp. 265–6).

In the past forty years, much has been made of Taylor's "philosophy of history" – much too much. Taylor himself consistently denied having a philosophy or even a systematic approach. These denials have the ring of truth. In all his work he tried to tell stories, to explain how one thing led to another, to answer the child's question: "What happened next?" But good stories have something to tell us, just as good jokes tell the truth. Such philosophy as may be found in *Origins* can be summed up as a warning to mistrust historical truths and parallels. We do learn from our mistakes, he says – we learn how to make new ones. The attempt to extract simple policies from the lessons of the 1930s was one of the enemies of clear thinking in the period that followed the Second World War: Munich and the argument over appeasement supplied "superficial parallels and superficial terms of abuse."[15] A conciliatory policy towards Russia "would not be rejected so firmly now were it not for the recollection of the appeasement towards Germany that failed a decade ago."[16] This warning against the historical cliches offered up by historians and statesmen is as valuable a message today as it was when first uttered.

These new essays on the origins of the Second World War are designed neither to honor A. J. P. Taylor nor to replace him. They undoubtedly testify to his influence. If anyone is to hold the first-mortgage on the subject, we are fortunate that that person should be someone able to write vigorous prose and to stimulate debate – even among those not yet born when the book was written. But Taylor has claimed that in writing *Origins* he wished to examine events in detail, and the details of what happened behind the scenes are available to us today in a way that was almost unimaginable when it was written. Not surprisingly, the specialists contributing to this edition, having had the opportunity to examine these events in great detail, have found much in his book that requires revision or reconsideration. They have found that some of the charges leveled at Taylor twenty-five years ago, especially those of contradiction and overstatement, were justified. They have also found that he made mistakes and overlooked material available to him, that he sometimes guessed wrong or allowed prejudice to blind him.

Nevertheless, one is left with the distinct impression that Taylor will continue to be read and re-read with interest and profit for decades to come. These essays have been collected with that premise in mind: to contribute to the ongoing debate by clarifying vital aspects of Taylor's interpretation, by synthesizing the work that has been done over the past quarter-century, and by offering fresh evaluations of major themes connected with the origins of the Second World War. This book is intended not to signal the end of the debate but to show where it stands today, and where new discoveries are being made.

Notes

1 I wish to express my gratitude to Kathy Burk for allowing me to read the early chapters of her forthcoming biography. Although she had not yet reached the post-1961 controversy in her writing, she assures me that nothing I say here will be contradicted by her!

2 A. J. P. Taylor, *The Origins of the Second World War*, Harmondsworth, 1964, p. 190. All references in this essay are to the Penguin paperback edition, which includes the 1963 Foreword, "Second thoughts."

3 A. J. P. Taylor, *The Struggle for Mastery in Europe*, Oxford, 1954, p. 5.

4 A. J. P. Taylor, *Rumours of Wars*, London, 1952, p. 25.

5 A. J. P. Taylor, *The Italian Problem in European Diplomacy, 1847–1849*, Manchester 1934, pp. 236–42.

6 Taylor, *Struggle for Mastery*, p. 324.

7 Taylor, *Struggle for Mastery*, p. 61.

8 A. J. P. Taylor, *The Habsburg Monarchy, 1809–1918*, London, 2nd edn, 1948, pp. 34, 56.

9 Taylor, *Habsburg Monarchy*, p. 232.

10 Taylor, *Struggle for Mastery*, p. xix.

11 Taylor, *Struggle for Mastery*, p. 294.

12 A. J. P. Taylor, *Bismarck*, London, 1955, p. 272.

13 Taylor, *Habsburg Monarchy*, p. 230.

14 Taylor, *Bismarck*, p. 268.

15 Taylor, *Rumours of Wars*, p. 76.

16 Taylor, *Rumours of Wars*, p. 80.

2 1918 and after

The postwar era

Sally Marks

The controversy over A. J. P. Taylor's *The Origins of the Second World War* centered on the prewar years and the outbreak of war. Taylor's dissent from the assumption that Adolf Hitler was the primary cause and his views on appeasement angered many, generating a debate on certain issues. Were Taylor's critics blinded by a conviction that Hitler caused the Second World War? Regarding other leaders of the 1930s, did Taylor equate ineptitude or error with evil? Above all, did Hitler "plan" the Second World War? On another level, Taylor was charged with abuse and misuse of documentation, dismissal of evidence, contradiction, overstatement, a narrow focus on diplomacy, and ignoring fundamental causes.[1]

In the uproar, another question bearing on fundamental causes was ignored: how sound are his early chapters addressing the pre-Hitler period? Taylor would argue, and few historians now disagree, that the reasons for the Second World War did not suddenly emerge in 1935 or 1936. After all, Hitler gained power in the Weimar Republic because many Germans thought he could resolve their discontents. His first success, in 1930, came during a recession but in an election dominated by foreign policy, though many grievances about the Versailles treaty had been partially or fully resolved. So why did his foreign policy have such appeal? Taylor dismisses this problem by claiming Hitler's policy was that of his predecessors,[2] but he also asserts that the entire interwar period forms a unit and that events at the end of the first war were vital in provoking the second. Certainly, what happened in 1918–19 affected what came after, especially in forming the attitudes of most Germans, and Eugen Weber claims "the 1930s begin in August 1914."[3] Thus, Taylor's early chapters on the failure to solve what he calls "the German problem" warrant examination.

Characteristically, Taylor starts with the balance of power. The unification of Germany created a great nation in Europe's center but one soon balanced by a Russo-French alliance. Even so, Germany nearly won the First World War. In early 1918, it was triumphant in the east and undefeated in the west, where an impasse existed in France. Yet by November, Germany had lost the war in the west. However, the armistice and peace treaty permitted it to remain a major entity only somewhat diminished in a Europe providing fewer neighboring checks upon it. This implied, after a period of recovery and of breaking treaty restrictions, potential renewed German continental dominance. Some, including many Britons, soon found this acceptable if domination were economic, and not military. For them, German recovery was desirable if peaceful, and their concern was German grievances, not fear of new aggression (pp. 24–30).

The Versailles treaty created Germany's grievances and confirmed its continuation as a great power. Taylor argues that, some territorial clauses aside, the treaty focused on providing security against Germany. He says it "lacked moral validity from the start," meaning that Germans did not deem it fair, that many others, especially in the English-speaking world, came to agree with them, and that Germans were united in their hatred of the Versailles *Diktat*, in their determination to break it and revert to continental domination. Without German cooperation, enforcement became difficult and the German problem continued unabated (pp. 30–3).

Taylor says that the Germans might have accepted the treaty had not one portion of it remained unsettled. Disagreement among the victors deferred decision about the amount Germany was to pay in reparation for economic damage to the victors. Taylor says the question remained open throughout the 1920s, exacerbating all sore points, generating emotion, and becoming a chronic grievance. In his view, the Germans blamed all woes on reparations, whether or not they were so related, and soon transferred this grievance to the entire treaty. Britain, despite initial avidity, had second thoughts, turned against the reparations clauses, and projected these feelings onto the whole treaty, excepting clauses to Britain's benefit (pp. 46–52).

British attitudes were important in the other problem Taylor cites, the lack of Allied unity. The narrow victory on the western front in 1918 derived from Russia's 1914 contribution and then a coalition of France, Britain, Italy, and America. Postwar communist Russia was self-absorbed and widely distrusted. American withdrawal was less than complete but soon substantial. Italy was not really interested in the German problem. That left the British and the French, who disagreed regularly about Germany. France feared future German aggression despite alliances with Poland and Czechoslovakia to replace the Russian tie. According to Taylor, Britain thought French fears foolish, was confident there would be no war, and wished to revive Germany in a peaceful Europe. In one pretense at compromise after another, the two powers canceled each other out. Then Britain offered a meaningless paper guarantee to France, confident it would never have to be honored if France gave up all else: great power status; treaty enforcement; and in part its eastern allies. Though the French initially balked at the price and struggled to enforce the treaty, Taylor says they learned the futility of this. Thus the paper guarantee emerged as the 1925 Locarno treaty. Taylor claims it ended the First World War and brought peace to Europe, whereas its repudiation in 1936 "marked the prelude to the second war" (pp. 34–9, 44–58).

In examining Taylor's analysis of the postwar period, one finds that most questions prominent in the debate are irrelevant, for they focus on the Nazi era. The charge of misuse of documentary evidence is extraneous, for Taylor cites no documentation earlier than 1932. Of the usual complaints, there remain dismissal of evidence, contradiction and overstatement, a narrow focus on diplomacy, and ignoring fundamental causes. Further, Taylor's chronological ambiguity makes it difficult to judge his generalizations, which often are pertinent for one point in the interwar period but not otherwise; without dates, their soundness cannot be tested. Moreover, one should ask whether he spotted the key pieces in the puzzle and put them together properly. As to this last, most difficult, problem, Taylor was perceptive about many of the pieces but not always about the links among them.

To be fair, one must take into account the evidence which was available when he wrote. In 1960–61, material about the Nazi years far exceeded that available on the earlier period. Taylor said he "attempted to tell the story as it may appear to some future historian, working from the records" (p. 22). For the postwar era, most archives now are open, those future historians have arrived, and the records have produced some surprises. Though Taylor cannot be charged with failure to read closed files, he did not explore much of what was at hand. His bibliography for the pre-Nazi years is skimpy. Many published documentary materials were not consulted, including Parliamentary Command Papers, *Documents diplomatiques*, and *Papers relating to the Foreign Relations of the United States*. Taylor's list of memoirs and monographs is also scant. Another problem in assessing his use of the evidence is the lack of citation of works listed in his bibliography. Therefore, while his interpretation of the postwar era often conflicts with opinions prevailing in 1961, one cannot determine whether his views were brilliant, perverse, research-based, or derived from others.

The charges of contradiction and overstatement are often sustainable for the first chapters. The early exegesis glitters but is marred by instability of viewpoint, contradiction, carelessness, a fatal cleverness, and illogicality. Examples abound. Taylor says the Rapallo treaty afforded "little chance of active cooperation between the two signatories" but that, once it lapsed, Germans regretted its "vanished intimacy" (pp. 52–3, 249). He misdates the Brest–Litovsk treaty as January 1918 (pp. 25, 71)[4] and claims: "Russia disappeared from view – her revolutionary government, her very existence ignored by the victorious Powers." (pp. 25–6). Though Russia was rarely a major factor in the early postwar equation, Taylor has overstated the case. On successive pages, he says that in the late 1920s (apparently) France "renounced the fruits of victory before the dispute over these fruits began", and that "[i]n 1929 the system of security against Germany, devised in the treaty of Versailles, was still complete" (pp. 62–3). Neither statement is strictly true, for both ignore the Anglo-German drive to dismantle the postwar security system which undid much of the treaty in a decade.

Taylor rightly says that the interwar era centered on the German problem, but illogically adds "if this were settled, everything would be settled" (p. 44), and argues that if Germany were treated as an equal, there would be no basis for reparations (p. 61), though inequality had never been a justification for payments. The rationale was reconstruction of the civilian damage done by German invasion, destruction, and seizures. Here Taylor is confusing matters and accepting Weimar's view, which indeed sought equality. To Germans, this meant removal of defeat and its consequences, and a reversion not to early 1918 but to early 1914.

Taylor's analysis of the postwar power balance is penetrating but does not differentiate between what it was and how it was then viewed. Granted, archival evidence clarifies the picture. He does well in distinguishing – at least for Germany – between the short-term power balance and what it was likely to be later if the treaty were not enforced. He sees that Germany would then revert to continental predominance, but again does not explore the distinction between reality and the perception of it, notably in Britain and America. Despite attention to reparations, he scants economic factors and emotional issues important in democracies. Public opinion and propaganda mattered in the 1920s in setting the outer limits of policy and fundamental assumptions, not least those of historians.

Finally, the issue of causation warrants the analysis of Taylor's opening chapters, for here he addresses underlying causes. Naturally, reviewers focused on later portions of the book, some praising the first section in passing.[5] Taylor asserts variously that the First World War, the armistice, or the treaty caused the Second World War. This is overstatement, contradiction, and simplification, and approaches preaching historical inevitability. Taylor begins his account in 1918–19 because he believes Allied failure to solve the German problem then laid the basis for the Second World War. He is right that the German problem was not solved (pp. 16, 23–8, 43–4, 71, 267), but to attribute the history of the next twenty years exclusively to events in those months is too categorical and omits other factors which require exploration, including the nature of the German problem.

Taylor never defines this question crucial to the continent's future, asking in effect on what basis Europe would be reconstructed.[6] He assumes a united Germany would be dominant and disruptive. In the Preface to the 1983 edition of *Origins*, he asks why Britain and France did not resist German reversion to great-power status.[7] He ignores how this was to be done, especially without Russian aid, and Allied assumptions, which he indicates elsewhere, about what had been accomplished by the 1918 military verdict; and he also forgets that the question was not whether Germany would be a great power, but on what terms. He disregards the nature of German nationalism, the self-delusions of the citizenry and the reasons for each. Taylor is right that Weimar Germany was resentful and revisionist, though his exploration of the reasons is inadequate. He asserts that both Hitler and his predecessors wished to revert to the situation of March 1918, which hardly explains why Hitler's foreign policy was more popular than Weimar's. He assumes a united Germany would drive by force toward an equality tantamount to continental predominance, that little or nothing could have been done to deter it (thereby contradicting his own 1983 question), and that Germany would revert to its place as "the greatest power in Europe from her natural weight" (p. 70). His conclusion that a war over the settlement between Germany and Britain and France "had been implicit since the moment when the first war ended" (p. 267) ignores how little of the 1919 settlement remained in September 1939 and how few of Hitler's goals dealt with treaty eradication; it ignores also the underlying reasons for German resentment, revisionism, and later larger aims, and what the victors could have done in 1918–19 and the 1920s to deflect what he considers the inevitable course of history. Taylor perceives many pieces of the puzzle but not their connections. For instance, he looks at British, French, and German attitudes but does not examine the effect of British policy assumptions upon Germany, France, the unraveling of the treaty, the German drive to regain continental predominance, and thus the history of the 1920s.

Taylor's approach to fundamental causes deals in absolutes from the outset, positing an either–or situation. In November 1918, he argues, the Allies could either break Germany up or accept its continental predominance and revert to the situation early in 1918 when Germany was triumphant in the east and undefeated in the west. Because they did neither, the German problem continued. In fact, both options were unrealistic. This was clear at the time, and neither was seriously considered. Accepting German predominance after a long, bitter war was politically impossible, amounting to surrender on the day of victory. Breaking up Germany was no solution, given the relative modesty of Allied territorial aims in Europe, Wilson's opposition to dismemberment, and Anglo-American eagerness to retire militarily except for token contingents. Without Russian collaboration, enforcement of disunification would have required a lengthy British and American military commitment politically impossible to both powers. Taylor says that in the armistice, the Allies committed themselves "almost without realizing it" to continued German unity. Elsewhere and more accurately, he notes that the Allies had no desire to dismember Germany but rather wished to demonstrate that aggression "could not succeed," and this they thought they had done (pp. 26–7).

Thus Taylor's solutions to the German problem – supremacy or destruction – were not viable in 1918. Were there other possibilities which neither the Allies then nor Taylor later considered? As he mentions, in 1918–19 a gap existed between reality and German popular perception of it. He says Germany was thoroughly defeated and its leaders knew that in November; a few pages on, he reports without comment that "no German accepted the treaty as a fair settlement between equals 'without victors or vanquished' " (p. 26). Here Taylor brushes a key factor, the popular German perception that the First World War was a draw and that Wilson's "just peace" should mean the *status quo ante bellum* with rectifications in Germany's favor.[8] However, Taylor fails to explain how this situation arose and what could have prevented it.

Some answers are obvious. The war was fought on the soil of the victors; they lay in ruins, not Germany. Clearly, German self-delusion was a factor, but the Allies permitted that, perhaps their greatest mistake. In November 1918 the victors could end the war or fight on. In retrospect, they probably should have fought on into Germany, but they did not know how near the end was. Further, as Taylor notes, beyond thinking their goal of German defeat accomplished, Britain and France were exhausted and feared American domination if the war continued (p. 26). Still, the document ending hostilities should have been called a surrender, not an armistice, a misleading term which fostered German illusions about the war's outcome. Taylor ignores this possibility and also another, not considered by the victors – that the surrender terms might have provided for a modest Allied occupation of Berlin and other key cities for a year. But the Allies feared more bloodshed and the spread of Bolshevism to their troops;[9] so, in the absence of Allied armies, the Germans were free to enter what Ernst Troeltsch called the "dreamland" of the armistice period.[10]

They clung to Wilson's "peace without victory" speech of January 1917 when the United States was neutral and he was seeking a negotiated peace. They became convinced that Wilson's 1917 statements about a peace "without victors and vanquished" and a "peace between equals" were part of the armistice terms, which they were not.[11] Forgetting the harsh treaties of Brest–Litovsk and Bucharest (not to mention plans, unknown to the public, to squeeze the last pfennig out of the Allies if Germany won), they naively assumed that the Reich's past expansion could serenely continue, that Wilsonian self-determination meant Germany would lose no territory, though the armistice terms indicated otherwise, and that it could annex Austria. But the Allies had no intention of converting victory into defeat by handing their foe the gateway to south-eastern Europe and the middle east: "Germany's enemies had not fought a war and made sacrifices only to end up by turning Little Germany into Greater Germany."[12] Thus, in their "dreamland," German expectations embarked on a journey away from reality.[13]

Playing the "if" game is usually futile, but German perceptions were so important that we may linger briefly. A durable peace must rest on what a defeated major power will accept, but what it will accept is affected by its perception of its circumstances. In 1814, Russia's army and tsar were in Paris. In 1871, the German empire was proclaimed at Versailles, and Prussian forces trooped through the Arc de Triomphe.[14] In 1918, the Allies occupied only the Rhineland. Had they paraded soldiers in Berlin and Munich, reality would have intruded. Chancellor Friedrich Ebert would not have hailed German troops in December 1918 with "As you return unconquered from the field of battle, I salute you,"[15] were Allied armies likely to be marching in Berlin the next week. Taylor attributes German refusal to accept the treaty simply to the continued existence of a united Germany. Had symbols of defeat been visible in German cities, perceptions of the nation's circumstances would have been different and, hence, perhaps also views of the treaty.

Ebert's statement reinforced German self-delusion about the war's outcome and the German army's *Dolchstoss* myth that it was undefeated in battle but had been stabbed in the back by pacifists, Jews, and socialists. Ebert, who needed army support, did not counter it, nor did the Allies. Between November and May, this myth led many Germans to a belief that Germany had not lost the war. The victors devising the peace in Paris proceeded on the premise of German defeat, which Weimar rejected. Thus, any treaty they were likely to produce would be viewed as unjust by most Germans. The terms, largely predicted by Gustav Stresemann, later Weimar's ablest foreign minister, did not surprise Germany's cabinet, but shocked the people and generated bitterness.[16]

Given their expectations, they found their territorial losses enormous. Actually, excluding those anchored in the fourteen points and the armistice (Alsace–Lorraine and territory to Poland) and the north-Schleswig plebiscite (promised by an 1866 Prussian treaty), the losses – thanks partly to self-determination – were minuscule, amounting to Eupen-Malmédy permanently and the Saar Basin provisionally. German outrage was also fueled by two myths launched by their foreign minister when he received the treaty at Versailles on May 7, 1919. Though he had not yet seen it, he denounced it for containing a war-guilt clause, whose inclusion his delegation assumed. Actually, the Allies did not intend Article 231 to connote war guilt, which it does not mention, and virtually identical clauses in the Austrian and Hungarian treaties were not so interpreted, but the German denunciation in a sense "created" a war-guilt clause. Article 231 was intended to establish a legal basis for reparations, and the wording, devised by John Foster Dulles of the United States, of "the responsibility of Germany and her Allies for causing all the loss and damage to which the Allied and Associated Governments and their nationals have been subjected as a consequence of the war imposed upon them by the aggression of Germany and her allies" was meant to *restrict* claims upon Germany.[17] However, the myth of Germany's supposedly "unilateral war guilt" was launched, as was that of the deliberate Allied starvation of countless Germans by maintaining the naval blockade. Though Allied warships remained in place against a possible resumption of hostilities, the Allies offered food and medicine after the armistice, but Germany refused to allow its ships to carry supplies. Despite that, and the efforts by its more conservative leaders to persuade American emissaries to delay shipments until Germany had a stable non-socialist government, Allied food arrived in Allied ships before the charge made at Versailles.[18]

A campaign initiated by the German foreign office spread these myths across the world, especially in English-speaking countries. Military and civilian notables were recruited in this effort, which was conducted throughout Weimar's history. Though the fact that Germany's invasion of Belgium had touched off the First World War was not seriously disputed, Germany focused on Article 231 and so-called "unilateral war guilt" hoping that, if one could refute German responsibility for the war, not only reparations but the entire treaty would collapse. A massive propaganda drive, including publication of forty volumes of carefully selected documents, was unmatched by France. The resulting distortion of the historical record has been termed disinformation. This campaign convinced many in the British establishment, whose own efforts reinforced the view that no one had caused the war into which Europe had somehow slid.[19] As it became a patriotic duty in Germany to further this argument, German historians and their supporters elsewhere did so faithfully, until Fritz Fischer examined the evidence and published his findings in 1961 to a storm of nationalist abuse.[20] Meanwhile, the propaganda and myths had forty years to become "fact." As that happened in Germany and the English-speaking world in the 1920s, the treaty was undermined, aggravating the German problem. Indeed, when Taylor says the treaty "lacked moral validity," edging close to implying that it was another "scrap of paper,"[21] he is paying unconscious tribute to German and Anglo-American propaganda.

Taylor claims that the treaty itself helped perpetuate the German problem. In this, he is perhaps right for the wrong reasons. The victors assumed a united Germany but also that it would accept defeat and a treaty, based approximately on the fourteen points, thus providing a somewhat reduced Germany in a redesigned Europe. They failed both to make defeat visible and to notice that the continental power balance was being arranged precariously, with a strong Germany surrounded largely by weak neighbors. The Paris debates showed that France and other neighbors of Germany, which also feared for the future, wanted German power reduced more than did Britain and America. As Taylor notes, the English-speaking nations thought the war had produced a final verdict and wished to go home (pp. 34–5). The clash of views led to compromises resulting in a treaty severe enough to generate intense resentment, but not sufficiently draconian to constrain Germany for long, particularly without effective enforcement. This situation created an instability that soon surfaced. Thus both the German problem and German self-delusion about the war's outcome continued.

The overriding difficulty with the treaty, however, was less its terms than German hostility to it because it represented defeat. Many historians, including Taylor, dwell on German hatred of the Polish Corridor (p. 51), and some argue that the boundary should have been drawn to include fewer Germans. However, since most Germans defined territory of "indisputably Polish populations" – which Wilson's fourteen points promised to Poland – as that containing a 90 percent Polish majority and rejected *any* territorial transfer as unjust, the exact line hardly mattered. Because of the peace conference's structure and the original plan to negotiate with the foe, the treaty was more severe than intended, but how much this mattered is uncertain, given German hostility to decisions implicit in the fourteen points, which the imperial government accepted. In fact, Weimar's sharpest protests centered on clauses anchored in the fourteen points (as far as Wilson's slogans could provide treaty bases at all). Since opinion in Germany was so hostile, its new leaders told the voters what they wished to hear, as most politicians do, reinforcing misperceptions of the war's outcome and determination to undo the treaty.[22]

If Germans acknowledged defeat at all, they argued that they were undefeated by continental powers or by European powers alone. This was true, if not necessarily relevant. The treaty assumed continuing Anglo-American participation in its enforcement, which did not occur. Both withdrew substantially, leaving a battered France to enforce alone, a task beyond its capacity, particularly against Anglo-Saxon resistance and without Russian aid. Taylor notes the withdrawal but underestimates the resistance and its significance, for the treaty soon ceased to represent the continental power alignment, especially after the 1922 Russo-German treaty of Rapallo. This fact only heightened French fears and German demands for treaty revision.

There is another factor which Taylor does not address directly. As he notes, the kaiser was gone, Germany had a democratic republic, and the Allies expected it to settle down and live in peace with its democratic neighbors (pp. 26–7). Perhaps they were naive in assuming that democracies are peaceful, but they, like Taylor, overlooked the tragedy of German democracy. The Weimar Republic was born of defeat and as psychologically deformed as the ex-kaiser; further, the Social Democrats, more democratic than other parties, were saddled with defeat and the armistice, neither their doing, along with the treaty and what followed. No wonder democracy was unpopular and deemed "unGerman." Domestic politics required Weimar coalitions to resist treaty enforcement to prove their patriotism; this policy was so successful that it became axiomatic. The fragility of the Republic and its concentration on foreign policy were factors in Germany's refusal to accept the treaty and its rapid fraying.

Taylor wonders why the Allies thought they could impose upon Germany a treaty it would accept. They thought that Germany accepted defeat and assumed that, since other defeated great powers had honored peace treaties, Germany would do the same; France had done so after the 1871 treaty of Frankfurt, also a *diktat*. Taylor notes that the Allies believed, at least at first, in the sanctity of contracts (pp. 34, 51). Again, with eyes to 1871, they assumed Germany would honor the treaty to liberate the Rhineland quickly. But in 1871, France knew it had lost. Moreover, the Allies ignored the infant Republic's lack of political roots and the adolescently assertive character of German nationalism, which was a constant threat to governments in an unpopular democracy.

Taylor suggests also that the treaty was unenforceable because Germany was responsible for implementing it. The Allies, assuming acceptance of defeat and the treaty by a sturdier German Republic than existed, expected German co-operation. For this reason, and because Britain and America rejected lengthy continental involvement, the treaty lacked sufficient enforcement clauses, especially automatic ones not requiring Allied negotiation. Taylor is right that the Allied assumption that Germany would carry out the settlement gave Weimar a weapon against the treaty (pp. 28, 31, 33), but he oversimplifies. Any treaty requires co-operation, but more important in the 1920s was an evaporation of the will to enforce in Britain, America, and usually Italy.

Of course Allied unity collapsed soon after the last shot was fired. It generally does. Also, American withdrawal from treaty implementation, erratic but rapid, threw the peace structure and the power balance awry, exacerbating Germany's perception of injustice, as also did the reversal of British policy from March 1919 on.[23] One must investigate the reasons for and effects of British policy, for it was British support of German resistance which made it effective. This Taylor does not do. Again, the archives and recent works clarify the picture, but the basic outlines can be found in books which he lists. And while the extent and speed of Anglo-American reversal were not evident in 1919 when key treaty decisions were made, France was slow thereafter to face facts, because it was no more eager to accept solitude than Germany was to accept defeat.

Taylor comes close to Britain's motive when he cites Ramsay MacDonald's 1932 remark about Britain needing to support both sides (p. 56), but he sees neither its implications nor that they predated 1924, to which he applies it. Britain began reverting in 1919 to its traditional role as the fulcrum in the power equation, seeking a strong Germany to balance France and block bolshevism. It never abandoned France entirely, encouraging false hopes here,[24] and never supported Germany completely, creating bitterness there.[25] But usually it sought concessions to Germany at French expense, both to lure Weimar westward from Russia and to weaken France. All British leaders pursued this largely instinctive policy, though Austen Chamberlain did so less than most others. It derived from isolationism, imperial crises, nostalgia for Britain's prewar economic and political predominance, reaction against the war's cost in blood and money, tradition, misreading the power equation, reluctance to enforce the treaty, and fear of France. Here Taylor's crystal-ball clouded. We now know that Britain fixed on the superficial situation and misjudged the long-term power balance. The momentary superiority of the French army and air force, along with France's submarine-building program, alarmed British leaders who seriously thought the next war might be against France.[26]

Thus Britain swung to the temporarily weaker power, inadvertently facilitating Germany's return to continental predominance – with profound implications for the western entente and its treaty enforcement. Taylor says that Britain and France blocked each other's policies but not that Britain did so better, having more allies and superior skills at propaganda and playing to the historical galleries. He notes that Allied threats were progressively less effective (p. 32), but not that Britain increasingly refused to threaten and gave Germany assurances behind France's back, which is why threats by continental victors lost force. Taylor adds that America constituted world opinion; here he is wrong. America could be useful, and each country wanted its support, but Britain was the key power for the continental players, above all for Germany,[27] which never defied the entente when it was united, only when Britain stood aloof or backed Berlin. As Britain moved from its allies toward the middle, and sometimes surreptitiously to the German side,[28] treaty enforcement dissolved.

Taylor sees that America was more involved in Europe than most realized, but should add that the involvement was sporadic, financial, and often unofficial. He overlooks the role played in the 1920s by New York bankers, giving MacDonald unilateral credit for the 1924 reparations settlement, when in fact J. P. Morgan and Co.'s agents were equally important in bringing France to heel (pp. 55–6). America supported Britain out of distaste for European embroilment, reluctance to bother, susceptibility to Anglo-German propaganda, and hope that Europe would "settle down."[29] It was much easier not to enforce the treaty; like Britons, Americans failed to see that unity rendered enforcement unnecessary.

Despite his denunciation of Italian fascism as illegal, "corrupting," and dishonest, and of Mussolini as "fraudulent" and "a vain blundering boaster without either ideas or aims," Taylor's treatment of Italy's revisionism, lack of genuine power status, and absence from involvement in the German problem is sound, though he errs in that thinking Italy (or France) liked the Locarno treaties (pp. 58–9). Italy preferred words to action and enjoyed German nationalism at French expense. Both before and after 1922, Italy skittered among the great powers, trying to sell itself to all sides at once. This effectively left France and Weimar's other neighbors, all weak, to face the German problem.[30]

With some reason, Taylor dismisses Italy from the postwar power equation. With less reason, he dismisses Russia, forgetting that its isolation in 1919 was temporary. Though Germany's "natural weight" would return it to power, evidently Russia's would not. Taylor's chronological vagueness is acute here, but in remarking with typical panache that had Russia ceased to exist as a great power, he speaks of "long years after 1918" and of "weakness for a generation." His claim that the victors ignored its existence and made no effort to "draw Russia back into European affairs" (pp. 25, 41, 49) dismisses Allied interventions in Russia in 1919 and overtures during the peace conference and at the 1922 Genoa conference.[31] He ignores Russian feelers from July 1919 on, which achieved trade treaties with western powers by 1921, and never examines the idiosyncratic lens through which Soviet leaders viewed Europe.[32] Taylor's concern is the German problem, but he should ask how Russia affected it. He seems to think Russo-German relations were defined by Germany's 1917 victory in the east and forgets that winning the next-to-last round is not what matters. He ignores not only Weimar's raising fears of bolshevism to gain western concessions but the effect of Soviet Russia upon Germany's power position. The history of east-central Europe and of the power balance was distorted by Russia's full and Germany's partial eclipse, permitting new states to emerge between them. Beyond acknowledging that Germany's position was strengthened by Russia's disappearance (p. 28), Taylor dismisses this situation.

Treaty enforcement was difficult without a Russian counterweight to Germany's east. Poland was the primary target of Weimar's territorial revisionism[33] and eastern Europe an area it hoped to dominate economically, though many states allied with France. Taylor thinks France preferred these smallish states to the prewar Russian tie (p. 42), which it did not, for it understood Germany's drive toward a new *Mitteleuropa* and wrote off the Polish Corridor by 1925.[34] Moreover, Soviet Russia's existence facilitated German penetration of the *cordon sanitaire* states, but it availed Germany far more than that. The 1922 Rapallo treaty, which Taylor dismisses as trivial (pp. 52–3), provided Russia's bridge to Europe, gave Germany maneuvering room against the west along with economic and military advantages,[35] and facilitated concessions from the victors. Weimar capitalized on this freer hand, though the tie weakened after 1926, when Germany needed it less, and again in 1929 when Russia turned inward.[36] Though France tried to compete there economically, it could not forgive the separate peace, canceled debts, and Marxist ideology; even fear of Germany could not bring it in the 1920s to seek an alliance on the prewar model.[37]

As Taylor sees, French policy stemmed from what Austen Chamberlain called its "nightmare horror" of German renascence.[38] France read the underlying power balance correctly, and saw a disparity more severe than Taylor perceives. He cites Germany's demographic advantage, but its younger population and higher birth-rate guaranteed a greater future advantage. While he notes that Britain wished to reintegrate Germany in European trade, he does not see the effect on France, for Lorraine's iron industry depended on reparations coal and German markets.[39] If France did not gain a German trade treaty (which Britain hindered) before the economic clauses of the Versailles Treaty expired in 1925, it would be at Berlin's mercy. And effective transfer of reconstruction costs from the losers to the winners added to Weimar's advantage, as did erasure of its war debts during the 1922–23 inflation, which was caused primarily by internal factors but which reduced the real value of Germany's domestic debt to less than 1 US cent. Weimar emerged debt-free while continental victors faced staggering domestic and foreign war debts and reconstruction costs.[40]

Further, France's predominance eroded as army equipment aged and military service was reduced from three years to one; moreover, by 1925 the national will was exhausted. France was no longer truly a great power. In 1921, a French diplomat remarked that "in the foreseeable future the difficulty will be to slide France reasonably smoothly into the ranks of the second-rate powers, to which she belongs."[41] Understandably, French leaders did not accept this and struggled to maintain France's artificial treaty predominance against Anglo-German revisionism. With Gallic illogicality, however, they wanted both deterrence and conciliation, treaty enforcement and a British alliance, for France's "English problem" was linked to its "German problem."[42] But Britain read French nightmares and efforts at partial treaty enforcement as vindictiveness or imperialism, fearing French hegemony would replace that of Germany.[43] Taylor reflects this outlook when he remarks that in 1929 danger remained of aggression by France, the continent's only great power because it had the only great army (p. 62). Though Taylor admits France had accepted defeat, his assertion ignores the Russian army (easily as large by 1929, especially in Europe), France's weakness, and how it could attack Germany without losing the Locarno tie to Britain.

Though Taylor rightly says France saw its eastern allies as assets against Germany, not as potential liabilities, he errs in thinking that they dominated French foreign policy (p. 42). Since a Russian treaty was not practical politics, the primary goal was always a British alliance, for Paris assumed the next war would resemble the last, when the British navy, empire, and ties to Wall Street saved France. Every French premier wished to revive the wartime alliance, but London's price proved prohibitive, higher than Taylor notes. Yet a frightened France continued to seek protection, whereas Britain, alarmed at the prospect of being drawn into another continental bloodbath and wanting to turn away from Europe, pressed France to concede more to Germany to pacify it.[44]

Germany wanted to break the treaty and regain the *status quo ante bellum*, undoing the 1918 military verdict; thus the postwar became the continuation of war by other means.[45] Germany fought in many ways, using John Maynard Keynes as an unofficial adviser and propagandist.[46] The key battlefield at first was reparations. Though the archives have proved him wrong on some points, Taylor commendably faced this topic when most historians avoided it. His assessment shows more comprehension of France's dilemma than many early accounts, though at times he approaches hinting that if France had only thrown away its costly victory without protest, all would have been well.[47] Saying that Britain was not ready "to underwrite every French claim against Germany" (p. 38) omits that London increasingly opposed all French claims, however well-grounded, particularly if Weimar was likely to refuse, creating a situation requiring Allied action. Taylor rightly says that the Germans "deliberately kept their economic affairs in confusion" to escape reparations; he deserves credit for not blaming German fiscal and monetary chaos on French vindictiveness and on reparations which mostly were not being paid.[48]

Because reparations schemes were excruciatingly technical, neither Taylor nor historians after him penetrated to their core, which was political, not financial, though the key documents were available early on. At the peace conference, Allied reparations experts knew German capacity to pay was somewhere between 40 and 60 (French and American estimates) milliard gold marks.[49] However, this could not be revealed to Allied electorates, who were led to expect that Germany would pay for reconstruction and "the costs of the war."[50] Thus the problem was to bury a realistic sum in misleading devices implying a vast figure. From the peace conference on, every reparations scheme used one or several red herrings to inflate the ostensible total. At Paris, the German reparations offer (contingent on massive territorial revision) did the same.[51] The ostensibly large figures fooled the public and the historians, partly because all governments wished to continue the fiction of immense totals. Britain and Germany cited them to press for treaty revision. Weimar's leaders used them to encourage Germans to blame all economic ills on reparations,[52] whereas cabinets of continental victors stressed them to assure electorates that Germany, not Allied taxpayers, would pay. Given the actual claims, the real question was whether Germany would contribute to Allied reconstruction costs or whether these would be added to Allied domestic and foreign war debts. As that had major implications for the power balance, reparations became the terrain on which the war continued.

The reparations struggle was complicated by its link to war-debts disputes between American creditors and European debtors, a subject on which the literature remains sparse.[53] When Taylor says that reparations were perpetually unsettled, he forgets they were settled in 1921 by the London Schedule of Payments, then unsettled at British–German–American insistence, as happened after each subsequent settlement. The resultant uncertainty derived from Germany's resistance with Anglo-American support. German threats of an export drive impressed the British, as did Keynes's pronouncements, which influenced opinion where it mattered. Taylor properly notes that German impoverishment derived from the war, not from reparations, but should add that its scale was modest compared to that of the continental victors, especially of France.

The key reparations battle came with France's "occupation" of the Ruhr in January 1923. Premier Raymond Poincaré opposed military action and hoped through 1922 for British cooperation in economic sanctions.[54] But, by December, he faced a British–American–German front against treaty application,[55] and saw coal for French steel production, funds for reconstruction of industrial areas, the treaty itself and France's wartime victory draining away. Caught between Germany, Britain and the powerful French Right, which urged action,[56] Poincaré lacked maneuvering room and so reluctantly moved narrowly to avoid becoming the loser of World War I. The Ruhr encirclement was profitable[57] and caused neither the German hyperinflation, which began in 1922 and ballooned because of German responses to the Ruhr occupation, nor the franc's 1924 collapse,[58] which arose from French financial practices and the evaporation of reparations. Poincaré won the battle, forcing Germany to acknowledge its treaty obligations, but lost the war because he failed to capitalize on his victory while he had the upper hand, and the Allies swung to the other side.

Poincaré lost the 1924 election more from the franc's collapse and ensuing taxation than from diplomatic isolation, so Edouard Herriot led France to the first of two decisive defeats. Herriot made mistakes before and during the London reparations conference but, given the British–American–German front against France, whether another premier could have salvaged more is questionable.[59] Taylor correctly gives MacDonald generous credit for the 1924 settlement. His policy did not differ from his predecessors' (and he gave France no more, except blither) but his style and tone did, and that mattered. Moreover, France was now at the mercy of American bankers who dictated many terms.[60] Reparations payments were sharply reduced, with gradual increases to a substantial amount – at which point Germany would seek new revision. France lost preponderance on the reparations commission, the right of sanctions against future German default, and hope of a German trade treaty before 1925.[61] Taylor notes that the treaty provided artificial compensations to France for Germany's inherently greater power, but omits that many were temporary and that in 1924 France lost several advantages vital to its economic future and to treaty enforcement, losses which affected the power balance, accentuating French weakness.

Taylor says that France learned "the folly of coercion" (p. 54). In fact, it learned the futility of seeking partial treaty enforcement without token British co-operation and American consent. Taylor assumes that because treaty enforcement largely collapsed in 1924–5 (while contradictorily assuming most of the treaty remained intact in 1939), it was inevitable that it do so. Actually, the treaty could have been enforced – with a different set of British and, perhaps, American assumptions and policies. Non-military actions to compel fulfillment were available – such as seizing customs receipts, taxing German exports to victors,[62] surprise disarmament inspections, requiring Germany to tax to the level of the victors (as the treaty specified), or to transfer some railway profits –

but these required a degree of Allied unity which did not exist. Taylor never considers non-military enforcement, but he knows Britain and the United States thought the war ended in 1918 and were not alarmed at the prospect of German resurgence; however, he ignores the implications of their short-sightedness. In truth, in 1924 the English-speaking nations arranged a crushing defeat of France and victory for Germany, unappreciated by the latter because it was not total. Thereafter, France's will sagged.

France's second defeat, against which it did not struggle, came when Britain rejected the Geneva Protocol and a pact with France in favor of the Locarno treaties, which formalized Britain's temporary return to the power equation's center.[63] French officials disliked the German proposal of a Rhineland pact but feared rejection would end all hope of a British guarantee. Aristide Briand agreed, and energetically pursued the scheme, not daring to fail again to gain the essential British guarantee, even if the pact gave parity to Germany.[64] Taylor's discourse on Locarno is sometimes confused, but he correctly concludes that the military guarantee was inoperable (p. 58). He errs in thinking any leader except Chamberlain and Stresemann liked the settlement. The other men of Locarno knew defeat when they saw it. French leaders had few illusions; early on, the treaties were interpreted as giving Germany a green light in the east.[65] When Stresemann refused any written declaration that he would not try to revise the Polish frontier by force,[66] the final treaties confirmed this view. Stresemann also argued, with technical accuracy, that the Locarno treaties did not exclude peaceful territorial change in the west,[67] and five days after the closing ceremony at Locarno he sought retrocession of Eupen-Malmédy from Belgium.[68] He also told Germans that, once circumstances changed, treaties were no longer valid; thus, when Germany rearmed, reconquest of Alsace–Lorraine could not be excluded.[69] In truth, Locarno changed little, neither French fears nor German revisionism. Relations among the powers remained strained and the German problem unresolved.[70]

Taylor says Locarno ended the First World War but omits who won. Locarno signified France's defeat and Germany's return to diplomatic equality and potential superiority. France had deployed all weapons short of war, not always wisely or well, trying to enforce the treaty and maintain its security, but was defeated by the combination of its allies with the enemy and the relaxation of its own will. By 1925, much of the Versailles system was gone, and more followed Locarno; what ensued in the next five years (the Depression aside) was implicit in the settlements. Britain continued to pursue *de facto* treaty revision, which never satisfied a Germany seeking outright renunciation; as Taylor notes, with more concessions, German resentment grew. Although he argues that "Locarno gave to Europe a period of peace and hope," (p. 58) it actually provided no solid peace, only a fragile respite of civility as Stresemann and Briand circled warily, seeking interim solutions politically possible to both, with Chamberlain as referee. In the late 1920s, the question was not whether the 1919 treaty would be revised by war or peace, as Taylor claims (pp. 54–60), but how soon revision would occur peacefully and when Germany would return to predominance. Both the principals saw what lay ahead; Stresemann tried to accelerate its advent, Briand to delay it. When Stresemann complained, influential British and American voices supported him.[71] Scarred by France's renewed 1926 financial crisis and trying to salvage something, in 1928, Poincaré and Briand accepted early evacuation of the Rhineland to gain a "final" reparations plan which lasted eighteen months.[72] In desperation, Briand pursued European union,[73] hoping to enmesh Germany in European integration and freeze the political status quo, because he knew the old weapons were gone.

Taylor's assessment of Briand and Stresemann is perceptive, though both were less sincere and Stresemann more skillful than he suggests. Historians have focused on these dominant figures of the late 1920s, tending to view both as less noble and more hard-headed than was previously the case. Stresemann is now seen as less a "good European" than a German nationalist, while some regard Briand as craven, or duplicitous, and as the first French appeaser. Taylor correctly views Briand's clouds of rhetoric as "romantic utterance" (p. 57) but omits that they stemmed partly from lack of diplomatic and military weapons. Taylor is right that Stresemann's task was more difficult than Bismarck's but oversimplifies in saying that Stresemann chose peace over war (pp. 54–5). Despite rapid improvement, Germany's position remained weak, and treaty revision by force was not yet feasible, as Stresemann noted. He substituted conciliation for confrontation as a more effective and less costly means to unchanged goals.

The reassessment of British policy, which was similarly consistent despite variations in technique and tone, downgrades it from far-seeing wisdom to blind ruthlessness encased in elevated rhetoric, for restoring Europe's strongest nation to continental predominance was not in Britain's interest. David Lloyd George's historical reputation has not improved, though MacDonald has gained a few admirers; Chamberlain emerges as an exceptionally nice man of limited stature. On the other hand, Mussolini is taken more seriously. Few would suggest that he had much moral standing, but even Briand of the ennobling rhetoric falsified his report of the Thoiry meeting, and behind Mussolini's posturing some historians discern considerable ability.

Most work published since *Origins* has derived from the opening of major archives. The Paris peace conference[74] and the international history of the 1920s enjoyed a vogue for some years because of new evidence, but nobody used it to test Taylor's ideas, for debate about his book centered on the 1930s. Such traumatic experiences as the Cold War and the Vietnam War had little effect on historical interpretation, perhaps because analogies were difficult to draw. Americans most influenced by the war in Vietnam focused on other topics. Shifts in interpretation occurred primarily as a result of which archives were opened, and when.

The German files were accessible first, so a batch of books reflected nostalgia[75] for "poor old Weimar," destroyed by the treaty, the Depression, and the wicked French. It was for long almost axiomatic that these factors alone caused Hitler's advent, though a few voices suggested otherwise;[76] the old view lingers, but one can now suggest that some responsibility fell to the citizenry. The

Weimar records are valuable, but western scholars using them wrote much nonsense about the need for German "reconstruction" when it was the victors who needed reconstructing; they argued, too, that the Maginot line threatened Germany – as if it could lumber across the frontier – and assumed wrongly that, since the *Reischsvervand der deutschen Industrie* representing the German iron–steel–coal complex was so dominant, the same must have been true of the *Comité des Forges* of French steel companies.

Next came American and British archives, reinforcing the German view. Of the two, the American files are the less important, unless the papers of bankers are added. The massive, minuted British records are invaluable – and misleading since few British officials questioned their own assumptions or the policy they conducted. As Taylor notes, "morality" mattered to the British (p. 183); others call it self-righteousness. Whichever it was, it played well to historians. Though one can infer from British files that Poincaré did not want to enter the Ruhr, few researchers did. Again, scholars adopted the viewpoint of what they read, and for some years assumptions about British far-sightedness and generosity were reinforced.[77]

Finally, French, Italian, and Belgian archives (and that of the League of Nations) offered new information and a corrective to one-sided evidence. The massive Belgian records compensate on German questions for the paucity of internal French memoranda and loss of some dossiers in the Second World War. Surviving French files reveal disarray, disorganization, and confused planning, not only among government departments but also in their dealings with elements such as the *Comité des Forges*; the contrast with German methods and comparative cohesiveness is startling. In administration and policy planning, France had not reached the twentieth century, a factor which influenced the power equation.[78] Poincaré-la-guerre emerges as a timid procrastinator, fearful of decisions and ignorant of monetary matters.[79] Italian files add to the evidence, and not only about Italy. Numerous books have appeared based on these archives, some providing a more balanced analysis.[80] Others improve on the evidence or suppress it to French benefit, as still happens with German records to enhance Weimar's reputation, for the craft imposes few controls on the practitioner.

Historians now have most of the evidence they can expect, except as to east-European archives. Though some private papers and a few government files remain closed, most German, west-European, and American records are available. To the east, whence the surprises, if any, will probably come, the situation varies from country to country and year to year, as material is opened or closed, apparently on bureaucratic whim. But for what one author called *Great Britain, France and the German Problem*,[81] evidence is plentiful and historians need only to master it. As D. C. Watt remarked,[82] the quantity of material renders the task daunting, but some scholars have the necessary fortitude.[83] And do they confirm or deny Taylor's arguments? Despite the lack of consensus, they do a bit of both.

The records confirm some of Taylor's judgments, and he was among the leaders in certain insights. He asserted that relaxing the treaty would render

Germany "as strong, or almost as strong," as before (p. 28); others since have seen that comparatively it was stronger.[84] Taylor's approach to the 1919 Polish settlement was calmer than others'. He pointed to German resurgence and internal pressures for German rearmament, since confirmed by archival research;[85] some still echo him in less-measured tones about Germany's innate right to rearm, failing to ask: rearmament to what end? Taylor's focus on reparations was sound, if not always accurate, and more judicious than some in the early literature. He was right that Germans blamed all woes on reparations and transferred their feelings to the entire treaty. He saw that Germans convinced London that reparations were unjust (and harmful to Britain's economy), leading it to apply this view of some clauses to most (pp. 49–50), though he ignores the parallel development and its significance. The absence of the vital connection is an instance of Taylor's failure to put the pieces together to discover why the interwar era went awry.

Since key clashes in the Franco-German struggle came over reparations, with implications for treaty enforcement and the power equation, historians have tackled this abstruse topic.[86] Many of their findings could have been ascertained earlier, had their elders consulted published documents instead of journalistic accounts. Historians returned to the texts, and to studies of economic theory, and reached a degree of consensus. Most now think the 1921 London Schedule of Payments probably lay within Germany's capacity to pay, had it been willing to try, and amounted to 50 milliard gold marks in nominal value, the present value being less. The rest of the ostensible 132 milliard gold marks (nominal value) represented camouflage to bridge the gap between feasibility and popular expectations and also, if possible, to provide worthless paper to exchange for American war-debt cancellation.[87] Most think the transfer problem, allegedly the barrier to substantial payments, was exaggerated. Certainly, there is no dispute about the importance of the issue.[88]

Historians agree with Taylor about the speed of Germany's return to predominance, but instead of ascribing this phenomenon to Germany's natural place and an inevitable process, they ask why it happened so fast. Instead of declaring the treaty devoid of "moral validity," they ask why Germans and others rejected it and why it disintegrated so quickly, noting that, because of the former, the answer to the latter was an anti-French coalition with powerful economic, financial, and propaganda weapons. These historians deem the German problem more complex than did Taylor, and they examine aspects in Taylor's beloved power balance which he ignored. They cast their net wider, focusing on German determination and self-delusion, the assertiveness of German nationalism, and British blindness in helping Berlin to reverse the 1918 military verdict. They emphasize French frailties, Belgian ambivalence in balancing between Britain and France, and pressure by American bankers toward "appeasement" of Germany. Instead of attacking Taylor's focus on the power equation, these historians examine economic, financial, ethnic, and domestic political and emotional factors which Taylor had scanted. In particular, they stress France's dependence on German coal, coke, and outlets, along with

Britain's obstruction of Franco-German economic arrangements. Though they agree that Germany had greater power potential than France in more senses than Taylor mentions, few view the postwar era with Taylor's determinism as an inevitable German drive "to restore the natural order of things" (pp. 22, 61).

When *Origins* appeared, some reviewers faulted Taylor's focus on diplomacy. But his postwar power balance operates in military terms, though no major wars were in sight and Germany had no usable military arm but instead relied on other weapons.[89] He talks of men available for armies, and of whether the 1919 settlement would be revised peacefully or by war, but not of other pieces of the power balance. This military focus is inadequate for analysis of an era when no country had aims in Europe achievable by war. Despite British fears of France, French fears of Germany, and Russian fears of the capitalist west, nobody seriously contemplated fighting. Stresemann talked privately of reconquest of Alsace–Lorraine when Germany was rearmed, but did he mean it? At best, this was last on his long agenda. Germany could not fight; the victors had no thought of doing so. Mussolini's oratory was bellicose but his escapades minor; nobody else even talked of war. Taylor says it was easier to continue war in 1918 than to threaten to renew it in June 1919, and threats of renewed war became less viable as time passed (p. 32). In fact, renewed war was not mentioned after June 1919. All actions the victors debated or took were limited sanctions for enforcement purposes. In the largest, in the Ruhr, Poincaré did not foresee passive resistance. Though he was playing France's last trump in a decisive contest, and despite France's critical shortage of troops and coal, he never considered barring money and food shipments to force the Ruhr back to work. Though Germany refused to feed conquered civilians in 1914–18, he was not so brutal.

Taylor's focus on force obscures other factors. This is why he dismisses Russia, ignoring its economic and military potential and Rapallo's importance, and says that "the only economic effect of reparations was to give employment to a large number of bookkeepers" (p. 42). This is why he claims there was no prospect of communism in Europe for twenty years after Russia's 1920 defeat at Warsaw, for he assumes Marxism could only arrive via the Red army (p. 44), and dismisses Stresemann's efforts to parlay the plaints of German minorities in *cordon sanitaire* states into east-European territorial revision.[90] This is why he scants British fear of continental involvement and nostalgia for an earlier era, ignores constraints imposed by public opinion on French and German leaders, and deems the Ruhr occupation a failure instead of examining the array France faced afterwards. This is why he thinks France threw away its victory after it was lost, and why he faults France for not being militarily aggressive in a period when it, like most countries, was seeking a stable peace.

This is also why Taylor barely mentions the 1930 Rhineland evacuation (p. 60). French forces there in 1929 and 1930 were scant but important as a bargaining counter, a deterrent to German moves eastward, and a symbol of German defeat; since recognition of that defeat had long since evaporated from Germany's collective consciousness, the occupation was a major grievance. When it ended, Berlin issued a fervently nationalistic proclamation.[91] The

French evacuation in June 1930 released the brake from pent-up German nationalism which exploded in the 1930 election, dominated by foreign-policy issues. However, the Nazis aside, the focus was on reversion to 1914.[92] Taylor ignores these facts, though Hitler bragged that he never accepted anything under the treaty and took his first stride toward power in that election.

This brings us to Hitler in comparison to his Weimar predecessors. True, his early diplomatic moves polished off items on Stresemann's list. But Weimar politicians were preoccupied with the Polish Corridor, whereas Hitler was not. Though the war which Taylor addresses, the European war of 1939, started there, Poland was not important in Hitler's thinking, for he saw it as either an obedient satellite or an area to cross en route to Russia.[93] Some Weimar leaders hoped to regain Alsace–Lorraine, but their wider aims did not extend far beyond the boundaries of 1914, *Anschluss* aside. They shrank from confrontation with Britain and would have swooned at the idea of attacking Russia. Granted, the opportunity was not yet there, but many Weimar notables were horrified when it happened, and Hitler had declared this as a primary goal long before it was possible.[94] Without becoming embroiled in continuity theory, one can say that Hitler's aims were more vast, his ideology different, and his methods more drastic than those of his predecessors. Weimar politicians wanted treaty revision; even in the 1920s, Hitler deemed that a mistake, and posited more sweeping goals.[95] Germany did not fight "specifically in the second war to reverse the verdict of the first and to destroy the settlement which followed it." Much of that was destroyed before Hitler took office, and much more had become so by 1939. Despite Taylor's assertion that Hitler's "foreign policy was that of his predecessors" (pp. 23, 70–1), his world view was far more grandiose.[96] Whether one looks back on the Weimar years from the perspective of the late 1930s or forward from the 1920s toward the Nazi era, the idea that the Second World War had been "implicit since the moment when the first war ended" (p. 267) is simplistic, and the concept of Hitler as one more Weimar politician struggling manfully against the shackles of Versailles contradicts the evidence from both eras.

Notes

1 Most major essays are collected in: E. M. Robertson (ed.), *The Origins of the Second World War*, London, 1971; W. R. Louis (ed.), *The Origins of the Second World War: A. J. P. Taylor and His Critics*, New York, 1972; and *Journal of Modern History*, vol. 49, 1977. Also K. L. Nelson and S. C. Olin, Jr, *Why War?*, Berkeley, CA, 1979, and W. H. Dray, "Concepts of causation in A. J. P. Taylor's account of the origins of the Second World War," *History and Theory*, vol. 18, 1978. And see the biographies by R. Cole, *A. J. P. Taylor*, New York, 1993, and A. Sisman, *A. J. P. Taylor*, London, 1994.

2 A. J. P. Taylor, *The Origins of the Second World War*, New York, 1961, p. 70. All citations are of this edition unless otherwise noted.

3 E. Weber, *The Hollow Years: France in the 1930s*, New York, 1994, p. 11.

4 This was corrected in the 1983 edition. In both, he misdates *Mein Kampf* and inflates into an orange the German lemon which Sir Eric Geddes wished to squeeze until the pips squeaked.

5 G. A. Craig terms the early chapters "masterly" in his essay "Provocative, perverse view of pre-1939", in Louis, *Origins*, p. 110. They are praised in Robertson, *Origins*, by T. W. Mason, pp. 105–6 and E. M. Robertson, p. 15.

6 R. Poidevin and J. Bariéty., *Les relations franco-allemands*, Paris, 1977, pp. 236–7.

7 Taylor, *Origins*, 1983 edn, p. xiv.

8 In March 1919, the American government privately reminded Germany that the Allies had won and rejected Germany's interpretation that the war lacked victors. See *Akten der Reichskanzlei, Weimar Republic* [hereafter *ARWR*]: *Das Kabinett Scheidemann*, Boppard am Rhein, 1971, p. 28.

9 J. F. V. Keiger, *Raymond Poincaré*, Oxford, 1997, p. 248; S. A. Schuker, "The Rhineland question," in M. F. Boemeke *et al.* (eds), *The Treaty of Versailles*, Washington, DC, 1998, pp. 275–312.

10 See K. Schwabe, "Germany's peace aims and the domestic and international constraints," and F. Klein, "Between Compiegne and Versailles," in Boemeke *et al.*, *Versailles*, pp. 37–68 and 203–20.

11 M. F. Boemeke, "Woodrow Wilson's image of Germany, the war-guilt question, and the treaty of Versailles," in Boemeke *et al.*, *Versailles*, pp. 603–14. For a study accepting German views, see A. Lentin, *The Versailles Peace Settlement*, London, 1991, pp. 6, 14. Whether Taylor does so is unclear: see *Origins*, p. 32.

12 H. Heiber, *The Weimar Republic*, trans. W. E. Yuill, Oxford, 1993, p. 38. Also I. Geiss, "The Weimar Republic between the Second and Third Reich," in M. Laffan (ed.), *The Burden of German History*, London, 1988, pp. 68–9.

13 M. Lee and W. Michalka, *German Foreign Policy*, Leamington Spa, 1987, p. 19.

14 N. Sauvée-Dauphin, "L'occupation prussienne à Versailles," in P. Levillain and R. Riemenschneider (eds), *La guerre de 1870/71 et ses conséquences*, Bonn, 1990, p. 231.

15 R. G. L. Waite, *Vanguard of Nazism*, New York, 1969 edn, p. 7.

16 K. Schwabe, *Woodrow Wilson, Revolutionary Germany, and Peacemaking*, trans. R. and R. Kimber, Chapel Hill, NC, 1985, p. 444n, and see pp. 300–29; M. Kitchen, *Europe Between the Wars*, London, 1988, pp. 1–4; Heiber, *Weimar Republic*, p. 36; Laffan, *Burden*, pp. 81–3; Lee and Michalka, *German Foreign Policy*, p. 19.

17 S. Marks, "Smoke and mirrors," in Boemeke *et al.*, *Versailles*, pp. 337–70.

18 E. Glaser-Schmitt, "The Making of the Economic Peace," in Boemeke *et al.*, *Versailles*; S. Marks, "German–American relations, 1918–1921," in *Mid-America*, vol. 53, 1971: 5.

19 W. Murray, "The collapse of empire," in Murray *et al.* (eds), *The Making of Strategy*, New York, 1994, pp. 396–7; A. P. Adamthwaite, *Grandeur and Misery*, London, 1995, pp. 86–8; H. H. Herwig, "Clio deceived," in K. Wilson (ed.), *Forging the Collective Memory*, Providence, RI, 1996, pp. 87–127; F. Fischer, *From Kaiserreich to Third Reich*, trans. R. Fletcher, London, 1986, p. 83.

20 Herwig, "Clio," p. 87; Lentin, *Versailles*, pp. 14–16; Keiger, *Poincaré*, pp. 271, 291; Fritz Fischer, *Germany's Aims in the First World War*, New York, 1967. Fischer echoed L. Albertini, *The Origins of the War of 1914*, London, 1952, 3 vols, but no German historian had accepted this interpretation.

21 In August 1914 the chancellor told the Reichstag that the 1839 treaties committing Prussia and, later, Germany to Belgium's defense, which Germany had just violated, were a "scrap of paper."

22 In March 1919, several Weimar cabinet members acknowledged German culpability in the war's outbreak but declined responsibility for their predecessors' actions. See *ARWR, Das Kabinett Scheidemann*, pp. 78–88.

23 In March 1919, Lloyd George's manufactured evidence about starving German children and his Fontainebleau memorandum started a trend. Baron Riddell, *Lord Riddell's Intimate Diary of the Peace Conference and After*, London, 1933, p. 210; United States, Department of State, *Papers Relating to the Foreign Relations of the United States: The Paris Peace Conference. 1919*, Washington, DC, 1942–7, 13 vols [hereafter *FRUS PPC*]: vol. 2, pp. 139–43; D. Lloyd George, *Memoirs of the Peace Conference*, 2 vols, New

Haven, CT, 1939; vol. 1, pp. 265–73. Britain had told Berlin that German war guilt was "undeniably established," *ARWR, Das Kabinett Scheidemann*, p. 85.

24 Comte de Saint-Aulaire, *Confession d'un vieux diplomate*, Paris, 1953, p. 644.

25 *ARWR, Die Kabinette Wirth I und II*, 2 vols, Boppard am Rhein, 1973, vol. 2, pp. 1,059–60.

26 Italy, Ministero degli affari esteri, *I documenti diplomatici italiani*, settima serie, Rome, 1953–, vol. 3, p. 320; Great Britain, Foreign Office, *Documents on British Foreign Policy 1919–1939* [hereafter *DBFP*], London, 1958– 1st series, vol. 16, p. 862; Belgium, *Documents diplomatiques belges. 1920–1940* [hereafter *DDB*], 5 vols, Brussels, 1964–6; vol. 1, pp. 360–1, 385–6, 412–14.

27 *ARWR, Das Kabinett Cuno*, Boppard am Rhein, 1968, pp. 49–50.

28 On 4 March 1921, Lloyd George officially cited the Frankfurt treaty to German delegates and then privately assured them that if German responsibility for the war were repudiated, the Versailles treaty would disintegrate. *DBFP*, series 1, vol. 15, p. 259; *ARWR, Das Kabinett Fehrenbach*, Boppard am Rhein, 1972, p. 510.

29 S. A. Schuker, *The End of French Predominance in Europe*, Chapel Hill, NC, 1976, and Schuker, "Europe's banker: the American banking community and European reconstruction, 1918–1922," in M. Petricioli (ed.), *A Missed Opportunity?*, Bern, 1995, pp. 47–60.

30 S. Marks, "Mussolini and Locarno," *Journal of Contemporary History*, vol. 14, 1979, pp. 423–39; also the collection, "Italy in the aftermath of the First World War," *International History Review*, vol. 8, 1986, pp. 27–82.

31 D. Stevenson, "The empty chair at the peace conference," in W. R. Keylor (ed.), *The Legacy of the Great War*, Boston, MA, 1997, pp. 55–61; C. Fink, *The Genoa Conference*, Chapel Hill, NC, 1984.

32 R. H. Haigh, D. S. Morris, and A. R. Peters, *Soviet Foreign Policy, the League of Nations, and Europe*, Totowa, NJ, 1986, pp. 7–8.

33 P. Krüger, *Die Aussenpolitik der Republik von Weimar*, Darmstadt, 1985, pp. 282, 284; M. Laffan, "Weimar and Versailles," in Laffan (ed.), *Burden*, p. 86.

34 S. Marks, "The misery of victory," *Historical Papers*, 1986, p. 120.

35 P. Krüger, "A rainy day," in C. Fink *et al.* (eds), *Genoa, Rapallo, and European Reconstruction*, Washington, DC, 1991, pp. 59, 64.

36 P. Krüger, *Versailles*, Munich, 1986, p. 146; J. Hiden, *Republican and Fascist Germany*, London, 1996, pp. 27–8.

37 J. Jacobson, "The Soviet Union and Versailles," in Boemeke *et al.*, *Versailles*, pp. 451–68, Jacobson, *When the Soviet Union Entered World Politics*, Berkeley, CA, 1994. R. Debo, *Revolution and Survival*, Toronto, 1979, and *Survival and Consolidation*, Montreal, 1992. On the Russo-German tie, see W. Laqueur, *Russia and Germany*, Boston, MA, 1965, and K. Rosenbaum, *Community of Fate*, Syracuse, NY, 1965.

38 D. Dutton, *Austen Chamberlain*, New Brunswick, NJ, 1985, p. 238.

39 Most of the Saar Basin's coal was anthracite, not bituminous coking coal.

40 Hiden, *Fascist Germany*, p. 113; S. D. Carls, *Louis Loucheur and the Shaping of Modern France*, Baton Rouge, LA, 1993, p. 9; G. D. Feldman, *The Great Disorder*, Oxford, 1993; C-L. Holtfrerich, *The German Inflation*, trans. T. Balderston, Berlin, 1986.

41 N. Jordan, *The Popular Front and Central Europe*, New York, 1992, p. 5.

42 R. J. Young, *Power and Pleasure*, Montreal, 1991, pp. 160–2, and *France and the Origins of the Second World War*, New York, 1996, p. 12.

43 R. A. Doughty, "The illusion of security," in Murray *et al.* (eds), *Strategy*, p. 474; J. R. Ferris, *Men, Money, and Diplomacy*, Ithaca, NY, 1989, p. 104.

44 P. M. H. Bell, *France and Britain, 1900–1940*, London, 1996; S. Marks, "Mesentente cordiale," in Petricioli (ed.), *Missed Opportunity*.

45 *ARWR, Das Kabinett Cuno*, p. 192.

46 Keynes's passion for Carl Melchior, the German reparations expert whom he met after the armistice, and his guilt as a pacifist at having aided London during the war, shaped his views. J. M. Keynes, *Two Memoirs*, New York, 1949; R. Skidelsky, *John*

Maynard Keynes, London, vol. 1, 1983, pp. 356–7, 364; J. M. Keynes, *Collected Writings*, 30 vols, New York, 1971–89; vol. 18, pp. 159–60.

47 Taylor claims (pp. 31, 48) that France retarded reparations settlements to remain on the Rhine. Actually, after many coal-payment defaults had demonstrated German bad faith, Paris argued the 5–10–15-year occupation terms would not begin. This security-based argument was a casualty of the 1924 settlement.

48 Taylor confuses Germany's economy, healthy compared to those of the continental victors, with its fiscal and monetary shambles. Germany falsified its economic data and postponed fiscal and monetary reform to gain reparations reductions. After mid-1921, cash reparations were a trickle, financed as earlier by foreign loans repudiated by Hitler. Beyond the export advantage, Germany profited (approximately totalling all payments in cash and kind through 1923) from the inflation until mid-1922, thanks to foreign speculation in the mark which, owing to its depreciation, equaled a direct capital transfer. K.-L. Holtfrerich, "Internationale Verteilungsfolgen der deutschen Inflation," *Kyklos*, vol. 30, 1977/8, pp. 271–91; S. A. Schuker, *American "Reparations" to Germany*, Princeton, NJ, 1988; Skidelsky, *Keynes*, vol. 2, p. 117; P. Krüger, *Deutschland und die Reparationen*, Stuttgart, 1973, pp. 182, 210; Heiber, *Weimar Republic*, p. 86.

49 P. M. Burnett, *Reparation at the Paris Peace Conference*, 2 vols, Washington, DC, 1940; vol. 1, pp. 25, 54–8. Britons on the peace conference's Commission on Reparation produced astronomical figures, but Keynes estimated 40–60 milliard, favoring the higher figure. Keynes, *Collected Writings*, vol. 16, p. 378. A milliard is an American billion, but "billion" has another meaning in Britain, so "milliard" is more exact. Whereas the paper mark depreciated rapidly, the gold mark held at 4 to the dollar and 20 to the pound.

50 Peace conference estimates of civilian damage were 60–100 milliard gold marks. The US Army Corps of Engineers' final figure, excluding damage in Russia, Poland, and Czechoslovakia, was 160 milliard gold marks. Burnett, *Reparation*, vol. 2, pp. 49, 46.

51 Marks, "Smoke and Mirrors"; Krüger, *Deutschland*, pp. 187, 198–9; Heiber, *Weimar Republic*, p. 67; J. M. Keynes, *The Economic Consequences of the Peace*, New York, 1920, pp. 222–3.

52 Krüger, *Deutschland*, pp. 210–13.

53 The sole major study remains D. Artaud, *La Question des dettes interalliées*, 2 vols, Lille, 1978.

54 When Poincaré decided to enter the Ruhr is unclear. Archival evidence suggests he hoped for united action until January 4, 1923. See also Schuker, *French Predominance*, pp. 21–5, Keiger, *Poincaré*, pp. 290–3; M. J. Carley, "The shoe on the other foot," *Canadian Journal of History*, vol. 26, 1991, pp. 581–7.

55 The American element consisted primarily of financiers.

56 Schuker, *French Predominance*, pp. 20–1; Carley, "Shoe".

57 Profits were held on the reparations account for all victors, but for technical reasons most went to Belgium. Profits (after Ruhr–Rhineland occupation costs) were nearly 900 million gold marks, *FRUS PPC*, vol. 13, pp. 487, 785. These figures should not be compared to the defunct London Schedule but to the four-year cessation of payments Britain demanded in January 1923.

58 Schuker, *French Predominance*, is definitive.

59 Schuker, *French Predominance*, pp. 386, 392.

60 J. Bariéty, *Les Relations franco-allemandes après la première guerre mondiale*, Paris, 1977; Schuker, *French Predominance*.

61 France's defeat was evident to contemporary observers. Bariéty, *Les Relations*, p.718; S. Marks, "The myths of reparations," in Keylor (ed.), *Legacy*, pp.155–67.

62 Britain did this for several years, but when France tried to do likewise Germany howled.

63 E. Goldstein, "The evolution of British diplomatic strategy for the Locarno Pact," in M. Dockrill and B. McKercher, *Diplomacy and World Power*, New York, 1996, p. 115.

64 For Briand's first effort toward a British treaty, see S. Marks, "Ménage à trois," *International History Review*, vol. 4, 1982, pp. 524–52.

65 A. Adamthwaite, *The Lost Peace*. New York, 1981, p. 65; Poidevin and Bariéty, *Les Rélations*, p.268; *DDB*, vol. 2, p. 213.

66 G. Stresemann, *Vermächtnis*, 3 vols, Berlin, 1932; vol. 2, p. 233.

67 Texts: Great Britain, Parliamentary Command Paper [hereafter Cmd] 2525, 1925; Stresemann's interpretation: *Vermächtnis*, vol. 2, pp. 232–3, and M. J. Enssle, *Stresemann's Territorial Revisionism*, Wiesbaden, 1980, pp. 109–12.

68 *DDB*, vol. 2, p. 399.

69 Enssle, *Stresemann's Territorial Revisionism*, pp. 85–6, 104, 113, 126, 128. Briand challenged Stresemann's view through diplomatic channels but not publicly lest he jeopardize ratification.

70 Dutton, *Austen Chamberlain*, p. 262.

71 J. Jacobson, *Locarno Diplomacy*, Princeton, NJ, 1972, Part 4.

72 *DBFP*, Series IA, vol. 5, p. 335. Texts of the Young plan and Hague conference documents: Cmd 3484, 1930, Cmd 3763, 1931, and Cmd 3766, 1931.

73 *DBFP*, Series 2, vol. 1, pp. 314–24.

74 Key recent works on the peace conference: A. Sharp, *The Versailles Settlement*, New York, 1991, Boemeke *et al.* (eds), *Versailles*, and Keylor (ed.), *Legacy*. My thanks to Prof. Keylor and Dr D. Mattern for pre-publication knowledge of the latter works. English-language studies: A. J. Mayer, *Politics and Diplomacy of Peacemaking*, New York, 1967; I. Floto, *Colonel House in Paris*, Åarhus, Denmark, 1973; K. Lundgreen-Nielsen, *The Polish Problem at the Paris Peace Conference*, Odense, Denmark, 1979; S. Marks, *Innocent Abroad*, Chapel Hill, NC, 1981; Schwabe, *Woodrow Wilson*; A. Walworth, *Wilson and his Peacemakers*, New York, 1986; L. S. Jaffe, *The Decision to Disarm Germany*, Boston, MA, 1985.

75 R. J. Schmidt, *Versailles and the Ruhr*, The Hague, 1968; D. Felix, *Walther Rathenau and the Weimar Republic*, Baltimore, MD, 1971, and, to a degree, H. J. Rupieper, *The Cuno Government and Reparations*, The Hague, 1979.

76 H. W. Gatzke, *Stresemann and the Rearmament of Germany*, Baltimore, MD, 1954; A. Thimme, "Stresemann and Locarno," in Gatzke (ed.), *European Diplomacy Between Two Wars*, Chicago, IL, 1972, pp. 73–93.

77 D. Marquand, *Ramsay MacDonald*, London, 1977.

78 The situation emerges in the archival material. See also Schuker, *French Predominance*, pp. 365–7, 385; J. Gillingham, *Coal, Steel and the Rebirth of Europe*, Cambridge, 1991, p. 14.

79 Keiger, *Poincaré*.

80 A. Cassels, *Mussolini's Early Diplomacy*, Princeton, NJ, 1970; R. J. B. Bosworth, *Italy and the Wider World*, London, 1996.

81 W. M. Jordan, *Great Britain, France and the German Problem*, London, 1943.

82 D. C. Watt, "Some aspects of A. J. P. Taylor's work as diplomatic historian," *Journal of Modern History*, vol. 49, 1977: 30.

83 English-language surveys: Adamthwaite, *Lost Peace*; S. Marks, *The Illusion of Peace*, London, 1976, and Kitchen, *Europe Between the Wars*. Monographs: P. S. Wandycz, *France and Her Eastern Allies*, Minneapolis, MN, 1962, and *The Twilight of French Eastern Alliances*, Princeton, NJ, 1988; Jacobson, *Locarno Diplomacy*; C. S. Maier, *Recasting Bourgeois Europe*, Princeton, NJ, 1975; Schuker, *French Predominance*; Gatzke, *Stresemann*; Anne Orde, *Britain and International Security*, London, 1978, and *British Policy and European Reconstruction after the First World War*, Cambridge, 1990; D. H. Aldcroft, *From Versailles to Wall Street*, Berkeley, CA, 1977; and K. L. Nelson, *Victors Divided*, Berkeley, CA, 1975.

84 F. H. Hinsley, "The origins of the Second World War," in Louis (ed.), *Origins*, p. 72; G. L. Weinberg, "The defeat of Germany in 1918 and the European balance of power," in Weinberg (ed.), *Germany, Hitler and World War II*, Cambridge, 1996.

85 E. W. Bennett, *German Rearmament and the West*, Princeton, NJ, 1979.

86 English-language works: Maier, *Recasting Bourgeois Europe*; Schuker, *French Predominance* and *American "Reparations"*; M. Trachtenberg, *Reparation in World Politics*, New York, 1980; G. D. Feldman, *Iron and Steel in the German Inflation*, Princeton, NJ, 1977, and *The Great Disorder*. Also the debate in *Journal of Modern History*, vol. 51, March 1979; Marks, "Myths," in Keylor (ed.), *Legacy*, and "Smoke and mirrors," in Boemeke *et al.* (eds), *Versailles*; A. C. Mierzejewski, "Payments and Profits," *German Studies Review*, vol. 18, 1995, pp. 65–86.

87 The 50 milliard included A Bonds (the 12 milliard unpaid balance on what Germany owed by May 1, 1921) and B Bonds. C Bonds constituted the rest of the 132 milliard, subject to arithmetical adjustments. Germany paid about 22 milliard gold marks, of which less than one-third was in cash, mostly borrowed. See *FRUS PPC*, vol. 13, p. 409; Schuker, *American "Reparations"*, pp. 106–8.

88 *Journal of Modern History*, vol. 51, March 1979. Little else has been written about the historiography of the 1920s except J. Jacobson's review articles, "Strategies of French foreign policy after World War I," *Journal of Modern History*, vol. 55, 1983, pp. 78–95, and "Is there a new international history of the 1920s?", *American Historical Review*, vol. 88, 1983, pp. 617–46; C. S. Maier, "Marking time: the historiography of international relations," in M.Kammen (ed.), *The Past Before Us*, Ithaca, NY, 1980, pp. 355–87, stresses American diplomacy. For an entirely different approach see Gordon Martel, "Reflections on the war-guilt question and the settlement: a comment," in Boemeke *et al.* (eds), *Versailles*, pp. 615–36,

89 R. M. Spaulding, "The political economy of German frontiers," in C. Baechler and C. Fink (eds), *The Establishment of European Frontiers after the Two World Wars*, Bern, 1996, pp. 231–3; Fischer, *Kaiserreich*, p. 83.

90 C. Fink, "The minorities' question at the Paris peace conference," in Boemeke *et al.* (eds), *Versailles*, pp. 249–74 and "The protection of ethnic and religious minorities," in Keylor (ed.), *Legacy*, pp. 227–38.

91 *DBFP*, Series 2, vol. 1, pp. 487–8.

92 *DBFP*, Series 2, vol. 1, p. 502.

93 G. L. Weinberg, *The Foreign Policy of Hitler's Germany*, 2 vols, Chicago, IL 1970, 1980: vol. 1, pp.13–14.

94 *Hitler's Secret Book*, New York, 1961, pp. 139, 145.

95 *Secret Book*, pp. 144–5; G. L. Weinberg, "Friedenspropaganda und Kriegsvorbereitung," in W. Treue and J. Schmädeke (eds), *Deutschland 1933*, Berlin, 1984, pp. 121–2.

96 G. L. Weinberg, *World in the Balance*, Hanover, 1981, pp. 76, 81–4, 89–90, and "Die Deutsche Politik gegenüber den Vereinigten Staaten im Jahr 1941," in J. Rohwer and E. Jäckel (eds), *Kriegswende. Dezember 1941*, Frankfurt-am-Main, 1984, pp. 73–9.

3 The end of Versailles

Stephen A. Schuker

When did the Versailles system break down? A. J. P. Taylor never quite makes up his mind in *The Origins of the Second World War*. He devotes almost one-third of his book to charting the successive stages in the disintegration of the peace settlement over the course of fifteen years. But he attaches at most secondary importance to these epiphenomena. He approaches the subject on the assumption that the Versailles treaty "lacked moral validity from the start."[1]

That does not necessarily reflect his own judgment, Taylor insists (not wholly convincingly). It represents, rather, the view of the Germans and the many people in the Allied countries who came to sympathize with them (p. xi). The essence of the matter lay in the balance of demography and economic resources. Those criteria indicated that Germany remained potentially by far the greatest power on the European continent after 1919; indeed the dissolution of Austria–Hungary, the withdrawal of Russia from international affairs, and the exhaustion of France and Italy rather worsened the disparity compared with relative strengths before the war. All Germans, Taylor notes, meant to shake off some part of the peace treaty as soon as it proved convenient to do so. They differed at most over timing (pp. 24, 28). The conclusion seems to follow with disarming simplicity. The treaty was doomed from the moment that the Allies agreed to make it with a united Germany, the great unified state created by Bismarck. "Given a great Germany...the only question was whether the settlement would be revised, and Germany become again the greatest Power in Europe, peacefully or by war" (p. 51).

Was the course of events, then, foreordained once the Allies had failed to march on Berlin in 1918 and to impose a dictated peace? Is Taylor not forgetting the caveat of the distinguished medievalist F. W. Maitland – which he quotes elsewhere to telling effect – that historians should avoid "after-mindedness" and remember that "events now long in the past were once in the future?"[2] Taylor, however, is not so easily pinned down. In 1919 the danger lay "in a hypothetical future; and who could tell what the future would hold?" Out-of-office Frenchmen might peddle separatism by the back door. "High-flying historians" might lament that the work of Bismarck remained intact. Yet after every great war alarmists had feared that the defeated power would strike again. It did so rarely, or else halfheartedly (pp. 23, 25).

Here is one example, among many, of the quintessential Taylor method. He rivets one's attention with an extraordinary claim, and then qualifies it, or contradicts it, before objections are raised. Like a bantam-weight boxer, nimble on his toes, he lands a darting blow here, executes a clever feint there, and dances out of range before the reader knows what has happened. He stands as the master of history presented as a seamless web of aphorisms: "Everything about Fascism was a fraud" (p. 56). "The greatest masters of statecraft are those who do not know what they are doing" (p. 72). Does it not seem churlish to ask for proof or to inquire about documentation? Usually diplomatic historians rely on the inductive method. They are fussy, even obsessive, about sources. But other ways exist of apprehending reality. "One should absorb the color of life," Oscar Wilde once remarked, "but one should never remember its details. Details are always vulgar."[3]

As a matter of fact, Taylor offers no footnotes for his interpretation of events before 1932. He provides but a handful for the period before 1935. Perhaps that does not matter much. He aims in his first chapters principally to set the stage for his discussion of Hitler's motives and of the proximate origins of the Second World War. And those are the subjects, too, with which his critics have exclusively concerned themselves. Not a single contributor to the collections edited by, respectively, E. M. Robertson and William Roger Louis deals at any length with Taylor's analysis of diplomacy before Hitler's assumption of power.[4] Yet Taylor evidently accords considerable significance to what happened earlier. This emerges by implication from the "Second thoughts" that he prepared for the 1963 reissue of his work. "My book has really little to do with Hitler,' he protests. "The vital question, it seems to me, concerns Great Britain and France." If Germany naturally sought to become a great power again, "why did the victors not resist her?" (p. xiv).

Clearly, this formulation suggests the importance of an inquiry into the shift in the power balance that began in the first years after the Versailles treaty came into force. When Taylor published in 1961, however, historians had available to them hardly any reliable data about policy formulation in the 1920s. Even for the 1930s, Taylor found little enough to go on – mainly the published volumes of British and German diplomatic documents, supplemented by statesmen's memoirs. The "extraordinary paucity" of original records, he concedes in his own memoirs with as much frankness as grace, "makes my book a period piece of limited value."[5]

For the 1920s the situation then appeared even more discouraging. Only the defeated Germans had been forced to open their archives. Elsewhere (except in the United States) the "fifty-year-rule" still held sway. Moreover, given the intense public interest in the immediate causes of the latest world catastrophe, European governments had relegated publication of official documentary collections on the 1920s to a lower and distant priority.[6] Taylor had perforce to rely for the early period on secondary accounts – and his bibliography suggests that most of these were general surveys not informed by primary research. What could he do but to mediate the impressions garnered from those works through his own experience of the 1920s as a politically conscious young man?

By his own account, Taylor came from an unusual family of Nonconformist Lancashire cotton merchants. With a competence of £100,000 sterling, his father had retired from business to join the Gas Workers' Union, deserted the Liberal Party for Independent Labour, and for twenty years displayed his militancy on the local Trades and Labour Council, hoping to transform himself into an authentic working man. His mother, not to be outdone, progressed from anti-conscription agitation in the First World War to a romantic communism that did not preclude acting as a conduit for Soviet funds to the British Communist Party. Taylor himself was a 17-year-old fifth-former of decidedly progressive views attending Bootham, the Quaker-run public school, when Poincaré occupied the Ruhr in 1923. He had become a Labour firebrand at Oxford who thrilled to the "revolutionary enthusiasm of the common people" in Russia by the time that the frock-coated representatives of the western powers negotiated the Locarno agreements two years later. When Hitler took over the Reich chancellery in 1933, Taylor had already won local notoriety as the brilliant university lecturer who served as chief spokesman for the Manchester Anti-War Council.[7]

Of course, no one with Taylor's temperamental independence and iconoclasm could remain in an intellectual straitjacket of any sort for long. Still, hardly anyone from this background in interwar Britain had a good word to say about the Versailles treaty. None would have defended the sanctity of international obligations or expostulated on the justice of reparations and war-debt payments. Few would have grasped the importance of a strong military establishment for Britain, let alone for France. Significantly, Taylor opposed rearmament by the National Government until the mid-1930s because he feared that Britain might take Hitler's side in a war against Russia. When his anti-Nazi sentiments overcame those scruples and he swung round on rearmament in 1936, he lapsed into political inactivity. To favor armament expenditure, whatever the circumstances, was an impossible position for a man of the Left![8] The wonder is not that vestigial traces of interwar Labour views turn up in Taylor's treatment of the period. The marvel is that Taylor the mature historian could so far transcend the sentiments of his youthful milieu as to approach objectivity at all.

Yet one must somehow explain a perceptible inconstancy in Taylor's interpretation of the 1920s. Can one speculate that this derives from the unresolved tension between Taylor's youthful recollections and his subsequent reflections as a historian? How else can the reader account for his disconcerting tendency to write on both sides of almost every issue? Let us examine, for example, his successive statements on the question with which we started – when and how the Versailles system broke down.

The German army had ceased to exist as a major fighting force after the war, Taylor tells us; no one had to worry about armed conflict with the Reich for years to come. Nevertheless, measures of coercion against Germany ultimately could not work. The decision whether to comply with the treaty remained in

German hands (p. 42; see also p. 29). At each confrontation from the 1918 Armistice to the 1923 Ruhr occupation, it became more and more difficult for the Allies to threaten an application of force against Germany. Yet, in fact, by 1921 much of the peace treaty was being enforced (pp. 28, 42). Resentment against the treaty increased with every passing year, largely because of reparations. On the other hand, appeasement began not with Neville Chamberlain, but with Lloyd George, who carried it through successfully. "Even reparations were constantly revised, and always downward, though no doubt the revision dragged out tiresomely long" (pp. 42, 48). The Locarno treaties of 1925 ended the First World War and ushered in a period of "peace and hope." Indeed, the most popular cry in Germany, as late as 1929, was "No More War." All the same, appeasement was not achieved, and when the occupying forces left the Rhineland in 1930 German resentment bulked larger than ever (pp. 55–9).

The conflict between France and Germany seemed bound to continue, Taylor asserts, so long as the illusion persisted that Europe remained the center of the world. On the other hand, it appeared that "treaty revision would go on gradually, almost imperceptibly, and that a new European system would emerge without anyone noticing the exact moment when the watershed was crossed" (pp. 58–9). The French had "never possessed" a mobile army capable, in case of need, of an independent offensive against the Reich. Consequently, French foreign policy stood in fundamental contradiction with French strategy. The system of security against Germany, however, as devised in the Versailles treaty, remained intact in 1929 (pp. 59–61).

More of this follows. No reason existed why the Depression should have increased international tension. In depressions most nations turn away from foreign affairs. The Brüning Government in Germany, however, had to seek successes abroad in order to counterbalance the hardships imposed by deflation at home, and the Japanese, too, had a good case for invading Manchuria, because their trading interests had suffered devastation there. "Men who are well off forget their grievances; in adversity they have nothing else to think about" (pp. 61–2). No real negotiations were possible at the 1932–3 disarmament conference because the German Government needed a "sensational success." Yet prevailing opinion "rightly feared" the collapse of Germany, not German strength, in the midst of the Depression; and actually the Reich remained "virtually disarmed" even when Hitler came to power. On the other hand, one could not assure security for France and equality of status for Germany at the same time. By insisting upon that fact, the French nevertheless "fired the starting pistol for the arms race," although characteristically they failed to run it (pp. 67, 74, 77). As for Hitler himself, he merely took over the policies of his predecessors and indeed of almost all Germans. In principle and doctrine, he seemed "no more wicked and unscrupulous than many other contemporary statesmen." If truth be told, he did not initially concern himself much with foreign affairs, but spent the bulk of his time at Berchtesgaden, "dreaming in his old feckless way." Still, showing little talent other than his gift for patience, he somehow within two years had broken the Franco-Polish alliance, foiled an "eastern Locarno," made a first move to subvert Austria, reclaimed the Saarland, and reintroduced conscription. The artificial security system of Versailles was dead. But never mind those achievements! They proved merely that "a system cannot be a substitute for action, but can only provide opportunities for it" (pp. 68, 71–2, 86).

Paradox after paradox – the mind reels as Taylor presses onward with his pellucid prose and opaque meaning. Yet Taylor reports in his memoirs that Boswell's *Life of Dr Johnson* became his favorite book in public school and remained so ever after.[9] Did he never, when fashioning his epigrams, recall the advice that Johnson ascribes to a college tutor: "Read over your compositions, and wherever you meet with a passage which you think is particularly fine, strike it out"? Of course, we would have been lexicographically the poorer had he done so. All the same, the best-advised passengers on this historical journey will take pleasure in the gems along the path and suspend belief about the destination.

Enough has been said of the artifices by which Taylor contrives to sustain the reader's interest. Let us pass to an analysis of his fundamental views – in so far as we can distinguish them from their pyrotechnic accompaniments. Taylor rightly points out that the history of Europe between the wars revolved around the German problem (p. 40). Italian irredentism, Hungarian revisionism, the territorial squabbles among the Habsburg successor states, and the continuing colonial rivalries of the Entente powers grew from local conflicts into serious threats to peace only when they impinged on the overriding issue – how to reconcile Germany to Versailles. Historians since Taylor have questioned his assumption that Soviet Russia abandoned its efforts to undermine other governments after 1920. They have further explored the raw competitive underside to Anglo-American cooperation, particularly outside Europe; and they have emphasized the difficulties caused by the rapid change in the Far East balance of power.[10] Generally, however, they have confirmed Taylor's judgment that international relations on the European continent turned on the two conventional topics – reparations and security.

Taylor recognizes that reparations figured as the dominant problem in the first years after 1919. But he devotes limited space to this complicated issue – perhaps out of discretion. Lord Palmerston had joked of the nineteenth-century Schleswig–Holstein dispute that only three men had ever understood it; and he, the only one who had not gone mad or died, had forgotten all about it.[11] Before the research of the last generation, reparations appeared to many as the Schleswig–Holstein question of the interwar period. Taylor makes no pretense of joining the circle of initiates; still, his instincts are right as often as they are wrong, and that rates as no mean accomplishment for a book published in 1961.

Taylor shrewdly concludes that Etienne Mantoux had the better of his controversy with John Maynard Keynes over reparations (p. 44).[12] The reparations actually required from Germany – as distinct from that country's legal liability – amounted to approximately 6 percent of German national income under the 1921 London Schedule of Payments.[13] That would have represented an appreciable claim on German resources, roughly comparable to the burden imposed on some western economies as a result of the explosion in oil prices during the 1970s. To transfer such a sum would have required genuine sacrifices. But it would not have constituted an insuperable burden for a nation resolved to limit domestic consumption sufficiently to meet the levy. It would not have reduced Germany, in the picturesque phrase that Taylor borrows from Keynes, to "a state of Asiatic poverty" (p. 44). In fact, the London Schedule marked the abandonment of the unrealistic proposals bandied about by some of the British and French delegates at the Paris peace conference and an adjustment of the bill to Germany's capacity to pay.

Taylor does not deal specifically with the London Schedule. He outlines with only the barest of brush strokes the many disputatious conferences of 1920–2 at which the French endeavored to compel payment, the Germans sought to evade it, and the British twisted uneasily between the two, increasingly coming to favor concessions with the hope of reviving their export trade. But he suggests correctly what the archives have since confirmed: that Poincaré occupied the Ruhr as a last resort in 1923 in order to oblige Germany to meet its financial obligations, and not with a view to promoting the disintegration of the Reich (p. 50).[14] He shows how France snatched defeat from the jaws of victory. Germany found itself obliged to abandon government-sponsored "passive resistance" in the Ruhr. France, however, could muster neither the financial strength nor the will to go it alone. Almost inevitably, fresh negotiations within an interallied framework led to a new *de facto* reduction of the reparations bill. The moral seemed to be that the Allies could reach a stable accommodation with Germany only by engaging the latter's voluntary cooperation, and not through compulsion (pp. 44, 50).[15]

Taylor does not traffic in economic statistics, but he perceptively observes that Germany ultimately emerged as the net gainer through the financial transactions of the 1920s (p. 44). Subsequent calculations reinforce his analysis. The Dawes plan of 1924 provided a four-year partial moratorium and reduced the projected reparations levy afterward to 3.3 percent of national income. The Young plan of 1929 marked a further limitation of the Allied claim on German resources, effectively to 2.6 percent. Moreover, the Reich never paid those sums in full. In 1932 the Lausanne conference canceled reparations altogether. For the whole period 1919–31, Germany transferred to the Allies, in cash and kind together, an average of only 2.0 percent of national income. At the same time, Germany experienced a windfall profit resulting from the devaluation of foreign-owned mark-denominated assets during the 1919–23 inflation. Then, after 1931, it defaulted on most private foreign investment. These items combined yielded a unilateral transfer equal to a startling 5.3 percent of German national income for 1919–31. On balance, the United States and, to a lesser extent, the European Allies subsidized Germany during the Weimar era, and not the other way round.[16]

So far Taylor has gotten it right – as his hero Evelyn Waugh might have said: "Up to a point, sir!"[17] Characteristically, he then reverses field. The foreign subsidy of the German economy, he asserts, provided "little consolation to the German taxpayer, who was not at all the same person as the German borrower"

(p. 44).[18] Hence the average German held the "more or less rational belief" that reparations pointed down the road to ruin.[19]

The United States "complicated the problem," Taylor contends, by insisting on repayment of Allied war debts. Thus Allied taxpayers obtained little relief from reparations because they saw the proceeds immediately transferred across the Atlantic. In addition, reparations fanned international suspicion and resentment all around. This happened in part because the French "cheated": some of them did not wish to be paid, and instead attempted to exploit the situation so as to keep troops in the Rhineland or to ruin Germany forever. Yet ultimately reparations did almost as much damage to democracy in France, where they led people to lose faith in the political leadership, as they did across the Rhine. More than any other issue, in sum, reparations "cleared the way for the Second World War." Economically, however, they produced but one effect after the various capital flows were balanced against each other: "to give employment to a large number of bookkeepers" (pp. 27, 32, 44–5, 47).[20] Here we have, in short compass, a distillation of every cliché that in Britain between the wars nourished self-righteous sentiment on the part of subscribers to the fashionable intellectual weeklies and readers of the *Manchester Guardian*. Each of the substantive claims, however, turns out upon further scrutiny to be seriously misleading.

The careful reader will observe here some gratuitous pulling of Uncle Sam's beard. Actually the American debt settlements of 1923–26 required no more than token payments from the continental Allies during the first decade, and the British could not reasonably complain about an annuity claiming a mere 0.8 percent of their foreign investment portfolio. An examination of the magnitudes involved does not substantiate the common references to a circular flow of funds.[21]

But Taylor's misconceptions go beyond technical economics. He appears to have lost from sight the point of reparations in the first place – to repair the damage wrought in a war for which Germany bore primary responsibility. He starts from the premise that both sides in the conflict "found it difficult to define their war aims," that both fought only for victory (pp. 19–20). No one who had assimilated Hans Gatzke's findings in *Germany's Drive to the West* could have sustained that point of view, even in 1961.[22] Studies published since then have rendered it wholly implausible. The discoveries of Fritz Fischer and his students, and the revelations from the diary of chancellor Bethmann-Hollweg's assistant, Kurt Riezler, have underscored the almost megalomaniacal annexationism of the German leadership, civilian as well as military, from the "September program" of 1914 down to the end of the war.[23] Scholars of Allied war aims have uncovered nothing comparable.[24] Taylor acknowledges this disparity in the "Second Thoughts" prepared for his 1963 edition. Indeed, with not atypical overstatement he now accuses Bethmann-Hollweg of having nurtured more extreme aims than had Hitler, because the former sought *Lebensraum* in the west as well as the east (p. xxv).[25] Unfortunately, Taylor gives no outward sign of thinking through the implications of the new evidence. If the nations of Europe in 1914 had blundered into war by mistake, a peace of reconciliation involving a sharing of financial burdens might have helped bind up the wounds. If, however, the elites of the new Republican Germany inherited the territorial appetites of their Wilhelminian predecessors, such largesse would prove neither expedient nor wise.

At no point does Taylor clearly articulate the central issue: that whether Germany paid reparations and how much it paid would largely determine the European balance of power in the 1920s. The costs of the most destructive conflict in history had already been incurred. Someone would have to pay for the treasure spent, the foreign investment lost, the land laid waste, the ships destroyed, the men cut down on the battlefield at the start of their most productive years. Someone would have to care for the maimed, the widowed, and the orphaned. War also spurs economic growth, of course. But in this case the greatest development had taken place in Asia and the Americas, and the burgeoning manufacturing capacity outside Europe would dislocate trade patterns and make recovery for the belligerents more rather than less difficult.[26]

At the peace conference European statesmen had maneuvered to induce the United States to subsidize victors and vanquished alike by canceling war debts and purchasing reparations bonds on commercial markets. American officials, however, had declined to fall in with those schemes. Some Wall Street bankers acknowledged that their country's new-found creditor status imposed special responsibilities. But economically the United States remained remarkably self-sufficient (compared, for example, with the situation after the Second World War). Political leaders in Washington, mindful that their constituents had already spent $40 billion on the war effort, recognized from the spring of 1919 on that public sentiment would not tolerate disbursing any more.[27] Europeans had to face the question squarely: would the taxpayers, bondholders, savers, and consumers of Germany assume the main burden of reconstruction, or would their counterparts in France, Britain, and other Allied nations have to foot the bill?

Taylor, with habitual eloquence, explains how reparations took on symbolic importance for Germans outraged by the punitive aspects of the peace (pp. 44–5). If the German government won its test of wills with the Allies and undermined the reparations clauses of the Versailles treaty, it would assume a stronger moral position in its efforts to revise the territorial provisions of the European settlement. Taylor neglects to add, however, that reparations also involved the transfer of real resources, which assumed critical importance in the boom-and-bust cycle and the prolonged period of trade disruption that followed the war.

If France, most importantly, could obtain sufficient coal, coke, and capital through reparations, it might hope to rebuild its devastated districts and to promote economic revival without overstraining the nation's rickety tax and financial system. In the generation before 1914 Germany had rapidly pulled ahead of France and Britain in industrial production. It had quadrupled its steelmaking capacity – the key to military power. Could France, having secured Lorraine minette ore and Saar coal through other Versailles treaty provisions, now deploy its reparations entitlement to make a comparable leap forward?[28]

Despite the deficient mechanisms in the Paris bureaucracy for shaping long-term economic policy, certain French officials perceived this challenge clearly. That is why Jacques Seydoux of the Foreign Ministry, for example, pressed so hard in the postwar years for reparations in kind. That is why, far from trying to "ruin Germany," he sought in vain to find a formula that would link the coal, steel, potash, and chemical industries of the two nations to their mutual advantage.[29]

Taylor evinces no demonstrable interest in such technical negotiations, possibly because he believes that a united Germany would have come to dominate Europe again.[30] Admittedly, the prospects for any outcome other than this appeared slim from the beginning. France would have had to create an industrial infrastructure enabling it to sustain permanently the diplomatic position secured for the moment by a paper treaty. For that purpose reparations appeared indispensable, yet insufficient. France would also have had to maintain an unshakable alliance with Britain. But the economic interests of the two erstwhile Allies diverged.[31] If the United States refused to act as *deus ex machina* by providing loans to Germany, how could one reconcile those interests? The British suffered from their own form of "devastated areas." Two million unemployed queued disconsolately for the dole in the Midlands, on Clydeside, and in Wales. Once war passions cooled, Britain could neither tolerate the transfer of cash reparations large enough to reduce the German standard of living nor encourage deliveries in kind coupled with Franco-German industrial linkages: both prospects might further reduce the Central European market for British goods. British difficulties in fact derived as much from the wrong mix of industries, unprofessional management, and backward labour relations as they did from the state of world trade. But few discerned this at the time.[32] The Franco-British conflict over reparations steadily deepened. As it festered, all hope of forcing compliance with the treaty as a whole slipped away.

If Taylor were writing today, presumably he would make more of the connections between economics and political power. In the past generation, practitioners of diplomatic history have changed the face of the discipline by investigating questions of that sort. Today it is a commonplace that reparations determined the outcome of the struggle for power in Europe between France and Germany. The war-debt controversy similarly figured as a central element in the duel between Britain and the United States for dominance in world finance. But, for all his brilliance, Taylor approaches diplomacy the old-fashioned way. He therefore mentions the 1924 London conference only in passing. He focuses instead on the Locarno meeting fourteen months later as the turning-point of the interwar era (pp. 53–4). Today, looking back, we see clearly that the London conference provided the first unmistakable augury of the demise of the Versailles system.[33]

At the London conference France agreed to evacuate the Ruhr without any significant *quid pro quo*. Germany might for a while meet its reduced obligations under the Dawes plan or successor schemes. It would never subsequently pay reparations on a scale sufficient to change power relationships. And when it defaulted, France pledged, in effect, not to take unilateral action again. Moreover, the last chance slipped by to strike a deal on coal and steel before Germany recovered its tariff sovereignty and took advantage of its natural strengths to dominate European heavy industry. In addition, France conceded a heretofore disputed legal point with an important bearing on security. The Allies confirmed that, whether Germany had met its disarmament obligations or not, the Rhineland occupation clock had begun to run. The occupation henceforth constituted a wasting asset. French troops would have to withdraw by 1935 in any case. Why squander scarce military resources and exacerbate ill-will by remaining until the final hour?

Taylor would have us believe that, after Germany had freely accepted the Locarno accords, the French could think of no rationale for preserving reparations or perpetuating one-sided disarmament of the Reich (p. 58). Actually, few Frenchmen suffered from a bad conscience – that malady principally afflicted their friends across the English Channel. But, through financial weakness and national lassitude, they had already made the decisive concessions. When they fussed about arrangements for leaving the Cologne zone in 1926, fumed about minor conditions for terminating Allied military control in 1927, and jockeyed tiresomely for reparations advantages before withdrawing the last skeletal divisions from the Rhineland in 1929–30, they knew that they were engaged in desperate rearguard actions.[34]

In discussing security problems of the 1920s Taylor offers his usual mixture of good sense and artful obfuscation. He makes a surprisingly favorable evaluation of the Versailles territorial settlements. The new borders, even in eastern Europe, rested on the "principles of natural justice, as then interpreted" (p. 26). Germany lost only land, Taylor adds, to which it held no entitlement on national grounds. With facile insouciance he dismisses even the most bitterly voiced German grievances: the Polish Corridor had a predominantly Slavic population; the arrangements for railway communications across that area to east Prussia seemed adequate; and the lost colonies had proven a drain rather than a source of profit (p. 47).

Other historians do not on the whole confirm the claim that the mass of Germans expressed indifference to an Austrian *Anschluss* in 1919 or that they cared little about the fate of German-speaking minorities in the Sudetenland and elsewhere (though undoubtedly German plenipotentiaries at the peace conference had felt obliged to rank their objectives and concentrate their fire).[35] But ultimately it makes little difference how much German resentment against the new boundaries originated in 1919 and how much developed later. No treaty enforces itself. Certainly the Versailles treaty could not do so. The Congress of Vienna a century earlier had reached a modicum of consensus by appealing to the universally acknowledged principles of legitimacy and compensation, suitably diluted with the equally familiar values of convenience and hypocrisy. The world of 1919 comprised too many ideological divisions to hope for a similar consensus. Only the application of superior force had won the war. Only the threat of force – whether applied through a Wilsonian "concert of right" or through the cruder equilibration of the balance of power – could keep the peace.

Taylor, however, employs all his ingenuity to show why the Allies could not maintain a preponderance of power on their side. He deprecates security arrangements as "artificial" expedients that "ran against the common sense of mankind." He embraces, apparently as his own, the reasoning of the (British) man-in-the-street: "The war had been fought to settle things. What was the good of it if now there had to be new alliances, more armaments, greater international complexities than before the war started?" (pp. 27–8). Taylor dismisses, one by one, every conceivable solution for maintaining the status quo. German disarmament could work only if the Germans chose to make it work. The Anglo-American guarantee to France, even if the US Senate had not tabled it without action, constituted no more than a long-term promise to liberate France after Germany had overrun it again. France erred in seeking a substitute for the prewar Russian alliance through arrangements with Poland and the Little Entente, since those states had backward and ill-equipped armies and would require assistance rather than provide it (pp. 31–9).[36] Some truth exists in these claims – although French planners understood their dilemma and the narrow range of possible solutions rather better than Taylor suggests. But does it follow that just a single option remained: to appease the Reich sufficiently to win over the Germans, and to allow German statesmen to set the diplomatic agenda and define the terms?

Some possibilities that Taylor excludes from discussion may merit more attention. He does not dwell on the fact that France had renounced separation of the Rhineland from Germany in return for a prospective Anglo-American guarantee. Nor does he explore whether, in the absence of such a guarantee, the French government should have returned to an aggressive Rhineland policy – as some military men and local agents urged.[37] He assumes, finally, that a British government with aspirations to enlarge the welfare state and the resolve to defend the empire as well could make no meaningful "continental commitment." The wish is clearly father to the thought. "It is easy to understand why the British felt distinct from the Powers of Europe," Taylor volunteers discreetly here, "and why they often wanted to withdraw from European politics" (p. 41). In his subsequent biography of Lord Beaverbrook, the hidden agenda emerges. He records his conviction that a policy of isolation, free of European alliances, figured as "the wisest course to follow in a world full of dangers" and seemed "also more honourable than to distribute guarantees which we could not fulfill."[38]

Why Taylor ranks Gustav Stresemann, the foreign minister in the middle years of the Weimar Republic, as "a great German, even as a great European, statesman" (p. 51) is evident. Stresemann sought to recover Danzig, the Polish Corridor, and Upper Silesia, to bring about *Anschluss* and to protect ethnic Germans living outside the borders of the Reich. But he would go about this in a peaceful way, for the present generation, and leave the west alone. He would pose no threat to British interests.[39] Taylor waxes enthusiastic over the Locarno treaties because they reconciled, at least on paper, Franco-British friendship with France's eastern alliances (p. 54). We can now show more explicitly than Taylor did that the treaties were meant to open the way for territorial revision in the east. If France went to the assistance of its Polish ally, and Germany then attacked France, the British guarantee of the western frontiers would not apply. The British Cabinet expected the French, in consequence, to adopt a defensive military strategy and to limit their eastern commitments. The Poles and the Czechs would draw closer to the German economic orbit. Forces would be set in motion that would gradually lead to peaceful change and so stabilize the continent.[40]

It is never easy, however, to manage peaceful change. British Foreign Office planners did not reckon with the increased urgency of German revisionism in the Depression; nor did they expect the Poles to ignore the relationships of power and to become ever more obdurate as time went on. All the same, the British government did not issue a blank check, in 1925 or later. Taylor does not stand on firm ground in drawing a direct comparison between the aims of Stresemann and Hitler. He goes beyond the evidence when he argues that Hitler merely sought satellites and not territorial gains, and also when he asserts in contradictory fashion that Hitler aspired to restore the great eastern conquests of Brest–Litovsk, but that many in the west accepted this as natural, even desirable (pp. 70, 80).[41]

If Taylor had wished to strengthen his case for the continuity of Weimar and Nazi foreign policy, he would have done better to focus more attention on the years 1930–3. The Brüning, Papen, and Schleicher cabinets did seek more radical concessions in foreign policy than had their predecessors, both to provide distraction from the pain of deflation and to head off the growing Nazi electoral menace. We now have more proof than Taylor did of the quantum leap in the military preparations of the *Reichswehr* in 1931–2.[42] One rubs one's eyes in disbelief at Taylor's portrayal of Arthur Henderson as a latter-day Austen Chamberlain, anxious to "reconcile disarmament and security" and to use disarmament as a "lever for increasing British commitments to France."[43] The Cabinet Secretary, Sir Maurice Hankey, was nearer the mark when he noted in September 1931 that British pacifism and Britain's disarmament policy drew inspiration less from idealism than from realization of the country's exhaustion and economic weakness, and that this derived in turn from "our insistence on maintaining a much higher standard of living than our economic circumstances justify."[44]

Whatever the mix of motives, Great Britain, like the United States, supported "equality of rights" for Germany throughout the Geneva disarmament conference of 1932–3. They both tried to persuade France to reduce its forces to a level that Germany was already planning to exceed. American leaders considered the balance of power immoral; British statesmen failed to perceive where the balance really lay. Taylor makes much of the slow pace of German rearmament in 1933–5 and speaks slightingly of the "false alarms" issued by Churchill and others (p. 75).[45] One wishes he had coupled this with an analysis of unreadiness in the British and French armed forces over the same period and an explanation of how Depression-era budgetary constraints determined the glacial pace of improvement.[46] Most Englishmen, he notes, believed in the early 1930s that "great armaments were themselves a cause of war" (p. 64).[47] Once they acted on that belief, the European structure erected at the Paris peace conference was bound to crumble. And crumble it did.

None of the objections made to *The Origins of the Second World War* – least of all those to the early chapters – appeared to bother Taylor a whit. In reply to earlier criticism, he pleaded the simplest of motives. He had sought to produce "a straightforward piece of hack diplomatic history."[48] He had tried to write without thinking that he was English, or a radical or a Socialist. He took no delight, "impish or otherwise," in shocking readers; he just put down what seemed to him right without worrying whether it would appear orthodox or not. If inconsistencies turned up, they usually resulted from his having learned better afterward.[49] Doubtless those explanations represent much of the truth. The French Socialists used to remark about Aristide Briand that he was "so guileful one ought not to believe the opposite of what he says."[50] Yet elsewhere Taylor observes, half in jest, that we have left behind the era of Ranke: nowadays we read diplomatic history "for purposes of entertainment."[51] If the office of history is to amuse, then Taylor stands without peer. Some four decades after publication of *The Origins of the Second World War*, students still read the book avidly. No doubt they will continue to do so far into the future, when the learned rebuttals of critics lie moldering on library shelves. Such scholarly longevity speaks for itself. André Gide, when asked whom he considered the greatest French poet, replied, "Victor Hugo, *hélas*." Taylor's sternest critics will scarcely improve the line.

Notes

1   A. J. P. Taylor, *The Origins of the Second World War*, London, 1961, p.28. Citations in this essay are of the latest American edition (New York, 1983), which uses arabic pagination as in the original, but employs roman pagination for the 1963 Foreword, "Second thoughts," and the "Preface for the American reader" (dating from 1966).

2   See Taylor's reference in *Origins*, p. 234; Maitland on after-mindedness in H. M. Cam (ed.), *Selected Historical Essays of F. W. Maitland*, London, 1957, p. xix.

3   Despite his nonchalance about certain minutiae, Taylor conceived himself as writing squarely within the empirical-history tradition. He proffered no theoretical challenge to objectivity on the model later made popular by the "postmodernists." Compare A. Megill (ed.), *Rethinking Objectivity*, Durham, NC, 1994, with R. J. Evans, *In Defence of History*, London, 1997.

4   E. M. Robertson (ed.), *The Origins of the Second World War: Historical Interpretations*, London, 1971; W. R. Louis (ed.), *The Origins of the Second World War: A. J. P. Taylor and his Critics*, New York, 1972.

5   A. J. P. Taylor, *A Personal History*, New York, 1983, p. 233.

6   The abbreviated run of *Documents diplomatiques belges, 1920–1940* reached completion in 1966 but Her Majesty's Stationery Office did not complete Series 1 and 1A of the *Documents on British Foreign Policy* (covering 1919–29) until 1986. Series A and B of *Akten zur deutschen auswärtigen Politik* (covering the years 1918–33) did not all appear until 1995. The Quai d'Orsay began to publish *Documents diplomatiques français* for the

1920s only in 1998, after a private German team under S. Martens took the initiative with *Documents diplomatiques français sur l'Allemagne, 1920*, Bonn, 1992–93. The original Russian series, *Dokumenty vneshnei politiki SSSR*, Moscow, 1959–77, revealed remarkably little; the much franker volumes on 1939–41 appeared only in 1995. The Italian, Swiss, and Austrian official series remain works in progress.

7 Taylor, *Personal History*, pp. 23–4.

8 Taylor, *Personal History*, pp. 125–8.

9 Taylor, *Personal History*, p. 60.

10 On Russian policy, see the standard synthesis by A. B. Ulam, *Expansion and Coexistence* revised edn, New York, 1974; J. Braunthal, *History of the International*, vol. 2: *1914–1943*, New York, 1967; R. Pipes, *The Bolshevik Regime*, New York, 1994, and *The Unknown Lenin*, New Haven, CT, 1996; R. K. Debo, *Survival and Consolidation*, Montreal, 1992; also the meticulously compiled evidence on Soviet subversion in Germany in W. T. Angress, *Stillborn Revolution*, Princeton, NJ, 1963. E. H. Carr, *Twilight of the Comintern, 1930–1935*, New York, 1982, still portrays Soviet policy as defensive, and some younger scholars who wrote before the opening of the Soviet archives agree. See, for example, J. Haslam, *Soviet Foreign Policy, 1930–1933*, New York, 1983. Helpful works on co-operation and competition in Anglo-American relations include: C. Parrini, *Heir to Empire*, Pittsburgh, PA, 1969; M. J. Hogan, *Informal Entente*, Columbia, MO, 1977; M. G. Fry, *Illusions of Security*, Toronto, 1972; S. V. O. Clarke, *Central Bank Cooperation, 1924–1931*, New York, 1967; B. J. M. McKercher, *The Second Baldwin Government and the United States, 1924–1929*, Cambridge, 1984; and B. J. M. McKercher (ed.), *Anglo-American Relations in the 1920s*, Edmonton, 1990. K. Burk, *Britain, America and the Sinews of War, 1914–1918*, London, 1985, provides background. R. N. Kottman, *Reciprocity and the North Atlantic Triangle, 1932–1938*, Ithaca, NY, 1968; C. A. MacDonald, *The United States, Britain and Appeasement, 1936–1939*, New York, 1981; B. M. Rowland, *Commercial Conflict and Foreign Policy*, New York, 1987; and D. Reynolds, *The Creation of the Anglo-American Alliance, 1937–1941*, Chapel Hill, NC, 1981, carry the story onward. On the Far East, the best works include A. Iriye, *After Imperialism*, Cambridge, MA, 1965; M. D. Kennedy, *The Estrangement of Great Britain and Japan, 1917–1935*, Manchester, 1969; I. H. Nish, *Alliance in Decline*, London, 1972; R. Dingman, *Power in the Pacific*, Chicago, IL, 1976; and J. Neidpath, *The Singapore Naval Base and the Defence of Britain's Eastern Empire, 1919–1941*, Oxford, 1981.

11 Quoted in E. Eyck, *Bismarck and the German Empire*, London, 1958, pp. 77–8.

12 Compare J. M. Keynes, *The Economic Consequences of the Peace*, London, 1919, and the still less temperate *A Revision of the Treaty*, London, 1922 with E. Mantoux, *The Carthaginian Peace*, London, 1946; reprinted Pittsburgh, PA, 1965. On Keynes's private motives for embracing the German cause, see S. A. Schuker, "The collected writings of John Maynard Keynes," *Journal of Economic Literature*, vol. 18, 1980, pp. 124–6; N. Ferguson, "Keynes and the German inflation," *English Historical Review*, vol. 110, 1995, pp. 368–91; and G. Martel, "The prehistory of appeasement: Headlam-Morley, the peace settlement and revisionism," *Diplomacy and Statecraft*, vol. 9, 1998, pp. 242–65.

13 On the London Schedule, Taylor could have consulted, but apparently did not, E. Weill-Raynal, *Les Réparations allemandes et la France*, 3 vols, Paris, 1947, esp. vol. 1, pp. 618–702. C. Holtfrerich, *Die deutsche Inflation 1914–1923*, Berlin, 1980, p. 221, summarizes recent work reconstructing German national income for the period. S. Marks provides the soundest orientation to scholarship on the reparations problem in: "Reparations reconsidered," *Central European History*, vol. 2, 1969, pp. 356–65; "The myths of reparations," *Central European History*, vol. 11, 1978, pp. 231–55; and "In smoke-filled rooms and the Galerie des Glaces: reparation at the Paris peace conference," in M. Boemeke, G. Feldman, E. Glaser (eds), *The Treaty of Versailles: A Reassessment after 75 Years*, Cambridge, 1998, pp. 337–70.

14 See S. A. Schuker, *The End of French Predominance in Europe*, Chapel Hill, NC, 1976, pp. 20–6; J. Bariéty, *Les Relations franco-allemandes après la première guerre mondiale*, Paris, 1977,

pp. 101–8; W. A. McDougall, *France's Rhineland Diplomacy*, Princeton, NJ, 1978, pp. 214–49; also J. F. V. Keiger, *Raymond Poincaré*, Cambridge, 1997. For a summary of the copious literature on passive resistance, see J.-C. Favez, *Le Reich devant l'occupation franco-belge de la Ruhr en 1923*, Geneva, 1969.

15 On negotiation of the Dawes plan and French financial problems, see Schuker, *French Predominance*, pp. 31–231; and Bariéty, *Relations*, pp. 289–320.

16 For economic analysis and statistics, see S. A. Schuker, *American "Reparations" to Germany*, Princeton, NJ, 1988; also A. Klug, *The German Buybacks, 1932–1939*, Princeton, NJ, 1993. Note that certain economists remain unconvinced: e.g. B. Eichengreen, *Golden Fetters*, New York, 1992; a minority of historians, including B. Kent, *The Spoils of War*, Oxford, 1989, continues to recycle older interpretations as well.

17 Quoted in A. J. P. Taylor, *Beaverbrook*, London, 1972, p. 678n.

18 Precisely what Taylor means by this remains puzzling, since the German states and municipalities – the greatest borrowers in 1925–28 – would otherwise have had to draw upon tax revenue, directly or indirectly, for the services that they provided.

19 G. D. Feldman, *The Great Disorder*, Oxford, 1993, shows that, whatever the economic balance, the German people paid a tremendous social price both contemporaneously and later for adopting inflationary policies after the First World War. But it does not follow that the actual reparations burden, as opposed to the subjective perception of that burden, forced Berlin to make the fiscal and monetary choices that perpetuated the inflation.

20 Keynes produced the original formulation: "The engravers' dyes, the printers' forms are busier. But no one eats less, no one works more." See "The progress of the Dawes scheme [entry for September 11, 1926]," in E. Johnson (ed.), *The Collected Writings of John Maynard Keynes*, London, 1978, vol. 18, pp. 277–82.

21 See B. D. Rhodes, "The United States and the war debt question, 1917–1934," Ph.D. thesis, University of Colorado, 1965, and "Reassessing uncle Shylock," *Journal of American History*, vol. 55, 1969, pp. 783–803; M. P. Leffler, "The origins of Republican war debt policy, 1921–1923," *Journal of American History*, vol. 59, 1972, pp. 585–601. On linkage of the debts with other issues, note R. A. Dayer, "The British war debts to the United States and the Anglo-Japanese alliance, 1920–1923," *Pacific Historical Review*, vol. 45, 1976, pp. 569–95; E. Glaser, "Von Versailles nach Berlin," in N. Finzsch *et al.* (eds), *Liberalitas*, Stuttgart, 1992, pp. 319–42; E. Wandel, *Die Bedeutung der Vereinigten Staaten von Amerika für das deutsche Reparationsproblem 1924–1929*, Tübingen, 1971; and especially the magisterial work by W. Link, *Die amerikanische Stabilisierungspolitik in Deutschland 1921–1932*, Düsseldorf, 1970.

22 H. W. Gatzke, *Germany's Drive to the West*, Baltimore, MD, 1950.

23 F. Fischer, *Griff nach der Weltmacht*, Düsseldorf, 1961, and *Krieg der Illusionen*, Düsseldorf, 1969; trans. as *Germany's Aims in the First World War* and *War of Illusions*, New York, 1967 and 1975; I. Geiss, *Der polnische Grenzstreifen, 1914–1918*, Lübeck and Hamburg, 1960; K. Riezler, *Tagebücher, Aufsätze, Dokumente*, ed. K. D. Erdmann, Göttingen, 1972; H. Afflerbach, *Falkenhayn*, Munich, 1994. For attacks on the *Sonderweg* thesis, however, see D. Calleo, *The German Problem Reconsidered*, Cambridge, 1978; also D. Blackbourn and G. Eley, *The Peculiarities of German History*, Oxford, 1984.

24 Standard works in this field include: V. H. Rothwell, *British War Aims and Peace Diplomacy, 1914–1918*, Oxford, 1971; D. Stevenson, *French War Aims against Germany, 1914–1919*, Oxford, 1982, and *The First World War and International Politics*, Oxford, 1988; M. Palo, "The diplomacy of Belgian war aims during the First World War," Ph.D. thesis, University of Illinois, 1977; S. Marks, *Innocent Abroad*, Chapel Hill, NC, 1981, pp. 5–102; also the magisterial study of economic war aims by G. Soutou, *L'Or et le sang*, Paris, 1989. On the earlier period, see D. C. B. Lieven, *Russia and the Origins of the First World War*, London, 1983; and J. F. V. Keiger, *France and the Origins of the First World War*, London, 1983.

25 Such a comparison appears unduly harsh in light of the appreciation by K. H. Jarausch, *The Enigmatic Chancellor*, New Haven, CT, 1973.

26 D. H. Aldcroft, *From Versailles to Wall Street, 1919–1929*, Berkeley, CA, 1977, pp. 11–77. For reflections on war as a stimulus to technological change and growth, see also A. S. Milward, *War, Economy, and Society, 1939–1945*, Berkeley, CA, 1977, pp. 1–17.

27 M. Leffler, *The Elusive Quest*, Chapel Hill, NC, 1979, pp. 3–39; D. Artaud, *La Question des dettes interalliées et la reconstruction de l'Europe, 1917–1929*, 2 vols, Lille, 1978; vol. 1, pp. 66–324; F. Costigliola, *Awkward Dominion*, Ithaca, NY, 1985; S. A. Schuker, "Origins of American stabilization policy in Europe, 1918–1924," in H.-J. Schröder (ed.), *Confrontation and Cooperation*, Providence, RI, 1993, pp. 377–407; E. Glaser, "The Making of the Economic Peace," in Boemeke *et al.* (eds), *The Treaty of Versailles*, pp. 371–400.

28 J. Bariéty, "Das Zustandekommen der Internationalen Rohstahlgemeinschaft als Alternative zum misslungenen 'Schwerindustriellen Projekt' des Versailler Vertrages," in H. Mommsen, D. Petzina, and B. Weisbrod (eds), *Industrielles System und politische Entwicklung in der Weimarer Republik*, Düsseldorf, 1974, pp. 552–68; "Le Rôle de la minette dans la sidérurgie allemande et la restructuration de la sidérurgie allemande après le traité de Versailles," *Centre de Recherches Relations Internationales de l'Université de Metz*, vol. 3, 1975, pp. 233–77; S. A. Schuker, "Frankreich und die Weimarer Republik," in M. Stürmer (ed.), *Die Weimarer Republik*, Königstein, 1980, pp. 93–112.

29 G. Soutou has written numerous articles on this subject, among them "Problèmes concernant le rétablisement des relations économiques franco-allemandes après la première guerre mondiale," *Francia*, vol. 2, 1974, pp. 580–96; and "Die deutschen Reparationen und das Seydoux-Projekt, 1920–21," *Vierteljahrshefte für Zeitgeschichte*, vol. 23, 1975, pp. 237–70. See also P. Krüger, *Deutschland und die Reparationen, 1918/19*, Stuttgart, 1973, pp. 134–7; and M. Trachtenberg, *Reparation in World Politics*, New York, 1980, pp. 155–91.

30 Taylor would have had available to him only the rather technical treatment of reparations in kind by Weill-Raynal, *Réparations allemandes*, vol. 1, pp. 368–592. Documentation on the political significance of the subject became available only subsequently.

31 A. Orde, *British Policy and European Reconstruction after the First World War*, Cambridge, 1990.

32 For a helpful introduction to this vast field, see S. Pollard, *The Development of the British Economy, 1914–1967*, London, 1969; and N. K. Buxton and D. H. Aldcroft (eds), *British Industry between the Wars*, London, 1979. For discussion from various viewpoints of British structural problems and why contemporaries delayed recognizing them, see S. Howson and D. Winch, *The Economic Advisory Council, 1930–1939*, Cambridge, 1977; L. Hannah, *The Rise of the Corporate Economy*, London, 1983; A. D. Chandler, Jr, *Scale and Scope*, London, 1990, pp. 235–392; and C. Barnett, *The Collapse of British Power*, London, 1972.

33 Schuker, *French Predominance*, pp. 295–382; Bariéty, *Relations*, pp. 475–747. For the subsequent negotiations on trade and economic issues, 1925–27, see also K.-H. Pohl, *Weimars Wirtschaft und die Aussenpolitik der Republik, 1924–1926*, Düsseldorf, 1979; B. Weisbrod, *Schwerindustrie in der Weimarer Republik*, Wuppertal, 1978; and C. S. Maier, *Recasting Bourgeois Europe*, Princeton, NJ, 1975, pp. 516–45.

34 The basic work remains J. Jacobson, *Locarno Diplomacy: Germany and the West, 1925–1929*, Princeton, NJ, 1972. The voluminous German-language literature finds reflection in P. Krüger, *Die Aussenpolitik der Republik von Weimar*, Darmstadt, 1985, pp. 207–506. Fresh material has appeared in C. A. Wurm, *Die französische Sicherheitspolitik in der Phase der Umorientierung, 1924–1926*, Frankfurt, 1979; E. D. Keeton, *Briand's Locarno Policy*, New York, 1987; V. J. Pitts, *France and the German Problem, 1924–1929*, New York, 1987; and F. Knipping, *Deutschland, Frankreich, und das Ende der Locarno-Ära, 1928–1931*, Munich, 1987. On military aspects, see M. Salewski, *Entwaffnung und Militärkontrolle in Deutschland, 1919–1927*, Munich, 1966; and J. M. Hughes, *To the Maginot Line*, Cambridge, MA, 1971. Several essays in G. Schmidt (ed.), *Konstellationen internationaler Politik, 1924–1932*, Bochum, 1983, also address these questions.

35   Given the confusion in Germany during 1918–19, and the illusions of German statesmen about what was achievable at the peace conference, it is not surprising that scholars have failed to reach a consensus on the importance of those objectives. K. Schwabe provides the most reliable general overview in *Deutsche Revolution und Wilson-Frieden*, Düsseldorf, 1971; revised version and ET: *Woodrow Wilson, Revolutionary Germany, and Peacemaking, 1918–1919*, Chapel Hill, NC, 1985. For public opinion during the subsequent period, see C. Höltje, *Die Weimarer Republik und das Ostlocarno-Problem 1919–1934*, Würzburg, 1958; and E. Hölzle (ed.), *Die deutschen Ostgebiete zur Zeit der Weimarer Republik*, Cologne, 1966. C. M. Kimmich, *The Free City*, New Haven, CT, 1968, covers Danzig; F. G. Campbell, *Confrontation in Central Europe*, Chicago, IL, 1975, and R. Jaworski, *Vorposten oder Minderheit?*, Stuttgart, 1977, deal with the German minority in Czechoslovakia from different points of view. N. Krekeler, *Revisionsanspruch und geheime Ostpolitik der Weimarer Republik*, Stuttgart, 1973, treats assistance to minorities in Poland; K.-H. Grundmann, *Deutschtumpolitik zur Zeit der Weimarer Republik*, Hanover, 1977, addresses the Baltic. One cannot speak with categorical assurance even about policy toward Austria: see S. Suval, *The Anschluss Question in the Weimar Era*, Baltimore, MD, 1974, pp. 3–20; and A. D. Low, *The Anschluss Movement, 1918–1919 and the Paris Peace Conference*, Philadelphia, PA, 1974.

36   On the Anglo-American guarantee, see L. Yates, *The United States and French Security, 1917–1921*, New York, 1957. The fundamental books on the eastern alliances, P. Wandycz, *France and Her Eastern Allies, 1919–1925*, Minneapolis, MN, 1962, and *The Twilight of the French Eastern Alliances, 1926–1936*, Princeton, NJ, 1988, emphasize the importance of the Polish and Czech connections; N. Jordan, *The Popular Front and Central Europe*, Cambridge, 1992, bathetically laments their abandonment. But numerous recent articles in *Relations internationales*, the *Revue d'histoire de la deuxième guerre mondiale*, and other journals have pointed to the frustrations experienced by the French in training armies and trying to turn a profit on their investments in eastern Europe. P.-E. Tournoux, *Défense des frontières*, Paris, 1960, examines the successive strategic plans of the French army and confirms what Taylor suspected – that they became steadily more defensive in the 1920s.

37   See J. M. King, *Foch versus Clemenceau*, Cambridge, MA, 1960; S. A. Schuker, "The Rhineland question: west European security at the Paris peace conference," in Boemeke *et al.* (eds), *The Treaty of Versailles*, pp. 275–312; and McDougall, *Rhineland Diplomacy*. There exists a large literature, much of it contentious in tone, evaluating the seriousness with which the French at various points viewed the Rhineland option. See K. D. Erdmann, *Adenauer in der Rheinlandpolitik nach dem Ersten Weltkrieg*, Stuttgart, 1966, still the most solid account despite later revelations about Erdmann's career under the Third Reich; E. Bischof, *Rheinischer Separatismus 1918–1924*, Bern, 1969; Centre de Recherches Relations Internationales de l'Université de Metz, *Problèmes de la Rhénanie, 1919–1930/Die Rheinfrage nach dem Ersten Weltkrieg*, Metz, 1975; G. Steinmeyer, *Die Grundlagen der französischen Rheinlandpolitik, 1917–1919*, Stuttgart, 1979; H. Köhler, *Novemberrevolution und Frankreich*, Düsseldorf, 1980, and *Adenauer und die rheinische Republik*, Opladen, 1986; H. E. Nadler, *The Rhenish Separatist Movements in the Early Weimar Republic*, New York, 1987; S. Jeannesson, *Poincaré, La France et la Ruhr*, Strasbourg, 1998; and S.A. Schuker, "Bayern und der rheinische Separatismus," *Jahrbuch des historischen Kollegs* 1997, pp. 75–111.

38   Taylor, *Beaverbrook*, p. xiii.

39   For useful discussions of Stresemann's aims, as set out in his September 7, 1925 letter to Crown Prince Wilhelm, see Hans Gatzke, *Stresemann and the Rearmament of Germany*, Baltimore, MD, 1954; and Gaines Post, *The Civil–Military Fabric of Weimar Foreign Policy*, Princeton, NJ, 1973. W. Weidenfeld, *Die Englandpolitik Gustav Stresemanns*, Mainz, 1972, and C. Baechler, *Gustave Stresemann*, Strasbourg, 1996, mount the barricades for the defense. W. Michalka and M. M. Lee (eds), *Gustav Stresemann*, Darmstadt, 1982, group twenty essays by leading specialists who have elucidated various aspects of Stresemann's policies.

40 For the explicit formulations by Cabinet members and by the Foreign Office legal adviser, see Schuker, *French Predominance*, pp. 389–90; also note the discussion in Jacobson, *Locarno Diplomacy*, pp. 12–44; and S. E. Crowe, "Sir Eyre Crowe and the Locarno pact," *English Historical Review*, vol. 87, 1972, pp. 49–74.

41 On the growing rigidity of Polish policy, see R. Debicki, *The Foreign Policy of Poland, 1919–1939*, New York, 1962; J. Korbel, *Poland Between East and West*, Princeton, NJ, 1963; and L. Radice, *Prelude to Appeasement: East Central European Diplomacy in the Early 1930s*, Boulder, CO, 1981. On French frustration with the Poles, see the review article by H. Rollet, "Deux mythes des relations franco-polonaises entre les deux guerres," *Revue d'histoire diplomatique*, no. 96, 1982, pp. 225–48. G. Weinberg, *The Foreign Policy of Hitler's Germany: Diplomatic Revolution in Europe, 1933–36*, Chicago, IL, 1970, esp. pp. 1–24, puts to rest in elegant fashion the notion of Hitler as a traditional diplomat. Neither J.-B. Duroselle, *La Décadence 1932–1939*, Paris, 1979, nor any of the monographs on which he based his synthesis, offer support for Taylor's quixotic notion that "most" Frenchmen came to favor German dominance of Russia on the model of the 1918 Brest–Litovsk treaty.

42 On foreign and military policy of the Reich in 1930–32, see particularly A. Rodder, *Stresemanns Erbe: Julius Curtius und die deutsche Aussenpolitik, 1929–1931*, Paderborn, 1996; E. W. Bennett, *Germany and the Diplomacy of the Financial Crisis, 1931*, Cambridge, MA, 1962 (1931), and *German Rearmament and the West, 1932–1933*, Princeton, NJ, 1979. The seriousness of German rearmament in those years remains disputed. Much depends on whether one examines industrial mobilization or immediate readiness, and short- or long-term planning. G. Meinck, *Hitler und die deutsche Aufrüstung, 1933–1937*, Wiesbaden, 1959, minimizes early efforts under Schleicher; M. Geyer, "Das Zweite Rüstungsprogramm, 1930–1934," *Militärgeschichtliche Mitteilungen*, vol. 16, 1975, pp. 125–72, and *Aufrüstung oder Sicherheit: Die Reichswehr in der Krise der Machtpolitik, 1924–1936*, Wiesbaden, 1980, esp. pp. 237–362, stresses elements of continuity. Note also E. W. Hansen, *Reichswehr und Industrie*, Boppard am Rhein, 1981, which explores industrial rearmament; and T. Vogelsang, *Reichswehr, Staat und NSDAP*, Stuttgart, 1962, which concentrates on political questions. G. Schulz's Introduction to I. Maurer and U. Wengst (eds), *Politik und Wirtschaft in der Krise: Quellen zur Ära Brüning*, 2 vols, Düsseldorf, 1980; vol. 1, pp. ix–civ, reviews the growing literature on Brüning's foreign economic policy; K. Borchardt, *Wachstum, Krisen, Handelsspielräume der Wirtschaftspolitik*, Göttingen, 1982, pp. 165–224, and W.L. Patch, *Heinrich Brüning and the Dissolution of the Weimar Republic*, Cambridge 1998, emphasize Brüning's limited maneuvering room.

43 The balance of scholarly opinion sheds a less unkind light on Ramsay MacDonald than it does on Henderson, although there is ample blame to go around. See D. Carlton, *MacDonald versus Henderson: The Foreign Policy of the Second Labour Government*, London, 1970; D. Marquand, *Ramsay MacDonald*, London, 1977; and H. Winkler, *Paths Not Taken: British Labour and International Policy in the 1920s*, Chapel Hill, NC, 1994.

44 S. Roskill, *Hankey: Man of Secrets*, London, 1972, vol. 2: *1919–1931*, pp. 544–5.

45 The debate continues over the pace of German rearmament before 1936. Still basic is the semi-official history: W. Deist, M. Messerschmidt, H.-E. Volkmann, and W. Wette, *Das Deutsche Reich und der Zweite Weltkrieg*, Stuttgart, 1979; vol. 1: *Ursachen und Voraussetzungen der deutschen Kriegspolitik*. K.-J. Müller, *General Ludwig Beck*, Boppard am Rhein, 1980, shows that the Reichswehr pushed Hitler as much as the other way round. W. K. Wark, *The Ultimate Enemy, 1933–1939*, Ithaca, NY, 1985, assesses the perceptions of British intelligence; R. J. Overy, "German air strength, 1933 to 1939," *Historical Journal*, vol. 27, 1984, pp. 465–71, calls attention to the difficulties of using nominal figures to evaluate German offensive strength in the air.

46 For Britain, see N. H. Gibbs, *Grand Strategy*, London, 1976, vol. 1; B. Bond, *British Military Policy between the Two World Wars*, Oxford, 1980, esp. pp. 161–214; G. C. Peden, *British Rearmament and the Treasury, 1932–1939*, Edinburgh, 1979; R. P. Shay,

British Rearmament in the Thirties, Princeton, NJ, 1977; and R. Middleton, *Towards the Managed Economy*, London, 1985. For France, see M. Vaïsse, *Sécurité d'abord*, Paris, 1981, esp. pp. 597–615; R. J. Young, *In Command of France*, Cambridge, MA, 1978, pp. 13–75; R. Frankenstein, *Le Prix du réarmement français*, Paris, 1982; and M. S. Alexander, *The Republic in Danger*, Cambridge, 1992.

47 For a notable example of the pro-disarmament mentality of the era, see P. Noel-Baker, *The First World Disarmament Conference, 1932–1933, and Why It Failed*, New York, 1979. M. Ceadel, *Pacifism in Britain, 1914–1945*, Oxford, 1980, sums up the *Zeitgeist* shrewdly. N. Ingram, *The Politics of Dissent: Pacifism in France, 1919–1939*, Oxford, 1991, demonstrates that Gallic contemporaries enjoyed no natural immunity to this illusion.

48 Taylor, *Personal History*, p. 234.

49 Taylor to E. B. Segal, November 21, 1964, in Louis, *Origins*, pp. 26–7.

50 Quoted in D. B. Goldey, "The disintegration of the *Cartel des Gauches* and the politics of French Government finance, 1924–1928," DPhil. thesis, Oxford University, 1961, p. 110.

51 Cited by E. B. Segal in Louis, *Origins*, p. 14.

4 Mussolini and the myth of Rome

Alan Cassels

The Second World War left behind ample scope for anguished historiographical debate in all the major powers involved in the conflict.[1] This has proved particularly true in Germany and Italy where historical disputes have followed an interestingly parallel course, extending well beyond the fact that the two countries were Axis partners in the war itself. Germany's notoriously "unmasterable past" raised the issue of Germany's collective guilt for Nazism.[2] To what extent did the origins of Nazism lie in German history and culture? Applied to the field of international relations, the question bore on Nazi expansionism after 1933. Was this simply a continuation of traditional German foreign policy, or was it the working-out of a peculiar Nazi *weltanschauung*? In answer to this foreign-policy question the Nuremberg Trials put the spotlight on Hitler, his immediate circle and Nazi ideology. Not until the 1960s did the scholarly search for the roots of the Third Reich's international aggression really switch to the pre-Nazi period. In large measure, this was due to the work of two historians. Fritz Fischer, first implicitly and then avowedly, connected German annexationist aims in the First World War to the Nazi search for eastern *Lebensraum* a generation later.[3] A. J. P. Taylor reached best-seller fame by provocatively depicting the *Führer* as no more than a conventional if unusually opportunistic German statesman.[4] Since the 1960s, therefore, no account of Nazi foreign policy can ignore the diplomatic legacy bequeathed by the Bismarckian, Wilhelmine and Weimar regimes.

Historical literature on Italy's role in the Second World War has undergone a similar metamorphosis. After Italy's entry into war in 1940, Winston Churchill singled out Benito Mussolini as the "one man and one man only [who] was resolved to plunge Italy...into the whirlpool of war."[5] Although at the time no more than a propaganda ploy to divide the Fascist Duce from the Italian people, it epitomized the view that Italy's recent belligerence could be laid exclusively at the door of the Fascist regime. After the war some Italians built on this idea to develop the "parenthesis" argument, namely, that Fascism was a disjunctive interlude in the "real history" of united Italy. Fascism, wrote Benedetto Croce, the most notable spokesman of this persuasion, "was an outgrowth extraneous to Italy's long history and repugnant to recent Italian traditions."[6] Over the past half-century this assertion has been increasingly challenged, even if one cannot isolate any clear-cut historiographical watershed equivalent to the Fischer–Taylor revisionism in the case of Germany. In Italy, opinion changed more gradually, but nonetheless in the same direction and for the same purpose as in German historical writing – to situate the Fascist experience in the *longue durée* of Italian history. And, as in the German paradigm, the most pertinent link between liberal and Fascist Italy is to be found in the pursuit of national *grandezza* – a position which has been argued most forcefully by Richard Bosworth in a series of publications.[7]

This was deducible, in fact, as early as 1951 with the publication of Federico Chabod's sophisticated analysis of Italian foreign policy towards the end of the nineteenth century.[8] Chabod drew attention to the legacy of the *risorgimento*, the renewal of Italian culture that underpinned the drive for the peninsula's political unification. Giuseppe Mazzini was only the most celebrated of those writers who had imbued the movement with a sense of mission – that it was the destiny of the Italian people to build a third Rome, a combined material and spiritual empire in succession to that of the caesars and the popes. The acquisition of Rome itself in 1870 to serve as the capital of united Italy gave an enormous boost to this messianic brand of imperialism.[9] In a psychohistorical way, it was a compensatory mechanism for the fact that the capture of Rome, like all earlier stages in Italian unification, had required the help of outside powers.

Yet the pretentious myth of Rome ran directly counter to Italy's true international situation. An uneasy status as the least of the great powers (or the biggest of the small fry) called for a cautious policy, avoiding costly adventures and adapting pragmatically to the interplay among the major international actors. Within the Italian foreign ministry these constraints were sometimes recognized, sometimes not.[10] But it was among Italy's political class, primed by an education in the classics, that the lure of *Romanità* was strongest. In these circles the Roman myth was regularly invoked to justify the Italian claim to participate in great power rivalries and in the scramble for Africa. Premier Francesco Crispi used it to justify the attempt to seize Ethiopia, which was foiled by the defeat of an Italian army at Adowa in 1896.[11] In 1911 Italy's capture of Libya was accompanied by allusion to ancient Rome's civilizing role in North Africa.[12] The vision of a third Rome also lay behind Italian demands for imperial gains at the close of the First World War, and behind the umbrage over the "mutilated victory" when they were not forthcoming. Mussolini came to office in 1922 partly on the back of this nationalist frustration, a surrogate for the nationalist hero, Gabriele D'Annunzio. The absorption of the Italian Nationalist Party and movement into the Partito Nazionale Fascista (PNF) a year later was wholly appropriate.[13] The Fascist regime thus advertised itself as the vehicle of Italian imperialism and ultranationalism, and in due course the myth of Rome became "a key element in the official vocabulary of Italian Fascism and…something of an obsession in the regime's cultural rhetoric."[14]

The full range of Fascism's international aspirations was not immediately apparent, however. In the 1920s Mussolini acquired the epithet of "a good European," a reputation gained in the main from his participation in the international efforts to resolve Franco-German squabbling, the culmination of which was Italy's signature on the Locarno pacts of 1925 as one of the four guarantors of European stability. In this connection, Rome queried why the Duce should not share the Nobel Peace Prize with the other Locarno architects.[15] After Locarno a personal friendship between Mussolini and the family of Austen Chamberlain, British foreign secretary, laid the groundwork for an Anglo-Italian entente lending Fascist Italy added international respectability. The perception of Mussolini as cooperative and amenable derived as much as anything from wishful thinking in a strife-weary world, especially on the part of the British and the Americans.[16] Moreover, it entailed ignoring alternative signals which indicated that Fascism was the veritable incarnation of hyperbolic Italian nationalism. As early as August 1923 Fascist Italy bombarded Corfu and landed a military force with the intent of annexing the Greek island. Thwarted by a veiled threat of British naval action, Mussolini immediately turned his attention to Fiume and succeeded (where D'Annunzio had failed) in seizing it from under Yugoslavia's nose. By 1927 Italy's intrigues in Albania had transformed that infant country into what approximated an Italian protectorate under a puppet ruler, Ahmed Zogu, who went on to take the title of King Zog I. All this should have been sufficient to burst Mussolini's bubble reputation as a statesman of moderation and a "good European."[17]

Even more significant in the light of what later unfolded was Fascist Italy's flirtation with revision of the 1919 settlement. Since the western powers had frustrated the dream of a new Roman empire at the end of the First World War, the temptation existed to bring defeated and disaffected Germany into play as a counterweight. In fact, Italy's adherence to Locarno notwithstanding, the first decade of the Fascist era was punctuated by numerous clandestine Italian overtures to German nationalism. In the midst of the imbroglio of France's occupation of the Ruhr, Mussolini saw fit to inquire whether Germany "would be in a position to immobilize part of the French army on the Rhine." It was a patent gambit to neutralize France, which was well disposed towards Yugoslavia, while Italy took possession of Fiume. Not surprisingly, the German chancellor, Gustav Stresemann, was not interested,[18] whereupon Mussolini turned to an alternative, and maybe preferred, method of enlisting Germany in Italy's cause. This consisted of cultivating the goodwill of German Nationalists on the right of the political spectrum in expectation that one day they would assume control of German policy. Contact was established with Germany's Nationalist Party and its paramilitary arm the *Stahlhelm*, and German generals were approached and, in violation of the treaty of Versailles, wooed with secret supplies of arms for the *Reichswehr*.[19]

Nor was the German National Socialist Workers' Party excluded from Mussolini's favors. Fascist Italian money probably flowed into the Nazi treasury. Mussolini may even have abetted Adolf Hitler's beer-hall *putsch* in 1923, and in its wake he afforded a comfortable sanctuary for some of the Nazi fugitives, most famously Hermann Goering.[20] Despite the ignominious outcome of Hitler's first bid for power, Fascist Italy continued to pay close attention to the Nazi movement,[21] for on two counts at least the Nazis stood out and apart from run-of-the-mill German nationalists. They described themselves as *fascist*, admittedly a nebulous term, but the presumptive imitation flattered Mussolini's thirsty ego.[22] Of much greater importance, however, was Hitler's unequivocal stand on the Alto Adige. The Paris peace conference's delimitation of the Austro-Italian border at the Brenner Pass had consigned more than 200,000 German-speaking former Habsburg subjects to the mercy of an intolerant Italian state. Hence German nationalists, not excepting Hitler, referred to the region south of the Brenner by its German name of the South Tyrol. But whereas all other pan-Germans put the South Tyrol/Alto Adige high on the irredentist list for inclusion in a future Reich, Hitler consistently repudiated any such objective. In *Mein Kampf* he castigated imperial Germany's diplomacy before 1914 for allowing Italy to slip out of the Triple Alliance; in the future, Italian friendship would have to be bought by abandoning the South Tyrol. This line of argument he reiterated publicly in speeches and in the *Völkischer Beobachter*, as well as privately to Mussolini.[23]

Readiness to traffic with Europe's revisionist groups did not stop with Germany. In the second half of the 1920s Mussolini turned to discontented elements in the Danube valley in order to weaken the Little Entente and offset French influence there, and he also began his long association with the Croatian separatists in Yugoslavia.[24] In 1928 he endorsed international revisionism before the Italian senate: "I have sometimes had occasion to point out that the treaties of peace are not eternal....Is there anyone who dares argue that the peace treaties...are a work of perfection?"[25] Yet despite this public avowal, most of the Duce's early revisionist activity was conducted *sub rosa* – even behind the back of Italy's diplomats. The Italian ambassador in Berlin, for one, was less than fully aware of all the ramifications of Mussolini's German policy, much of which was handled by his man in Berlin, Major Renzetti.[26] While the majority of Italy's foreign ministry officials were nationalistic enough to imagine they could use the "wild" Mussolini to frighten the western states into concessions, they were less ready to contemplate deserting the victorious First World War coalition.[27] But their influence was circumscribed, and it declined with the passage of time. The Duce, whether or not he held the foreign-ministry portfolio himself, always kept the strings of Fascist foreign policy in his own hands. And, from the outset, Mussolini was prepared to employ a diplomatic strategy as reckless as his goals were extravagant; both methods and ambition placed him on the extremist wing of Italian nationalism.

The pace at which Fascist Italy moved to realize its Roman empire was inevitably contingent on the situation at home. For several years Mussolini's first concern was to secure his position in Rome, which he did in two ways. First, by constructing, in the wake of the Matteotti affair of 1924, a one-party dictatorship.[28] Second, by agreeing a series of *modi operandi* with Italy's old power structure – the *latifondisti*, the *Confindustria*, the armed forces, the monarchy and, above all in 1929, the Catholic Church. These alliances resulted in the transformation of Italian Fascism, in the phraseology of Renzo De Felice, from a movement into a regime, denoting a shift from radical innovation to bureaucratic stultification.[29] Indeed, the PNF's abandonment of any serious program of social and economic change was glaringly revealed when the Great Depression brought widespread distress to Italy.[30] Having betrayed its pristine revolutionary rhetoric, then, Fascism by the opening of the 1930s lacked any *raison d'être* other than imperial expansion in conformity with the myth of Rome. Accordingly, in 1932 Mussolini ordered that military plans be drawn up for the conquest of Ethiopia, the east-African territory which had successfully resisted Italy's civilizing mission in the 1890s – the most humiliating reversal experienced by any colonial power in the scramble for empire. The Duce's directive thus stemmed from a long Italian imperialist tradition and, it is worth noting, was issued before Hitler reached office. Although the Ethiopian venture would end by entrapping Mussolini in Hitler's net, Fascist Italy was at first inhibited from pursuing its planned African campaign by alarm at the resurgence of a German nationalism increasingly located in the Nazi movement.

As one who had anticipated the renewal of German nationalist pretensions, Mussolini was appropriately the first to advance a plan to meet the exigency. His Four-Power Pact, floated in 1932, predicated embracing – and controlling – Germany within a new concert of Europe (to the detriment of the League of Nations, always a Fascist *bête noire*). As inducements, some revision of the postwar settlement was proffered; parity in armaments was openly touted, and adjustment of Germany's borders hinted at. But this revisionist dimension offended France and its eastern allies, and in the end killed Mussolini's project.[31]

The failure of the Four Power Pact threw Mussolini back on his own devices for coping with the German menace. The touchstone of Italo-German relations was the double-edged problem of Austrian integrity and the sanctity of Italy's Brenner frontier. Whatever promise Hitler might make about the South Tyrol, his program envisaged *Anschluss*, which would see German troops camped on the Brenner. Italy's palpable need to preserve an independent Austria as a buffer had prompted Mussolini for some years to intervene surreptitiously in internal Austrian politics in the hope of installing and patronizing a congenial govern-ment in Vienna. By 1934 his preferred client was Engelbert Dollfuss, the Austrian conservative and quasi-fascist chancellor. It was with the Duce's encouragement that Dollfuss attacked the Austrian Socialists in February, precipitating a state of tension in his country which, four months on, led to the first Hitler–Mussolini meeting in Venice. However, the encounter did nothing to dispel the incompatibility of the two leaders' aims in Austria, in part because Hitler went on at great length in German without benefit of an interpreter.[32] The innate misunderstanding sprang into the open almost at once when, in July, the Viennese Nazis murdered Dollfuss in a coup intended to bring about *Anschluss*. Mussolini had the embarrassing task of informing Frau Dollfuss, who was his guest in Rome, of her husband's assassination. He relieved his feelings politically by threatening Italian military intervention in Austria. Regardless of his own implication in the Vienna *Putsch* (still a matter of some conjecture), Hitler immediately disowned the Austrian Nazis who were left to stew in their own juices. Having preached the need for Italian friendship for fifteen years, the Führer remained true to his precept and *Anschluss* was postponed.[33]

Mussolini emerged from the episode triumphant, but was nonetheless shaken by the demonstration of the fragility of Austrian independence. He was therefore still open to cooperation with the west to curb renascent German nationalism. When in March 1935 Nazi Germany announced conscription and the building of an air force, Britain and France proposed a conference to discuss the new international situation, and Mussolini promptly offered hospitality at Stresa. The verbal rebuke administered to Hitler by this Stresa Front in April 1935 was ineffectual, but Mussolini's signature on the communiqué marked a step away from his tolerance of German rearmament in the Four-Power Pact. Furthermore, the anti-German gesture at Stresa was backed up by Franco-Italian military staff talks and exchange of military intelligence.[34]

The Four Power Pact, the Dollfuss affair and the Stresa Front all suggested that the German danger occupied first place in the Duce's diplomatic thinking. Yet within weeks of Stresa he seized on an earlier incident on the border of Ethiopia and Italian Somaliland to launch a full-scale attack on the former. On the surface, the assault on Ethiopia appears a foolhardy diversion from Italy's international priority – security on its north-eastern frontier; an instance perhaps of the delusion that Italy was strong enough to keep several irons in the global fire, which was certainly a commonplace conceit among the advocates of a new Roman empire. On the other hand, Mussolini's timing of his Ethiopian war was not completely illogical. *Anschluss* was temporarily on hold; full German military recovery was some years away; and even the internal stability of the Nazi regime was problematical. In these circumstances a swift victory in East Africa might not only impress the world, and even give Hitler pause for thought, but afford the Duce time to resume guard on the Brenner before the Austrian question flared up again. This reckoning was strengthened by the attitude of France and Britain, the two colonial nations with territory adjacent to Ethiopia. In January 1935 the French premier, Pierre Laval, had led Mussolini to believe he had France's approval of Italian designs on Ethiopia in return for Italy's continued opposition to *Anschluss*. At Stresa the western signatories allowed the final communiqué pledging support for the status quo to carry the restrictive phrase "in Europe." Shortly after, Italian military intelligence purloined from Britain's Rome embassy a copy of the Maffey report, an interdepartmental study compiled in London, which confirmed that an Italian conquest of Ethiopia would not jeopardize vital British interests.[35] All of which could justifiably be taken as a green light for Italy to go ahead in Africa.

In the event, Mussolini's gamble on a quick success paid off; the Italo-Ethiopian war was over by May 1936. But there was to be no Italian return to the Stresa Front nor to the watch on the Brenner. Ironically, the Ethiopian affair had exactly the reverse effect. The catalyst was the League of Nations' condemnation of Italy's aggression and the imposition of sanctions with the ostensible approval of Britain and France.[36] Mussolini was incensed, in spite of Laval's assurance that military sanctions were ruled out and Britain's refusal to close the Suez Canal to Italian military transports. In truth, the support of the western powers for the League was time-serving: the government in London facing re-election was swayed by a poll indicating the League's popularity with the public, and France was dragged along in Britain's wake. Anglo-French discomfort with sanctions was disclosed for all to see in December 1935 when the Paris press published – and thereby scuttled – an offer to buy-off Mussolini with two-thirds of Ethiopia if he would stop fighting (Ethiopia to be compensated out of British and French neighboring possessions). Whether Mussolini would have accepted this Hoare–Laval plan remains moot.[37] What is beyond dispute is that the Duce's vilification of the alleged duplicity of the west was stimulated further.

The raucous breach with the west furnishes the essential backdrop to the pivotal chapter in the story of Italian Fascism. In the new year 1936, immediately following the collapse of the Hoare–Laval plan, Mussolini relinquished his protection of Austrian integrity. "If Austria," he told the German ambassador in Rome, "were...in practice to become a German satellite, he would have no objection." This statement so astonished the ambassador that he asked for it to be repeated. Hitler, after similar initial skepticism, grasped the opportunity to accomplish a drastic alteration in Austria's status. Berlin promised diplomatic recognition of Fascist Italy's Ethiopian empire in exchange for Mussolini's blessing on an Austro-German "gentleman's agreement," which was duly concluded on July 11. It declared Austria to be "a German state" whose foreign policy must henceforth accord with that of the Third Reich, and provided too for the entry of pro-*Anschluss* elements into the Viennese cabinet.[38] After such an Italian capitulation to pan-German interests, *Anschluss* itself was now only a matter of time. Mussolini had effectively forsaken the western Allies and entered the camp of Nazi Germany.

Throughout the Ethiopian affair Mussolini, aiming to ward off strict sanctions, had intimated that he might throw in his lot with Hitler. Nevertheless, his actual reversal of allegiance strains credulity and continues to puzzle historians, if only because it seemed so unnecessary. After all, British and French lukewarm support for the League of Nations had hardly impeded Italy's conquest of Ethiopia. On the other side of the ledger, Hitler had not done much to earn the Duce's gratitude. For a start, the Führer regarded the attack on Ethiopia as a distraction from Italy's appointed role in his grand scenario, which was to contain France in the Mediterranean. His stance during the crisis was ambivalent. Nazi Germany, while refusing to join in League sanctions, did not markedly step up strategic supplies to Italy to fill the sanctions gap, and some German arms even reached the Ethiopian army.[39] In brief, Mussolini's *volte face* owed little to normal diplomatic or realist calculation. Clearly, he was driven by personal pique at what he called Britain's "mad sanctionist policy," and by the personal animosity existing between himself and Anthony Eden, who had succeeded Samuel Hoare as British foreign secretary. But a more cogent explanation is to be found in the social Darwinism inherent in Fascist policy, which became dominant in the mid-1930s.

According to this social Darwinian view, nation states were engaged in endless struggle with each other or, as Mussolini once wrote, "strife is the origin of all things."[40] In the competitive international anarchy states could be divided into those on the rise and those in decline; Mussolini's favorite adjectives for the two categories were, respectively, "virile" and "effete." He took it for granted that Britain and France had entered a period of decline, and so after Ethiopia his imperial appetite turned to British and French possessions. To be sure, his evidence for the western nations' decadence was impressionistic, not to say suspect. He accepted as literal truth sensationalist rumors of drunkenness, sexual perversion, and the crippling materialism supposedly rife in the "plutodemocracies," and he relished demographic figures – the low French birth-rate, a surplus of spinsters in Britain, populations too old to fight.[41] Anglo-French behavior in the Ethiopian affair served to vindicate his judgment; vacillation over sanctions and the British Government's surrender to public opinion were held to be self-evident proofs of weakness. Conversely, Nazi Germany's exploitation of the League of Nations' turmoil during the Ethiopian crisis in order to remilitarize the Rhineland was deemed to signify national virility.

However, social Darwinism went beyond mere admiration of the strong. It was an offshoot of the school of natural law which presumed history to unfold along lines of preset and immutable rules. In other words, a law of history dictated whether at any given moment a specific nation was rising or falling. Mussolini wholeheartedly accepted the notion of predetermination in international politics. Early in 1936 he informed a German visitor that "between Germany and Italy there is a common fate...Germany and Italy are congruent cases. One day we shall meet whether we want to or not. But we want to! Because we must!"[42] As the years passed his speeches became more and more peppered with references to "*destino*." For Italy's ultranationalists, their country was foreordained to be the imperial successor to the western powers. But if it was assured that a tide of history ran in Italy's favor, what need was there to take measures to attain the goal? Reliance on providence alone to provide goes some way to explaining the almost total neglect in Fascist Italy of serious planning and preparations for war.[43] For that matter, the entire myth of Rome rested on the conviction that a new Roman empire was written in the stars; it allowed the question of Italy's capacity for the task to be brushed aside.

Myths, of course, are staple ingredients of ideological constructs, and the Roman myth helped to induce an ideological mindset. Italian Fascism, it must be conceded, lacked a monocausal ideology comparable to Marxism–Leninism or the Nazi racial *weltanschauung*. This is not to say, however, that the Fascist regime and its Duce did not function within an ideological frame of reference, especially in international relations. Dogmatism, combativeness, intolerance, not to mention the terrible simplifications of social Darwinism, were characteristic of an ideological cast of mind.[44] This suited the *zeitgeist* of the late 1930s, as world politics tended to polarize around communism and fascism. The Spanish Civil War, widely if naively adjudged a contest between these two "-isms," supplied a perfect example. When Mussolini himself, on the very morrow of the Ethiopian war, thrust his country into the Spanish conflict, geopolitical motives combined nicely with propaganda against Soviet "popular frontism." The same ideological rationale came into play the following year when Italy joined the Anti-Comintern Pact.[45] In a more positive ideological context, Mussolini and Hitler had no trouble recognizing each other as fellow-fascists. A. J. P. Taylor spotted the quintessence of the new Italo-German relationship to which Mussolini gave the name "Axis": it was "ideological similarity."[46]

Mussolini's personality, social Darwinism and ideological thinking, then, combined to create Fascist Italy's pro-German orientation. In addition. it is worth observing that history was here repeating itself. In 1882 Italy had joined Bismarck's Germany and Austria–Hungary in the Triple Alliance, and subsequently, during the Crispi period, many of Italy's elite out of admiration for German power, wealth, and culture copied Teutonic fashions.[47] Half a century on, another political *rapprochement* between Rome and Berlin was followed by Italian affectation of German manners and mores. In the latter instance, unfortunately, one element of Nazi-German culture imported by Italy was antisemitism. Not at the behest of Hitler but in manifest imitation, Mussolini introduced race laws into Italy in 1938.[48] The wheel had come full circle in Italy's search to fulfill the myth of Rome. Partnership with Germany had been superseded by alliance with the western powers in the First World War; now it was back to collaboration with Germany once more.

Mussolini was loath to admit the true extent of Italy's absorption into the Nazi orbit, and it is just possible that he sincerely believed his stance to have been a neutral one. He was, after all, capable of immense self-deception to the point of believing his own propaganda.[49] At any rate, this circumstance has opened the door to a good deal of historiographical discussion about the nature and degree of Mussolini's commitment to Hitler. Some have claimed that the Duce actually sought to preserve "equidistance" and operate as a *peso determinante* (decisive weight) between the western states and Nazi Germany up until a few months before entering the Second World War in June 1940. This school of thought takes its cue from the work of Renzo De Felice, the acknowledged dean of Mussolinian studies, although he has been accused of immersing himself so deeply in contemporary Fascist documentation as to have swallowed some of its more self-serving commentary.[50] Any thesis pleading the case for a Mussolinian equidistant strategy of necessity lays stress on two Anglo-Italian agreements, signed in January 1937 and April 1938, which bound the two powers to uphold the status quo in the Mediterranean and the Middle East.[51] Called – in the style of the day – "Gentleman's Agreements," these accords, taken at face-value, implied that Mussolini was appeasable. Predictably, there were those in the west who, in light of the greater peril of aggression from Nazi Germany, were eager enough to placate Mussolini.[52] Thus, some historians have argued that the western powers missed a chance to build on these agreements, appease Mussolini further, and in the process break the Rome–Berlin Axis.[53] A variation on this theme is the contention of one Italian scholar that the failure to attain a lasting

Anglo-Fascist *détente* should be attributed to the British government's negotiating in bad faith and denial of Italy's legitimate interests.[54]

But the idea that Mussolini was open to western overtures, that in fact he was striving to play an even-handed game between the democracies and Hitler, constitutes a minority opinion.[55] For the reality was that Fascist diplomacy after Ethiopia was anything but impartial. Even the Gentleman's Agreements were not axiomatic pro-western gestures. It is significant that Rome consistently rejected a triple pact which would include France as well as Britain.[56] In this context, the agreements can be construed as a Mussolinian diplomatic stratagem to split the western Allies. This conjecture is given substance by the Duce's obstinate refusal to honor the spirit of his understandings with Britain. For instance, implementation of the second Gentleman's Agreement, also known as the Easter accords of 1938, was delayed for six months by the ongoing presence of Italian forces in Spain despite promises of withdrawal.

Furthermore, in the sequence of international crises leading up to the onset of the Second World War, Fascist Italy's record showed an unmistakable bias in favor of Germany, and even more emphatically against Britain and France. Mussolini's acquiescence in *Anschluss* in March 1938 was a foregone conclusion; he had forfeited any other option two years earlier. The crisis over the Czech Sudetenland six months later was a different matter altogether. If Mussolini's foreign minister, Count Galeazzo Ciano, is to be believed – and there is no reason to doubt him – his Duce was minded to fight alongside Nazi Germany, though no Italian interests were directly engaged.[57] And maybe it was Mussolini's professions of loyalty that persuaded Hitler to accede to his eleventh-hour request for one last round of negotiations. Mussolini emerged from the ensuing Munich conference as the savior of European peace, and Britain rewarded him by activating the Easter accords and recognizing Italian rule over Ethiopia. But none of this sat well with his image as warrior–leader, and en route to Munich he had grumbled that war was averted, because "we could have liquidated France and Great Britain for ever."[58] This reaction breeds the suspicion that Mussolini was not content to use the Axis to blackmail the western powers into concessions, but wanted war for its own sake – an experience to harden the Italian people and an opportunity to displace Italy's old-fashioned establishment.[59] On the international stage bellicosity was yet another bond with the other war-lover in Berlin.

Mussolini's estrangement from the western Allies, discernible from his conduct at Munich, sprang into full view over the winter of 1938. On November 30 the Italian parliament witnessed an orchestrated demonstration by Fascist deputies who asserted Italy's right to the French territories of Tunisia, Corsica, Nice and Savoy. The key to achieving these ambitions in actual fact lay in London rather than Paris. In the first place, Mussolini hoped to persuade the appeasement-minded British administration to put pressure on the French to yield; this was his purpose in inviting prime minister Chamberlain and foreign secretary Halifax to Rome in the new year of 1939.[60] If this gambit failed, as it did – not because Britain would not lean on France but because the French would not budge[61] – then the alternative was to turn to military force. And the foremost obstacle to an Italian military campaign overseas was British sea power. This the Duce spelled out in a secret session of the Fascist grand council in February 1939, the only occasion he addressed this body at any length on international affairs. It was a frank exposition of foreign-policy goals which bears comparison with Hitler's notorious disquisition, minuted by colonel Hossbach. Mussolini began with the premise that a state's freedom is "proportional to its maritime position," and went on to voice the familiar lament that Italy was a "prisoner in the Mediterranean and the more populous and powerful Italy becomes, the more it will suffer from its imprisonment. The bars of this prison are Corsica, Tunisia, Malta, Cyprus: the sentinels of this prison are Gibraltar and Suez." From this situation he drew two conclusions:[62]

1   The task of Italian policy, which may not and does not entertain any territorial objective on the European continent save Albania, is first to break the prison bars.
2   Once the bars are broken, Italy's policy can have only one watchword: to march to the ocean. Which ocean? The Indian Ocean by linking Libya with Ethiopia by way of the Sudan, or the Atlantic by way of French North Africa.

On the walls of the basilica of Maxentius in Rome were affixed maps showing side-by-side the conquests of classical Rome and Fascist Italy. The march-to-the-ocean injunction suggested that Mussolini took this cartographical imagery seriously. So far-ranging an empire necessitated that not just France but even Britain should submit to Italy's will. Indeed, Britain rather than France was Mussolini's long-range target, for it was Britain's pre-eminent imperial status that he really coveted. Egypt being the geopolitical crux of this aspiration, Radio Bari directed a stream of anti-British propaganda to the Middle East.[63] Anglo-Italian relations went further downhill when Hitler's extinction of Czechoslovakia prompted Italy to invade Albania on Good Friday 1939. Britain's response was a series of unilateral guarantees to those small states deemed under threat by the Axis powers. Whereupon Mussolini complained of British "encirclement" (shades of Kaiser Wilhelm II whom the Duce so resembled), and he asked London whether the Easter accords "possessed any further value."[64] A token and disingenuous gesture to international equidistance.

In reality, notional equidistance had already given way to outright solidarity with Nazi Germany by means of negotiations for a military–political pact. The transformation of the informal Rome–Berlin Axis into a formal alliance had been in the offing since the *Anschluss*. It was delayed while an effort was made to inveigle Japan into a tripartite agreement. This proving fruitless, Mussolini had determined as early as January 1939, the eve of Chamberlain's Rome visit, on a bilateral Nazi–Fascist accord. It was finally signed on May 22 and christened the "Pact of Steel". The manner of its negotiation reflected Mussolini's growing subservience to his Axis partner: the Italians accepted *verbatim* a German draft and agreed to a comprehensive engagement without the customary diplomatic reservation of a defensive *casus belli*.[65] Such cavalier behavior in so momentous an undertaking is hard to credit, and is explicable solely on the grounds that Mussolini and Ciano assumed Italy to be left with sufficient room to maneuver. This fond hope arose from the fact that before signing the Pact of Steel the Italians, in a rare burst of honesty, had admitted that their country could not be ready for war until 1942 at the earliest, to which the Germans had replied that they had no intention of launching war for several years – and then only in consultation with Italy. A week after the conclusion of the pact the Duce dispatched general Ugo Cavallero to Berlin with a memorandum restating this verbal understanding.[66] Here may be perceived Mussolini's ultimate formula to make good the myth of Rome. An Italian empire would be won on the battlefield with the help of Nazi Germany, but Fascist Italy would fight at a time and in a way of its own choosing. When Italy fought it would be in company with Germany, yet it would not be fighting Germany's war; it would fight what Mussolini later came to call his "parallel war." A parallel war, of course, presupposed that Duce could manipulate the Führer; it proved Mussolini's most calamitous delusion of all.

The Italian miscalculation was soon exposed. Visiting Salzburg and Berchtesgaden between August 11 and 13, Ciano learned that the Germans planned to invade the Polish Corridor within a few weeks, regardless of the near-certain war with the western democracies which the move would spark.[67] In Rome debate was immediately joined over whether to honor Italy's commitment under the Pact of Steel. Mussolini's first inclination was to stand by Hitler, but he was eventually dissuaded by reports of his nation's unpreparedness for war. This was a victory for those moderate Italian nationalists who, while themselves not immune to the myth of Rome, did not share Mussolini's extreme interpretation of it and, most assuredly, disliked his compact with Nazism as the agency for consummating it. Prototypical, and very influential in August 1939, was King Victor Emmanuel III. Some Fascist hierarchs also now vented their reservations about the German alliance. One who, later in his memoirs, would make much of his opposition to war was Dino Grandi, although how much weight the opinion of this erstwhile Fascist foreign minister and ambassador to the court of St James's still carried is open to doubt.[68] Of more significance, Ciano, following his Salzburg conversations with Hitler and foreign minister Ribbentrop, had conceived a profound distrust of the Nazis and counseled neutrality in the coming war.[69]

Mussolini tried to save face by submitting an impossible list of war supplies required from Germany before Italy entered the war. In Berlin the communication was interpreted, as it was intended, as a declaration of neutrality. Still anxious to cut a figure in the international drama, the Duce offered an unsolicited mediation proposal. The French evinced some interest, but Germany and Britain gave it short shrift.[70] The rebuff seemed to illustrate Italy's position at the bottom of the pecking order of great powers and, by extension, of the marginal role that the country played in bringing on the Second World War. As

Taylor dismissively puts it: "The most Italy could do was hit the headlines, not raise an alarm."[71] Yet, on receiving the news of Mussolini's desertion, Hitler evinced genuine shock; neither the Cavallero memorandum nor his generals' contempt for Italy's military capability had apparently registered with him.[72] If the Führer had known from the start of the Polish crisis that Italy would not fight, would he have stepped back from war? Probably not, but clearly trust in the Pact of Steel was one of several factors emboldening Hitler to force the issue. The Italian impact on British policy can also lead to counterfactual speculation. The driving force behind British appeasement was the triple threat, that is to say, fear of having to fight Germany, Italy and Japan simultaneously.[73] Had Fascist Italy not adopted so warlike a posture in the Mediterranean, one can reasonably presume that London would have been less inclined to appease and, however unwittingly, encourage Hitler. For a lesser power which did not even join in the hostilities in 1939, Italy's contribution to the outbreak of the Second World War was not negligible.

Staying out of war at the outset did not mean that Mussolini renounced his dream of empire. He eschewed the word "neutrality" since it embarrassingly recalled liberal Italy's policy in 1914; instead, he employed nonbellicosity which connoted, his entourage soon discovered, an intent to enter the war at the earliest propitious moment.[74] A parallel war against the democracies was still on the agenda. Consequently, negotiations with Britain over the blockade of Germany were difficult. In particular, an attempt to reach a commercial arrangement which would mitigate the blockade's worst effects on Italy was abruptly halted on Mussolini's orders in February 1940.[75] Ominously, the Duce evaded US endeavors to obtain a pledge of continued Italian neutrality (or nonbelliger-ency).[76] The Nazi *blitzkrieg* in north-western Europe in May and the prospective collapse of France brought on the moment of truth. Besides the patent chance of making depredations on the western states' colonial empires, what also weighed with Mussolini was the scarcely veiled German hint that, without participation in the war, Italy would be treated as a second-rate power in Hitler's looming new world order.[77] A desperate French premier traveled to London with a proposal to buy off Mussolini with an offer of colonial concessions, but he was blocked by Churchill. In any case, when approached by the French alone, the Duce showed no interest.[78] On June 10, 1940, from the famous balcony overlooking the Piazza Venezia he announced Italy's entry into the Second World War in customary social-Darwinian terminology: "An hour signaled by destiny is sounding.…This is a struggle between peoples fruitful and young against those sterile and dying."[79]

In the event, Italy gained next-to-nothing from the fall of France. Then in October came the real test of the parallel war: unannounced to Hitler beforehand, Italian forces invaded Greece. But Fascist Italy's dismal military performance in the Balkans, coupled with other disasters in the Mediterranean and North Africa, resulted in Germany assuming almost complete control over all Axis operations in these theaters. By the end of 1940 the fantasy of a parallel war had been exploded.[80]

So, was June 10, 1940 "Mussolini's war?" Or was it "the natural result of Italian history?"[81] The answer, as to all such simplistic queries, is "Both." The myth of a third Rome antedated Fascism. As one of those "assumptions' or *mentalités* behind foreign-policy making, its force might not have been quantifiable, but it was plainly visible in the rhetoric of the liberal era before, during, and after the First World War. In his pursuit of the myth of Rome Mussolini, then, was no radical innovator, and he appeared to carry most Italians with him at first. The Corfu affair was a transitory setback, and was offset by the acquisition of Fiume. The slow penetration of Albania could be counted a success, and the conquest of Ethiopia was undeniably popular. The first half of the 1930s saw at least a passive Italian consensus in the Fascist regime's favor.[82] Mussolini's slide in public esteem began in 1936, and must be ascribed overwhelmingly to the Axis, an "iron cage" in which he trapped himself.[83] The rudiments of his idea of using Germany to forge a new Roman empire went back to the early 1920s, and once it materialized the Axis was put ahead of all other considerations. Italians did not so much resent the German tie *per se* as the Duce's deference to it – from the import of an antisemitism alien to Italy to the subordination of Mussolini's parallel war to Hitler's geopolitical priorities. To a certain extent, Italy's miserable war effort of 1940–43 resulted from the feeling of ordinary Italians that this was not their war. But it was among Italy's political class, those who had helped Mussolini into power and served him, that the myth of Rome was most pervasive and its achievement most keenly anticipated. Even in these quarters, and before June 10, 1940, many of the so-called Fascist *fiancheggiatori* (flankers) had been expressing unease about the German connection. When they followed the Duce into the maelstrom of war, it was not with any confidence that he could now deliver a Roman empire, but rather out of nearly twenty years of habit.

Like Hitler, Mussolini inherited a nationalist tradition and put his own stamp on it. The Fascist leader contributed an ideological disposition, albeit less fanatical than Hitler's, and the same fatalistic social Darwinism which permitted him to fix his gaze on the end without troubling about the means. These traits were endemic in the hothouse atmosphere generated by the Rome myth, which asked to be accepted as an article of faith and relied for fulfillment on Italy's star being in the ascendant. On the other hand, Mussolini's elevation of social-Darwinian ideology to be the *deus ex machina* of his diplomacy set him at least narrowly apart from mainstream Italian nationalism. It was a distinction of degree more than of kind, and it concerned methods and tactics, not aims. After 1936 Fascist foreign policy amounted to an all-or-nothing gamble that placed all Italy's eggs in the German basket. This was a strategy based in the last analysis on a rash belief in a favorable tide of history. As such, it tested the credence in destiny of many old-guard Italian nationalists, and indeed stretched it to breaking-point. In Germany Hitler's analogous recklessness, born of blind confidence in his historic mission, alienated numerous conservative and pragmatic nationalists. The Italo-German parallelism held good to the end. On 25 July 1943 the Italian political class belatedly mustered sufficient will to depose the Duce; the following year their German counterparts tried to assassinate the Führer.

In each case, the leader's identification with a hypernationalist ideal, which was proving unrealizable, had become absolute. Banal though it may sound, one cannot comprehend either Italian or German history in the Second World War by reference to one man without the set of historic ideas he arrogated, or to the ideas without the man who came to embody them.

Notes

1 See, for example, the exercise in comparative historiography by R. J. B. Bosworth, *Explaining Auschwitz and Hiroshima: History Writing and the Second World War, 1945–1990*, London, 1993.

2 C. S. Maier, *The Unmasterable Past: History, Holocaust, and German National Identity*, Cambridge, MA, 1988.

3 F. Fischer, *Griff nach der Weltmacht*, Düsseldorf, 1961; *From Kaiserreich to Third Reich: Elements of Continuity in German History, 1871–1945*, London, 1986.

4 A. J. P. Taylor, *The Origins of the Second World War*, London, 1961.

5 Churchill speech on BBC, 23 December 1940, *The Churchill War Papers*, vol. 2: *Never Surrender, May–Dec. 1940*, M. Gilbert (ed.), London, 1994, pp. 1284–8.

6 Quoted in C. Sprigge's Introduction to B. Croce, *Philosophy, Poetry, History: An Anthology of Essays*, London, 1966, p. lvii.

7 *Italy, the Least of the Great Powers: Italian Foreign Policy before the First World War*, Cambridge, 1979, chs 1, 2; "Italian foreign policy and its historiography," in *Altro Polo: Intellectuals and Their Ideas in Contemporary Italy*, R. Bosworth and G. Rizzo (eds), Sydney, 1983, pp. 65–85; *Italy and A Wider World, 1860–1960*, London, 1996, chs 1, 2. Also on the question of continuity in Italian foreign policy, see S. C. Azzi, "The historiography of Fascist Italy," *Historical Journal*, vol. 36, 1993, pp. 187–203.

8 F. Chabod, *Storia della politica estera italiana dal 1870 al 1896: Le premesse*, Bari, 1951. The work has now been translated into English under the title *Italian Foreign Policy: The Statecraft of the Founders*, Princeton, NJ, 1996.

9 Chabod, *Statecraft*, Part 2: "The idea of Rome." With few exceptions, however, Italian historians have been slow to follow Chabod either in seeking the roots of Italian foreign policy in sociopolitical culture, or in locating twentieth-century Italy's pursuit of grandeur in post-unification mythology.

10 For an exemplary portrait of Italy's old-guard diplomats as moderate and responsible, see R. Guariglia, *Ricordi, 1922–1946*, Naples, 1950. Bosworth, *Italy, Least of the Great Powers*, ch. 4, demonstrates that they were not so immune to delusions of national grandeur as their memoirs would suggest.

11 C. J. Lowe and F. Marzari, *Italian Foreign Policy, 1870–1940*, London, 1975, pp. 9–10, 54–68. See also the essays in *Adua: Le ragioni della sconfitta*, A. Del Boca (ed.), Rome, 1997.

12 C. Segrè, *Fourth Shore: The Italian Colonization of Libya*, Chicago, IL, 1974, pp. 22, 25, 39–40.

13 On nationalist sentiment in post-First World War Italy, see M. G. Melchionni, *La vittoria mutilata*, Rome, 1981; H. J. Burgwyn, *The Legend of the Mutilated Victory*, Westport, CT, 1993; M. Ledeen, *The First Duce: D'Annunzio at Fiume*, Baltimore, MD, 1977; R. De Felice, *D'Annunzio politico, 1918–1938*, Bari, 1978, Parts 1, 2; A. De Grand, *The Italian Nationalist Association and the Rise of Fascism in Italy*, Lincoln, NE, 1978.

14 "Romanità", in P. V. Cannistraro (ed.), *Historical Dictionary of Fascist Italy*, Westport, CT, 1982, p. 461.

15 Ministero degli Esteri, Italy, *I documenti diplomatici italiani* [henceforth *DDI*], series 7, vol. 4, no. 532. On Italy at Locarno, see S. Marks, "Mussolini and Locarno: Fascist

foreign policy in microcosm," *Journal of Contemporary History*, vol. 14, 1979, pp. 423–39.

16 See the following articles by P. G. Edwards: "The foreign office and Fascism, 1924–1929," *Journal of Contemporary History*, vol. 5, no. 2, 1970, pp. 153–61; "The Austen Chamberlain–Mussolini meetings," *Historical Journal*, vol. 14, 1971, pp. 153–64; "Britain, Fascist Italy and Ethiopia, 1925–1928," *European Studies Review*, vol. 4, 1974, pp. 359–74; "Britain, Mussolini and the 'Locarno–Geneva system,' " *European Studies Review*, vol. 10, 1980, pp. 1–16. For American opinion, see D. F. Schmitz, *The United States and Fascist Italy, 1922–1940*, Chapel Hill, NC, 1988, chs 3, 4.

17 Mussolini's imposture is the theme of my *Mussolini's Early Diplomacy*, Princeton, NJ, 1970.

18 *DDI*, series 7, vol. 2, p. 238 n. 3; nos 360, 373.

19 Cassels, *Early Diplomacy*, pp. 160–6.

20 Cassels, *Early Diplomacy*, pp. 166–74; M. Palumbo, "Goering's Italian exile," *Journal of Modern History*, vol. 50, 1978, no. 1, D1035.

21 Instances of ongoing Italian interest in the Nazis are to be found in *DDI*, series 7, vol. 5, no. 680; vol. 6, no. 322; vol. 7, nos 413, 576; vol. 8, nos 367, 377, 384; vol. 9, nos 180, 254, 262, 289.

22 Use of the generic name "fascist" papered over some substantive ideological differences between the Italian and German movements: witness the failure to establish a Fascist International, M. Ledeen, *Universal Fascism: Theory and Practice of the Fascist International, 1928–1934*, New York, 1972. The latest attempt to create a typology of fascism is S. Payne, *A History of Fascism, 1914–1945*, Madison, WI, 1995, esp. pp. 3–19, 487–95.

23 A. Hitler, *Mein Kampf*, trans. R. Manheim, New York, 1943, pp. 128–30, 628–30, 655–66; K.-P. Hoepke, *Die deutsche Rechte und der italienische Faschismus*, Düsseldorf, 1968, pp. 159–65; D. J. Rusinow, *Italy's Austrian Heritage, 1919–1946*, New York, 1969, pp. 215–18.

24 H. J. Burgwyn, *Il revisionismo fascista: La sfida di Mussolini alle grande potenze nei Balcani e sul Danubio, 1925–1933*, Milan, 1979; S. Troebst, *Mussolini, Macedonien und die Mächte, 1922–1930*, Cologne, 1987; J. J. Sadkovich, *Italian Support for Croatian Separatism, 1927–1937*, New York, 1987.

25 B. Mussolini, *Opera omnia* [henceforth, *OO*], E. and D. Susmel (eds), Florence–Rome, 1951–84, vol. 23, pp. 176–7.

26 Hoepke, *Die deutsche Rechte*, pp. 248, 306–8.

27 Guariglia, *Ricordi*, pp. 14–16; Legatus [R. Cantalupo], *Vita diplomatica di Salvatore Contarini*, Rome, 1947, pp. 73–8.

28 A. Lyttleton, *The Seizure of Power: Fascism in Italy, 1919–1929*, 2nd edn, Princeton NJ, 1988, ch. 10ff.

29 This theme is adumbrated in the early volumes of De Felice's life-and-times' biography, *Mussolini*, Turin, 1965–98; 4 parts in 8 volumes. It is expressed more briefly in R. De Felice, *Fascism: An Informal Introduction to its Theory and Practice*, New Brunswick, NJ, 1976, pp. 43–55, and in M. Ledeen, "Renzo De Felice and the controversy over Italian Fascism," *Journal of Contemporary History*, vol. 11, 1976, pp. 269–82.

30 S. B. Clough, *The Economic History of Modern Italy*, New York, 1964, pp. 246–51; M. Clark, *Modern Italy*, 2nd edn, London, 1996, ch. 13.

31 K. Jarausch, *The Four Power Pact*, Madison, WI, 1965; G. Giordano, *Il Patto a Quattro nella politica estera di Mussolini*, Bologna, 1976.

32 Auswärtiges Amt, Germany, *Documents on German Foreign Policy, 1918–1945* [henceforth, *DGFP*], series C, vol. 3, nos 5, 7, 10; G. L. Weinberg, *The Foreign Policy of Hitler's Germany*, vol. 1: *Diplomatic Revolution in Europe, 1933–1937*, Chicago, IL, 1970, pp. 100–1.

33 G.-K. Kindermann, *Hitler's Defeat in Austria, 1933–1934: Europe's First Containment of Nazi Expansionism*, Boulder, CO, 1988.

34 W. I. Shorrock, *From Ally to Enemy: The Enigma of Fascist Italy in French Diplomacy, 1920–1940*, Kent, OH,, 1988, ch. 7.

35 The secret Laval–Mussolini accord is documented in *DDI*, series 7, vol. 16, nos 391, 399, 403; on the background, see F. Lefebvre D'Ovidio, *L'intesa italo-francese del 1935 nella politica estera di Mussolini*, Rome, 1984. For what was both said and implied at Stresa, see E. Serra, "La questione italo-etiopica alla conferenza di Stresa," *Affari Esteri*, vol. 9, 1977, pp. 313–39. Italian knowledge of the Maffey report was first revealed by M. Toscano, *Designs in Diplomacy*, Baltimore, MD, 1970, pp. 412–14. The overall appraisal of Italy's international position in 1935 in E. M. Robertson, *Mussolini as Empire Builder: Europe and Africa, 1932–1936*, London, 1977, explains why it seemed to Mussolini a propitious moment for a colonial excursion.

36 G. Baer, *Test Case: Italy, Ethiopia, and the League of Nations*, Palo Alto, CA, 1976, chs 2, 3.

37 R. Mori, *Mussolini e la conqista dell'Etiopia*, Florence, 1978, pp. 217–20, argues persuasively that he would not.

38 *DGFP*, series C, vol. 4, nos 485, 506, 525; series D, vol. 1, nos 152, 155. Berlin's diplomatic recognition of Italian Ethiopia was announced on October 24, 1936.

39 M. Funke, *Sanktionen und Kanonen: Hitler, Mussolini und der Abessinienkonflikt, 1934–1936*, Düsseldorf, 1970, pp. 48–81. For Italy's place in Hitler's global strategy, see his *Mein Kampf*, pp. 620, 664–5, and *Hitler's Secret Book*, New York, 1961, pp. 173–4.

40 *OO*, vol. 15, p. 216.

41 Some of the Duce's unorthodox sources of information are detailed in D. Mack Smith, *Mussolini's Roman Empire*, London, 1976, pp. 92–5.

42 Quoted in R. H. Whealey, "Mussolini's ideological diplomacy," *Journal of Modern History*, vol. 39, 1967, p. 435.

43 B. R. Sullivan, "The Italian armed forces, 1918–1940," in *Military Effectiveness*, vol. 2: *The Interwar Period*, A. R. Millett and W. Murray (eds), Boston, MA, 1988, pp. 169–217.

44 The phenomenon of an ideologue without an ideology, or the distinction between ideology and ideological thinking, is explored in my *Ideology and International Relations in the Modern World*, London, 1997.

45 J. F. Coverdale, *Italian Intervention in the Spanish Civil War*, Princeton, NJ, 1976, pp. 12–13, 78–82; G. Ciano, *Diplomatic Papers*, M. Muggeridge (ed.), London, 1948, pp. 138–41, 244.

46 Taylor, *Origins*, p. 111. Mussolini's Axis speech is in *OO*, vol. 28, pp. 67–71. Incidentally, the axis metaphor was not new in Mussolini's vocabulary; he had once described Germany alone as the axis of world affairs, *OO*, vol. 20, p. 31.

47 Clark, *Modern Italy*, pp. 97, 120; D. Mack Smith, *Italy: A Modern History*, revised edn, Ann Arbor, MI, 1969, pp. 265–6.

48 M. Michaelis, *Mussolini and the Jews: German–Italian Relations and the Jewish Question in Italy, 1922–1945*, Oxford, 1978, ch. 5.

49 D. Mack Smith, "Mussolini: artist in propaganda," *History Today*, vol. 9, 1959, pp. 223–32.

50 R. De Felice, *Mussolini il duce*, vol. 2: *Lo Stato totalitario, 1936–1940*, Turin, 1981; chs 5, 6.

51 C. Seton Watson, "The Anglo-Italian Gentleman's Agreement of January 1937," in *The Fascist Challenge and the Policy of Appeasement*, W. J. Mommsen and L. Kettenacker (eds), London, 1983, pp. 266–82; D. Bolech Cecchi, *L'accordo di due imperi: L'accordo italo-inglese del 16 aprile 1938*, Milan, 1977.

52 See, for example, A. L. Goldman, "Sir Robert Vansittart's search for Italian cooperation against Hitler," *Journal of Contemporary History*, vol. 9, no. 1974, pp. 93–130.

53 For example, R. A. Lamb, *Mussolini and the British*, London, 1997.

54 R. Quartararo, *Roma tra Londra e Berlino: Politica estera fascista dal 1930 al 1940*, Rome, 1980.

55 A telling critique, of De Felice in particular, is M. Knox, "The Fascist regime, its foreign policy and its wars: an anti-Fascist orthodoxy?", *Contemporary European History*, vol. 4, 1995, pp. 347–65. A recent survey, H. J. Burgwyn's *Italian Foreign Policy in the Interwar Period, 1918–1940*, Westport, CT, 1997, attempts to find a "middle ground" between De Felice and his critics.

56 P. Brundu Olla, *L'equilibrio difficile: Gran Bretagna, Italia e Francia nel Mediterraneo*, Milan, 1980.
57 G. Ciano, *Diary, 1937–1938*, A. Mayor (ed.), London, 1952, pp. 161–3.
58 Ciano, *Diary*, 1937–1938, p. 166.
59 M. Knox, "Conquest, foreign and domestic, in Fascist Italy and Nazi Germany," *Journal of Modern History*, vol. 56, 1984, pp. 1–57. The same postulate informs P. Morgan's *Italian Fascism, 1919–1945*, Basingstoke, 1995.
60 P. R. Stafford, "The Chamberlain–Halifax visit to Rome: a reappraisal," *English Historical Review*, vol. 98, 1983, pp. 61–100.
61 Shorrock, *From Ally to Enemy*, pp. 264–7.
62 *OO*, vol. 37, pp. 151–2.
63 C. A. MacDonald, "Radio Bari and Italian propaganda in the Middle East and British counter measures, 1934–1938," *Middle Eastern Studies*, vol. 13, 1977, pp. 195–207. On the Anglo-Italian imperial rivalry, see also my own "Deux empires face à face: La chimère d'un rapprochement anglo-italien, 1936–1940," *Guerre mondiales et conflits contemporains*, no. 161, Jan., vol. 41, 1991, pp. 67–96.
64 Foreign office, Great Britain, *Documents on British Foreign Policy, 1919–1939*, series 3, vol. 5, no. 652. The British, hoping always to detach Mussolini from the Axis, replied that they considered the Easter accords to be still valid, *DBFP*, no. 708.
65 M. Toscano, *The Origins of the Pact of Steel*, Baltimore, MD, 1967, ch. 4. The text of the pact is printed in an appendix.
66 Ciano, *Diplomatic Papers*, pp. 283–4; *DDI*, series 8, vol. 12, no. 59.
67 *DDI*, series 8, vol. 13, nos 1, 4, 21.
68 D. Grandi, *Il mio paese*, Bologna, 1985, ch. 45; P. Nello, *Dino Grandi: Un fedele disubbidiente*, Bologna, 1993, pp. 359–64.
69 G. Ciano, *Diary, 1939–1943*, M. Muggeridge (ed.), London, 1947, pp. 120–9.
70 P. R. Stafford, "The French government and the Danzig crisis: the Italian dimension," *International History Review*, vol. 6, 1984, pp. 48–87; R. A. C. Parker, "The British government and the coming of war with Germany, 1939," in *War and Society*, M. R. D. Foot (ed.), London, 1973, pp. 3–15.
71 Taylor, *Origins*, p. 40.
72 F. Halder, *Diaries*, Boulder, CO, 1976, vol. 1, p. 28; P. Schmidt, *Hitler's Interpreter*, London, 1951, p. 146; Weinberg, *Foreign Policy of Hitler's Germany*, vol. 2: *Starting World War II, 1937–1939*, Chicago, IL, 1980, pp. 637–8.
73 L. R. Pratt, *East of Malta, West of Suez: Britain's Mediterranean Crisis, 1936–1939*, Cambridge, MA, 1975, pp. 4, 30–2.
74 M. Knox, *Mussolini Unleashed, 1939–1941: Politics and Strategy in Fascist Italy's Last War*, Cambridge, 1982, pp. 44–59.
75 W. N. Medlicott, *The Economic Blockade*, London, 1952, vol. 1, ch. 8.
76 S. Welles, *The Time for Decision*, New York, 1944, pp. 78–89, 135–47.
77 "If Italy was content with a second-rate position in the Mediterranean, then she need do nothing more," *DGFP*, series 9, vol. 3, no. 1. Interestingly, this explicit Hitlerian threat is contained in the official German record of the Hitler–Mussolini meeting on the Brenner in March 1940, but not the Italian. See Ciano, *Diplomatic Papers*, pp. 361–5, reprinted in *DDI*, series 9, vol. 3, no. 578.
78 On these last-minute maneuverings to keep Italy out of war, see Cassels, "Deux empires face à face," pp. 92–5.
79 *OO*, vol. 29, pp. 43–5.
80 Knox, *Mussolini Unleashed*, ch. 6.
81 Bosworth, "Italian foreign policy and historiography," p. 79.
82 R. De Felice, *Mussolini il duce, Gli anni del consenso, 1929–1936*, Turin, 1974; vol. 1.
83 Ennio Di Nolfo's phrase quoted in Burgwyn, *Italian Foreign Policy*, p. 228.

5 A. J. P. Taylor and the problem with France

Robert J. Young

Rereading *The Origins of the Second World War*, more than three decades after its first appearance, is like bumping into a familiar face at a school reunion. Years ago we, the new boys, had been cautioned about this celebrity. Our mentors distrusted his judgment, though they admired his "style' – in part a temperament distinguished by audacity, in part an inspired pen that too often made the complex appear simple. It was clear to us then, even if the reasoning behind it were less so, that Taylor's *Origins* had passed some tests magnificently and failed others rather miserably. Whatever the final assessment of his peers, we undergraduates knew that Taylor had been responsible for an historical event of its own kind. Almost forty years later that publishing event of 1961 remains, as Taylor said of the war itself, "a matter of historical curiosity."[1]

It is a mark of this book's impact to be able to say that it remains central to a debate that still bubbles away over the war's origins. Of course, scholars may persist in saying, as they have for nearly forty years, that Taylor got it wrong, or at least much of it. They will continue to insist, as indeed they must, that his evidence was often inadequate for his case, if not overtly incompatible with it. An historical *agent provocateur*, he invited the blows of those who found his grasp of economics rudimentary, his interest in ideology moribund, his predilection for contrived aphorisms excessive. And yet he was never chased from the field, never made to surrender. They may have worked around him; for a while they may even have ignored him; but in the end they have had to return to his field.

Taylor opened the first edition of *Origins* with a chapter entitled "Forgotten problem." It was here that he acknowledged some of the archival obstacles that he had encountered and which, by his own admission, may have contributed to the "perhaps misleading impression that international relations between the wars were an Anglo-German duologue" (p. 38). Misleading or not – and it was – this is what Taylor concentrated on. Accordingly, it was here that one might have expected him to vent his enthusiasm. He did not disappoint. Taylor tackled Hitler's Germany and Chamberlain's England with the zeal of an iconoclast. Hitler, contrary to all that had been said, had no great design, plan or blueprint, but succeeded. Chamberlain, contrary to popular wisdom, had a plan, knew what he wanted, but failed. Hitler was no man of action, but rather a procrastinator, one who excelled in waiting. Chamberlain was no chinless temporizer, but rather a resolute decision maker who was impatient for peace. After Taylor, many of the old truths looked decidedly shop-worn. One of the best exponents of paradox since Karl Marx, Taylor played games with all previous judgments, often agreeing with two opposing views and so discrediting both. "Though the object of being a Great Power is to be able to fight a great war, the only way of remaining a Great Power is not to fight one" (p. 15). The Rhineland crisis of March 1936 was a turning-point in that it "opened the door for Germany's success," though it also "opened the door for her ultimate failure." What better paradoxical illumination could one seek, lest it be that "the defect of this explanation is that, since it explains everything, it also explains nothing" (pp. 134–5)?

This is vintage Taylor: unconventional insight articulated by means of paradox and, sometimes, riddle-like aphorism. "Only a country which aims at victory can be threatened with defeat" (p. 134). "Wars, when they come, are always different from the war that is expected. Victory goes to the side that has made fewest mistakes, not to the one that has guessed right" (p. 151). "After all, standing still is the best policy for anyone who favours the *status quo*, perhaps the only one" (p. 306). As Taylor once said of Metternich, "most men could do better than this when shaving," for what do such maxims really mean?[2] Are they intended to instruct, or merely titillate? Explanation alone could make or unmake their profundity. Until it does, one can only echo Captain Corcoran's response to a torrent of enigmas: "Though to catch your drift I'm striving. It is shady – it is shady."

Frankly, this is an overlooked quality of *Origins*. It was a rare and singular gift which permitted Taylor to be as controversial when he was being abstruse as when he was being crystal-clear. For example, one can understand the picture of Hitler as day-dreamer, a man who had no desire or plan for war, a man whose international goals were more modest than those of his predecessors. One may object or protest, but the point is clear enough. But precisely what is one to understand from the way Taylor brandished the vocabulary of morality in international affairs? Here, the point is not at all clear. Sometimes we are led to believe that fascism had such a corrupting effect that the leaders of Britain and France were beset by a "moral and intellectual fog", so much so that they "came to believe that an unscrupulous policy was the only resource" (pp. 141, 194). So far so good. Yet appeasement, by Taylor's telling, was the work of a British government whose motives were "of the highest" and who made this "high-minded attempt at the impartial redress of grievances." Then, presumably, the fog rolled in again, for by the time of the Munich conference, appeasement "had lost its moral strength" (pp. 212, 228) And then it lifted, just in time to make it obvious that for the British "morality counted for a great deal," and that a British prime minister had actually succeeded in getting the French, even the Czechs, "to follow the moral line" (pp. 234–5).

One such illustration normally would be enough to demonstrate the frequent patches of confusion, but in this instance the point is too important for doubts to be allowed to linger. This is a study which purported to address Britain and

France more than Germany, and specifically the question of why they did not resist Hitler. As such, the issue of their moral motivation certainly became very central to the book, despite Taylor's claim that he never mixed business with morality (pp. 7, 9). The historian, so he assured readers of his first edition, must only elucidate, never judge – an admirable counsel of self-restraint, provided one is sure of being able to distinguish one from the other. When it comes to his remarks on the French, however, Taylor's claim seems a little tarnished. From where he sat, beside the Thames, the fog over Paris never seemed to lift. Never do the French catch sight of even a few errant rays of moral enlightenment, except of course when they are hoodwinked into following "the moral line." How all of this fits into premier Daladier's despairing protestations is anyone's guess, for it seems to have been he, in April and September 1938, who resisted the very principle of appeasing Hitler at the expense of "independent peoples" (pp. 234–5, 201, 225).[3]

As he was to do with the British and the Germans, so Taylor would do with the French, stirring up the water with a great stick in an effort to catch a glimpse of the foreign policy of the Third Republic and the attitudes behind it. Paradoxically, however, the less certain he was of the French, the less he wrote, and the less he wrote, the greater was his impact. In the case of Britain and Germany, on which he wrote immeasurably more, Taylor has been challenged and corrected, repeatedly. In the case of France, few even bothered. In 1961, or subsequently, one would not have turned to *Origins* for a considered analysis of French policy; but, for a provocative and witty study of the coming of a world war, why not? Accordingly, hundreds of thousands read Taylor, while a few score looked for something better on France, in some cases even in works written in French. More than three decades later, it still shows.

I once commented on those many studies of international relations which had skimmed over interwar France with only the slightest regard. A "Great Power" by the standards of the day, France was duly located on the right side of the Channel and then dismissed with comments which were as dogmatic as they were brief. Yet every such passage left a trail of slips and innuendoes, all of them suggesting a country that had lost its way, that had become unmistakably degenerate.[4] At the time, A. J. P. Taylor was far from my thoughts. But on rereading *Origins* the conviction grows that his work had contributed substantially to that earlier impression. Certainly when it came to the French, Taylor was no revisionist. Quite the reverse. An Englishman, as he said, "by birth and preference,"[5] Taylor tended to confirm what his compatriots had known for a century or two, namely that the French were a thoroughly difficult lot. One might choose to upend cherished interpretations, even give Stalin the benefit of the doubt, but some truths were indeed self-evident and needed defending more than rethinking.

Some historians of France are certain to dislike Taylor's treatment of the interwar Third Republic. Much of what he had to say about the French will seem questionable in the extreme, whether it was when he saw fit to link them with the British or when he was more determined to disassociate them from the high-minded thinking of Whitehall. In the former case a series of examples comes to mind: "western policy mainly turned" on Britain; "western statesmen strove to keep them [the Americans] out"; "British and French statesmen...sincerely believed...that Hitler would be content and pacific if his claims were met"; both "Great Britain and France in 1938 were for 'peace at any price'." (pp. 234–5, 201, 225). Unlike the second and third of these extraordinary assertions, the first and last are only half-mistaken. Fundamentally, however, what is off-putting is the assumed ease with which the French could be packaged with the British – when it was convenient to do so.

Sometimes, of course, it was altogether too inconvenient. For whatever this means to the "western" policy above, appeasement was presented very much as an English invention. The French do not subscribe to it as a positive way of reconciling differences. Rather, for them, it is merely an expedient to get them off the hook and free them from the obligation to defend the Czechs, "not a dangerous...but perhaps an ignoble policy" (p. 233). In other ways, too, the French were different, and had to be assessed by Taylor in quite discrete ways. For example, he said they made "no attempt to protect the French frontier with Belgium" with the same assurance that he claimed the Baldwin government had imposed a Spanish non-intervention policy on Léon Blum (pp. 149, 158). Neither claim has the evidence on its side. Nor is there substance, indeed credibility, to the claim that the French failed to appreciate the significance of Germany becoming "the dominant Power in Eastern Europe." And whatever could have possessed Taylor to say that the French "did not fear defeat if war were thrust upon them" in 1938? (pp. 203, 233). Such affirmations, all of them, are baseless, at least as so tersely expressed in *Origins*. In fact, the French stepped up their fortification program along the Belgian frontier in 1936. They actually initiated the policy of non-intervention in Spain, instead of buckling to pressure from London. They were only too conscious of what the consequences might be for their own security if Germany acquired the resources of eastern Europe. They certainly did fear military defeat at the hands of the Germans in 1938, if they were to face Germany on their own, without benefit of an Allied coalition. Taylor's inability to appreciate this point alone suggests a degree of misunderstanding that one cannot help but find frankly puzzling. Surely something had obscured the vision of this often remarkably insightful and undeniably gifted historian.

Part of his problem with the French was source-related. He knew from the start that there were difficulties to overcome, in particular the unevenness of the published diplomatic documentation, rich on the British and German sides but impoverished on the French and Russian (p. 37). Consequently, compensating as he could with a mixed array of other published sources, Taylor took the plunge, as he had to, assuring himself that there was little to be gained by waiting for the release of further archival material. In fairness, who would have wished otherwise? Nevertheless, it is also fair to suggest that Taylor – intent as he was on working with a broad continental canvas – did not come close to exhausting the supply of very important French materials. By all appearances he did consult

Paul-Boncour, Bonnet, and Flandin, but he overlooked Baudouin, Cot, Fabry, Laval, Monzie, Reynaud, Tardieu, and Zay. General Gamelin he read, but evidently not Armengaud, Bourret, Gauché, Jacomet, Minart, Nollet, Prételat, Réquin, or Weygand. More remarkable, the eleven volumes of reports and testimonies produced by a French parliamentary commission just after the war seemed to have escaped Taylor's attention.[6] Though such criticism may be mistaken for cavil by some, the scholar will acknowledge the point. The fact is that Taylor, for all his Anglo-German research, made no extraordinary or even great effort to consult many of the French sources which were available to him and which he would have found instructive.

Another part of the problem comes from what one is tempted to call a cultural bias. In a word, it is this which makes it easy for many English to think ill of the French, a state of mind which is known to have been reciprocated by the French when given half a chance. The trick, of course, is to be able to sort out informed from uninformed bias, a service sometimes afforded by one historian or another. The "despairing cynicism" of the French in the 1930s, Taylor wrote, their "lack of faith in their leaders and in themselves," had a "long and complicated origin which has often been dissected by historians" (p. 72). Reassured by the reasoned analyses of these entirely unidentified scholars, and satisfied by the very predecessors whose other judgments he was in the process of discarding, Taylor was ready to confront the French. What ensued was a scattering of cryptic, unflinching, unsubstantiated, judgmental remarks about the French. Indeed, *Origins* is peppered with the language of some apprehensive day-tripper to Calais.

"Characteristically," the French failed to see the implications of their decisions on disarmament policy in April 1934. Faced with a renascent Germany, they "looked plaintively to London." Weak in spirit and devoid of resolution, they were responsible for "dragging the British down with them" for, as everyone knows, "weakness is infectious" (pp. 107, 197, 209). Daladier, when not being "sullen," either "gave way" or "wriggled and dodged." He, the "most representative of French politicians" led a people who regularly had "acquiesced in" or "allowed" one German challenge to succeed after another, a people which had "supposed all along that the advantages won in 1919 and subsequently…were assets which they could supinely enjoy, not gains which they must fiercely defend" (pp. 216, 219, 225, 322, 233). Indeed, for all of his assurance that appeasement was a positive policy, generated by Chamberlain without reference to military calculations, Taylor wrote of the prime minister's dilemma before the Commons in September 1938: "He could not stress the unwillingness of the French to fight, which had been the really decisive weakness on the western side" (p. 236). Despite gallant attempts to be the impartial exponent, and not the judge, there is little doubt that Taylor was manifestly more successful when it came to treating England's enemy than he was her ally.

Force of assumption, undiminished by a thorough reading of French source materials, does much to explain Taylor's handling of France. As a result, he was not merely unpredictable – he was often unreliable. It is, however, a tribute to his native perspicacity and instinct that he could be as insightful as he sometimes was. He was error-prone; he demonstrated no profound sense of France's plight between the wars; yet he still saw what so many others had not. It was he who recognized the fact that the Hoare–Laval proposal of December 1935 was not a wicked French invention, indeed, was not French at all and only arguably wicked. He also saw that the absence of a French military reaction in March 1936 was the result of a deliberate government policy, arranged in advance of the German initiative, and not the panic-induced paralysis of a government taken by surprise. In a similar vein, Taylor's few sentences on the subject correctly implied that the French government had no intention of doing anything about the *Anschluss* in March 1938. And he did not miss the fact that the Daladier government assumed more and more of the diplomatic initiative in the wake of the Munich conference, and especially after the fall of Prague and the guarantee to Poland (pp. 126, 130–8, 175–87, 264–336). Each of these examples he may have read perversely, in ways that were consistently unflattering to the French; nevertheless, on the surface, when it came to specific policy at particular moments, Taylor was indeed able to "get things right" much of the time (p. 10). Considering the liabilities with which he was working in the late 1950s – some more avoidable than others – that is a respectable record. Indeed, it may have been far better than many comparable studies which noticed France only through peripheral vision. But clearly it was not good enough.

Taylor, even when he got it "right," demonstrated little interest in interwar France and, accordingly, no great understanding. Two illustrations come to mind: his practised inability to see either skill or acumen behind French foreign policy in the 1930s; his failure to ask why the French seemed so anxious to keep in step with Britain, why they were "terrified at losing even the thin shreds of British support" (p. 109). Both deficiencies derive from the same source – the ineradicable impression that, at worst, the French were craven and, at best, that they had been reduced to some catatonic state by the specter of a new war. Out of this leaps the argument that the British were forced to take the initiative, forced to sort everything out, with the French "dragging protestingly along behind" (pp. 202, 246).

The first illustration concerns foreign minister Pierre Flandin in March 1936. Taylor said, fairly, that the Sarraut government had decided in advance not to resist a German remilitarization of the Rhineland with force. Yet Flandin went to London and threatened to use the army unless the British government offered some new and further assurances for French security. Taylor saw this as mere bravado, and concluded that Flandin simply caved in when Baldwin condemned the notion of any kind of military riposte. After all, Flandin had never been serious about such action in the first place. Fair again, but all that Taylor can discern in this is a typical Frenchman "concerned to take his responsibility across the Channel and to leave it there" (p.132) He made no connection between Flandin's apparent change of heart and the British decision of the same week to commit Britain "for the first time in her history – to peacetime alliance with a continental Great Power"; no connection between this milestone – designed only for restraining France, for "ceaselessly holding her back" – and Flandin's triumphant return to Paris where he announced the dawning of a new day in Anglo-French relations. If ever he suspected it, Taylor certainly never acknowledged even the possibility that a British government had been finessed. As for the retort that it was the French who had been finessed and unwittingly harnessed, one has only to invoke Taylor's murmured aside: "not that the French needed much restraining" (p. 148). If not, then what explains his "alliance," unless Flandin's bluff had worked and the British government had felt compelled to defuse the situation?

Edouard Daladier receives similar treatment in the course of the Czech crisis of 1938. After Chamberlain's meeting with Hitler at Berchtesgaden, a series of Anglo-French meetings took place in London in the last two weeks of September. Daladier, by Taylor's record, had proven obstreperous. However much he "wriggled," he seemed to have a nasty habit of "returning to the question of principle." For their part, the British "were urging the French not to take the offensive." They even declined the possibility of a last-minute meeting between Chamberlain and Daladier, just on the eve of the Munich conference, for fear that the French premier "would once more try ineffectually to coordinate resistance" (pp. 225–6, 228). The trick was to keep the pressure on Daladier until he was trapped, but the premier had demanded something in exchange, one "essential condition." His acquiescence was contingent upon a British agreement to share in a formal guarantee to the forthcoming rump Czech state. Chamberlain, the moralist, balked at such a commitment, but finally relented. Daladier, Taylor's weak cynic, though "convinced in his heart that Germany was aiming at something far greater," had stood firm. As a result, he managed to commit Britain "to opposing Hitler's advance in the east." No mean achievement this, had it been deliberate; but of course it was not, not by Taylor's light. Rather, Daladier "had built better than he knew" (pp. 219–20). In short, he had succeeded by blunder and pure chance – a familiar Taylor motif – unaware of what he had done, or why. How many times can one afford to lift the glass to the blind eye?

There was something else that Daladier had demanded, and got, in London. This was the inauguration of more formalized staff talks with the English. Indeed, this was the one thing that Daladier was really after. All of his grudging concessions to Chamberlain, over a period of several months, need to be considered in the light of his determination to put some teeth into the "alliance"; with Britain. This conclusion, to be sure, makes sense only if one rejects yet another of Taylor's contentions, namely that military considerations were not central to British policy in 1938 and that neither Britain nor France in 1938 seriously envisaged the possibility of being defeated by Germany. This is not the place, nor is there space, to argue this point. Sometimes, à la Taylor, it is enough to rely on simple refutation. Recent research certainly raises many questions about his judgment of British policy – even to some extent where Chamberlain himself is concerned – and who but Taylor would suggest that the French were incapable of admitting the possibility of defeat?[7] Clearly, they were not.

Accordingly, they were intensely interested in promoting joint Anglo-French planning through the medium of extended staff talks. To secure agreement here, the French government was prepared to adopt a policy in which it did not believe, and which it actually considered to be inimical to the peace of Europe. Taylor, distracted by seeing the French "dragged helplessly behind," caught little if any of this (pp. 202, 246).

But what made Britain so important to the French? Here is the second illustration of the problem Taylor has with France. For him the answer lay in the tirelessly repeated assertion that they were resolved to avoid war at any cost. This, of course, was neither argued nor substantiated, only reiterated. The combination of this technique, and the cultural bias previously discussed, meant that the French emerged gutless from Taylor's mold. In the absence of clear historical exposition, there would appear to be no rhyme or reason to their fear of finding themselves at war. But just as there is another construction that can be placed on Flandin and Daladier, so there is another that may illuminate further the condition of France between the wars. Since the argument has been advanced before, and more thoroughly than is possible here, it should be sufficient to sketch its outline – namely that French foreign and military policy may profitably be appraised with some reference to the "guerre de longue durée."

This notion of a long war of attrition, similar to that which ended in 1918, was central to French official thinking between the wars.[8] Little wonder, therefore, that they found the prospect of some future war both awesome and repellent. Nevertheless, for twenty years the conviction endured that the Germans were bent on revenge, that France would be the principal adversary and the first victim of German attack. In the absence of outside assistance, the struggle would be uneven. Indeed, Germany was likely to win, thanks to its superior industrial and demographic resources. Short of resigning themselves to such an outcome – an alternative that even Taylor discarded when he said they did not fear defeat – the French had to rebuild a coalition of allies, one that could be used to deter Germany from an act of revenge, or to defeat it if deterrence should fail. To that end, with very mixed results, the government of the Third Republic sought to enlist the co-operation of Belgium, Poland, Czechoslovakia, Romania, Yugoslavia, Italy and Russia. Each, for a time, was part of what is often called the French alliance "system." The term, though an exaggeration, is probably better than having French policy confused with alleged attempts to establish a new continental imperium. This was not what the French were after. Rather they wished to have at the ready allies who would help to defend France. As such, the contradictions between their reciprocal undertakings to each "ally," and their much remarked upon "defensive" military strategy, are perhaps more apparent than real.

The keystone of this system, however, was supposed to be Britain. It was to Britain that successive French governments turned for economic and financial support. The delayed onslaught of the Depression in France had presaged a similarly delayed recovery, one that was not very apparent until the last quarter of

1938. Accordingly, French governments depended heavily on British fiscal co-operation and accommodation in order to engineer the economic recovery which the German danger had made imperative. Without that recovery, and the attendant acceleration of French rearmament, the chances of deterring Germany were reckoned to be slight. If deterrence failed, the argument for an Anglo-French alliance was all the more compelling.[9] In the event of an actual German attack, the best the French could hope to do by themselves was to secure a military stalemate. Thereafter, and in theory, the resources of the allies could be brought to bear against the initial German siege, and latterly to permit a war-winning strategic offensive. But all of this would take time, indeed, several years: time during which British coal could be delivered to France's wartime industries; time for essential raw materials from the French and British empires to be carried to France in British merchant ships; time for the British navy to join with that of France in an economic blockade of Germany, and to assist in the passage of troops from North Africa to France, or from France to some future theater of military operations in eastern Europe. In short, British assistance was more than simply desirable, it was held to be indispensable. And this is what Taylor chose *not* to explore, the possibility that something other than moral lethargy lay behind French behavior.

Certainly he was right to say that General Gamelin expressed confidence in military victory in 1938 – a victory entirely and expressly predicated on the presence of a broad anti-German coalition. But this did not exist, as the general, and the premier, well knew. The British government, in particular, refused to contemplate a military confrontation with Germany in 1938. That said, it was understandable why the French themselves declined to run the risk of war without firm and prior assurances of British support. They were alarmed not merely at the prospect of war itself – which overall they were more prepared to countenance than was Chamberlain – but also by the possibility, even the likelihood, that they would be defeated in a strictly bilateral war with Germany. Far from being craven, some might call this common sense. Others, were they to follow Taylor's own nostrum, might even see French policy as a coarse mixture of principle and pragmatism, and as such the work of "every statesman of any merit" (p. 129). Certainly it is unclear why we should call "ignoble" Daladier's grudging consent to something he knew to be wrong, when Chamberlain's refusal to admit to any kind of wrong-doing was deemed to be "high-minded."

Nevertheless, the spell of the late Professor Taylor endures. Even we, his sometime critics, continue to see him as mentor and to follow his example. For even as we are provoked by him, we may be inclined to reply in kind, over-accentuating our arguments, implying a degree of self-assurance and of consensus that may not be there. The foregoing analysis is a case in point, for the fact is that it remains a maverick view, shared by probably a minority of scholars and, more certainly, by an even smaller minority of general readers. In other words, Taylor still reigns, the lion whose tail is occasionally bitten by some mouse; but, to use Donald Watt's sobering metaphor, "the mouse remains a mouse and the lion a lion."[10] It may be just as well, for the mice too have had their differences.

Those differences have a long history, indeed too long to be invoked in its entirety here. Suffice to say that ever since the sudden collapse of France in 1940 there have been interpretive clashes among historians over the causes of that defeat. And some of those interpretations have been consistent with Taylor's reading of interwar events in general and the behavior of France in particular.[11] There is, for example, the work of the late Professor Jean-Baptiste Duroselle, a legendary figure in postwar French scholarship and author of a weighty tome called *La Décadence.*[12] Published in 1979, this provocatively titled book had overtones of Taylor's work of twenty years earlier. Here we find a survey of the principal flaws which had reduced the French republic to ignominy in the decade that preceded its military collapse. To begin with, there was a fundamental structural problem manifest in an overly powerful legislature and an emasculated executive branch; this accounted for the sixteen different governments that presided over France's destiny between 1932 and 1940. From this chronic upheaval came the associated problem of long-range planning for the purpose of international affairs. Hence we have Duroselle's root cause of the uncertainty and indecisiveness which he detected in the country's foreign policy; but there was something more, something more serious. He was reluctant to suggest a lethal blemish in the "national character," and was only slightly more willing to attribute this suspected decadence to the self-seeking, bourgeois, governing class. More credible, or so he determined, was the prospect of linking whatever had been wrong with France to the discredited Marshal Pétain, the defeated and dismissed General Gamelin, the exiled and forever taciturn Alexis Léger. Here was proof that the carnage of the First World War had denied the country really first-class leadership when it came to facing her destiny in the interwar period. Here, in the Third Republic, "men proved weaker than fate."

His successor at the Sorbonne caught the same odor of decadence. "Decay was in the air," wrote René Girault. "They were preparing for defeat." For him, the lack of will-power was at the heart of the decadence, at once its symptom and cause. Like Professor Duroselle, he was convinced that internal political divisions had proven so fractious that there was no longer one France but two, two nations divided over an ideological vision of where the greatest danger lay: in the Left or in the Right. Hence, there was no unified, single, national will; and in its absence, France gave to all observers the impression of being the new sick man of Europe. Such imagery seemed none too harsh for another of Girault's Paris-based colleagues. If anything, Serge Berstein was even more convinced that prewar rot pretty much explained the military disaster of 1940. The country had dissolved in a sea of "national decadence," its interwar military policy had been "inane," and its intellectual leadership woeful.[13]

Clearly, Taylor would be quite at home with all of this, entirely familiar with the broad outline of this enduring view of interwar France. What could be more encouraging than to have the support of three such eminent French historians? Together, and expressly, they have ensured that the brief but sweeping judgments of *Origins* will retain their relevance for years to come. Appraised in this light, therefore, one must acknowledge that Taylor's version of France remains very much in the historical mainstream, despite the dissidence and doubts that have been expressed earlier in these pages.

And if further proof were needed, one might turn to a few examples of Anglophone scholarship in the 1980s and 90s, works which are roughly consistent with Taylor's view of France. Toward the end of his massive work on the immediate origins of the war, Donald Watt observes, matter of factly, that the French republic was in its "penultimate stage of decay" led by a buck-passing foreign minister in a buck-passing "French system of government."[14] However reluctantly, the Yale-based scholar Piotr Wandycz settled upon decadence as an explanation for France's flaccid policy toward eastern Europe in the 1930s, a conclusion shared with more enthusiasm by Nicole Jordan, who is struck not only by France's impotence but by her cynicism and dishonesty.[15] The same dishonesty has caught the eye of the Ottawa-based historian, Michael Carley, who has attributed much of it to capitalist machinations. Simply put, Rightist influences in France's public and private sectors, people blinded by their animus toward the Soviet Union, severely underestimated the threat posed by Nazi Germany.[16] Whereas Carley puts a particular ideological twist on the concept of Decadence, the eminent historian Eugen Weber is prepared to use it more conventionally. As an entrée to a recent chapter entitled, simply enough, "The decadence," Weber invokes a saying about Frenchmen being "always inferior to circumstances" and quickly subscribes to the impressions cast by Professor Duroselle.[17] For his part, Anthony Adamthwaite is more circumspect about the language of decadence. Indeed, he finds it inappropriate. At the same time, however, he concludes his most recent book on interwar France with the remark that what was missing by the late 1930s was courage, a quality intended to depict the national character, and a language not far removed from Taylor's own moralistic verdicts on France.[18]

It would take a debunker of Taylor's own talent and stature to overturn all such dismal verdicts on the failures of interwar France. In fact, no one has yet tried, and no one seems likely to. The instances of brilliant policy brilliantly conducted are rare in human affairs, and rarer still in the eyes of tough-minded historians. This is neither more nor less true of France than elsewhere, despite the disturbing proclivity of some observers – French included – to represent France as perpetually exceptional. However, common sense, to invoke one of Taylor's favorite devices, would tell us that interwar France, like prewar or postwar France, is likely to disclose a rather mixed legacy: on the one hand, oversights, mistakes, missed opportunities; and, on the other hand, instances of success and achievement, some delivered through good planning, others through good fortune. Not surprisingly, this is indeed what we do find once we discard the blurring vocabulary of French decadence.

Take, for instance, the matter of French public morale in 1939. While refraining from calling it defeatist in character, Taylor detected a state of crippling enervation. The French were, he judged, "at a loss what to do" and "therefore decided to let things happen" (p. 322). Yet Professor Duroselle himself led the way in countering this particular over-simplification. In a public-opinion poll taken shortly after the Munich settlement, some 70 percent of French respondents believed that Britain and France had to resist any future demands from Berlin; and a subsequent poll indicated that a substantial majority were actually in favor of military action in the event that Germany should attempt to seize the Baltic port of Danzig. The prospect of war did not please them, but they had had enough of being bullied.[19] Far from being supine, they had been conditioned to think of resistance by patriotic school textbooks and state-sponsored cinema, by a surfeit of popular literature on France's imperial resources and by a wave of media hype about the reappearance of the Anglo-French alliance.[20] Saddened though they certainly were by the prospect of renewed fighting, they were now nonetheless resolved to stand up to Hitler. Indeed, pacifism, which had been in the ascendant in 1938, had become the refuge of a minority in 1939, as the public mood swung in favor of resistance. Though incapable of regenerating the boisterous but naive spirit of belligerence of 1914, the French nation stoically accepted the coming of war in August 1939.[21]

The growing mood of resistance was in turn associated with the considerable upswing of the French economy through 1938 and 1939. Indeed, so substantial was the acceleration of industrial production that Professor Duroselle understood why some contemporaries had considered it miraculous. Without it, he said, there certainly would not have been the "remarkable" progress made in aerial rearmament.[22] Two economic historians, Jean Bouvier and Robert Frank, added their assent. What is more, they used this economic recovery to explain the contrast between French international policy in 1938 and in 1939. In 1938 the overall economic situation was so troubled that Daladier could not accept the risk of war. A year later, when the economic mood was so much brighter, there was an appreciable increase in the nation's determination to check Hitler.[23] Such conclusions render two services. First, they credit the Daladier government with an actual *reason* for having gone along with Chamberlain in 1938. Second, they certainly suggest that the spirit of resistance was quickly rekindled once there were some identifiable grounds for renewed economic optimism.

Similar conclusions may be drawn from the adjacent arena of military rearmament. Far from shunning war as part of some adamant refusal to countenance its return under any circumstance, the French government was coldly pragmatic. It was concerned about the potentially disastrous disparity between actual French and German military capacities.[24] This appraisal, offered by a team of scholars working for the army's historical directorate, adds to the list of legitimate reasons why Daladier acted as he did in 1938. By the same token, the rearmament progress that was recorded through 1938 and 1939, especially in the air, certainly contributed to the government's decision to accept war only a year after it had rejected it at Munich. By 1939 the country was spending more on national defense than it had in 1914, and a higher percentage of its national income.[25] France still remained vulnerable, and doubtless unprepared for undertaking a major offensive, but the combination of its domestic arms' revival, the recent loss of Czechoslovakia and the threatened loss of Poland, made both its potential and its need for resistance that much more obvious. By the spring of 1940 the rhythm of its arms' production had become even more impressive, yet another omen for those who would be captivated by images of French despair, resignation, or apathy.

Then there is the related matter of military planning, a subject which can embrace everything from strategy to doctrine, and from rearmament administration to tactical theory. Once more, there are scholars who have expressed doubts about Tayloresque characterizations of interwar France. If none speaks of brilliance, a good number perceive foresight and well-honed professionalism. Such was true of Jeffery Gunsburg. Neither he nor the accomplished French scholar Henri Michel, whose Foreword appears in Gunsburg's book, was much drawn to the "moral decay" argument. In fact, Gunsburg was impressed by the technical proficiency of the French army in 1940, and explained its collapse within the context of a much broader Allied defeat.[26] A similar chord has been struck by Martin S. Alexander, a British scholar who regards as "old-fashioned" the decadence-inspired critiques of French policy makers in the 1930s. In fact, Alexander writes, the often maligned general Maurice Gamelin understood the German military peril more fully than most of his contemporaries, which is why he became the "architect of a program of unprecedented peace-time defensive preparation."[27] Colonel Robert Doughty is equally chary about using decadence as an explanation. The French failure, he asserts, "was not one of stupidity, decadence, disloyalty or defeatism." Nor, thanks to the intense rearmament effort of the late 1930s, was it due to any truly decisive material imbalance between the French and German land forces. Rather, it stemmed from a "vulnerable strategy" and "inadequate tactical doctrine."[28] More recently, we have had the judgment of Eugenia C. Kiesling, who also rejects sloth and stupidity as explanations for French doctrinal shortcomings. As for decadence, she ignores the idea altogether, preferring to seek explanations in the army's organization and training.[29]

Students of foreign policy have also contributed to a more sympathetic, more realistic, impression of interwar France. Whereas Taylor acknowledged the growing mood of resistance in 1939, he was at a loss to explain it beyond panic and desperation. Professor Duroselle subsequently enlarged our understanding by exploring French foreign policy in the last year of peace. In the course of that exploration he made it clear that neither Daladier nor Bonnet, unlike Chamberlain, had any illusions about Hitler's trustworthiness. That was why they were not prepared to make significant economic concessions to Germany, why they were not prepared to forsake French interests in eastern Europe, why they were not happy with British foot-dragging over negotiations with Russia, and why Daladier in particular was not going to trade French territory for the sake of appeasing Mussolini.[30] More recently, we have had the work of William I. Shorrock and John E. Dreifort, neither of whom finds either complete ineptitude or, for that matter, brilliance in French foreign policy. While sharply critical of the Popular Front's Italophobia, the former stresses the severe constraints imposed on France by her eastern allies and by the perverse caution of the

British government. Dreifort detects the same kind of constraints when it comes to French policy toward the Far East, constraints imposed by the Americans on the one hand and by the British on the other.[31] And, more recently still, we have had fresh insights from Peter Jackson who has examined the history of the Anglo-French guarantee to Romania in the spring of 1939. The evidence, Jackson argues, does not suggest an underlying French decadence, or drift, or, in this case, even indecision. Rather, the French government, driven by its own strategic interests, prevailed upon London to join in a guarantee of Romanian security against German attack. In this context, too, one can speak of French vigor and initiative.[32]

In other words, the evidence supports – as it usually does – a wide range of interpretive impressions. Even without benefit of knowing what happened in 1940, one could say that this was a country plagued by economic distress, ideological division, social fragmentation, and security anxiety. And one could say with assurance that not all of these problems were addressed with aplomb and dispatch – any more than problems of similar magnitude were deftly resolved elsewhere. That said, I am inclined to agree with Michael Miller's observation that French "self-assuredness" between the wars has been underrated, and also with William Irvine's analysis of French domestic political opinion in the years just prior to the collapse. France, he writes, "was morally and materially ready to confront Nazi Germany" by the summer of 1939. That is why, "it was not decadence that led to 1940." Rather, it was 1940 "that has led us to view the late Third Republic as decadent."[33] This was not an incompetent, morally bankrupt, all-thumbs regime. Or if it were, we would be hard pressed to explain the stunning economic revival in the last year before the war, the attendant burst in rearmament, the stiffened public resolve to say "no" to Hitler once the material conditions for resistance had perceptibly improved. Such, at any rate, seems to me the most compelling interpretation, and partly because its claims are generally more modest and measured than those tossed off in *Origins*.[34]

Whatever one thinks of the notion that there was something fundamentally and peculiarly wrong with France in the 1930s, there is one final bone to pick with the late Professor Taylor. In his "Second Thoughts" of 1963 he prescribed that the historian's "sole duty is to find out what was done and why." A related dictum, however, proscribes the historian from considering "what ought to have been done" (p. 26). The argument, though he offers none, presumably is that otherwise we would spend too much time fecklessly speculating on the historical "what ifs." Many will share this concern, but many may also worry that such a proscription may also disguise irresponsibility within a cloak of good intentions. For Taylor, history is deceptively simple. Tell it how it is and why, exposition and not judgment. But if it is exposition left unmeasured against any realistic yardstick of probabilities and "what ifs," it may also be exposition for which the historian cannot be held responsible. Unchecked from this quarter, and smitten by one's own impartiality, it becomes easy to fudge the difference between explanation and judgment. And so Taylor is intent on "explaining," sometimes magnanimously, where the British and French went wrong, how they misread Hitler and completely misunderstood him, thought he was planning to do them in, when he was not. Hitler was only waiting; waiting for his chance to extract more concessions. Their mistake, Taylor explains, beyond their basic misreading, was to have resorted to concessions, whether from drift or deliberation.

Is that it? Should they have seen that Hitler was an arch opportunist, not a planner, and then denied him his opportunities? That would have left the initiative to him, would have put pressure on him, but with what likely result? We do not know. Taylor does not know. All we know is that such a disobliging approach had been characteristic of French policy over reparations and disarmament, a policy that had drawn much criticism from London and one which Taylor himself liked no better than the over-supple policy of concessions in the later 1930s. Indeed, one has the nagging impression that the French can never get things quite right. Their disarmament policy earlier in the decade was criticized for being too rigid and unbending – which, for the most part, it probably was.[35] In 1938 their policy was similarly condemned, partly because it appeared tough, and partly because it proved weak. Flexible or unyielding, French policy just never seemed quite in time with the beat followed in Whitehall. That led to contemporary British criticism and complaints, a perspective which Taylor seemed to find eminently justified. Moreover, it is not clear from Taylor how, when, or why the French – had they understood Hitler the way he did – might have changed from hard to soft policy, or vice versa. Neither is it clear how the British – endowed with Taylor's vision – might have responded to a more perspicacious French policy. It was enough for him to know where they went wrong. It was not necessary to test or confirm it; no flicker of interest from him over what would or could have happened had they known what he knew. This, it must be reckoned, is the behavior of a judge, one who is forever appraising negligence, if not culpability, and who recognizes no obligation to justify any judgment. If it is not ostensibly a verdict, it is ostensibly more than an explanation. This, however, did not much concern Taylor, a man not really given to second thoughts. Over the years he surrendered little ground, made few concessions, other than the late-in-life decision to minimize brushes with academic colleagues. "My view is that they should get on with writing books in their way and I will get on with writing them in mine."[36] Never before has that advice seemed more sound for those whom he has left behind.

Notes

1 A. J. P. Taylor, *The Origins of the Second World War*, London, 1964, p. 336. All references are to this Penguin edition, which contains his supplementary essay entitled "Second Thoughts."

2 See "Metternich," in A. J. P. Taylor, *Grandeur and Decline*, London, 1967, p. 23.

3 There is some irony to this criticism. Taylor has been criticized for having treated Hitler as some ordinary German, despite the enormity of the crimes committed by his regime. By so doing, Taylor has been charged with having abdicated his moral responsibility as an historian. Here he is being criticized for making too many moral judgments about the French, principally by means of implication and insinuation. For

the earlier criticism, see C. Robert Cole, "Critics of the Taylor view of history," in E. M. Robertson (ed.), *The Origins of the Second World War*, London, 1971, pp. 142–57. See also the articles by Oswald Hauser and John W. Boyer in the Special Issue of *Journal of Modern History*, vol. 49, 1977, pp. 34–9, and 40–72.

4 Robert J. Young, *In Command of France: French Foreign Policy and Military Planning, 1933–1940*, Cambridge, MA, 1978, p. 1.

5 A. J. P. Taylor, "Accident prone, or what happened next," *Journal of Modern History*, vol. 49, 1977, p. 18.

6 These and other materials are surveyed in Robert J. Young (ed.), *French Foreign Policy, 1918–1945. A Guide to Research and Research Materials*, Wilmington, DE, 1991.

7 In 1938 the British chiefs of staff admitted their uncertainty as to whether the Germans were capable of delivering a knockout blow against England from the air. For his part, the prime minister warned his cabinet in August that the country could not face the prospect of war with much confidence. See R. A. C. Parker, "Perceptions de la puissance par les décideurs britanniques, 1938–1939: le Cabinet," in René Girault and Robert Frank (eds), *La Puissance en Europe, 1938–1940*, Paris, 1984, p. 48. See also Parker's more recent *Chamberlain and Appeasement. British Policy and the Coming of the Second World War*, London and New York, 1993.

8 Conference paper by Philippe Masson, "La marine française et la stratégie alliée, 1938–39," presented to the Colloque Franco-Allemand, Bonn, 1978. See also Eleanor M. Gates, *End of the Affair: The Collapse of the Anglo-French Alliance, 1939–1940*, Berkeley, CA, 1980, pp. 3–17; and Robert J. Young, "La Guerre de Longue Durée: some reflections on French strategy and diplomacy in the 1930s," in Adrian Preston (ed.), *General Staffs and Diplomacy Before the Second World War*, London, 1974, pp. 41–64.

9 See the two papers by René Girault and Robert Frankenstein entitled, respectively, "The impact of the economic situation on the foreign policy of France, 1936–1939," and "The decline of France and French appeasement policies, 1936–1939," in Wolfgang J. Mommsen and Lothar Kettenacker (eds), *The Fascist Challenge and the Policy of Appeasement*, London, 1983, pp. 209–26, and 236–45.

10 D. C. Watt, "Some aspects of A. J. P. Taylor's work as diplomatic historian," *Journal of Modern History*, vol. 49, 1977, p. 33.

11 For a fuller discussion of the history of these interpretive debates, see the historiographical chapter in my *France and the Origins of the Second World War*, London, 1996, pp. 37–59.

12 J.-B. Duroselle, *La Décadence, 1932–1939*, Paris, 1979.

13 René Girault, "Les décideurs français et la puissance française en 1938–1939," in *La Puissance en Europe*, p. 39; Serge Berstein, *La France des années 30*, Paris, 1988, pp. 80, 169.

14 Donald Cameron Watt, *How War Came. The Immediate Origins of the Second World War*, London, 1989, p. 617.

15 Piotr Wandycz, *The Twilight of French Eastern Alliances, 1926–1936*, Princeton, NJ, 1988; Nicole Jordan, *The Popular Front and Central Europe: The Dilemmas of French Impotence, 1918–1940*, Cambridge, MA, 1992; and "Maurice Gamelin, Italy and the eastern alliances," *Journal of Strategic Studies*, vol. 14, 1991, pp. 428–41.

16 Michael J. Carley, "End of the 'low, dishonest decade': failure of the Anglo-French Soviet alliance in 1939," *Europe–Asia Studies*, vol. 14, 1993, pp. 303–41; and "Prelude to defeat: Franco–Soviet relations, 1930–1939," *Historical Reflections / Réflexions Historiques*, vol. 22, 1996, pp. 159–188.

17 Eugen Weber, *The Hollow Years: France in the 1930s*, New York, 1994, pp. 111–46.

18 Anthony Adamthwaite, *Grandeur and Misery. France's Bid for Power in Europe, 1914–1940*, London, 1995, p. 231.

19 Duroselle, *Décadence*, pp. 355–6. See also his *L'Abîme, 1939–1945*, Paris, 1982, pp. 17–18. This conclusion has been questioned by the remarkable, not to say extraordinary, construction advanced by a psychohistorian who perceives a "suicidal group fantasy" at work on the inexorable road to 1940. See Stephen Ryan, "Reflections on the

psychohistory of France, 1919–1940," *Journal of Psychohistory*, vol. 2, 1983, pp. 225–41.

20 See, for example, the following articles which appeared in a single issue of *Relations Internationales* (no. 33, 1983), addressed to "Images de la France en 1938–1939": Christine Sellin, "Les manuels scolaires et la puissance française," pp. 103–11; Rémy Pithon, "Opinions publiques et représentations culturelles face aux problèmes de la puissance. Le témoignage du cinéma français, 1938–1939," pp. 91–101; René Duval, "Radio–Paris," in Olivier Barrot and Pascal Ory (eds), *Entre deux guerres. La création entre 1919 et 1939*, Paris, 1990, pp. 129–46.

21 See Maurice Vasse, "Le pacifisme français dans les années trente," *Relations Internationales*, no. 53, 1988, pp. 37–52; and Norman Ingram, *The Politics of Dissent. Pacifism in France, 1919–1939*, Oxford, 1991.

22 Duroselle, *Décadence*, pp. 444, 457.

23 Jean Bouvier and Robert Frank, "Sur la perception de la 'puissance' économique en France pendant les années 1930," in *La Puissance en Europe*, pp. 182–3. For the contribution of the Comité des Forges and the Conféderation du Patronat to this new mood, see H. Coutau-Bégarie, "Comment les Français se sont préparés à la guerre," *Revue d'Histoire Diplomatique*, vol. 97, 1983, p. 347. For the range of industrial responses to accelerated rearmament, see Richard Vinen, *The Politics of French Business, 1936–1945*, Cambridge, 1991.

24 Général J. Delmas, "La perception de la puissance militaire française," in *La Puissance en Europe*, pp. 127–40.

25 On the subject of French rearmament, see the work by Robert Frankenstein, *Le prix du réarmement français, 1935–1939*, Paris, 1982; and Jean Crémieux-Brilhac, *Les Français de l'An 40*, vol.2: *Ouvrier et Soldats*, Paris, 1990. On military strategy more generally, see Gordon Martel, "Military planning and the origins of the Second World War," in Brian McKercher and Michael Hennessy (eds), *Military Planning and the Origins of the Second World War*, Westport, CT, 1999.

26 Jeffery A. Gunsburg, *Divided and Conquered: The French High Command and the Defeat of the West, 1940*, Westport, CT, 1979. For a dissenting, if familiar, view of the French army, see the peculiarly self-possessed work by Williamson Murray, *The Change in the European Balance of Power, 1938–1939*, Princeton, NJ, 1984.

27 Martin S. Alexander, *The Republic in Danger. General Maurice Gamelin and the Politics of French Defence, 1933–1940*, Cambridge, 1992. For his remarks on the historiography, see "Did the Deuxième Bureau work? The role of intellgence in French defence policy and strategy, 1919–1939," *Intelligence and National Security*, vol. 6, 1991, p. 302; and "The fall of France, 1940," *Journal of Strategic Studies*, vol. 13, 1990, pp. 12–21.

28 Robert A. Doughty, *The Seeds of Disaster. The Development of French Army Doctrine, 1919–1939*, Hamden, CT, 1985, p. 188; *The Breaking Point. Sedan and the Fall of France, 1940*, New York, 1990, p. 245.

29 Eugenia C. Kiesling, *Arming Against Hitler. France and the Limits of Military Planning*, Lawrence, KS, 1996, pp. 6, 144. See also Elizabeth Kier, *Imagining War. French and British Military Doctrine Between the Wars*, Princeton, NJ, 1997.

30 Duroselle, *Décadence*, chs 12–15. See also Elisabeth du Réau, *Edouard Daladier, 1884–1970*, Paris, 1993, pp. 310–54.

31 William I. Shorrock, *From Ally to Enemy: The Enigma of Fascist Italy in French Diplomacy, 1920–1940*, Kent, OH, 1988; John E. Dreifort, *Myopic Grandeur. The Ambivalence of French Foreign Policy toward the Far East, 1919–1945*, Kent, OH, 1991.

32 Peter Jackson, "France and the guarantee to Romania, April 1939," *Intelligence and National Security*, vol. 10, 1995, pp. 242–72.

33 Michael B. Miller, *Shanghai on the Métro. Spies, Intrigue and the French Between the Wars*, Berkeley, CA, 1994, p. 5; William D. Irvine, "Domestic politics and the fall of France in 1940," *Historical Reflections/Réflexions Historiques*, vol. 22, 1996, pp. 86, 90.

34 Contrary to the suggestions of Douglas Porch, far from subscribing to the decadence view, I have spent the last thirty years contesting it. See my *France and the Origins of the*

Second World War, London and New York, 1996, and his *The French Secret Services. From the Dreyfus Affair to the Gulf War*, New York, 1995, p. 144.

35　See Maurice Vaïsse, *Sécurité d'Abord. La politique française en matière de désarmament, 9 décembre 19 30–17 avril 1934*, Paris, 1981. See also his "Against appeasement: French advocates of firmness, 1933–1938," in *The Fascist Challenge and the Policy of Appeasement*, pp. 227–35.

36　Taylor, "Accident prone," p. 17.

6 Misjudging Hitler

A. J. P. Taylor and the Third Reich

Richard Overy

In 1981 A. J. P. Taylor was invited by the German Historical Institute in London to give a lecture on the origins of the Second World War. Twenty years had elapsed since the publication of Taylor's own account. He took the lecture as the opportunity to go back over those twenty years and to reflect on whether his interpretation had stood the test of time. Characteristically, he made few if any concessions to his many critics. The evidence missing from his original volume, and its subsequent "Second thoughts," was material that he believed only confirmed his view of British and German behavior in the 1930s. Above all, he stood by his argument that Hitler was merely interested in treaty revision, like Stresemann or Brüning: "I think one can see a pattern, that [Hitler] was operating within a framework of revisionism, at any rate until 1939, and was then caught in a situation where he was prepared to make peace."[1]

No single aspect of Taylor's argument has occasioned more criticism than his judgment of Hitler's political intentions and behavior in the years leading to war.[2] Revisiting the subject in 1981 Taylor refused to see Hitler as anything more than representative of the long thrust of German history towards domination of Europe, a latter-day Bismarck whose rhetoric and world-historical fantasies weighed little against his evident opportunism, and whose role in the conduct of German foreign policy was limited in 1939. Consistent with this interpretation, Taylor rejected the view that Hitler's ambitions in the USSR in 1941 had anything to do with the search for economic empire or ideological confrontation. He argued instead that Hitler seized the opportunity afforded by having a large mobilized army on his hands to "knock Russia out" in the hope of winning the negotiated peace with Britain that he failed to get in 1939 or 1940.[3]

It has always been tempting to dismiss Taylor's views on German foreign policy either as an unintended defense of Hitler, and as such morally repugnant, or as an extension of Taylor's robust prejudices against Germany exposed in his earlier writings, and so morally irresponsible. Taylor, of course, was writing at a time when Hitler was widely regarded as the man who planned the war of 1939, a uniquely evil tyrant who held his people in a mesmeric trance. Taylor's reaction to this characterization was understandable, and it was to a great extent rooted in the available scholarship and the published sources. Taylor sought to make Hitler plausible: "Hitler had no clear-cut plan and instead was a supreme opportunist, taking advantages as they came."[4] In Taylor's hands Hitler was no more a monster, but a vain power-seeker whose ideological rhetoric amounted to mere incantations, "phrases to produce the popular roar." Hitler was not possessed of "genuine beliefs," but "craved for power" alone.[5]

More than thirty years of scholarship on German foreign and military policy in the 1930s, and on the role of Hitler himself, threaten to make Taylor's view of Germany nothing more than a historiographical curiosity. Yet it is important to remember in the first instance what Taylor got right. German policy in the 1930s was rooted in the longer course of German history and did not represent a sharp rupture with the past. It can be clearly demonstrated that the main elements in Hitler's view of foreign policy derived in almost a straight line from the radical nationalism of the pre-1914 Reich. These elements were three: the pan-German longing for the territorial unity and independence of all racial Germans; the pursuit of *Lebensraum* (living-space) in order to achieve the proper match between the territory and the economic needs of a people (with the strong implication that space should rightfully be allocated to peoples with superior cultures and forms of social organization); the pursuit of *Weltpolitik*, or global policy, in which the united and enlarged state engaged in worldwide imperial politics.[6]

Taylor, of course, did not express the continuities in this way. He acknowledged that Hitler came from a Viennese pan-German background, but he did not accept that Hitler's ideological baggage mattered at all. In reality it mattered a great deal. The infant *Deutsche Arbeiter Partei* (DAP) founded by Anton Drexler in 1919, which was the immediate forerunner of the Nazi Party, was directly linked with the pan-German *Vaterlandspartei* founded by Alfred Hugenberg in September 1917 to rally patriotic support for the German war effort, and with the radical nationalist Thule Society. Both organizations sought the moral and spiritual regeneration of Germany, the unity of all Germans and the predominance of the German race in Europe. Drexler found both organizations too dominated by bourgeois intellectuals, and set up his own party. The DAP admitted Adolf Hitler in September 1919, and the following year changed its name to the *Nationalsozialistische Deutsche Arbeiterpartei* (NSDAP).[7] The new Party's twenty-five-point program included demands for the unity of all Germans, and the right to living-space. These ambitions owed something to the Versailles settlement and German revisionism, but in effect their pedigree considerably pre-dated Versailles. Hitler's program did not simply amount to treaty revision, as Taylor claimed in 1981, but rested on a popular radical nationalist discourse which held racial unity and violent economic imperialism at its core.

During the 1920s Hitler became an important spokesman for nationalist circles in Germany that kept alive these prewar ambitions. German nationalism itself was always a fractured movement. Many Germans, across the political spectrum from right to left, sought revision of some kind. The terms of the Versailles settlement were never accepted, and the well-known efforts of Gustav Stresemann, foreign minister from 1924 to 1929, and Heinrich Brüning, chancellor from 1930 to 1932, to ameliorate or remove treaty restrictions scarcely merit repetition.[8] Germany was reabsorbed into the states system when the

Treaty of Locarno was signed in 1925, respecting the western frontiers of Germany established in 1919, and when Germany was permitted to join the League of Nations a year later. The Allied Control Commission in Germany, charged with monitoring the disarmament clauses of the treaty, left in 1927. In 1930 the occupation forces were finally withdrawn from the Rhineland. The most hated symbol of German inferiority, the annual payment of reparations to the Allies for German "war guilt," were finally suspended at the Lausanne conference of 1932. It is almost certain that if Hitler had not come to power in 1933, another German government would have continued the revisionist thrust and might have achieved through negotiation much of what Hitler ultimately achieved by a defiant unilateralism.

The other elements of German nationalism in the 1920s were potentially more dangerous, but were for much of the period confined to the radical nationalist fringe. Hitler expressed them in *Mein Kampf*, which Taylor dismissed as fantasy, and more elaborately in his so-called "Second book," dictated in 1928 but not published until 1961, when it appeared in German and in English. This latter book came too late for Taylor's first edition, but whether he would have treated it any more seriously than he did *Mein Kampf* is open to question. Yet the second book, even more than the first, shows Hitler's rejection of what he called the "patriotic-national bourgeois" circles in Germany, who had sold the Reich "to an organization of pimps, pickpockets, deserters, black marketeers and hack journalists."[9] Hitler was not concerned just with treaty revision, with its strong implication of a "restoration" of the Germany of pre-1914, but saw in Germany's future the building of a solid racial core, the race-contest with international Jewry, and the build-up of sufficient military power to allow Germany to seize an economic empire in the spaces of the ill-defined "east."[10] This hardly constituted a clear program, but it reflected a unique strand in German nationalism that transcended treaty revision, or conventional balance-of-power politics, and ultimately embraced just what the Nazi regime in fact embarked upon – ethnic cleansing on a grotesque scale and a grandiose imperialism in the east. The distinction between the cautious foreign and military policy of German revisionists in the inter-war years, and the violent pursuit of a race-based New Order is too fundamental to be dismissed lightly. Hitler had beliefs, borrowed beliefs perhaps, but beliefs nonetheless. They were not, in Taylor's trivial formulation, "the conversation of any Austrian café or German beer-house,"[11] but quite the reverse. Hitler's ideological outlook was widely echoed in universities and professional associations colonized by a nationalist intelligentsia that also gazed beyond revisionism.[12]

Taylor was right, however, in another respect. Hitler did not act alone in the conduct of foreign policy in the 1930s, neither did he dictate its course exclusively. There were continuities of personnel and policy across the divide of 1933. There was not one but several strands in the formation of German foreign policy in the 1930s, what Wolfgang Michalka has called "a plurality of conceptions."[13] For much of the period between 1933 and 1939 foreign policy was run by traditional career diplomats whose nationalism was based on a cautious revisionism and the reassertion of Germany's power-political position that had been lost between 1914 and 1919. They were represented by the German foreign minister Constantine von Neurath, a conservative nationalist who was appointed before Hitler came to power, and kept his office until 1938. Neurath, together with conservatives in the armed forces' leadership and in economic affairs, was concerned that the pace of revision should not prejudice the establishment of domestic stability, nor invite the dangerous intervention of other states. Hitler left much of the day-to-day conduct of diplomacy in Neurath's hands, just as he left economic policy to Schacht, and the practical achievement of rearmament to the armed forces. Up until 1939 and the German demand for the return of Danzig and renegotiation of the terms of the Polish Corridor (which conservatives cared about more fervently than any other aspect of revision), little that Hitler had achieved ran counter to the conservative view of revision (except the *Anschluss* with Austria, with its implicit rejection of Bismarck's conception of a Prussia-centered Germany). Where conservatives parted company with Hitler was over the methods used to achieve revision, methods which ran much greater risks than they were prepared to accept.[14]

The conservatives also shared further preferences in foreign policy. They hoped, as before 1914, to secure the friendship of Britain; they disliked Poland but courted Russia; they favored the establishment of some kind of economic/political bloc in central and eastern Europe (the prewar vision of *Mitteleuropa*); they were hostile to collaboration with Italy (Albert Speer recalled after the war that President von Hindenburg had once asked Hitler never again to enter Germany into alliance with Italians[15]); finally, they wanted colonies and the reintegration of Germany with the wider world economy. Some of these preferences Hitler himself shared. Up until 1937 he too favored an alliance with Britain, and had written so in the 1920s. Hitler was not a particular enthusiast for Italy, despite the fact that it was governed by a fellow-radical nationalist. Hitler was all for constructing a system of alliances and trade agreements in eastern Europe, and did so right through to 1939 culminating with an agreement with the USSR. There always existed sufficient congruence between Hitler and the conservative nationalists to blur the differences, and it was in this sense that Taylor could claim that Hitler's foreign policy was "that of his predecessors, of the professional diplomats at the foreign ministry, and indeed of virtually all Germans."[16]

There was more, of course, to German foreign policy in the 1930s than either Hitler or the foreign ministry. The current view is that the Third Reich operated in a polycratic way, with no single and consistent agenda and with a high level of systemic tension generated by rivalry between the Party leaders. Alfred Rosenberg, the Party's official ideologue, harbored the idea of a German-dominated Eurasia made up of ethnically defined states freed from Bolshevik rule; Hermann Göring played a major part in securing better relations with Poland, and with Italy, and tried to act as a brake on Hitler in 1938 and 1939 when he felt the risks his leader played were too great.[17] Above all, Joachim von Ribbentrop, one of the Party's foreign affairs' advisers, pursued a policy derived more from pre-1914 *Weltpolitik*: the pursuit of colonies; re-entry into global politics along with Italy and Japan; and a possible reconciliation with Russia to cover potential conflict with Britain. Some historians have seen his appointment as foreign minister in February 1938 to replace von Neurath as evidence that von Ribbentrop now played a prominent part in formulating German foreign policy,[18] particularly as he followed Hitler in 1937 in promoting a strongly anti-British line, and apparently secured the German–Soviet Pact in August 1939. Though his influence now seems to have been far short of decisive, von Ribbentrop did clearly play some part in shaping Hitler's attitude toward the balance of power in the critical months leading to war, particularly in his efforts to persuade Hitler to call Britain's bluff over Poland.[19] Yet none of the leading Nazis with foreign-policy interests, Von Ribbentrop included, was able to impose them on Hitler in any systematic way.

Finally, Taylor was surely right to view the outbreak of war in 1939 as part of a broader crisis of the international order of which Hitler was able to take particular advantage, as did Japan and Italy. Hitler clearly did perceive opportunities to exploit as the League system broke up in the 1930s. The two global powers, Britain and France, faced pressures on all fronts, domestic, foreign, and imperial to which, in Hitler's view, they manifestly failed to respond with vigor. All the revisionist states profited from the partial decline of Britain and France; Hitler hoped to exploit that decline when he sought war with Poland in 1939. Not all historians accept that Hitler wanted to isolate Poland and avoid a general conflict, but the evidence weighs heavily in favor of this interpretation. Take, for example, the notes of Hitler's army adjutant, Gerhard Engel, published in 1974. On August 22, 1939 he recorded Hitler's views, expressed at a conference with his generals: "He repeats again, he is convinced that Poland remains isolated, England and France would only bluff, and he does not intend to settle business with these in the foreseeable future." On August 27 Engel heard Hitler again argue that Britain would not intervene. Two days later Hitler was determined to finish off Poland "but indeed wants no war at all with the others."[20] Hitler's immediate entourage was less sanguine about the chances of avoiding a general war, but as Göring concluded in one of his postwar interrogations: "[Hitler's] main idea was to try to keep the western powers out of the war....As we saw it he held much too rigidly to this."[21]

Hitler was not, of course, acting in wilful disregard of reality. He was supplied with a diet of information, some of it culled from intercepted diplomatic traffic between France, Britain and Poland, that seemed to confirm western hesitancy. It is known that intelligence information which contradicted this interpretation was deliberately withheld from him.[22] For a man already predisposed to see in the democracies only signs of decadence and double-dealing, the accumulating weight of evidence suggested that Poland would be left in the lurch. Hitler's decision to invade Poland was a risk, but one which he judged to be worth taking, even more so after the German–Soviet Pact, which ended any prospect of a revived strategy of "encirclement" which he, like any German statesman, was anxious to avoid. In this sense he might well appear the unprincipled opportunist of Taylor's version of 1939, seizing a favorable moment to complete the program of German revanchism for which millions had voted for him in 1932. Hitler did not break down the European political order. It was already deep in crisis when he delivered the fatal blow in 1939.[23]

The weaknesses of Taylor's argument about Germany and Hitler lie not in the realm of diplomacy but in that of domestic politics. His insistence that Hitler had only a limited program of treaty revision, which was widely approved by the conservative elites and by the German people, blinded him to the dynamic nature of the dictatorship, and in particular to the sharp break in domestic politics that occurred between 1936 and 1938. The structure and aims of German foreign policy, and the means to achieve them, altered fundamentally in the mid-1930s at the expense of the conservative nationalists who had applauded the early stages of treaty revision. This was not perhaps immediately evident from the formal foreign-office archive on which Taylor relied, which reflected what Klaus Hildebrand has called "seemingly familiar historical phenomena," but behind the conventional diplomacy of the late 1930s lay, in Hildebrand's words, "a dogma which took over everything," driven by the "destructive excess of [Hitler's] historical vision."[24]

The break in the mid-1930s was rooted in one of the most important documents of the whole period, the strategic memorandum that Hitler drew up at Berchtesgaden in August 1936, which has come to be known as the "Four-Year Plan Memorandum." Its significance derives from the fact that Hitler hardly ever put pen to paper throughout the entire dictatorship, but on this occasion the substance of his thoughts was sufficiently important to the future development of German policy for him to set them down himself. Hitler treated the document with a solemn self-importance. When it was written he summoned Göring to Berchtesgaden where he discussed its contents and presented him with one of only four copies. Others were given to Fritz Todt, the engineer who was responsible for Hitler's grandiose construction plans, and to general Werner von Blomberg, the war minister.[25]

Hitler's central argument was simply that the world had reached a historic climacteric: the French Revolution had worked its evils on European culture for more than a century, and its natural progeny, Bolshevism, in alliance with world Judaeism, was poised to do to Europe what the barbarian invasions had done to ancient Rome. "No nation," Hitler argued, "will be able to avoid or abstain from this historical conflict."[26] The western powers had forfeited leadership of the world struggle, corrupted as they were by democratic values and infected by Marxism. Germany stood in the way of the worldwide triumph of Judaeo-Bolshevism, aided by Italy and Japan. Hitler regarded conflict as inevitable if Europe were to avoid "the most gruesome catastrophe" since "the downfall of the states of antiquity." All other aims paled into insignificance. Hitler called for a program of massive militarization, and the unrestricted mobilization of the nation's economic resources to prepare for the apocalyptic struggle: "the political movement among our people knows only one goal, the preservation of our existence..."[27]

Taylor makes no mention of this memorandum, and that he would have taken it at all seriously is questionable. It did not constitute a clear program of objectives, and was couched in the same language of historical generality already evident in *Mein Kampf*. Hitler was obsessed with the weight of the historical moment he confronted and the struggle for the future which that moment made necessary. The memorandum was not a detailed statement of policy; rather, it had the quality of an oracular pronouncement, pointing the way towards the harsh historical path that Germany must tread. What distinguishes the memorandum from Hitler's other writing is both its timing – for it was written well into the dictatorship rather than in the years of political apprenticeship before 1933 – and its practical consequences.

The 1936 memorandum cannot be regarded simply as some flight of fancy, for it was developed as the basis for a complex and far-reaching transformation of German foreign, economic, and military policy. It is well to remember that it was written shortly after the outbreak of the Spanish Civil War and Hitler's decision to send military assistance to help the nationalist rebels. There were, of course, practical reasons to explain German intervention. Valuable raw materials – pyrites, wolfram – were imported from Spain and had to be safeguarded for German rearmament.[28] Göring was keen to find an opportunity to try out aircraft capabilities and tactics. But intervention in Spain was also prompted by the fear that Spain might undergo a communist revolution that would hem in the fascist powers. The election of the Popular Front government in France in June, with Communist support, posed a further threat. Taken together with the knowledge of Soviet modernization and rearmament, Hitler's belief in an imminent reckoning of accounts with Bolshevism appears anything but fanciful.

It can scarcely be coincidence that the two states singled out in Hitler's memorandum as "standing firm in the face of the world peril,"[29] Italy and Japan, now became more closely aligned with Germany. Up until 1936 both the German foreign ministry and the general staff had worked to create close links with China rather than with Japan,[30] whose value as an ally and as a market was not regarded as high. Hitler, however, influenced by von Ribbentrop, took a rosier view of Japan, whose anti-Soviet stance he shared. Four days after the outbreak of the Spanish Civil War, Hitler spoke with the Japanese ambassador at Bayreuth, where he agreed to pursue negotiations for a pact with Japan and approved a secret protocol on benevolent neutrality. The discussions led to the drafting of the Anti-Comintern Pact on October 23 1936, and its final signature in Berlin in November, despite the continued hostility of the foreign ministry to any policy that threatened Germany's links with China.[31]

Intervention in the Spanish Civil War also drew Germany into alignment with Fascist Italy. Again this was not the preference of the foreign ministry, nor was it an alignment altogether welcomed by either Mussolini or Hitler. The Italian leader had refused Franco's request for aid until news came of German assistance. Isolated after the Ethiopian war, and uncertain of German ambitions in central Europe, Mussolini was interested in closer links with Germany. When Count Ciano, the newly appointed Italian foreign minister, visited Berlin in the autumn of 1936 he was warmly received. In November Mussolini announced the Rome–Berlin Axis, which was little more than a statement of mutual goodwill in defense of the Fascist ideal. A year later Italy formally joined the Anti-Comintern Pact, following further assiduous negotiation by von Ribbentrop.[32]

The re-alignment with Italy and Japan, expressed as a front against international Marxism, made little strategic or military sense (nor did Germany, in the end, derive much benefit from the connection). The German army thought that Italy would be of more use to them as an enemy than as an ally; the generals were keen to continue assistance to the nationalist Chinese against Japan. But the alignment was made because it conformed with Hitler's desire publicly to sustain the struggle against the Bolshevik menace. The reorientation also coincided with a more substantive shift in Hitler's foreign-policy outlook away from the idea of a British alliance, around which his pre-1933 diplomatic conception had been based, to one in which Britain and France became obstacles to be overcome or set aside. The development during 1937 of a policy *ohne England*, without England, has been explained too often to be repeated here, but it represented another important step away from conservative world policy and the search for German colonies.[33]

The colonial question united a great many nationalists in Germany. It was always assumed that at some point the return of colonies would be negotiable, and in the context of declining world trade and raw material shortages German leaders expected colonies to play an important part in sustaining Germany's world-economic position. When, in 1936, Hjalmar Schacht, minister of economics, and a spokesman for conservative business circles in Germany, began his own program of negotiations with western statesmen over the return of colonies, he did so from traditional social-imperialist motives: colonies could be used to divert the enthusiasm of radicals in the Nazi Party, and to soften economic conditions at home in order to avert a revival of socialist agitation.[34] Hitler paid lip-service to this aspect of revisionism for as long as it gave him the prospect of keeping diplomatic lines open to London, but there seems little doubt that he was not essentially committed to the return of colonies at that juncture – though he would not have refused them had the opportunity arisen. He argued in the second volume of *Mein Kampf* that German interests lay fundamentally in "the strengthening of continental power by the winning of new soil and territory in Europe," a priority to which he remained consistently committed.[35]

Indeed, negotiations over colonies foundered on British insistence that Germany should trade a colonial settlement for promises of good behavior in eastern Europe, and were finally broken off in March 1938, after Schacht had been forced to resign as economics minister. Göring told a British contact in February 1937 that the regime wanted "a free hand in Eastern Europe" but was happy to leave colonies to the British.[36] The changing focus of German foreign policy in 1936–37 was strongly driven by ideology rather than *Realpolitik*. Intervention in Spain, closer ties with Japan and Italy, the gradual rejection of any deal with Britain that did not grant a free hand to construct living-space in the east, all stemmed from the desire to confront international Marxism and to remodel the "east" in Germany's favor. This reorientation was not achieved without important political changes, since much of it was driven by the more radical elements in the Party who regarded the regime's conservative allies in the armed forces, the economy, and the ministerial apparatus as a brake on policies that were more assertively National Socialist. In this sense the changing direction of German foreign policy was intimately related to the changing course of German domestic politics. Between late 1936 and the spring of 1938 conservatives were slowly eased out of key areas of responsibility and were replaced by Party appointments. Göring was given wide responsibilities for economic policy and rearmament in October 1936, when the Second Four-Year Plan was formally established, loosely based on Hitler's memorandum of August.[37] Göring set out to develop a comprehensive program of autarky, or self-sufficiency, which cut across Schacht's aim to expand exports and living standards. By November 1937 Schacht was sufficiently disillusioned with the new direction in economic policy to resign, leaving the field clear for Göring and another Party hack, Walther Funk, to dominate economic policy thereafter.

The armed forces were also unhappy with the implications of Göring's appointment, which relinquished, in their view, too much of a say in rearmament, over which they had exercised close control since 1933. Conservatives in the army feared, as did Schacht, that an irresponsible economic policy and excessive levels of remilitarization would invite the danger of social unrest and hence undo much of the valuable work done since the late 1920s in repairing Germany's military base. Nor were von Neurath and the foreign-office officials satisfied with the increasing intervention of von Ribbentrop, and the tendency, explicit since the 1936 negotiations with Japan and Italy but evident even before that, to sidestep the foreign office altogether in the conduct of foreign affairs. They were well aware that any congruence between Hitler's policy and their conservative nationalism was now more apparent than real, a distinction between what Hildebrand has called "revisionist Great Power policy" and Hitler's "expansionist race policy."[38]

The rumblings of discontent did not go unnoticed. When in November 1937 Hitler chose to reveal to von Neurath and senior military leaders his view of how foreign and military policy would develop, the response was muted, even hostile. In the spring of 1938 the political revolution was completed. The foreign minister was replaced in February by von Ribbentrop, who personified the shift in the power balance between the Party and the traditional elites. That same month the war minister, von Blomberg, and the army commander-in-chief, von Fritsch, were forced to resign on trumped-up charges of sexual scandal. Whether or not Hitler was privy to the plots that ensnared Germany's most senior soldiers is still unclear, but he used the crisis as the opportunity to face the logic of his growing personal power by abolishing the war ministry and establishing a supreme headquarters (OKW) with himself as the supreme commander of the armed forces.[39]

The political significance of this decision is often overlooked. It was without precedent to establish a supreme headquarters organization in peacetime. The innovation was an expression of Hitler's recognition that only he understood the nature of the grand tasks that lay before Germany and should therefore hold the reins of military strategy in his own hands. The creation of the OKW revealed publicly the alteration in the relationship between the military and society. Military affairs were now dominated by the Führer in a more direct way than any other area of state, a situation that greatly reduced the ability of the military leadership to influence decisions about strategy in the broadest sense, as they had done before 1914. By the middle of 1938 the key areas of policy in which the conservatives had played a major part since 1933 – foreign affairs, economic reconstruction and remilitarization – were now the province of Party bosses close to Hitler. Many of them regarded this as a dangerous development, which prejudiced the revival of German international strength and domestic stability in which they, like their pre-1914 forebears, had a powerful vested interest. Conservative disillusionment was manifest, though it did not prevent many of them continuing to work with the regime. Senior generals toyed with overthrowing Hitler in 1938 and again in 1939, though their hostility to Hitler's risk-taking was much weakened in the case of Poland because of their long-held desire to emasculate the peace settlement in the east. In January 1939 Schacht, who had remained head of the Reichsbank, submitted a lengthy critique of financial policy, echoed in a long memorandum on the threat and consequences of inflation forwarded by the army.[40] Schacht was sacked for his pains, but conservative anxieties about the political ambitions of the new elite survived through to the failed July plot in 1944.[41]

The establishment of the OKW was, above all, indicative of the changing nature of the dictatorship. Up to 1938 there was considerable room for maneuver in military and diplomatic affairs for those who did not necessarily follow the Party line. Policy issues were argued out, and decisions taken without automatic recourse to the Führer. From early 1938 Hitler assumed a more central role, both by virtue of his new office, but also because the men in charge of foreign affairs and economic development were his creatures, who discussed issues with him regularly and in detail. Though Göring or von Ribbentrop might disagree or recommend, they depended ultimately on Hitler's goodwill, and were always hostage to the fact that he now held the political initiative.

The changing structures of decision-making meant that Hitler assumed an exceptional prominence, at the same time as the structural pressures that might have limited or modified his strategic ambitions were much reduced. This model does not suggest a simple "intentionalist" approach, which Taylor, for one, would have rejected. In effect Hitler constructed a political apparatus between 1936 and 1938 which allowed his own ideas and ambitions a degree of force in the formation of policy that no German statesman, even Bismarck, had ever enjoyed.[42] The structural changes in fact magnified the significance of intentions. Hitler did not, of course, do everything himself. He created what might be called a "climate of permission" for the radicals in his entourage, and in the Party and ministerial apparatus, to push on further and faster with plans for racial hygiene and economic imperialism. However, they too could operate only to the extent that their activities could be reconciled when necessary with Hitler's current priorities, ill-defined as they often were.

Under these circumstances it is essential to establish just what those intentions were. Here the significance of the strategic memorandum of 1936 becomes clear. In it Hitler developed lines of policy – some of them very specific – which indicated the overall conceptual framework he was working with in the mid-1930s. First, he expected some kind of major conflict, provoked by the threat posed by Bolshevism and world Jewry, but by no means confined to them. There are other fragments of evidence from the same period which show that he had privately recognized that such a world-historical conflict was imminent and inescapable. Second, he believed that Germany would survive that contest only by developing into an economic and military superpower. The following passage in the memorandum was put in italics: "*The extent of the military development of our resources cannot be too large, nor its pace too swift.*" Such a program could be achieved, Hitler continued, only by subordinating all other national and social tasks to the one aim of strengthening Germany materially and psychologically. Finally, Hitler remained committed to the idea of seizing *Lebensraum* at the appropriate time, in order to secure the material foundation for global superpower status.[43]

These were broad goals and general expectations, certainly no blueprint for aggression of the kind Taylor so resolutely criticized. The most obvious thing that can be said about them is that between 1936 and 1945 Hitler's regime gave form and substance to them all. German society was heavily militarized and the economy diverted to vast strategic projects; living-space was carved out of central and eastern Europe; finally, Hitler decided in 1940 to launch the predicted reckoning with Bolshevism, and in 1941 with the Jews. While it is obviously tempting to argue that the thought was father to the deed, the actual course of events after 1936 clearly depended on circumstances and opportunities, and was neither pre-planned in any deliberate sense, nor remotely predictable. The paradox can best be explained by recognizing that Hitler operated at two distinct levels. The broad ideological and geopolitical aspirations acted as permanent reference points or markers in the day-to-day conduct of affairs; on the other hand Hitler acted like any politician in responding opportunistically to events or an altered set of conditions.[44] Improvisatory and reactive tactics in diplomacy are no more inconsistent with a broad strategic vision than they are on the battlefield.

Evidence of how the two levels interacted can be exemplified by a document for which Taylor had little respect: the so-called "Hossbach memorandum." The memorandum, written by Colonel Friedrich Hossbach, an army adjutant, is the record of a meeting at the Reich Chancellery on November 5, 1937. Taylor was skeptical of its provenance and authenticity, and of the views it purported to express, partly, no doubt, on grounds of scholarship, but partly because the document – taken at face-value – made it hard for him to argue that Hitler was at heart a moderate revisionist with no discernible program. The authenticity and accuracy of Hossbach's account should now no longer be in doubt.[45] Hitler used the meeting with senior representatives of the armed forces and von Neurath to give them a detailed insight into his views on foreign policy, and in particular the acquisition of living-space for the German people in Europe in a future great power conflict. This time, however, he gave a rough timetable, and an indication of his immediate priorities. The final date for the conflict over living-space he fixed at 1943–45, when the great military programs would be complete and potential enemies not yet so heavily armed. The exact timing of the conflict and against whom it would be fought depended on circumstances. Hitler never confined himself to the promised conflict in the east. But he expected to be able to incorporate Austria and to conquer Czechoslovakia, his initial aims, when the opportunity arose, and that, he told his audience, might be sooner rather than later.[46]

Both the projected date for conflict and the plans for *Lebensraum* are inde-pendently confirmed – indeed Hitler's colleagues made little secret of German aims in central Europe. In February 1937 Göring was reported to have told a British acquaintance: "Austria will come into our Reich of its own free will, but if the Czechs remain unyielding, we shall have to take Böhmen und Mähren [Bohemia and Moravia]. We don't want the province of Slovakia...some day the Corridor and Danzig must come back into the Reich."[47] It was Göring too who told another British visitor in December 1937: "First we shall overrun Czechoslovakia, and then Danzig, and then we shall fight the Russians."[48] Hitler had told Goebbels earlier in 1937 that the "great world conflict" would come in five or six years' time, and perhaps be over by 1950, the approximate date by which Albert Speer had been told to complete the "victory" buildings in Berlin.[49]

It is no doubt possible, even if the Hossbach memorandum is taken at face value, to argue that it amounts to little more than treaty revision in its final stages, as Taylor suggested. But such a perspective is convincing only if the issue of *Lebensraum* is set aside, for the conquest of territory outlined in November 1937 took Germany beyond treaty revision, just as the hints of world conflict suggest a vision of the 1940s that transcended revisionism entirely. There is not enough evidence to demonstrate a clear blueprint, and it would be surprising if any statesman, however committed to long-term aspirations, would draw one, but the balance between long-term aims and short-term goals suggest that Hildebrand's idea of a *Stufenplan*, moving on step-by-step from immediate revisionist goals to the seizure of living-space, and ultimately a contest for world power, may more accurately reflect Hitler's outlook.

Even the "step-by-step" formulation is, perhaps, too programmatic to be explained by what Hitler actually said before 1939. At the height of the struggle with the Soviet Union, in November 1942, he told an audience that three years beforehand he "could not even have suspected this outcome"[50] – who indeed could have done so? Hitler did not plan to destroy Poland and wage war on the

Soviet Union in the sense that the Schlieffen Plan before 1914 predicated for years a war with Russia and France, but neither course was inconsistent with his more general views about the prospect of war and its proximate cause. On the basis of the prewar evidence there is little that can be known with certainty about Hitler's detailed plans for the future, beyond the stated intention to destroy Poland and dominate eastern Europe, as Taylor maintained. But there are elements of a broader conception that cannot be disregarded if sense is to be made of what followed on from the war with the Poles. These were not necessarily shared by all of Hitler's colleagues, and certainly not by the German public as a whole, but because by the late 1930s Hitler had come to play such a central role in the establishment and conduct of foreign policy it is his views that bear the greatest historical weight.

First, Hitler was obsessed with the idea of waging war at some time. War was for him a necessary condition of the international system, as the struggle for survival was natural to the evolutionary process. War was the instrument for altering the conditions for a people's existence. War was the means to keep a people aware of its historic racial mission and to build a population committed to self-sacrifice and physical regeneration. When he looked at the Czech issue in 1938 he chose war above any of the other options for resolving German–Czech disputes. In 1939 Danzig and a revised Corridor might have been acquired by negotiation, but in April 1939 he made it clear that war against Poland was his preferred option. In the same speech in November 1942 he reflected on the dangers that might have overtaken Germany if Britain had decided to give him Danzig: "I have felt a shiver run down my spine when I read these proposals again, and I can only thank Providence for dictating a different course...". "War," as he wrote in 1936, was part of Germany's "destiny."[51]

Second, Hitler saw the solution to this destiny in turning Germany into an economic and military superpower capable of absorbing any and every crisis by striking the opponent with massive force. "If you want to lead a war," he told Goebbels in November 1937, "then this must be its name: destruction of the enemy with every means."[52] The key to becoming a superpower was to seize living-space in central and eastern Europe by force, so that Germany could get access to the resources that the post-1919 German state lacked. At the least it required the establishment of the Greater Economic Area (*Grossraumwirtschaft*) that began to take shape in the late 1930s as a complement to the strategy of domestic autarky. Food, materials, and labor were essential to sustain a large war effort whoever the enemy was and however long the war lasted. Hitler's concern was to avoid the risk-taking of 1914 by ensuring that Germany possessed sufficient armed might to be able to emerge from the imminent re-ordering of the world system as the victor.

Third, Hitler remained a consistent enemy of Bolshevism and Judaeism to the extent that ideology colored some of the critical choices made in German foreign policy. That is not to say that Hitler had definite plans in the late 1930s to annihilate Europe's Jews and destroy the Soviet Union. But he believed that Jewish world opinion was mobilized to stir up anti-German hatred in Britain and

America, and thus sow the seeds of conflict between them – a belief that fits ill with the idea that in foreign policy the Hitler regime was governed by balance-of-power rationality. He also regarded Soviet Marxism as the most serious threat posed to Europe's future, and although he could make a pact with the devil in August 1939, it is impossible not to see the decision taken in 1940 to move eastwards as a product of the ideologically inspired battle with Bolshevism as much as it stemmed from calculations of military expediency or *Realpolitik*. Hitler's worldview was shaped by these preconceptions and governed the choices he made when he was face-to-face with the issues of ethnic cleansing and living-space in 1941.[53]

Some of this outlook was shared by those around Hitler, even by wider circles in the radical nationalist constituency. For German conservative nationalists, however, the sum of Hitler's views on foreign and military policy ran directly counter to the conservative agenda. They did not want to risk waging war, though they were prepared to make Germany defensible if war should break out. They did not share the more fantastic elements of Hitler's vision of superpower status, though they hoped to constitute some form of central European power bloc dominated by Germany through political pressure and economic collaboration, which might restore Germany as an equal of the other great powers. They disliked the risks for social peace that the costs of becoming a military superpower entailed, and were fearful that if the German people were forced to accept sacrifices through heavy arms' spending there might be a return to the revolutionary crisis of 1918–19. Finally, they did not share Hitler's savage xenophobia and the "barbarous utopia" it presaged in the 1940s, though many of them became instruments in the attempt to achieve it. The problem faced by those who might have opposed the radical aspects of Hitler's strategy lay in the shifting political balance, which favored a Hitler-centered system and promoted the more radical elements of the Party to the forefront of German politics. The possibilities for resistance or dissent did not disappear entirely, particularly in the more routine day-to-day conduct of foreign or military policy, but they were greatly restricted by the nature of the political structures that emerged after 1936.

Taylor had one more string to his bow. Using the work of the American economist Burton Klein, Taylor argued in his 1963 supplement "Second thoughts" that the economic evidence confirmed his argument that Germany had not armed heavily in the 1930s, and had indeed a very narrow military base, designed to achieve the kind of quick Bismarckian victories that a limited revision required. Taylor felt that he, like everyone else in the 1930s, had been tricked by Hitler and that there had been "no overwhelming advance in armaments" after all. The arms' gap was "pure myth."[54] Hitler, Taylor concluded, was "pretending to prepare for a great war" but in fact "put butter before guns."[55]

Klein's work on the German economy, first published in 1959, was based upon his experience as a young economist on the United States Strategic

Bombing Survey team in 1945, which was sent to Germany to assess the economic and moral impact of bombing on the beaten enemy. The investigation arrived at the conclusion, after a few weeks' study, that Germany had armed only lightly, in width, during the 1930s and had then maintained a "peace-like" war economy in the first two years of war until forced to adopt fuller mobilization in 1942. The motive for limited rearmament was believed to be political – Hitler was thought to be anxious to improve living standards to avoid a social crisis. Although there was little detailed evidence to suggest that these were actual policy choices, Klein based his argument on the fact that German weapons' production was relatively modest in 1939–42, while the output of "consumer goods" was maintained at almost a constant level in the first years of war.[56] This was the kind of opportunistic rearmament that matched the brief opportunistic wars Hitler was believed to favor.

Once again the strategic memorandum of 1936 is the starting-point for a very different interpretation of German rearmament in the 1930s. Until then military procurement was left to the armed forces, who built upon the Second Rearmament Plan drawn up in 1932 and introduced in 1933.[57] Military spending was relatively low during this early period, constituting only 1.3 percent of GNP in the period 1932–35. Priority was given to the slow build-up of the military infrastructure of the state which had been dismantled in 1919–20, and to the re-establishment of a specialized armaments industry. The military capability of the armed forces was extremely limited, and aroused fears that Germany's neighbors might intervene to prevent the restoration of German armed power. In 1935 conscription was reintroduced, leaving the armed forces with the substantial and expensive administrative task of rebuilding mass armed forces after almost two decades of enforced disarmament. In 1936 the armed forces suggested a new armaments program, published in August, which was to expand the peacetime army to 800,000 men and complete the final phase of the remilitarization programme. This, too, was an expensive short-term project, but it was widely assumed that once the necessary level of military reconstruction had been achieved the yearly costs of maintaining the system would reach a plateau, or might even decline.[58]

This period of cautious military reconstruction was brought to an end in 1936, when Hitler's memorandum made it clear that he wanted "the premier army in the world" and the mobilization of resources for war preparation on the largest scale. The economy, Hitler wrote, has no other task than the "self-assertion of the nation." He continued: "Parallel with the military and political rearmament and mobilization of our nation must go its economic rearmament and mobilization, and this must be effected in the same tempo, with the same determination, and if need by with the same ruthlessness as well." The memorandum concluded with the injunction that "the German economy must be fit for war in four years."[59]

There were practical explanations for the decision to increase the scale and tempo of rearmament in 1936. The economy was stronger and the state more stable than it had been in 1933, when a great rush for arms might have compromised the economic revival and resurrected social tensions. The international situation deteriorated sharply in 1936 with the Ethiopian crisis, during which the western states showed their willingness to resort to economic pressure on Italy, and with the Civil War in Spain. Hitler sensed that the unraveling of the existing order was now underway. In February 1937 Goebbels recorded in his diary a conversation with Hitler: "He expected a great world conflict in five or six years. In 15 years he would have liquidated the Westphalian peace. He developed grandiose visions of the future. Germany will be victorious in the coming conflict or will live no more."[60] For Hitler the most dangerous development was the modernization and rearming of the Soviet Union, and he referred to the "menacing extent of this development" in the memorandum. When he discussed rearmament with Goebbels in January 1937 he measured German achievements against "Russia's strength"; in a speech that same year Hitler told his audience that on the issue of rearmament "the USSR as the leader of the tempo should show the way."[61]

Above all, rearmament was governed by Hitler's conception of the nature of modern war. He accepted the widely held view that future conflicts, like that of 1914–18, were likely to be on a large-scale and costly, drawing on the full material and moral resources of the nation. Here he was at one with much of the military leadership in Germany, which had since the mid-1920s been urging the case for a "defense-based economy" (*Wehrwirtschaft*). The concept was widely discussed and understood in 1930s' Germany. At root it represented a strategy designed to avoid the mistakes of the First World War: the provision of adequate foodstuffs to prevent internal unrest; the supply of essential war materials from domestic resources to avoid the effects of blockade; the preparation of detailed mobilization plans for industry and labor to ensure their rapid and effective conversion to war production; the reorientation of domestic priorities to ensure that developments in key areas such as transport, energy, and communications conformed with potential military requirements.[62]

The object was to ensure that Germany would be capable of fighting a "total war" if called upon to do so (though it obviously did not exclude fighting wars of lower intensity). Hitler did not have a particular war in mind. His aim seems to have been to create the sinews of a military and economic superpower which would then be in a position to emerge victorious from any possible conflict that might develop in the 1940s, a vision not very different from the one that had driven the Soviet build-up in the 1930s. The record that we have of Hitler's thoughts on the nature of war preparation all point in this direction, most famously in his address to the generals on May 23, 1939:

> Everybody's Armed Forces and Government must strive for a short war. But the Government must, however, also prepare for a war of from ten to 15 years' duration. History shows that wars were always expected to be short. In 1914 it was still believed that long wars could not be financed....However, every state will hold out as long as it can....The idea of getting out cheaply is dangerous, there is no such possibility.[63]

In 1939 Colonel Thomas, head of the OKW war economy staff, recorded Hitler's view "that any mobilization must be a total one," and in September 1939, when Britain and France declared war, that is what he ordered.[64]

Throughout the period 1936–39 the language that Hitler used to describe mobilization and war preparation was entirely consistent with the views expressed in the memorandum – the nature of military preparation "cannot be too large, nor its pace too swift." The view that he deliberately ran a calculated risk by preferring butter to guns is a speculation rooted in nothing more than the impression that Germany was less-heavily armed in 1939 than the generation that had lived through the 1930s, Taylor included, were led to expect. From 1936 the regime made no attempt to hide the fact that sacrifices would have to be made to satisfy the broad ideas of the "defense-based economy."[65] The clearest way to demonstrate the military priority of the regime lies in the macro-economic picture. By 1938 Germany's GNP was 39 percent greater than in 1928, the pre-Depression peak, but aggregate consumer expenditures were only 9 percent higher than a decade before, and in per capita terms had increased by only 4 percent, an increase largely accounted for by the higher proportion of adults in the population in the late 1930s.[66] As a proportion of national income, private consumption fell from 71 percent in 1928 to 59 percent in 1938, a fall of exceptional magnitude in an economy the size of Germany's. The additional spurt of growth in the economy in the late 1930s was almost all accounted for by war-related projects and high state spending.

The consequences of the increased tempo in 1936 were many. The military budget expanded rapidly, taking up 17 percent of GNP in 1938–39. In the last peacetime year 52 pfennigs out of every mark the German government spent went on defense. These were not remotely moderate proportions. In 1913, at the height of the pre-1914 arms race, the German government spent an estimated 3 percent of GNP, and devoted 24 percent of a much smaller state budget to defense purposes. In the 1960s western states spent between 3 and 7 percent of GNP on the military. There can be no question but that the level of military spending in the late 1930s in Germany was exceptionally high by any peacetime measurement.[67]

Why then did Klein, and afterwards Taylor, argue that German preparations were limited? Part of the explanation lies in a misreading of the regime's economic priorities in the 1930s. In 1936 Hitler used the August memorandum as the opportunity to bring the economy into relation with his military thinking. The instrument for achieving this was a new Four-Year Plan organization, set up in October 1936 under Göring who saw his new office as the centerpiece of a broad strategy for creating a defense-based economy. The Four-Year Plan was ostensibly concerned with the achievement of self-sufficiency, or autarky, in a range of sectors deemed to be vital for a blockade-free war economy. These included chemicals, iron-ore production, aluminum, synthetic rubber, synthetic textiles, synthetic fuel oil and foodstuffs. There was never any intention to achieve full self-sufficiency, and ultimately the regime intended to enlarge the resource base by taking over or controlling the material resources of central and eastern

Europe. Nevertheless the programs that were initiated were very large in scale, absorbing almost two-thirds of all industrial investment in Germany between 1936 and 1939. Investment in the new iron-ore and iron producer set up in 1937 – the *Reichswerke "Hermann Göring"* – topped 800 million RM before the outbreak of war; state investment in synthetic rubber production was 280 million RM, out of a total investment of 940 million. These sums were vastly greater than the amounts spent on weapons production, since they were large, complex, and capital-intensive sectors. They were the fruit of what Hitler had called "economic rearmament", a concept now generally described by the term "indirect rearmament" to distinguish it from the regular military budget which devoted considerably less to investment purposes and spent a great deal on wages and administration.[68]

Indirect rearmament took many other forms. Agriculture was given subsidies and technical aid to try to raise yields. Labor was retrained in skills more appropriate for a war economy, 1.2 million in total. The Four-Year Plan also became involved in expanding the machine-tool industry, and the research and development of a range of new substitute products. The broad framework for war preparation set up by Hitler in 1936 meant that much of the economy was engaged by 1939 on war-related activity, either direct or indirect. By May 1939 it was estimated by *Reichsgruppe Industrie* (Reich Group Industry) that 21 percent of the workforce was engaged on direct orders for the armed forces (28 percent in manufacturing).[69] If precise details on the labor force of the other strategic sectors built up under the Four-Year Plan were available, the final claim on the civilian workforce for war-related activity would be considerably higher, perhaps as high as one-third. To have more than one-quarter of the manufacturing workforce engaged on war contracts suggests not a regime committed to a strategy of "butter before guns" but an exceptional diversion of resources away from civilian consumption and exports.

The second explanation for Klein's argument lies in the comparatively low level of finished weapons produced in 1939. Taylor had scant regard for British and French rearmament, but he was surprised to discover that Germany was producing at levels that were no higher. The reason for the apparent discrepancy between national commitment to defense and the output of finished weapons lies partly in the large diversion of resources in Germany to establish the economic foundation for future war-making (raw materials and factory capacity), but largely from the fact that German forces were not yet prepared for a general war in 1939, and had not expected to fight one. The major arms programs were set up only in 1938 and 1939, and were far from ready when war broke out. In the summer of 1938 an explosives plan was drawn up which dwarfed the output figures of the First World War; in October Göring was ordered by Hitler to treble the general level of arms output and to expand the air force five-fold; in January 1939 Hitler authorized the naval Z-Plan (Z = *Ziel*, or "goal") for a large battle-fleet by the late 1940s, a decision that has encouraged some historians to see Hitler moving towards a global strategy, *Weltpolitik*, in the late 1930s.[70] All of these many programs were to be realized by 1942 at the earliest, the time when

Hitler had suggested in the "Hossbach" meeting that German armaments would reach their peak in relation to those of other great powers.

These armaments plans were to provide Germany with its superpower status. They are entirely incompatible with a policy of short local wars and a limited commitment to military spending. Indeed, many in the military and the ministerial apparatus regarded Hitler's programs as completely unrealizable under the economic conditions of the late 1930s, and were opposed to what they saw as Hitler's financial and political irresponsibility. By then the re-orientation of the economy was difficult, if not impossible, to reverse, for Hitler was committed to his vision of massive German military power and the defence-based economy. Had a general war not broken out in September 1939, it is difficult to believe that Hitler would have abandoned the attempt, having gone so far down the road to achieving the "room for maneuver" that the economic and military preparations allowed him.[71] As he saw it, war preparation was a task for which the German people would have to make sacrifices in the present to secure a rosy future for the race: "However well-balanced the general pattern of a nation's life ought to be there must at particular times be certain disturbances of the balance at the expense of other less vital tasks....For this task [rearmament] involves life and the preservation of life, and all other desires...are unimportant."[72]

In the end Taylor misjudged Hitler, just as many in the 1930s misjudged him. Unable to take Hitler's writing seriously, he assumed that Hitler was in the tradition of German *Realpolitik*, another in the line of German statesmen and soldiers who, since Bismarck, had sought German power in Europe and, without scruple of principle, used any opportunity to achieve it. With little interest in, or sympathy for, German domestic politics, he failed to see the relationship between the dynamic transformation of the dictatorship and the development of German foreign and military policy, which were transformed in the late 1930s by the shift towards economic empire-building, ethnic cleansing and a military build-up based on the ideas of the "defense-based economy." Because war broke out over Danzig, an issue long on the revisionist agenda, Taylor assumed that Hitler was just another revisionist, who had misjudged the temper of the western states. Hitler was a revisionist, but he was also a geopolitical fantasist; he was an opportunist, but he was also a dreamer. He did not plan the Second World War any more than he planned the Holocaust, but it was not mere historical accident that found him trying to remodel the world order and slaughter Europe's Jews between 1939 and 1945.

Notes

1 A. J. P. Taylor, "1939 revisited," German Historical Insitute, London, Annual Lecture 1981, 1982, p. 9.
2 See A. Sisman, *A. J. P. Taylor: A Biography*, London, 1994, pp. 294–301; R. Cole, *A. J. P. Taylor: The Traitor Within the Gates*, London and New York, 1993, pp. 190–203.
3 Taylor, "1939 revisited," pp. 14–15.
4 A. J. P. Taylor, *A Personal History*, London, 1983, p. 299.
5 A. J. P. Taylor, "The supermen: Hitler and Mussolini," in *Europe: Grandeur and Decline*, London, 1967, p. 221.

6 See particularly W. D. Smith, *The Ideological Origins of Nazi Imperialism*, Oxford, 1986, esp. pp. 244–52.

7 J. Hatheway, "The pre-1920s origin of the National Socialist German Workers' Party," *Journal of Contemporary History*, vol. 29, 1994, pp. 448–53.

8 See the discussion in A. Rödder, *Stresemanns Erbe: Julius Curtius und die deutsche Aussenpolitik, 1929–1931*, Paderborn, 1996; K. Hildebrand, *Das vergangene Reich: Deutsche Aussenpolitik von Bismarck bis Hitler, 1871–1945*, Stuttgart, 1995, esp. pp. 557–9.

9 T. Taylor (ed.), *Hitler's Secret Book*, New York, 1961, pp. 89–90.

10 On Hitler's foreign policy conception, see G. Stoakes, *Hitler and the Quest for World Dominion*, Oxford, 1986, esp. pp. 209–23. On differing perceptions of the "east," see M. Burleigh, *Germany Turns Eastwards*, Cambridge, 1988.

11 A. J. P. Taylor, *The Origins of the Second World War*, London, 1961, p. 98.

12 On varieties of nationalist outlook, see M. Laffan, "Weimar and Versailles: German foreign policy, 1919–33," in M. Laffan (ed.), *The Burden of German History, 1919–1945*, London, 1988, pp. 91–9. On the nationalist intelligentsia, see G. Mosse, *The Crisis of German Ideology: Intellectual Origins of the Third Reich*, London, 1970; F. Stern, *The Politics of Cultural Despair: A Study in the Rise of the German Ideology*, Berkeley, CA, 1961.

13 W. Michalka, *Von Ribbentrop und die deutsche Weltpolitik, 1933–1940*, Munich, 1980, p. 305.

14 Hildebrand, *vergangene Reich*, pp. 632–7; H.-A. Jacobsen, *Nationalsozialistische Aussenpolitik, 1933–1938*, Frankfurt am Main, 1968, pp. 32–3. On von Neurath see J. L. Heinemann, *Hitler's First Foreign Minister*, Berkeley, CA, 1979, esp. pp. 162–83. For a full statement of the conservative nationalist outlook see W. Michalka (ed.), *Deutsche Geschichte, 1933–1945: Dokumente zur Innen-und Aussenpolitik*, Frankfurt am Main, 1993, pp. 128–34, doc. 105, notes by the state secretary in the foreign office, Bernhard von Bülow, 13 March 1933.

15 Imperial War Museum (IWM), London, Speer collection box S362, Interrogation report 19, part II: Examination of Albert Speer, p. 1. On the central-European economic bloc, see B.-J. Wendt, "Aspects économiques d'une politique de securité nationale entre le revisionnisme et l'expansionnisme," *Revue d'histoire de la deuxième guerre mondiale*, vol. 39, 1989, pp. 47–59.

16 Taylor, *Origins*, p. 97. On Anglo-German relations, see D. Aigner, *Das Ringen um England: das deutsch–britische Verhältnis*, Munich, 1969.

17 On Rosenberg, see S. Kuusisto, *Alfred Rosenberg in der nationalsozialistischen Aussenpolitik, 1933–1939*, Helsinki, 1984; on Göring, see A. Kube, *Pour le mérite und Hakenkreuz: Hermann Göring im Dritten Reich*, Munich, 1986, esp. chs 3–4.

18 See especially Michalka, *Von Ribbentrop*.

19 For a more sober assessment of von Ribbentrop's capacity to influence Hitler, see S. Kley, *Hitler, Von Ribbentrop und die Entfesseung des Zweiten Weltkrieges*, Paderborn, 1996, pp. 326–43; M. Bloch, *Von Ribbentrop*, London, 1992, pp. 250–62.

20 G. Engel, *Heeresadjutant bei Hitler, 1938–1943: Aufzeichnungen des Majors Engel*, Stuttgart, 1974, pp. 58–60. There are many more examples.

21 IWM, FO 645, Box 156, Göring interrogation, September 24, 1945, p. 6.

22 For example, in August 1939 the German ambassador to London, von Dirksen, made repeated efforts to get his views on British firmness communicated to Hitler, but was stifled by von Ribbentrop. See Ministry of Foreign Affairs of the USSR, *Documents and Materials relating to the Eve of the Second World War*, vol. 2: *The Dirksen Papers (1938–9)*, Moscow, 1948, pp. 190–1 (memorandum by H. von Dirksen on the development of political relations between Germany and Britain, September 1939).

23 See particularly W. Murray, *The Change in the European Balance of Power, 1938–1939*, Princeton, NJ, 1984; W. Mommsen, L. Kettenacker (eds), *The Fascist Challenge and the Policy of Appeasement*, London, 1983.

24 K. Hildebrand, "Reich–nation state–great power: reflections on German foreign policy, 1871–1945," German Historical Institute, London, Annual Lecture 1993, London, 1995, pp. 22–3.

25 W. Treue, "Der Denkschrift Hitlers über die Aufgaben eines Vierjahresplans," *Vierteljahrshefte für Zeitgeschichte*, vol. 3, 1954.

26 J. Noakes and G. Pridham (eds), *Nazism, 1919–1945: A Documentary Reader*, vol. 2: *State, Economy and Society*, Exeter, 1984, p. 281 (all quotations from the memorandum are from this translation).

27 Noakes and Pridham, *Nazism*, vol. 2, pp. 282–3.

28 C. Leitz, *Economic Relations Between Nazi Germany and Franco's Spain, 1936–1945*, Oxford, 1996, ch 1.

29 Noakes and Pridham, *Nazism*, vol. 2, p. 282.

30 J. Fox, *Germany and the Far Eastern Crisis, 1931–1938: A Study in Diplomacy and Ideology*, Oxford, 1982, chs 3, 5.

31 Fox, *Far Eastern Crisis*, pp. 200–1.

32 D. Mack Smith, *Mussolini's Roman Empire*, London, 1976, pp. 95–8; W. C. Frank, "The Spanish Civil War and the coming of the Second World War," *International History Review*, vol. 9, 1987, pp. 389–406. On the dilemmas of Italian policy, see E. di Nolfo, "Der zweideutige italienische Revisionismus," in K. Hildebrand, J. Schmädeke, and K. Zernack (eds), *1939: an der Schwelle zum Weltkrieg*, Berlin, 1990, pp. 94–114.

33 See Aigner, *Das Ringen um England*, and, more recently, G. T. Waddington, "Hitler, von Ribbentrop, die NSDAP und der Niedergang des Britischen Empire, 1935–1938," *Vierteljahrshefte für Zeitgeschichte*, vol. 40, 1992, pp. 273–306.

34 On Schacht's campaign for colonies see A. J. Crozier, *Appeasement and Germany's Last Bid for Colonies*, London, 1988, pp. 171–98. Schacht's comment on Party radicals is documented in the Phipps Papers, Churchill College, Cambridge, I 1/17, Phipps to Eden, 10. 22. 36.

35 E. Jäckel, *Hitler's Weltanschauung: A Blueprint for Power*, Middletown, CT, 1972, p. 36.

36 The Christie Papers, Churchill College, Cambridge, 180/1 5, contain notes of a conversation with Göring on February 3, 1937. "Don't forget," Christie reports Göring as having said, "in the Europe Plan we guarantee the British Empire."

37 Details in R. J. Overy, *Goering: The "Iron Man"*, London, 1984, pp. 46–52.

38 G. Niedhart, "The problem of war in German politics in 1938," *War and Society*, vol. 2, 1984, pp. 56–8. There is a full discussion of the arguments over rearmament and economic policy in A. E. Simpson, "The struggle for control of the German economy, 1936/7," *Journal of Modern History*, vol. 21, 1959, pp. 37–45. See, too, Hildebrand, *vergangene Reich*, pp. 633–7.

39 On the fall of von Blomberg and von Fritsch, see H. Deutsch, *Hitler and his Generals: The Hidden Crisis, January–June 1938*, Minneapolis, MN, 1974, pp. 80–7, 98–104.

40 Army memorandum reproduced in M. Geyer, "Rüstungsbeschleunigung und Inflation: zur Inflations Denkschrift des OKW von November 1938," *Militärgeschichtliche Mitteilungen*, vol. 23, 1981, pp. 121–86. On the finance ministry's objections, see L. Schwerin von Krosigk, *Staatsbankrott: Finanzpolitik des Deutschen Reiches, 1920–1945*, Stuttgart, 1974, pp. 281–5. Schacht details in H. Schacht, *76 Jahre meines Lebens*, Bad Wörishofen, 1953, pp. 491–7.

41 See P. Steinbach, "The conservative resistance," and T. Childers, "The Kreisau circle and the twentieth of July," both in D. C. Large (ed.), *Contending with Hitler: Varieties of Resistance in the Third Reich*, Washington, DC, 1991, pp. 89–118. This is not to say that the Conservatives were unable to take any initiative, or even argue with Hitler, which his generals regularly did. See H. Koch, "Hitler's 'programme' and the genesis of Operation 'Barbarossa,' " *Historical Journal*, vol. 26, 1983, pp. 894–7.

42 Hildebrand, "Reich–nation state," pp. 22–3. On the centrality or otherwise of Hitler, there is now a vast literature. See the discussion in I. Kershaw, *The Nazi Dictatorship*, 3rd edn, London, 1993, pp. 59–79.

43 Noakes and Pridham, *Nazism*, vol. 2, pp. 282–4. On Hitler's world aims, see the discussion in M. Michaelis, "World power status or world dominion?" *Historical Journal*, vol. 15, 1972, pp. 345–59.

44 This was a conclusion arrived at by the prosecutors at the Nuremberg Trials. See Michaelis, "World power," p. 336.

45 See J. Wright and P. Stafford, "Hitler, Britain and the Hossbach memorandum," *Militärgeschichtliche Mitteilungen*, vol. 42, 1987, pp. 78–84, for a full discussion of its authenticity. See, too, B.-J. Wendt, *Grossdeutschland: Aussenpolitik und Kriegsvorbereitung des Hitler-Regimes*, Munich, 1987, pp. 11–37.

46 Minutes of the conference in the Reich Chancellery, November 5, 1937, *Documents on German Foreign Policy*, series D, vol. 1, pp. 29–39.

47 Report of meeting with Göring, July 28, 1937, in the Christie Papers, 18/1 5.

48 Lord Gladwyn, *The Memoirs of Lord Gladwyn*, London, 1972, p. 66.

49 E. Fröhlich (ed.), *Die Tagebücher von Joseph Goebbels: Sämtliche Fragmente*, 4 vols, Munich, 1987, vol. 3, p. 55; A. Speer, *Inside the Third Reich*, London, 1970, p. 154.

50 W. Maser (ed.), *Hitler's Letters and Notes*, New York, 1974, p. 189–90.

51 Noakes and Pridham, *Nazism*, vol. 2, p. 282; Maser, *Hitler's Letters*, p. 190. On Hitler's commitment to war, see J. Fest, "Hitlers Krieg," in N. Frei and H. Kling (eds), *Der nationalsozialistische Krieg*, Frankfurt am Main, 1990, pp. 103–21.

52 Goebbels, *Tagebücher*, vol. 3, p. 348.

53 See particularly Jacobsen, *Aussenpolitik*, pp. 446–8, 452–60; K. Pätzold, "Antikommunismus und Antibolschewismus als Instrumente der Kriegsvorbereitung und Kriegspolitik," and Y. Bauer, "Antisemitismus und Krieg," both in Frei and Kling (eds), *nationalsozialistische Krieg*, pp. 122–36, 146–61. Bauer concludes: "Hitler's war was from first to last a war against the Jews."

54 Taylor, "1939 revisited," pp. 6–7.

55 Taylor, "Second thoughts," in *Origins* (1963 edn), pp. 17–18.

56 See B. H. Klein, *Germany's Economic Preparations for War*, Cambridge, MA, 1959, and an earlier article which Taylor did not see, "Germany's preparations for war: a re-examination," *American Economic Review*, vol. 38, 1948. The genesis of the thesis of limited war is discussed in J. K. Galbraith, *A Life in Our Times*, London, 1981, pp. 212–25.

57 H. J. Rautenberg, "Drei Dokumente zur Planung eines 300,000-Mann Friedenheeres aus dem Dezember 1933," *Militärgeschichtliche Mitteilungen*, vol. 22, 1977, pp. 103–39.

58 Details in W. Deist, *The Wehrmacht and German Rearmament*, London, 1981, pp. 36–53. Costs for the army were to rise sharply during 1937–39 and then, for the 1940s, fall back to an annual level little higher than that of 1936.

59 Noakes and Pridham, *Nazism*, vol. 2, p. 283. In his "Secret book" (p. 96) Hitler had written: "[I]n the future the enlargement of people's living space...will require staking the whole strength of the people."

60 Goebbels, *Tagebuch*, vol. 3, p. 55.

61 Goebbels, *Tagebuch*, vol. 3, p. 33; Notes of a 1937 speech by Hitler, Christie Papers, 180/1 5.

62 On the theory of *Wehrwirtschaft*, see W. M. Stern, "Wehrwirtschaft: a German contribution to economics," *Economic History Review*, series 2, vol. 13, 1960–1, pp. 270–81. For a useful summary of the concept, see E. Hesse, "Wehrwirtschaft auf lange oder kurze Sicht?" *Der deutsche Volkswirt*, vol. 10, 1936, pp. 1,384–5. The background can be found in H.-E. Volkmann, "Aspekte der nationalsozialistischen 'Wehrwirtschaft,' 1933 bis 1936," *Francia*, vol. 5, 1977, pp. 513–38.

63 *Documents on German Foreign Policy*, series D, vol. 6, p. 577.

64 IWM, EDS files, Mi 14/377 (file 2), Thomas memorandum, March 28, 1939, p. 2; Mi 14/328 (d), OKW conference, September 3, 1939, pp. 1–2.

65 In December 1936, for example, Germany's most important economic journal, *Der Deutsche Volkswirt* (vol. 11, December 24, 1936, p. 625) included the following in a leading editorial on government economic policy: "It requires the sacrifice of living-standards, at least temporarily...in the end it is better to limit the demand for luxuries in order to build up ourselves what is necessary for food, clothing, housing and [military] security."

66 Klein, *Economic Preparations*, pp. 251–3; C. W. Guillebaud, *The Economic Recovery of Germany*, London, 1939, pp. 204–6.

67 R. J. Overy, *War and Economy in the Third Reich*, Oxford, 1994, p. 20.

68 On the Reichswerke, see Overy, *War and Economy*, pp. 190–1; on chemicals, A. Bagel-Bohlan, *Hitlers industrielle Kriegsvorbereitung, 1936 bis 1939*, Koblenz, 1975, pp. 117–21; on synthetic rubber, G. Plumpe, "Industrie, technischer Fortschritt und Staat. Die Kautschuksynthese in Deutschland, 1906–1944/5," *Geschichte und Gesellschaft*, vol. 9, 1983, p. 594.

69 Statistical material on the German manpower position during the war period, July 31, 1945, table 7, in IWM, Speer Collection, FD 3056/49.

70 On naval rearmament, see M. Salewski, *Die deutsche Seekriegsleitung, 1939–1945*, 2 vols, Frankfurt am Main, 1970, vol. 1, pp. 58–65; see, for example, G. Weinberg, "Hitler and England, 1933–1945: pretense and reality," in *Germany, Hitler and World War II*, Cambridge, 1995, who argues that changed armaments priorities indicate a clear intention to turn westward in 1939. This is a view that sits ill with the reality of German naval and air planning. Neither service was ready to face Britain in 1939, and their operational studies carried out that year made this situation clear to senior German commanders.

71 For Hitler's views on massive military build-up, see the interesting remarks of Albert Speer in Speer interrogation, July 13, 1945, in IWM, Box 8368:

> [Hitler] anticipated an intensification of the war...he had repeatedly drawn attention to the dangers of the second front or of additional theatres of war....He knew the supply figures of the last war in detail and could reproach us with the fact that output in 1917/18 was higher than we could show for 1942. I only knew that these were the requirements which had been fixed in his mind for a long time. They were in nearly every case three to six times the armament production of 1941.

72 Noakes and Pridham, *Nazism*, vol. 2, p. 282.

7   Appeasement

Paul Kennedy and Talbot Imlay

It is all too easy to comment upon the deficiencies contained in a book published thirty-eight years ago on the basis of the then available evidence, and to list the changes that would be needed to bring that volume up to date with more recent scholarship.[1] Both the questions asked by historians, and the materials open to them (especially in respect of twentieth-century sources) change significantly from one decade to the next. If historians are, in E. H. Carr's phrase, part of a vast caravan winding through time, it is hardly surprising that perspectives about "appeasement" have altered between 1961 and 1999 – a much more considerable period of time than that between the end of the Second World War and the publication of A. J. P. Taylor's book. Since the past three decades have also seen the opening up of the vast trove of British official records[2] on the interwar years, it is inconceivable that *The Origins of the Second World War* would not be "dated" in many respects – as its author later acknowledged.[3] What may perhaps be more surprising is the extent to which many of Taylor's judgments and (for want of a better word) "hunches" have stood the test of time. This was true when the first edition of this collection of essays appeared in 1986; and because there have been no dramatic advances in the scholarship on appeasement, it remains true today.

A greater difficulty in an essay such as this is to deal with a single strand – that of British appeasement policy – in isolation. To do so is difficult not merely because British attitudes and actions were, in Taylor's book, integrated into the overall story of why the Second World War occurred but because our own judgments of how well-founded, say, were Whitehall's worries about the size of the Luftwaffe will be affected by new researches on German aerial rearmament. Similarly, our assessments of British policy towards Poland, Russia and the USA in the 1930s can be placed in a different light by newly released archival materials from those countries, as well as from France, Japan and other actors. Above all, the issue of how well, or how poorly, the British understood Hitler's real intentions can be fully analyzed only by reference to scholarship on German policy, which is outside the bounds of this particular essay.[4] Students wishing to comprehend British appeasement will always need to understand other, non-British, perspectives as well.

The enormous literature on "the meaning of appeasement"[5] can be dealt with briefly here, since its significance for our purposes lies chiefly in the way Taylor's revisionist work challenged a well-established orthodoxy. Although appeasement originally was a positive concept – as in the "appeasing" of one's appetite – the failure of Neville Chamberlain's policies turned it into a pejorative term by 1939, a tendency which grew ever stronger as the costs of the war mounted and the full horrors of Nazi policy were gradually revealed. Since Hitler was by then regarded as the Devil incarnate, it followed that Chamberlain and Daladier's diplomacy in the late 1930s had been hopelessly misconceived and morally wrong.[6] Instead of standing up to the führer's manic ambitions, they had weakly appeased them.

Taylor's revisionism assaulted this orthodoxy on both the intellectual and the moral front. In his view, the restoration of Germany as a leading power, if not *the* leading power, in Europe was natural and inevitable. The Versailles settlement was an artificial, spatchcocked one, leaving ethnic minorities on the wrong side of hastily drawn boundaries; and it was seen as inadequate and unfair not only by all Germans but by most enlightened Britons, once their wartime anger had subsided. Changes, said Taylor, were therefore fairly inevitable: "The only question was whether the settlement would be revised and Germany become again the greatest Power in Europe, *peacefully or by war*" (p. 79; emphasis added). Far from being a madman, Hitler was merely another in a line of German statesmen – like Stresemann, for example – who thought that he could get revisions by negotiation, since the British in particular were making sympathetic noises. The führer's distinctiveness lay not in what he wanted but in the fact that, when negotiations for border rectifications became tense, he had better nerves than anyone else and possessed the gambler's instinct for knowing when he could get away with a risky deal, and what his opponent's weaknesses were. Because the German case for revision was a sensible one, and because Hitler had strong nerves while the appeasers did not, he could always rely upon other governments to rush forward and offer an improved settlement to satisfy German claims. This was particularly true after May 1937, when Neville Chamberlain assumed the premiership in Britain. He was determined to start something:

> Of course he resolved on action in order to prevent war, not to bring it on; but he did not believe that war could be prevented by doing nothing....He believed, too, that the dissatisfied Powers – and Germany in particular – had legitimate grievances and that these grievances should be met...he had no difficulty in recognizing where this injustice lay. There were six million Germans in Austria, to whom national reunification was still forbidden by the peace treaties of 1919; three million Germans in Czechoslovakia whose wishes had never been consulted; three hundred and fifty thousand people in Danzig who were notoriously German....Here was a program for the pacification of Europe. It was devised by Chamberlain, not thrust upon him by Hitler.
>
> (p. 172)

While this policy of revision worked successfully in the two crises of 1938 – that is, concerning the incorporation of Austria and the Sudeten Germans into the Reich – it broke down over the Polish issue in the year following. By that time, and especially after the German acquisition of the rump state of Czechoslovakia in March 1939, British public opinion wanted Chamberlain and his cabinet colleagues to take measures to "stop Hitler." In a tragicomedy of good intentions going astray, the British government – with France in its wake – found itself tied into binding military commitments to a stubborn and reckless Polish regime under Beck. Since Chamberlain was still determined to settle things peacefully and was sending messages to that effect to Berlin, Hitler felt that he could proceed to solve the Danzig dispute by hints of action but without serious risk of war with the west; indeed, with the very strong chance that Chamberlain would arrange things in just the same way as he had done at Munich. It was only because the Poles declined to be as conciliatory as the Czechs that Hitler's – and Chamberlain's – expectations went awry. Although none of them planned to be at war with each other, by September 3 that very state of affairs existed. Far from being a maniac, Hitler had acted in a rational (if calculated) manner. But the appeasers, having willingly undermined the European status quo on numerous occasions in the 1930s, had now bungled things, and had gone to war "for that part of the [1919] peace settlement which they had long regarded as least defensible" (p. 335).

The cries of outrage which greeted the publication of such views thirty-eight years ago are understandable, and perhaps even more so now in the light of recent scholarship on the Holocaust.[7] On the one hand, there was Taylor's refusal to make moral judgments, or to give much weight to the significance of Nazi ideology, domestic politics, and racial doctrines. Then there were the critics who were alarmed at the possible implications of Taylor's suggestion that German hegemony in Europe was "natural," and ought not to have been resisted; if that applied to Hitler's Germany in the 1930s, might it not also apply to Khrushchev's Russia in 1961 – the year of the Berlin crisis as well as of the publication of Taylor's book? Above all, there were those infuriated by his flippantly throwaway style and sweeping remarks: that Hitler had no "preconceived plan" (p. 98); or that the Hoare – Laval scheme was "perfectly sensible" (p. 128); or that Munich was "a triumph for all that was best and most enlightened in British life" (p. 235); or that "it seems from the record that [Hitler] became involved in war through launching on 29 August a diplomatic manoeuver which he ought to have launched on 28 August' (p. 336). All this was strong stuff.

The greatest indignation was, of course, reserved for Taylor's implicit (and sometimes explicit) "de-demonization" of Hitler, an interpretation that many critics thought untenable on both moral and factual grounds.[8] By contrast, Taylor's view of the British appeasers appeared less controversial, if only because the prevailing image of Neville Chamberlain was already a negative one. *The Origins of the Second World War* may have portrayed Britain's appeasement policy in a more dynamic and purposeful way than was hitherto imagined, but by showing how eager London was to comply with, or even anticipate, the führer's wishes, it still seemed unflattering. Consequently, the notion that policy was both unwise and immoral was scarcely shaken, as could be seen in Gilbert and Gott's swingeing indictment, *The Appeasers*, published two years later.[9] Taylor himself might not wish to draw moral judgments about Chamberlain, or Samuel Hoare, or Horace Wilson, but many other historians were very willing to do so.

Apart from his general argument that British appeasement policy unwittingly contributed to the outbreak of the Second World War, Taylor offered detailed remarks on the leading British personalities in this story, the arguments they deployed, and the phases they went through. All of this was based upon published British and German diplomatic documents for the interwar years, and upon older memoirs and biographies. Within another decade, however, virtually the entire official records for the 1930s (not to mention more and more private collections) were opened to historians – giving them the unexpected opportunity to measure Taylor's book, and other works, against the government's own documents. By an Act of 1967 the Labour government reduced from fifty years to thirty years the period of time in which public records were kept confidential, though there were exceptions. Had that not happened, historians today would only now be digesting the cabinet files on, for example, "colonial appeasement" in 1937, and much of what follows in this essay would have been impossible to write. For the past thirty years, therefore, there has been a vast swathe of scholarly books and articles dealing with British appeasement policy, although it would be fair to say that, during the past decade, there have been distinct signs of a tapering-off in the originality of viewpoints and arguments.

Many of Taylor's observations, it ought to be said at once, have stood the test of time rather well. His somewhat cynical view of statesmen, strengthened no doubt by his years of studying Bismarckian diplomacy, put him in good stead in describing the role of people such as Simon, MacDonald and Hoare. Recent biographies – of Hoare, Simon, even Eden – have fleshed out their personalities but have not fundamentally altered Taylor's portrait.[10] His coverage of Sir Nevile Henderson's debilitating functions as British ambassador in Berlin – constantly toning down the firmness of the foreign office's messages, and making deprecating noises to his German listeners about the Jews or the Czechs or the Poles – have required no amendments now that the files are open.[11] Above all, Taylor's observations on Halifax, although brief, ring very true: the foreign secretary's aloofness, his sense of conscience (occasionally fostered by his foreign-office staff) his sensitivity to what the Conservative Party and the country at large would think fair, made the "Holy Fox" one of the few people – perhaps the only one – who could influence the prime minister during the Munich and Prague crises (p. 188–9 and ff.).[12]

By contrast, the portrait of Chamberlain in these pages seems one-dimensional. Taylor captures the prime minister's personal decisiveness and sense of purpose, the businessman-turned-politician who knew how to run an organization on efficiently utilitarian lines; and many a later book, benefiting from the cabinet papers, has shown how *dirigiste* was the administration that

Chamberlain controlled.[13] On the other hand, historians who have gained access to the prime minister's private letters, especially those to his sisters, have shown Chamberlain to be increasingly uncertain about Hitler as 1938 turned into 1939. One week's expressions of confidence that all was going well, and that the likelihood of war was fading, mingle with much more gloomy assessments in the week following.[14]

No doubt these shifts of mood can be explained in part by the fluctuating reports of happenings on the continent, but Chamberlain's letters suggest a more complex figure than Taylor presents: sometimes briskly efficient, sometimes proud and privately boastful of his successes, sometimes worried and even bewildered at the turn of events. Perhaps this is why recent studies present such contradictory interpretations, with Aster returning to the "guilty men" view, Charmley portraying the prime minister as a far-sighted *realpolitiker*, and Parker seeking to draw a balance. We still await the second volume of Professor Dilks's biography of Chamberlain[15] before we have the full picture, but the image which is emerging has already shown how difficult it is to assess the prime minister's character in a few swift sentences. As it is, this continued focus on the "high politics" of the Chamberlain cabinet distracts scholarship from broader issues.

On the internal politics of Great Britain in the interwar years, and their effect on foreign policy, Taylor has not much to say, although the remarks he makes are usually accurate enough. For example, he shrewdly notes that Baldwin's pro-League statements in 1935 were intended to outwit the Labour Party just as a general election was pending. Similarly, Taylor's discussion of the spring 1939 considerations of an Anglo-Russian alliance to assist Poland nicely captures the dilemma in which Chamberlain found himself; if London negotiated with Moscow (which the prime minister and his colleagues greatly disliked) and was successful, it would be seen as vindicating the arguments of such varied critics of the government as Churchill, Lloyd George, and the Labour Party; if London refused to negotiate, or did so and failed to reach a settlement with Stalin, it would be blamed – by the British public, by a suspicious Hitler, and by posterity (as indeed it was). While Taylor does not provide Maurice Cowling's full picture of the internal political dynamics of appeasement diplomacy – that is, of a Chamberlain needing a successful "deal" with Germany not only to preserve peace but to secure his own political position and confound his critics to the left and the right[16] – he does hint at this domestic dimension.

Researches into the internal political aspects of British policy have therefore tended to supplement Taylor's version rather than replace it. Cowling, for example, has gone even further in his argument, suggesting that Chamberlain's deeper concern was that another great war (with its total mobilization of national resources) would lead to significant advances by Labour and the Trades Union movement – just as the First World War had done. The preservation of peace was, therefore, intricately linked with the fate of the Conservative Party, a fact which (Chamberlain felt) the more reckless or "irregular" Tories like Churchill did not comprehend.[17] Just as such an account does not contradict

Taylor, so also do the writings about the "anti-appeasers" scarcely affect his picture: for the message of such works has generally been that Chamberlain's opponents, too, were uncertain of how to respond to the unprecedented circumstances of the late 1930s. There were all sorts of divisions among the ranks of the Conservative critics, although this still remains inadequately researched (there is no study of the Tory Party and foreign policy, for example, and little use of constituency records). What we do know is that some Conservatives disliked the appeasement of Germany, but strongly urged the appeasement of Italy; most of them – even Churchill – softened their attacks when the prospect of being invited to join the government seemed closer; the "Eden group" tried to keep its distance from the "Churchill camp," and so on. In the same way, the Labour Party was neither as forthright nor as consistent in its criticism of appeasement as it later liked to think. Attlee and his colleagues (who deserve fuller study) were very wary of being portrayed as warmongers, and warier still of co-operation with the old imperialist war-horses on the right of the Conservative Party. The revelation of such uncertainties gives us a better idea nowadays of how Chamberlain was able to preserve his commanding position in British politics for so long.[18]

British public opinion – the press, varied pressure-groups and the legendary "man in the street" – is not a key feature in *The Origins of the Second World War*. To be sure, Taylor refers to that general mood of pacifism, non-interventionism, and dislike of "foreign politics" which conditioned the entire interwar period and made every administration, from Lloyd George's coalition onward, reluctant to accept commitments in Europe and eager to see an amicable settlement of all international disputes. Over the past three decades, the study of British public opinion – especially the ideas and movements associated with pacifism, the Peace Ballot and the League of Nations' Union, but also strands of opinion on the Right[19] – has become a major growth industry. The press's views of Germany, the Left Book Club, the public's attitude towards the Abyssinian crisis, or the Spanish Civil War, have all found their historians.[20] Here again, we are talking about additions to Taylor's version of events, not challenges to it.

Public opinion's two most significant disruptions of the official policy of appeasing the dictators occurred, first, in late 1935, when the news of the Hoare–Laval pact provoked an explosion of discontent against this undermining of League of Nations' principles; and, second (and more importantly), in the spring of 1939, when large segments of British public opinion, including many former supporters of Chamberlain's appeasement policies, decided that Hitler had to be stopped and urged all manner of embarrassing proposals upon the government: guarantees to east-European states, an alliance with Russia, further rearmament, closer ties with the French, and so on. Taylor gives a good account of how Chamberlain became increasingly trapped between two uncontrollable forces – the exogenous force of Hitler, moving to further actions or threats of action, and the endogenous force of a resentful British public – but much more might have been said about the vital change in mood and circumstances. There is little or nothing in his account, for example, of the anger and disgust produced in Britain by news of the *Kristallnacht*, (November 9, 1938), nor of the rabid speeches of late 1938 in which Hitler denounced Chamberlain's interfering diplomacy and proclaimed the Munich settlement a victory for brute force – exactly the opposite of what the prime minister was saying.[21]

Where Taylor seems less correct is in his assumption (which he repeated on many occasions in the 1960s and 1970s) that the Munich agreement was overwhelmingly supported by the British press, with only *Reynold's News* in opposition. In fact, both left-of-center papers like the *Manchester Guardian*, the *Daily Herald* and the *News Chronicle*, and the distinctly right-wing *Daily Telegraph*, wanted a firmer line taken toward Nazi Germany, and were joined in this by many individuals.[22] What is even more significant, and until recently less well-known, were the persistent and very determined efforts made by Chamberlain and his colleagues to control the media – by influencing the press lords and editors, by getting critical talks suppressed on BBC Radio, by censoring the contents of the newsreels shown at the enormously popular cinemas – so as to give to the world the impression that the nation was behind the prime minister and his policies.[23] In view of this recent evidence, the older idea of a general consensus in British public opinion in favor of appeasement which broke only with the news of the German entry into Prague in March 1939 now looks distinctly wrong. The much more likely position was that opinion was already divided during the Czech drama, although this was obscured by the combination of the government's censorship efforts, the reluctance of Chamberlain's critics to appear as warmongers, and the cautiousness produced by natural apprehension at the prospect of a major war. As soon as the shudders of relief at the avoidance of hostilities were over, however, the sense of unease returned, reinforced by one of shame at the fate of the Czechs, and anger at Hitler's speeches and programs. Seen in this light, the uproar over the Prague crisis was but one step (even if the most important one) in the dramatic switch of British public opinion against appeasement.[24] This metamorphosis of British opinion, and the government's efforts to steer it, still requires more work.

Appeasement – in the older sense of an attempt to settle differences by negotiation and concession – was not a new feature in British diplomacy: as historians have pointed out, many elements of appeasement went back to Gladstone's time, or even further.[25] What was quite new, and altogether more difficult for the British government to handle, was the unprecedented state of the international system after 1919. By that time, the USA was by far the most powerful financial and industrial (and, potentially, military) state in the world – yet it rapidly abandoned most of its diplomatic responsibilities, even while the ups and downs of its enormous economy continued to affect trade, investment, and prosperity across the globe. The other great continent-wide power, Russia, had been shattered by the First World War and was now ruled by the mysterious and threatening Bolsheviks. The Austro-Hungarian empire had dissolved into a cluster of intensely jealous rivals. By contrast, Germany's territories (despite reductions in size, especially in the east) remained basically intact; and its power potential, as measured in terms of population, industrial capacity, and national efficiency, was great – greater than France's in the long run. If and when the Germans organized themselves to assert their claims for a revision of the 1919 treaty, they would be inherently in a very strong position. Neither the "successor-states" of eastern Europe nor a nervous, politically fragmented, and economically weaker France would be able to resist for more than a relatively short period – unless aided by another Great Power. Yet, with the USA excluding itself, and the USSR in partly enforced, partly self-chosen isolation, only Britain remained; and it found it less easy to escape into isolation, much as it wanted to.

This fundamental change in the international balances as compared with the pre-1914 era Taylor captured very well, illuminating basic trends to which he had already drawn attention in his important earlier work, *The Struggle for Mastery in Europe, 1848–1918*.[26] The First World War, then, had not "solved" the German question: if anything, it had made it "ultimately more acute." "If events followed their course in the old 'free' way," Taylor suggested, "nothing could prevent the Germans from overshadowing Europe, even if they did not plan to do so" (p. 48). To be sure, Britain could have carried out her traditional balance-of-power policy, but many things conspired to make that seem less useful than ever before. In the first place, for the entire 1920s it was Germany's weaknesses and France's (and even Poland's) strengths which caught the eye. Second, as noted above, the British public in the post-Versailles era did not want any further commitments in Europe; and, like most British ministers, soon came to feel that the 1919 boundaries ought to be revised – by peaceful means, of course, and under the aegis of the newly created instrument of the League of Nations. The fact that Japan now appeared as a potential threat in the far east, where Britain had much more substantial interests than any other European country, also made it easy "to understand why the British felt distinct from the Powers of Europe and why they often wanted to withdraw from European politics" (p. 68). After the Abyssinian crisis and the Spanish Civil War had revealed not only a new potential enemy in the form of Mussolini's Italy but how ineffectual was the League of Nations, the international reasons for settling German grievances seemed more pressing than ever – or so it appeared to the firm-minded Chamberlain when he took over in 1937.

In discussing the general external structure in which the British government now had to carry out its diplomacy, Taylor's book is very lucid. It is also essentially correct in its portrayal of British policy toward potential allies among the other Great Powers. Thus, London's dismay at the difficulties of persuading the United States' government to do anything substantial either in Europe or in the far east, and Neville Chamberlain's personal suspicion that the Americans were "all words, and no actions," have been amply confirmed in the excellent studies by David Reynolds and Callum MacDonald.[27] In the same way, Taylor's picture of the far greater dislike shown by Chamberlain and his colleagues towards the Soviet Union – as a general threat to the western order of things and, more specifically, in the context of a possible Anglo-Russian alliance to support Poland in 1939 – has not been shaken by the newer literature. And, since Taylor distinguishes between this general mistrust of Russia, on the one hand,

and a (non-existent) policy of trying to provoke a German–Russian war, on the other, his portrayal is much more balanced than those strained pro-Moscow writings which seek to explain appeasement as fundamentally an anti-Marxist device (pp. 256, 279ff.).[28] Finally, he nicely captures the ambivalent British feelings towards France: resenting it for being the "disturber of the peace" and so paranoically anti-German in the 1920s, disliking the fact that its very existence (not to mention its unwise obligations in eastern Europe) made British isolation from the continent possible, and yet also fearful, at least by late 1938 or early 1939, that the French government was suffering such a crisis of morale that it might agree to everything demanded of it in Berlin unless it were given firmer British backing. In this latter sense, too, the six-month period following Munich was a watershed in British policy and strategy: for the "continental commitment," avoided by Whitehall for some twenty years, could not in the last resort be repudiated.[29]

The individual phases of British appeasement policy in the interwar years are dealt with by Taylor in a less balanced way, even if one readily concedes that the importance which historians attach to individual episodes must, to some degree, be a matter of choice as well as of existing documentary evidence. Only forty-seven pages are devoted to the 1920s; while the period from the Manchurian crisis to the *Anschluss* gets 100 pages; and the Czech and Polish crises of 1938–39 command nearly 150 pages. (It is chiefly for this reason that our own comments have focused heavily upon the late 1930s as well.) There is a fair-sized coverage of such topics as the Locarno pact of 1925 (pp. 81–6), the disarmament conference of 1932–33 (pp. 93–107), and the Abyssinian crisis of 1935–36 (Chapter 5); and while the very substantial literature has added many further details to our knowledge of those negotiations, the differences which have emerged have more to do with moral and ideological perspectives – for example, Frank Hardie's strongly disapproving account of *The Abyssinian Crisis*[30] – than they do with historical accuracy. Taylor's remarks on the role of pessimistic admiralty opinion in influencing British policy in 1935 is, for example, amply confirmed in the late A. J. Marder's article on that point.[31] But it is curious that there are only two pages (pp. 90–2) on the very important Manchurian crisis of 1931–39,[32] and less than a half-page (p. 118) on the Anglo-German naval treaty of 1935, toward which the British government attached such importance and which has, in consequence, attracted the attention of a number of scholars.[33] There is also very little in *Origins* about the various schemes for "colonial appeasement," that is, the satisfying of German grievances by the return of some of her former colonies. In fact, this was not especially important to a dictator intent in the first place on revising the European order; but it did obsess many Germans and consume the attention of many Britons (both for and against such a colonial deal), and was a major strand in British appeasement policy for some time – as recent works show.[34]

In a wide-ranging and clever article on appeasement published in 1965, after the appearance of Taylor's book but before the opening of the official records, Donald Watt presciently suggested that, when further evidence was available, it was probably going to be difficult to maintain the simplistic older line according to which the appeasers merely "lacked guts." Watt felt that a future investigation of the files might reveal, *inter alia*,

> the fears of Britain's Conservative leaders of the unrealism of current British opinion, and the existence of a degree of military weakness in 1935–36 which paralyzed Britain's military planners, giving them years of sick apprehension as their daily companion. It may reveal three services so unable to agree on a common strategy that one was imposed on all three of them by the Treasury, obsessed not with Britain's economic strength at home, but with the state of her gold and dollar balances, her foreign investments, and her earning power abroad. It may reveal a Commonwealth divided on everything else but its dislike of Versailles and its wish for non involvement in European affairs.[35]

Some of these aspects are indeed referred to by Taylor, but only briefly, such as defense weaknesses, or the influence of the treasury; and the role of the dominions, or the empire as a whole, is not mentioned at all. Yet if one feature of the historiography of appeasement since the opening of the official records stands out, it is the massive attention which has been paid to the evidence of Britain's frightening economic and strategical–global weaknesses in the 1930s.

Taylor is brief but reasonably good in referring to "economic appeasement," presumably since the published German and British documents detailed at least some of the efforts made by Whitehall to soften German resentments by offers of trade credits, access to raw materials, exchange arrangements, and outright loans; but his remarks upon the baneful influence of the treasury on British rearmament now look very dated. As a flood of works has shown, it was simply not true that a nice burst of Keynesian "pump-priming" by means of higher armaments' spending would have solved Britain's problems, reducing unemployment and strengthening the armed services. It is of course likely that in the early 1930s some extra expenditure on the forces would have had beneficial effects in strategic, industrial, and employment terms; but the amount of cash that was needed to rebuild a two-ocean navy, to provide the Royal Air Force with both its fighter defenses and its long-range bombers, and to equip the army for a European field role – all of which the chiefs of staff desired – was well beyond the industrial and financial capacity of the country. The long economic decline, exacerbated by the world slump after 1929, had eroded the British industrial base to an alarming extent. There were incredibly few skilled workers, especially in the vital engineering trades. There were insufficient machine-tools. There were few modern factories, and no modern shipyards. What was more, simply throwing money at these problems could never produce easy and fast solutions; it might, indeed, weaken the British economy still further by provoking inflation, hurting the balance of payments, and producing bottlenecks. For such an ailing patient, only a gentle stimulus seemed proper.[36]

By the late 1930s, the treasury's arguments were proven to be correct, even when – or, rather, especially when – it had lost its battle to keep defense spending down to levels which it judged to be economically safe. The great increases in government expenditures by that time, and the large defense loans, did cause inflation; the many orders abroad for the machine-tools, steel, aircraft, and instruments which a weak British industry could not produce itself, drastically raised the amount of imports; yet the transition of the economy from a peacetime to a wartime basis meant that the proportion of manufacturers devoted to exports was falling rapidly. The balance of payments was worsening, the standard rate of income-tax was higher than at any time since 1919, and the floating of government loans to pay for defense was weakening Britain's credit and leading to a run on sterling. With the treasury warning in early 1939 that the continuation of defense spending at the present rate "may well result in a situation in which the completion of our material preparations against attack is frustrated by a weakening of our economic stability, which renders us incapable of standing the strain of war or even of maintaining those defenses in peace,"[37] it was perhaps not surprising that Chamberlain still strove for a compromise settlement of the Danzig issue.

But if the treasury's words were gloomy, they were nothing like as dark as those of the chiefs of staff, the "Cassandras in gold braid," as Correlli Barnett has described them.[38] Years of underfunding, together with the constraints imposed by the Ten-Year Rule, had left Britain and its empire in a dreadfully weak position militarily – as the service chiefs were eager to explain after 1932, when the first attempts to assess the defense requirements of the empire were made. A whole series of reports were then laid before a worried cabinet for the next six years, always with the same depressing message. The Royal Navy had been run down far below Washington treaty standards, and was incapable of sending a "main fleet to Singapore" and of maintaining a one-power standard in European waters, hence the admiralty's concern to restrain German naval rearmament by the 1935 treaty.[39] There was not one adequately defended base throughout the entire empire. A minuscule army could not possibly play a role in preserving the European equilibrium – which is why the chiefs of staff frowned upon talks with the French military in 1938, and repeatedly warned the cabinet that Britain could not do much to help Czechoslovakia.[40] Above all, perhaps, there was the weakness in the air: far from the British being in a position to deter Germany by means of a long-range bomber force, it seemed itself much more vulnerable to aerial attack from the imposing Luftwaffe.[41] Going to war against one of the dictator states would be difficult enough; fighting all three was impossible. Appeasement was the only solution. Or, as the chiefs of staff pointed out in December 1937:

> [W]e cannot foresee the time when our defence forces will be strong enough to safeguard our trade, territory and vital interests against Germany, Italy and Japan at the same time…. [We cannot] exaggerate the importance from the point of view of Imperial Defence of any political or international action which could be taken to reduce the number of our potential enemies and to gain the support of potential allies.[42]

Here was an argument for appeasement which at first sight was utterly compelling. Yet apart from a brief mention of Britain's supposed vulnerability to aerial attack – which Chamberlain used in order to cow cabinet critics during the Munich crisis – the reader gains little sense from Taylor's account of the significant role of defense weaknesses in appeasement policy. This is not a charge of negligence on his part: the mass of evidence was simply not available to scholars in the late 1950s.

As if this catalogue of gloom were not enough, the global international crisis of the 1930s threatened to split the British empire apart. Ever since 1919 Afrikaners and French-Canadians – not to mention, after 1921, the fiercely independent Irish Free-Staters – had bitterly opposed any idea of "imperial defense" and expressed even more hostility to the notion of being dragged into a war in consequence of European quarrels. And while Australia and New Zealand were more willing to cooperate with Britain, they too were worried that European issues would divert resources from the more immediate danger of Japanese aggression in the Pacific. In addition, the dependent empire was much less tractable than in the days of Disraeli or Salisbury. A widespread Indian nationalist movement, Egyptian discontents, a potential civil-war situation in Palestine by the late 1930s, were all pinning down British troops and resources and, last but not least, reinforcing Whitehall's arguments for not being committed to Europe.[43] Moreover, these fissiparous movements *within* the empire could not be completely separated from the *external* threats to the Mediterranean route and especially to the British possessions in the far east – a region whose significance, were one to measure it in terms of books published on that aspect of British policy alone – overshadowed everything else![44]

Not only did the chiefs of staff and the treasury have contradictory ideas of the British government's existing priorities – with one side pressing for more defense spending, and the other pressing for financial stability – but their prognostications for a future conflict, should one actually come, were actually at odds. From the armed services' viewpoint, Britain had a chance of successfully fighting Germany and Italy only if the war were a long one, during which the population and material resources of the empire could steadily be mobilized. In the treasury's opinion, Britain could afford to fight only a short war, since it would very swiftly run out of gold and dollar holdings.[45] Impaled on the horns of this dilemma, was it surprising that cabinet ministers should endeavor to avoid a conflict of any kind?

Because the official archives have revealed this catalogue of industrial, financial, strategic and imperial weaknesses with which successive British governments grappled in vain during the interwar years, the tendency of recent writings has been much more emphatic (and even sympathetic) toward the appeasers. In consequence, the "guilty men" interpretation of the 1940s and 1950s looks unbalanced and unfair. Far from finding Chamberlain's policy in the late 1930s inexplicable, it now seems quite understandable to many historians. As one of them has put it: "If one begins to tot up all the plausible motivations for appeasement…one sees that these are far more than enough to explain it. It was massively over-determined; any other policy in 1938 would have been an astounding, almost inexplicable divergence from the norm."[46]

All this newer evidence of British weakness affects Taylor's arguments only indirectly. To the extent that many of these writings have suggested that appeasement was unavoidable and predetermined, they do place Chamberlain and his colleagues in a more favorable light than that in which they appeared in *Origins*. But such materials would probably not have affected his central thesis, that the coming of war in September 1939 was an accident, and one caused more by the erratic moves of the appeasers and the stubbornness of the Poles than by Hitler's own calculations. Nor, one suspects, would they have altered his own skeptical view that the politicians rarely consulted "their military experts in a detached way before deciding on policy. They decided policy first; and then asked the experts for technical arguments with which this policy could be justified" (p. 155). It was because of that habit, Taylor writes, that even when British leaders used such "practical arguments" as aerial weaknesses during the Czech crisis it was to reinforce their own conviction that appeasement was morally right (p. 254).

Given the weight of this newer evidence, few historians today will be as cynical and cavalier as Taylor was then about the role of military (or treasury) advice on British policy. None the less, his remarks may be useful in reminding us that strategic memoranda are not the "be-all and end-all" of historical causation, and that we still have the task of properly integrating the newer evidence into our larger understanding of what appeasement meant.

As noted above, the weakness of the older "guilty men" argument appeared to be that it denounced Chamberlain and his colleagues for a failure both of morality and of willpower without much appreciation (or knowledge) of the difficulties under which British governments of the 1920s and 1930s labored. By contrast, most of the later works have focused upon the seemingly compelling strategic, economic, and political motives behind British policy at that time, but without much concern for the moral and ideological aspects of it. That is to say, the mass of cool treasury memoranda and the well-honed strategic assessments of the chiefs of staff, available for everyone to see in the Public Record Office, now occupy such a prominent position in the story that they are in danger of overshadowing those very important personal feelings behind appeasement: the contempt and indifference felt by many leading Englishmen towards east-central Europe, the half-fear–half-admiration with which Nazi Germany and Fascist Italy were viewed, the detestation of communism, the apprehensions about future war.

Of course the warnings of the treasury and the chiefs of staff about Britain's impending financial and strategical bankruptcy were important; but the facts are that such statements were not infallible, and that they were sometimes used by Chamberlain to justify policies he already wanted to pursue. For example, as Correlli Barnett and Williamson Murray have pointed out, both the chiefs of staff and the cabinet were making some excessively gloomy predictions during the Czech crisis. Germany's own weaknesses were not considered. The value of the Czech army was ignored. Britain's vulnerability to aerial attack was repeatedly stressed, but without consideration of whether the Luftwaffe would or could throw itself against London while Germany was engaged in a central European war. Furthermore, the cabinet minutes reveal that when some ministers (Duff Cooper, Stanley) actually wanted to take a stronger stand against Hitler, despite the risks to Britain and its empire, they were swiftly overwhelmed by counter-arguments from Chamberlain and his friends.[47] Objectors within the cabinet had to be silenced, just as the press and the BBC had to be controlled. Even when, by early-to-mid 1939, British public opinion was moving strongly against appeasement, when Britain's aerial defenses were much improved, and when the dominions were more supportive of a firm line, Chamberlain and his fellow-appeasers were still seeking, in secret rather than in the open, to buy off Hitler. After Prague, making concessions to Germany was neither as logical nor as "natural" as it might have been in 1926 and 1936; on the contrary, it seemed to many a policy lacking in both practical wisdom and moral idealism. Yet it was still being attempted by Downing Street, which suggests that the convictions of individuals – in this case, Chamberlain's – must play a central part in our explanation of British policy, which cannot be fully understood simply in terms of "objective" strategical and economic realities.

Appeasement, then, is not a simple phenomenon which can be defined in a few sharp words. Older histories tend to see it as a shameful and bankrupt policy of surrender to the dictator-states. Taylor has portrayed it as a series of well-meaning bungles which eventually embroiled both Hitler and the west in a war neither of them desired. Some scholars have seen it as a natural and rational strategy in the light of Britain's weaknesses in the world by the 1930s. Others have pointed out that it was, albeit in a more intensified form, a normal continuation of the British diplomatic tradition of attempting to settle disputes peacefully.

Appeasement was, in fact, all of the above, and needs to be understood as such. It also needs to be investigated at different levels of causality, so that distinctions can be made between the nebulous, sometimes confused mentality of the appeasers on the one hand, and the cluster of military or economic or imperial or domestic–political motives which justified, or seemed to justify, concessions to the dictators on the other. Only when it is approached in such a way will the historians rise above simplistic one dimensional descriptions, and deal with appeasement as the complex, variegated, shifting phenomenon which it really was. This essay, then, closes with a call for further work on appeasement. Taylor's book, together with the opening of official and private archives, provoked and inspired a flood of scholarship on British policy in the 1930s. Although the tide has ebbed, it should be clear that many subjects remain inadequately explored. One can hope that the recognition of appeasement's complex nature will spur scholars to examine all aspects of British policy before the Second World War.

Notes

1 This essay is concerned with the text of the original (1961) edition of Taylor's *The Origins of the Second World War*, and not with the "Second thoughts" Foreword of the 1963 edition, nor with either "War origins again," *Past & Present*, no. 30, 1965, or "1939 revisited," the 1981 Annual Lecture of the German Historical Institute, London.

2 Intelligence records remain a notable exception, and thus far only official historians have gained access to them. See F. H. Hinsley *et al.*, *British Intelligence in the Second World War: Its Influence on Strategy and Operations*, vol. 1, London, 1979. For efforts to trace intelligence records by roundabout means, see D. Dilks, "Appeasement and intelligence," in D. Dilks (ed.), *Retreat from Power*, 2 vols, London, 1981, vol. 1, pp. 139–69; and Wesley K. Wark, *The Ultimate Enemy: British Intelligence and Nazi Germany, 1933–1939*, Ithaca, NY, 1985.

3 Taylor, "1939 revisited".

4 See Chapter 6, "Misjudging Hitler," in this collection of essays; G. L. Weinberg, *The Foreign Policy of Hitler's Germany*, 2 vols, Chicago, IL, 1970 and 1980; N. Rich, *Hitler's War Aims*, vol. 1, New York, 1973; W. Carr, *Arms, Autarky and Aggression*, London, 1972; E. Jäckel, *Hitler's World View*, Cambridge, MA, 1981; K. Hildebrand, *The Foreign Policy of the Third Reich*, London, 1973; Wilhem Deist *et al.* (eds), *Germany and the Second World War*, vol. 1: *The Build-Up of German Aggression*, Oxford, 1990, are all helpful here.

5 The general survey literature is now so large as to be almost beyond control; but historiographical pieces to note are D. C. Watt, "The historiography of appeasement," in A. Sked and C. Cook (eds), *Crisis and Controversy*, London, 1976; D. Dilks, "Appeasement revisited," *University of Leeds Review*, 1972, pp. 38–49; P. Kennedy, "Reading history: appeasement," *History Today*, October 1982, pp. 51–3. There are also very important analyses by German scholars such as B. I. Wendt, G. Schmidt, G. Niedhart, W. Gruner, R. Meyers, and others – some flavor of which can be gleaned from the important collection, edited by W. J. Mommsen and L. Kettenacker, *The Fascist Challenge and the Policy of Appeasement*, London, 1983, and summarized in part in P. Kennedy, "The logic of appeasement," *Times Literary Supplement*, May 28, 1982.

6 The works by Wheeler Bennett, Namier, and Churchill are very much in this tone, as are pro-Moscow books and articles. For a recent restatement of this view, see Sidney Aster, " 'Guilty Men': The case of Neville Chamberlain,' " in Robert Boyce and Esmonde M. Robertson (eds), *Paths to War: New Essays on the Origins of the Second World War*, London, 1989, pp. 233–68.

7 The literature on the Holocaust is massive, but see Raul Hilberg, *The Destruction of the European Jews*, New York, 1985 edn; Michael Burleigh and Wolfgang Wippermann, *The Racial State: Germany, 1933–1945*, Cambridge, 1991; Christopher Browning, *Ordinary Men: Reserve Battalion 101 and the Final Solution in Poland*, New York, 1992; Saul Friedlander, *Nazi Germany and the Jews*, New York, 1997. A useful historiographical summary is Michael Marrus, *The Holocaust in History*, Hanover, NH, 1987.

8 Some sense of this outrage can be gleaned from contributions in E. M. Robertson (ed.), *The Origins of the Second World War*, London, 1971, and W. R. Louis (ed.), *The Origins of the Second World War: A. J. P. Taylor and His Critics*, New York, 1972. The most sustained repudiation of the Taylor line is in volume 2 of Weinberg's *Foreign Policy of Hitler's Germany*, which is meaningfully subtitled *Starting World War II, 1937–1939*. D. C. Watt's panoramic study also identifies Hitler as chiefly responsible for the war: see *How War Came: The Immediate Origins of the Second World War, 1938–1939*, London, 1989, p. 610. See also Deist *et al.*, *Germany and the Second World War*, vol. 1.

9 M. Gilbert and R. Gott, *The Appeasers*, London, 1963.

10 David Dutton, *Simon: A Political Biography of Sir John Simon*, London, 1992; Robert Rhodes James, *Anthony Eden*, London, 1987; David Dutton, *Anthony Eden: A Life and Reputation*, New York, 1997.

11 Compare Taylor's remarks on Henderson with A. L. Goldman, "Two views of Germany: Nevile Henderson vs. Vansittart and the foreign office, 1937–39," *British Journal of International Studies*, vol. 6, 1980, pp. 247–77. A good recent treatment of Henderson is D. C. Watt, "Chamberlain's ambassadors," in Michael Dockrill and Brian McKercher (eds), *Diplomacy and World Power: Studies in British Foreign Policy, 1890–1950*, Cambridge, 1996, pp. 145–54.

12 Compare M. Cowling, *The Impact of Hitler*, Cambridge, 1975, pp. 271ff. R. A. C. Parker also has some astute comments on Halifax in *Chamberlain and Appeasement: British Policy and the Coming of the Second World War*, London, 1993, pp. 122–3; as does D. C. Watt, *How War Came*, pp. 79–80. Also see Andrew Roberts, *The "Holy Fox": A Biography of Lord Halifax*, London, 1991.

13 Cowling, *Impact of Hitler*; Colvin, *The Chamberlain Cabinet*, London, 1971; K. Middlemas, *Diplomacy of Illusion*, London, 1972; C. Barnett, *The Collapse of British Power*, London and New York, 1972. The best recent study of Chamberlain is Parker, *Chamberlain and Appeasement*.

14 Some of these ups-and-downs are covered in L. W. Fuchser, *Neville Chamberlain and Appeasement*, New York, 1982. See also D. C. Watt's perceptive essay, "Misfortune, misconception, mistrust: episodes in British policy and the approach of war, 1938–1939," in M. Bentley and J. Stevenson (eds), *High and Low Politics in Modern Britain*, Oxford, 1983, pp. 214–54.

15 Aster, *Guilty Men*; John Charmley, *Chamberlain and the Lost Peace*, London, 1989; Parker, *Chamberlain and Appeasement*. D. Dilks, *Neville Chamberlain*, vol. 1, Cambridge, 1984, only goes to the year 1929.

16 Cowling, *Impact of Hitler*.

17 Cowling, *Impact of Hitler*. Charmley, in *Chamberlain and the Lost Peace*, argues this point with particular gusto, suggesting even that resistance to German expansion to the point of war was not in Britain's long-term strategic interests. Charmley, however, downplays the potential costs to Britain – both material and moral – of a German conquest of Europe.

18 N. Thompson, *The Anti-Appeasers*, Oxford, 1971, confirms Cowling's descriptions of these divisions, as does D. Carlton in his critical biography *Anthony Eden*, London, 1981. For a study of an earlier period which makes use of Conservative constituency records, see Stuart Ball, *Baldwin and the Conservative Party: The Crisis of 1929–1931*, New Haven, CT, 1988. The best study of Labour's foreign policy remains J. F. Naylor, *Labour's International Policy*, London, 1969, pp. 252ff. But also see Ben Pimlott, *Labour and the Left in the 1930s*, Cambridge, 1977, and *Hugh Dalton*, London, 1985.

19 The literature is now too extensive to be listed in its entirety, but readers can consult M. Ceadel, *Pacifism in Britain 1914–45*, Oxford, 1980; D. S. Birn, *The League of Nations' Union, 1918–1945*, London, 1981; D. Lukowitz, "British pacifists and appeasement," *Journal of Contemporary History*, vol. 9, 1974, pp.115–28. For the right (apart from the works on fascism in Britain), see R. Griffiths, *Fellow-Travellers of the Right*, London, 1980.

20 F. R. Gannon, *The British Press and Germany, 1936–39*, Oxford, 1971; J. Lewis, *The Left Book Club*, London, 1970; D. Waley, *British Public Opinion and the Abyssinian War, 1935–36*, London, 1975; K. W. Watkins, *Britain Divided: The Effect of the Spanish Civil War on British Public Opinion*, London, 1963.

21 On which, see Weinberg, *Foreign Policy of Hitler's Germany*, vol. 1, pp. 516ff.; T. Taylor, *Munich: The Price of Peace*, London, 1979, pp. 937ff. See also the excellent analysis of the erosion of pro-appeasement feelings during late 1938 and early 1939 in L. Kettenacker, "Die Diplomatie der Ohnmacht," in W. Benz and H. Graml (eds), *Sommer 1939. Die Grossmächte und der Europäische Krieg*, Stuttgart, 1979, esp. pp. 239, 247ff. Watt, in *How War Came*, pp. 99–108, treats the shift in official opinion.

22 This is not to say that the *Telegraph* or the *Manchester Guardian* did not share, to some extent, the relief that war had been avoided in 1938, but their line was altogether much firmer than the government's. See Gannon, *British Press and Germany*;

Thompson, *The Anti-Appeasers*, pp. 165ff.; P. Kennedy, "Idealists and realists: British views of Germany, 1864–1939," *Transactions of the Royal Historical Society*, series 5, vol. 25, 1975, pp. 154ff.

23 A. Adamthwaite, "The British government and the media," *Journal of Contemporary History*, vol. 18, 1983, pp. 281–97. Also see Richard Cockett, *Twilight of Truth: Chamberlain, Appeasement, and the Manipulation of the Press*, London, 1989.

24 Kettenacker, "Die Diplomatie der Ohnmacht."

25 P. Kennedy, "The tradition of appeasement in British foreign policy, 1865–1939," *British Journal of International Studies*, vol. 2, 1976, pp. 195–215; I. W. D. Gruner, "The British political, social and economic system and the decision for peace and war: reflections on Anglo-German relations, 1800–1939," *British Journal of International Studies*, vol. 6, 1980, pp. 189–218; M. Gilbert, *The Roots of Appeasement*, London, 1966.

26 A. J. P. Taylor, *The Struggle for Mastery in Europe, 1848–1918*, Oxford, 1954. Also see P. Kennedy, *The Rise and Fall of the Great Powers: Economic Change and Military Conflict from 1500 to 2000*, London, 1988, pp. 275–343.

27 D. Reynolds, *The Creation of the Anglo-American Alliance, 1937–41*, London, 1981; C. A. MacDonald, *The United States, Britain and Appeasement*, London, 1981.

28 Compare G. Niedhart, *Grossbritannien und die Sowjetunion, 1934–1939*, Munich, 1972, as well as the two very good articles by Niedhart and Hewdon, in Mommsen and Kettenacker (eds), *Fascist Challenge*. Also see Parker, *Chamberlain and Appeasement*, pp. 216–45, which echoes Taylor on Chamberlain's anti-Soviet prejudices. Also useful is Anita Prazmowska, *Britain, Poland and the Eastern Front, 1939*, Cambridge, 1987. The pro-Moscow versions are briskly (perhaps too briskly?) dealt with in D. N. Lammers, *Explaining Munich: The Search for Motive in British Policy*, Stanford, CA, 1966.

29 For the military aspects, see especially M. Howard, *The Continental Commitment*, London, 1972, chs 4–6. For the general political and cultural side see A. Wolfers, *Britain and France Between Two Wars*, New York, 1966 (first published 1940); J. C. Cairns, "A nation of shopkeepers in search of a suitable France, 1919–1940," *American Historical Review*, vol. 79, 1974, pp. 710–43, and the brief but pertinent comments in E. M. Gates, *End of the Affair*, London, 1981, pp. 895ff. More recent treatments are Martin S. Alexander, *The Republic in Danger. General Maurice Gamelin and the Politics of French Defence, 1933–1940*, Cambridge, 1992, pp. 236–78; P. M. H. Bell, *France and Britain, 1900–1940*, London, 1996, pp. 167–231.

30 See F. M. Hardie, *The Abyssinian Crisis*, London, 1974, whose definition of appeasement (p. 4) is "not mere failure to resist an act of aggression but connivance at it." For Abyssinia, see also Gaines Post, Jr, *Dilemmas of Appeasement: British Deterrence and Defense, 1934–1937*, Ithaca, NY, 1993, pp. 81–115. Locarno and its results are covered in J. Jacobson, *Locarno Diplomacy: Germany and the West, 1925–1929*, Princeton, NJ, 1972; A. Orde, *Britain and International Security, 1920–1926*, London, 1978. The 1932–3 Disarmament conference is covered in the excellent book by E. W. Bennett, *German Rearmament and the West 1932–1933*, Princeton, NJ, 1979.

31 A. J. Marder, "The Royal Navy and the Ethiopian crisis of 1935–36," *American Historical Review*, vol. 75, 1970, pp. 1,327–56.

32 On which see the important study by C. Thorne, *The Limits Of Foreign Policy: The West, the League and the Far Eastern Crisis of 1931–1933*, London, 1972.

33 E. H. Haraszti, *Treaty-Breakers or Realpolitiker? The Anglo-German Naval Agreement of June 1935*, Boppard, 1973; D. C. Watt, "The Anglo-German naval agreement of 1935," *Journal of Modern History*, vol. 28, 1956, pp. 155–75; J. Dülffer, "Des deutsch–englische Flottenabkommen vom 18. Juni 1935," in W. Michalka (ed.), *Nationalsozialistische Aussenpolitik*, Darmstadt, 1978, pp. 244–76.

34 On the German side, see W. W. Schmokel, *Dream of Empire: German Colonialism, 1919–1945*, New Haven, CT, 1964, and K. Hildebrand, *Vom Reich zum Weltreich*, Munich, 1969. On the British side, see Andrew Crozier, *Appeasement and Germany's Last Bid for Colonies*, London, 1988, and the coverage in Gilbert and Gott's *Appeasers*.

35 D. C. Watt, "Appeasement, the rise of a revisionist school?", *Political Quarterly*, vol. 36, 1965, pp. 191–213.

36 For Keynes, see Roger Middleton, *Towards a Managed Economy: Keynes, the Treasury and the Fiscal Policy Debates in the 1930s*, London, 1985; P. F. Clarke, *The Keynsian Revolution in the Making, 1924–1936*, Oxford, 1988. For obstacles to rearmament, see R. A. C. Parker, "British rearmament 1936–9: treasury, trade unions and skilled labour," *English Historical Review*, 1981, pp. 306–43; G. A. H. Gordon, *British Seapower and Procurement Between the Wars: A Reappraisal of Rearmament*, London, 1988. For the political economy of rearmament, see the relevant and provocative sections of Keith Middlemass, *Politics and Industrial Society: The Experience of the British System since 1911*, London, 1979, and Correlli Barnett, *The Audit of War: The Illusion and Reality of Britain as a Great Power*, London, 1996 edn. For a challenge to the notion of decline, see Gordon Martel, "The meaning of power: rethinking the decline and fall of Great Britain," *International History Review*, vol. 13, 1991, pp. 662–94.

37 Cited in R. P. Shay, Jr, *British Rearmament in the Thirties: Politics and Profits*, Princeton, NJ, 1977, p. 243. Also very important is G. C. Peden, *British Rearmament and the Treasury, 1932–1939*, Edinburgh, 1979. Many of these points are summarized in P. Kennedy, "Strategy versus diplomacy in twentieth-century Britain," *International History Review*, vol. 3, 1981, pp. 45–61.

38 Barnett, *Collapse of British Power*, ch. 5, analyzes the role of the strategic advisers; but see also N. Gibbs, *Grand Strategy*, vol. 1, London, 1976, and R. Meyers, *Britische Sicherheitspolitik, 1934–1938*, Düsseldorf, 1976. The general findings of these works are reviewed in P. Kennedy, "Appeasement and British defence policy in the inter-war years," *British Journal of International Studies*, vol. 4, 1978, pp. 161–77.

39 British naval policy is covered in S. Roskill, *Naval Policy Between the Wars*, 2 vols, London, 1968 and 1976. The strategical "juggling-act'" is covered nicely in L. R. Pratt, *East of Malta, West of Suez: Britain's Mediterranean Crisis, 1936–1939*, Cambridge, 1975.

40 Howard's *Continental Commitment* covers the army's dilemma well, but the most thorough study now is B. Bond, *British Military Policy Between the Two World Wars*, Oxford, 1980.

41 Among the innumerable studies on air policy and aerial defense, see U. Bialer, *The Shadow of the Bomber: The Fear of Air Attack and British Politics, 1932–1939*, London, 1980; H. Montgomery Hyde, *British Air Policy Between the Wars*, London, 1976, and M. Smith, *British Air Strategy Between the Wars*, Oxford, 1984.

42 Cited in Howard, *Continental Commitment*, pp. 120–1.

43 Barnett, *Collapse of British Power*, is best here; but see also R. Ovendale, *Appeasement and the English-Speaking World*, Cardiff, 1975; R. Meyers, "Britain, Europe and the dominions in the 1930s," *Australian Journal of Politics and History*, vol. 22, 1976, pp. 36–50; and Max Beloff, *Imperial Sunset*, vol. 2: *Dream of Commonwealth, 1921–42*, London, 1989.

44 W. R. Louis, *British Strategy in the Far East, 1919–1929*, Oxford, 1971; C. Thorne, *Allies of a Kind*, Oxford, 1978; S. L. Endicott, *Diplomacy and Enterprise: British China Policy, 1933–1937*, Vancouver, 1973; A. Trotter, *Britain and East Asia, 1933–1937*, Cambridge, 1975; B. A. Lee, *Britain and the Sino-Japanese War, 1937–1939*, Stanford, CA, 1973; W. D. McIntyre, *The Rise and Fall of the Singapore Naval Base*, London, 1979; J. Neidpath, *The Singapore Naval Base and the Defence of Britain's Eastern Empire, 1919–1941*, Oxford, 1981; A. J. Marder, *Old Friends, New Enemies: the Royal Navy and the Imperial Japanese Navy*, Oxford, 1981; P. Haggie, *Britannia at Bay: The Defence of the British Empire Against Japan*, Oxford, 1981; P. Lowe, *Great Britain and the Origins of the Pacific War, 1937–1941*, Oxford, 1977; A. Shai, *Origins of the War in the East: Britain, China, and Japan, 1937–41*, London, 1976.

45 See, again, Kennedy, "Strategy versus diplomacy."

46 P. W. Schroeder, "Munich and the British tradition," *Historical Journal*, vol. 19, 1976, p. 242. Also see Charmley, *Chamberlain and the Lost Peace*, p. 210–12.
47 Barnett, *Collapse of British Power*, pp. 505–20. For more assessments of the balance, see W. Murray, *The Change in the European Balance of Power, 1938–1939*, Princeton, NJ, 1984, esp. ch. 7.

8 Debating the role of Russia in the origins of the Second World War

Teddy J. Uldricks

The central characters in A. J. P. Taylor's *The Origins of the Second World War* are Hitler and a succession of British and French statesmen. Soviet Russia is ascribed a lesser role, as earlier critics have pointed out.[1] For Taylor, the really important action takes place in Berlin, London and Paris, not Moscow. This is a serious weakness because, by "tilting" his analysis to the west, Taylor limits himself to an incomplete and interpretively distorted account of Europe's descent into war. Ironically, this western orientation leads Taylor seriously to underestimate the influence of anti-Communism and Russophobia within the British leadership.

The Soviet state is largely absent from the early chapters of the book. In Taylor's view Russia had fallen from the ranks of the Great Powers by 1918. He even goes so far as to refer in several places to the "disappearance" of Russia.[2] It is certainly true that the Bolshevik regime did not at first enjoy the same material base of military strength relative to the other European powers that its imperial predecessor had possessed, and that this shift in the balance of power benefited Germany. Yet, contrary to Taylor, the USSR had not disappeared. In fact, the western nations – mesmerized by the threat of revolution – may well have accorded more attention to communist Russia than they ever had paid to the Romanov empire. This oversight, fostered by Taylor's disinclination to give weight to ideological factors in international relations, causes him to misinterpret western policy in a number of important ways. For example, he criticizes the Allies for leaving Germany united and, thus, still potentially the strongest country on the continent. But this judgment misses the critical point that the victors, for all their hatred for the defeated enemy, felt that they needed Germany intact as an anti-Communist rampart in central Europe.[3]

Similarly, Taylor's aversion to the ideological factor causes him to write of the Bolsheviks' "sense of security" during the decade after the First World War (pp. 40–1). He assumes that the Soviet leaders must not have felt threatened, because he knows in hindsight that no other power attacked or even seriously planned to strike the USSR after the end of foreign intervention in the Russian Civil War. Bolshevik perceptions were, in fact, quite different. The belief that the imperialist powers intended to renew their bloody assault on the homeland of socialism was an article of faith in the Kremlin. The Dawes plan, the Locarno accords, German membership in the League of Nations and the Young plan were each interpreted in Moscow as parts of a concerted imperialist strategy to undo the October Revolution. These fears may have been unrealistic, but they were real.[4] Having dismissed these fears as either rhetorical or manipulative devices, Taylor underrates the tremendous importance the Rapallo treaty had for the Russians (pp. 52–3).[5] Both emotionally and ideologically, it was the centerpiece of the Soviet diplomatic system. It gave the Bolsheviks some minimal reassurance that a united phalanx of capitalist powers was not yet poised to crush the Soviet experiment.

Taylor's treatment of Soviet foreign policy, and also of the USSR as a factor in the diplomacy of other powers, is somewhat better for the 1930s than for the previous decade: his self-proclaimed historical "intuition" seems to serve him better in this period.[6] There is for the 1930s a somewhat more extensive coverage of Moscow's significance in European affairs, though the amount of attention accorded Soviet Russia is still not proportional to its actual role in the origins of the Second World War. The Soviet Union still did not fully re-emerge, in his view, as a European Great Power until the signing of the Nazi–Soviet Pact in August 1939 (p. 216). Taylor is also willing to give Soviet anxieties more credence in the Hitler era. He sees that the Kremlin perceived every diplomatic combination which excluded them (Mussolini's projected Four-Power Pact, the Munich conference, etc.) as a conspiracy against the USSR. He recognizes that the defensive pacts which the USSR signed with France and Czechoslovakia did not allay those fears and suspicions. Because the French refused to give it substantive military content, the Franco-Soviet agreement remained an "empty" gesture (p. 85).[7] That, in turn, vitiated the alliance with Prague, which was dependent on relations between Paris and Moscow.

The subject of British views of and policy toward the USSR is, on the whole, perceptively handled in *The Origins of the Second World War*. Taylor demonstrates that the British government constantly rebuffed the attempts of the Kremlin to draw it and France into a system of collective security against the menace of Nazi aggression. Far from aiming at alliance, it was the exclusion of the Soviet Union from European affairs that was a consistent British objective. Chamberlain did not trust the Kremlin, nor did he respect its strength. Moreover, he assumed that an alliance with Russia would provoke Hitler, thus making war more, rather than less, likely. The only really significant gap in Taylor's description of British policy toward the USSR is, once again, the omission of its ideological underpinnings. He seriously underestimates the strength of anti-Communism as a motive force in British foreign policy, not only toward Soviet Russia, but in regard to Germany as well.[8] Thus, Taylor notes, the great purges (especially the destruction of the Soviet officer corps) reinforced the Prime Minister's belief that the USSR was scarcely worth having as an ally, but he misses the more important point that Chamberlain was doctrinally opposed to any real alliance with the Communist state – even had Stalin been a benevolent ruler instead of a bloody tyrant.[9]

French foreign policy and diplomacy is treated in much less detail. Taylor follows the traditional interpretation of France as a self-imposed captive of

British policy. The French, as he notes, grew more anxious for a binding military convention with the USSR as the German threat continually mounted in the late 1930s. A powerful Franco-Soviet alliance never emerged, however, due to British opposition. Instead of recreating the Triple Entente, Paris had to choose between two alternative dual alliances – London or Moscow.

The steady progression of German advances from the announcement of rearmament to the absorption of Czechoslovakia finally produced a partial reassessment of British appeasement. After the German seizure of Prague, London responded more positively to the Soviet collective security campaign. Yet even at this juncture, Taylor suggests, "the British government, in fact, were not interested in solid military co-operation with Soviet Russia; they merely wanted to chalk a Red bogey on the wall, in the hope that this would keep Hitler quiet" (p. 246). Opening talks with Moscow was also a strategy for keeping their French ally in line. The British reluctantly took the lead in negotiations with the Soviets during 1939, Taylor suspects, because they feared that if they did not do so, France might make binding military commitments with the USSR which could subsequently drag Britain into war as well (p. 226).

The negotiations between the western powers and the Soviet Union in the spring and summer of 1939 never had much chance of success. The two sides came to the talks with divergent goals and expectations. The British still hoped that war could be avoided. If it could not be prevented, they thought that western forces, together with those of Poland, would bear the brunt of the fighting. Given the purge-ravaged condition of the Red Army, they looked to Russia as only a supply base, not as the main striking force of the prospective alliance. In addition, western strategy anticipated a long war of attrition, much like the First World War, in which Germany would be worn down by a prolonged blockade. The Soviet role in such a conflict would be limited to supplying and supporting a static eastern front in Poland and Romania. The Soviets saw things differently. They had little faith that war could be avoided, and even less confidence in the Polish army. They sought an alliance with Britain and France that included iron-clad military commitments, in which the Soviet army would play an aggressive and leading role from the onset of hostilities. They were convinced that only a great Franco-Soviet offensive on two fronts could prevent German victory. Differing forecasts of war or peace as well as divergent expectations of the nature of a possible conflict, thus erected further barriers to co-operation between the western democracies and the USSR (p. 247).[10] Chamberlain doubted the value of a defense pact with the Soviet Union, but he was sure that, if such a treaty were signed, the presence of the Red Army in east-central Europe would be neither necessary nor desirable. Therefore, he saw no need to force the Poles or the Romanians to grant transit rights to large Soviet military formations. The Polish regime's refusal to permit the passage of Soviet troops was allowed to stand as the apparent barrier to an Anglo-Russian alliance which the British government did not want in the first place (pp. 205–6, 247).

In contrast to his relatively thorough and insightful treatment of British relations with the USSR, Taylor's characterization of Nazi policy toward

Bolshevik Russia is completely inadequate. The source of this problem – the fundamental error which runs throughout the book – is the author's failure to take Hitler's ideas seriously. Taylor cannot believe that anyone would make the insane (and ultimately suicidal) National Socialist racist doctrines the basis for national policy. Instead, he treats Hitler as if the Nazi dictator were a rational and practical, if rather wicked, English statesman. Having dismissed Hitler's racist ideology as meaningless rhetoric with no bearing on the operative goals of the Reich, Taylor has lost touch with the wellsprings of Nazi behavior. Refusing to admit the racist core of the *Lebensraum* doctrine, he must try to explain it as an "economic" idea. That, in turn, leads him to waste time refuting the economic explanation of Germany's entry into the war (p. 105).[11] Taylor notes that Hitler was gravely concerned about the explosive growth of Soviet economic power, but denies that he had any long-range plans to attack the USSR. Hitler could not have harbored any aggressive intent toward Russia because, in Taylor's judgment, he did not adequately prepare for a major war (pp. 211–12). That might be a justifiable assumption in regard to a Bismarck or a Palmerston, but not to Hitler. In reality, his conception of *Lebensraum* necessitated the conquest of the Ukraine and the extermination of its population.

As noted above, Taylor does not devote to the motives and actions of Soviet diplomacy the attention he gives to those of Germany, Britain, or even France. The primary motives of Stalin's foreign policy during the 1930s, in his view, were fear of attack by one or more of the imperialist powers and the desire to stay out of a European war. Taylor argues that the principal objective of Soviet diplomacy, from the beginning of the collective security campaign in 1934 to its bankruptcy in 1939, was the construction of a solid military barrier to Nazi aggression, in cooperation with the western democracies. The USSR, like Britain, occasionally entertained the possibility of closer ties with Germany, but he dismisses these gambits as mere "soundings," unrepresentative of the overall thrust of Soviet policy. Throughout the period, a defensive pact with London and Paris, not an offensive alliance with Berlin, remained Moscow's primary goal (pp. 224–6, 232–3, 249). This controversial interpretation (with which I agree) is discussed in more detail in relation to the historiographical issues below.

Taylor is considerably less critical of Soviet diplomacy during the 1930s than many other western historians. He considers the collective security strategy to have been rational and appropriate to Russian national interest. He assumes the Kremlin pursued this course straightforwardly until finally deflected from it in 1939 by continual western rejection. Decreasing Soviet aid to the Republican forces in Spain is, therefore, seen as a reaction to the growing Japanese menace in the far east, rather than as an early sign of Moscow's disenchantment with the west (pp. 158–9). On the hotly-debated issue of whether the Soviets would have come to the aid of Czechoslovakia during the Munich crisis, had the Czechs and the western powers stood their ground, Taylor suspects that they would (p. 167). In the matter of transit rights for the Red Army through eastern Europe, however, he admits the possibility that Stalin may have had territorial designs on his neighbors but he still criticizes western statesmen for rationalizing the rejection of an alliance with the USSR on such hypothetical grounds. He is willing to accept the Soviet contention that a major Russian offensive through Poland and Romania was necessary to defeat Germany (pp. 246–8). He also believes that the Kremlin was reluctant to abandon its collective security campaign as late as August 1939, and he even suggests that Molotov may have deliberately stalled negotiations with Germany in order to give the democracies one more chance (p. 250). When the Soviets finally chose to deal with Hitler, Taylor contends, "the Russians, in fact, did only what western statesmen had hoped to do" (p. 252). Finally, he argues that the Nazi–Soviet Pact should not be considered an aggressive alliance – a conclusion which is difficult to support in view of Soviet territorial gains and the degree to which the Soviet economy functioned as the primary supplier of several otherwise unobtainable resources for the German war machine from September 1939 to June 1941.

The Nazi–Soviet Pact and, more broadly, the nature and aims of Soviet foreign policy throughout the 1930s have been subjects of intense debate. The controversy encompasses extreme polarities and a wide spectrum of opinion between them. At one extreme is the official interpretation sponsored by the former Soviet government, according to which the USSR pursued a clear, unambiguous, and even noble policy of building a European-wide shield of collective security against Nazi aggression. This diplomatic course was based not on cynical self-interest or the desire for aggrandizement but on high principle, since the Soviet Union was said to represent the forces of historical progress and was, therefore, bound to take the lead in opposing the barbarous and retrogressive schemes of Nazi Germany. If collective security ultimately failed, it was not for lack of unstinting and sincere Soviet effort, but rather because of the treacherous failure of the western democracies to oppose Hitler's murderous plans. In the words of the authoritative *History of Soviet Foreign Policy*, co-edited by former foreign minister Andrei Gromyko:

> When the nazis seized power in Germany, the threat of another world war became very real in Europe. However, at the time it was still possible to avert fascist aggression through the concerted efforts of countries desiring peace. Had the Soviet proposals for collective security been put into effect it would have been possible to erect a powerful barrier to any aggressor....But this project was wrecked by the joint efforts of the fascist states and Poland with British encouragement....In this atmosphere the Soviet Union never for a moment relinquished its efforts to create a system of collective security.[12]

Soviet commentators also minimized the significance of the Russo-German non-aggression treaty and rationalized it as necessitated by the grave threat of German and Japanese attacks on the USSR, combined with the betrayal of the cause of collective security by Britain and France. The Soviets contended that the pact could not be considered in any sense an alliance with Nazi Germany, while they ignored, and sometimes even denied the existence of, the secret protocol that divided all of eastern Europe between Hitler and Stalin.[13]

At the opposite extreme is the allegation that collective security against aggression was never the Kremlin's real objective, but only a front behind which Stalin sought throughout the decade to woo a reluctant Hitler into an aggressive alliance.[14] Robert Tucker has advanced an especially radical version of this interpretation. He contends that, as far back as 1925, Stalin determined to divide the capitalist states against each other and maneuver them into a mutually destructive inter-imperialist war, from which the USSR would emerge unscathed and in a strong position to expand territorially all along its borders. To bring about this war Stalin allegedly aided Hitler's rise by deliberately steering the policy of the Comintern and the German Communist Party on a suicidal course. The Nazi–Soviet Pact was, in this view, always implicit in Stalin's plans, while the collective security line was never anything more than a mask for his designs and a bait to attract Hitler.[15] Arguing along similar lines, R. C. Raack contends that Stalin wanted the outbreak of war in Europe as much as Hitler did. Stalin is said to have anticipated a prolonged war of attrition which would weaken both Germany and the western democracies, breed revolution throughout Europe, and thereby create an opportunity for the Red Army to aid proletarian insurrections in the west.[16]

There is very little evidence to support these theories. Lacking any direct evidence, Tucker must rely on a painstaking (and often strained) exegesis of certain portions of Stalin's published writings. Yet the Soviet dictator's statements were sometimes ambiguous and often ran counter to the thesis Tucker is trying to sustain.[17] The ambitious and aggressive policy of collusion with Germany, which Tucker ascribes to Stalin, is not a continuation of the Rapallo orientation, as he claims. The Rapallo policy, though certainly designed to split the imperialist camp by courting Weimar Germany, was a defensive strategy aimed at preventing the outbreak of a war in central Europe that could easily draw in the USSR. The course of action which Tucker describes is a reckless high-risk strategy. Hitler was that sort of desperate gambler; Stalin was not. Tucker also has suggested that the purges were necessary to clear away the opposition within the Bolshevik elite to an opportunistic deal with Hitler. Thus the great purges provide evidence, he argues, for his theory that collective security was always a ruse.[18] The problem with this argument is that Stalin had the wrong people killed. Among Soviet diplomats, for example, numerous senior officials with a strongly pro-Rapallo orientation, such as Nikolai Krestinskii and Lev Karakhan, were purged, while many of their pro-western colleagues, like Litvinov, Ivan Maiskii and Aleksandra Kollontai, were spared.[19]

A less extreme version of the theory that Stalin always preferred cooperation with Germany (whether Weimar or Nazi) to a defensive alliance with the western powers is advanced by Gerhard Weinberg. Although his major two-volume study concentrates on German foreign policy, Moscow's policy toward Berlin is an important sub-theme which is explored in some detail. He is especially interested in contacts between David Kandelaki, head of the Soviet trade mission in Berlin, and Hjalmar Schacht.[20] Although their tentative discussions did not lead to a Russo-German rapprochement, Weinberg is convinced that Stalin tolerated the collective security line only as a poor second choice while repeated Nazi rejections of Soviet feelers kept his preferred alternative – an agreement with Hitler – out of reach. Weinberg's version of Stalin's alleged preference for Germany over the democracies is certainly more temperately argued and more thoroughly researched than Tucker's or Raack's, but it, too, lacks sufficient evidence to be convincing. It makes 98 percent of all Soviet diplomatic activity in the 1930s a brittle cover for the remaining covert 2 percent. Lacking conclusive evidence to the contrary, it is more reasonable to assume that Soviet representatives spent the majority of their time and effort trying to accomplish their real objectives. Similarly, enormous energy was expended to propagate the Popular Front line in the Comintern and all foreign communist parties. These efforts were counterproductive to achieving a rapprochement with Nazi Germany. Moreover, the eventual abandonment of collective security and signing of the Nazi–Soviet Pact did incalculable harm to the communist movement around the world.[21] This suggests that the policy shift in August 1939 was not the culmination of a long and covert campaign, but a painful reorientation forced on Moscow by the failure of its collective security strategy.

When Taylor wrote *Origins* there was very little Soviet documentary and memoir material available on which to build an interpretation of Soviet conduct. His bibliography lists "Soviet Russia: Nothing." Since 1961 useful sources have appeared. The *Dokumenty vneshnei politiki SSSR* series began publication in 1957 and continued with a new volume each year until 1977. The series stopped suddenly, without any explanation, after the appearance of volume XXI, containing documents for 1938. The editors and, more importantly, the leadership of the Communist Party of the Soviet Union could not bring themselves to release sensitive, and potentially embarrassing, materials about the shift from collective security to the pact with Hitler in 1939. Not surprisingly, these published documents tend to show the Soviet Union pursuing a consistent and principled policy of anti-Fascism throughout the decade. Nonetheless, this official collection contains a great deal of valuable material, although it was tendentiously edited to support the party line.[22] Unfortunately, the editors omitted all documents relating to secret attempts by Kandelaki, Karl Radek, and Sergei Bessonov to seek a rapprochement with Berlin. Other governments, most notably the French and the Italian, have since 1961 issued substantial documentary collections which contain important evidence of Soviet diplomatic activities.

An interesting memoir, Evgenii Gnedin's *Katastrofa i vtoroe rozhdenie*, provides some glimpses behind the scenes of Soviet diplomacy.[23] Gnedin was first secretary at the Soviet embassy in Berlin and then press spokesman at the foreign Commissariat in Moscow during the latter half of the 1930s. In 1962 he was asked to prepare a report on Russo-German relations in the 1930s, in connection with a Central Committee investigation into the past "miscalculations and errors" of Molotov. In other words, Gnedin was requested to help with the compilation of politically damaging material against the former foreign commissar now in disfavor. The anti-Molotov project was subsequently scrapped, however, and Gnedin's commission to prepare the report was withdrawn. Gnedin did not abandon his research, although his work could not be published in the increasingly conservative Kremlin atmosphere after the fall of Khrushchev. Finally, in 1977 his writings began to appear abroad.

Gnedin believes that Stalin permitted Molotov to pursue a foreign policy different from the official collective security campaign then being waged by Litvinov. Under Molotov's direction, Gnedin contends, various non-diplomatic personnel (Kandelaki, Bessonov, and Radek) surreptitiously attempted to weld a Russo-German alliance. These initiatives were kept hidden not only from the western states, but were also carried out behind the backs of the foreign commissar and his diplomats. Gnedin angrily condemns Stalin and Molotov for undermining the anti-fascist and collective security policies. Gnedin's works contain a great deal of useful information about the Soviet system in the 1930s and the 1960s, but they are not an entirely reliable guide to Soviet diplomacy leading up to the Nazi–Soviet Pact. The author did not have access to Soviet archives, not even when he was preparing a quasi-official report for the Central Committee, so his memoirs rely heavily on personal recollection of events forty years old. The result is a number of obvious errors and discrepancies. Beyond that, as a relatively junior member of the Foreign Commissariat, Gnedin did not have access to Stalin or Molotov. Lacking either personal experience or uncensored documentary sources upon which to draw, his reconstruction of their activities is largely hypothetical. In addition, Gnedin was discharged from the diplomatic service in May 1939, so he has no direct knowledge of the events leading up to the Russo-German pact. Gnedin's judgment also has been affected (quite understandably) by his experiences as a prisoner in the *GULAG* system. He knows that Stalin and Molotov were evil men, so he assumes that they must have conducted an evil foreign policy.[24] Though informative in a number of respects, Gnedin's writings are something less than the all-revealing "insider" memoirs that they at first appear to be.

Moreover, in the absence of definitive documentary evidence, a number of other equally plausible explanations of the Radek–Kandelaki–Bessonov contacts can be advanced. For example, the German scholar Ingeborg Fleischhauer argues that these approaches to Berlin cannot be considered serious attempts by Moscow to secure an alliance with Germany. Instead, she contends, the Nazi–Soviet Pact had its origins in the persistent efforts of German diplomats who urged a Russo-German entente upon both Hitler and Stalin. She also suggests that German diplomats deliberately manipulated their reports back to Berlin so as to facilitate a Russo-German rapprochement and preserve peace.[25]

Memoirs and collections of diplomatic documents more recently available have been utilized extensively in two major studies of prewar Soviet foreign policy published in the 1980s. Jiri Hochman elaborates (with considerably more scholarly apparatus) on Gnedin's thesis that Molotov, with Stalin's blessing, systematically undermined Litvinov's attempts to build an anti-Nazi alliance.[26] Hochman, a veteran of the "Prague Spring" who emigrated to avoid further imprisonment after the Soviet crackdown, is disillusioned that Stalinist foreign policy was not "principled." He argues vehemently that, despite Litvinov's high-sounding rhetoric, the Soviet Union worked assiduously to ensure the failure of collective security. He is eager to prove the Soviet Union ill-intentioned at every turn. The Soviets, Hochman claims, did not want to strengthen their pact with France, did not wish to solve the troop transit issue with their east-European neighbors, never intended to come to the aid of Czechoslovakia under any circumstances and, finally, used the purges to dissolve the (supposed) resolution of Britain and France to take a firm stand against German aggression.

Hochman simply has not understood the real nature of the collective security campaign. When it fails to live up to the altruistic and "principled" image created by communist propagandists, Hochman rejects it, root and branch, as a thoroughly unprincipled and devious stratagem. Ironically, he commits the same error as apologists for the Soviet regime who claimed that the responsibility for failing to stand up to Hitler in time to prevent a disastrous war can be attributed to only one side. In actuality, both the USSR and the western democracies appeased Germany; both pursued short-sighted policies aimed at keeping themselves out of an approaching war, rather than at preventing or winning it. Hochman's work is also marred by his use of sources. He cites numerous documents from the Czech and Romanian archives, repositories that are generally closed to all except a few loyal to the regime, but does not discuss the provenance of these items. Worse still, he buttresses several points critical to his analysis with reference to a work entitled *Notes For a Journal*, which its publishers attribute to Maksim Litvinov.[27] Hochman does not seem to know that such knowledgeable Kremlinologists as Bertram Wolfe and Philip Mosely have denounced this work as a forgery. He makes no comment as to why he feels justified in employing this dubious source. He also follows the annoying practice, whenever he cannot find documents to prove his point, of assuming that such documents exist but are missing or have been suppressed. In fairness, it must also be said that even readers who reject the author's thesis will profit from reading this book. The discussion of negotiations with Romania for troop transit rights, for example, is more detailed than in any other study.

Jonathan Haslam's *The Soviet Union and the Struggle for Collective Security in Europe*, which appeared at about the same time as Hochman's book, is a much superior treatment of the subject.[28] Haslam used the full range of then available archival and published sources (except for a handful of east-European archival documents cited by Hochman), and he did so with great care. The most interesting aspect of Haslam's work is his ability to expose opposing factions within the Soviet foreign policy-formulating process. In his view the principal opponents of Commissar Litvinov, and therefore of the collective security strategy as well, were Molotov and Andrei Zhdanov. Haslam calls their foreign policy-orientation "isolationism," by which he means a combination of doubt about the possibility of achieving security in alliance with the democracies, nostalgia for the days of Rapallo-style cooperation with Germany and a desire to insulate the USSR from the war about to burst over Europe by avoiding commitments to any of the imperialist powers. Stalin, he believes, did not take a resolute position on either side of the argument between Litvinov and the isolationists. Instead, the Soviet dictator followed the alternative that appeared most likely to protect his state from a disastrous war – which meant the collective security line for most of the 1930s, until he despaired of its success at the end of the decade. Given the fragmentary evidence available, delineating Kremlin factions is a perilous enterprise for any scholar, but Haslam's conclusions are carefully reasoned and suitably tentative.[29]

This approach contrasts strongly with many earlier accounts of Soviet foreign policy in the 1930s which were influenced by the Cold War and by the then-dominant totalitarian model of Soviet behavior. That model depicts the Soviet state as a totalitarian monolith in which policy debates and political process, as normally understood, simply did not exist. Instead, this view portrays Stalin as the sole political actor in the Kremlin. He appears as a virtually omniscient, though diabolical, political chess master who plots his nefarious course many moves in advance. The model also suggests that totalitarian states require foreign enemies, war, and territorial conquests in order to maintain their domestic stability. Haslam's abandonment of the totalitarian perspective and his emphasis on genuine political differences in the Kremlin is supported by the work of Paul Raymond, who characterizes the Politburo debate over foreign policy options in the 1930s as "controlled pluralism." He sees the Soviet elite divided over a complex of crucial domestic and foreign policy issues, with Litvinov, Marshal Tukhashevskii, and others advocating collective security, while Molotov, Kaganovich, and others argued for a re-establishment of the old Berlin–Moscow nexus.[30] R. Craig Nation agrees that an "important body of opinion within the party hierarchy, including leaders closely linked to Stalin such as Viacheslav Molotov, Andrei Zhdanov, and Lazar Kaganovich, never accepted the legitimacy of Litvinov's program…"; but he cautions that "the most basic reality working to undermine support for collective security in Moscow was the unwillingness of the western powers and their eastern European allies to engage themselves unambiguously."[31] That conclusion is reinforced strongly by Michael Jabara Carley, who demonstrates the consistent and tenacious opposition of London and Paris to any collective security arrangement with Moscow.[32]

Haslam's book, along with the work of Geoffrey Roberts (discussed below), are the most realistic treatments now available of the evolution of Soviet foreign policy from collective security into the Nazi–Soviet Pact. Not only does Haslam attempt to demonstrate the diversity of opinion within the Kremlin leadership, he also gives full weight to the plethora of Soviet fears – fear of German aggression, fear of an anti-Soviet alliance between Germany and the western powers, fear that the democracies would "buy off" the fascist regimes by encouraging them to move eastward, fear of a Japanese attack, etc.[33] He avoids the trap of seeing Soviet policy as either sublimely "principled" or diabolically unprincipled. Instead, along with Taylor, Haslam assumes that the Kremlin elite was searching for whatever course would best protect the interests of the Soviet Union. Thus, Stalin's "preferred" policy is neither a defensive alliance with Britain and France nor a pact with Germany, but whatever policy would provide the greatest degree of security. Given the almost unrelenting hostility of the Nazi regime, the only alternative (before August 1939) was the collective security line.[34]

Haslam's interpretation of two crucial periods, the Czech crisis of 1938 and the dual set of negotiations in the summer of 1939, are particularly well argued and based on thorough research. He demonstrates that Stalin followed Litvinov's collective security line throughout 1938, as opposed to the "isolationist" alternative, and that the Soviets would have aided the Czechs against a German attack (at least if France did so, too). The Kremlin was still convinced that a show of resolution by Britain, France, and Russia together would have forced Hitler to back down, but the western powers were determined to appease Germany, so they undermined Soviet efforts for joint action.[35] Haslam places the blame for the breakdown of the collective security drive and for the signing of the Nazi–Soviet Pact squarely on Britain. He believes that Stalin did not make the final decision for a deal with Hitler until August. Up to that point, Soviet diplomacy still sought an alliance with the democracies, but their mutual suspicions and vastly different reading of the international situation prevented such an agreement.[36] "Confronted with the evident unwillingness of the Entente to provide immediate, concrete and water-tight guarantees for Soviet security in Europe...the Russians were left with little alternative," Haslam contends, "but an agreement with Germany creating a condominium in Eastern Europe."[37]

While debate over the nature and objectives of Stalin's foreign policy raged in the west, the writing of international history in the USSR remained caught in the icy grip of party orthodoxy well into the 1980s. Then, suddenly, that grip was broken in the *glasnost* era. Echoing poet Evgenii Evtushenko, Mikhail Gorbachev called for filling in the "blank spots" of Soviet history. However, Gorbachev initially had no wish to disseminate information which might embarrass the Soviet Union or undermine the legitimacy of Communist Party rule. The pace of change was slow at first. Well into the mid-1980s traditionalist senior historians still published essentially orthodox accounts of Soviet diplomacy before the Second World War, and they continued to deny the existence of the secret protocols to the Nazi–Soviet Pact. Inevitably, however, history soon became a weapon in the wider struggle between conservatives and reformers. Among the latter, Iurii Afanas'ev admitted the existence of the secret protocols, while Mikhail Semeriaga argued that it had been a mistake to accept a pact with Hitler rather than intensifying the pursuit of an alliance with Britain and France.[38] Seeking independence for Latvia, Lithuania, and Estonia, Baltic nationalists published the previously secret protocols, and Baltic historians denounced the Nazi–Soviet Pact and all that flowed from it as an illegitimate imperialistic conspiracy between Hitler and Stalin.[39]

The campaign to replace the pieties of party orthodoxy with a candid look at the Soviet past had become unstoppable. Colonel-general Dmitri Volkogonov, with access to state, party and military archives, published a massive, bombshell biography of Stalin. In the chapters on the origins of the Second World War, Volkogonov argues that Stalin consistently and sincerely pursued a collective security agreement with Britain and France, that Soviet forces would have come to the assistance of Czechoslovakia in 1938 had the western powers done so as well, and that Stalin agreed to a pact with Hitler only when it became apparent in August of 1939 that London and Paris would not conclude a binding military alliance with the USSR. At the same time, Volkogonov is highly critical of Stalin for the Great Purges, which undermined Soviet defenses and alienated potential allies in the west, and of territorial ambitions embodied in the secret protocols.[40] Although Volkogonov had uniquely wide access to previously closed archives, a trickle of important diplomatic documents began to appear in specialized journals and mass-circulation newspapers. Then in 1990, the Soviet foreign ministry published a two-volume collection of documents covering the period from September 1938 to May 1939. After the collapse of the USSR, the new Russian Federation government, with no mandate to defend the Soviet past, published a two-volume documentary compendium covering the whole of 1939.[41] Publication of the secret protocols in the 1990 collection had required a long period of study and debate by a special commission of the party's Central Committee under the leadership of Aleksandr Iakovlev, a leading reformer on the Politburo.[42]

Even the previously taboo issue of Soviet approaches to Germany during the 1930s was finally broached in Soviet scholarship. Using newly available archival material, Nikolai Abramov and Lev Bezymenskii address David Kandelaki's contacts with German officials. They readily admit these contacts, as well as the Kremlin's desire to avoid conflict with the Third Reich and to maintain a mutually beneficial economic relationship with Berlin. Yet, they reject the view that Kandelaki's probes amounted to a *sub rosa* alternative foreign policy conducted secretly by Stalin and Molotov. They demonstrate that Litvinov knew about Kandelaki's missions and that they constituted part of a unified, if multifaceted, foreign policy. The authors also suggest (as do the western historians Fleischhauer and Roberts) that these gambits were aimed at German officials, especially Schacht and Göring, who were thought to be less hostile toward the USSR than Hitler.[43]

Not everyone in Russia welcomed the tide of historical revisionism sweeping the country. Viacheslav Molotov, the man who signed the Nazi–Soviet Pact and its secret protocols, continued to claim in a series of published interviews that there never was a secret territorial deal between Stalin and Hitler. Similarly, the published memoirs of long-time Soviet Foreign Minister Andrei Gromyko repeated the orthodox view of Soviet diplomacy in the late 1930s.[44]

These dramatic revelations from the Soviet archives and the vigorous debate among Russian historians about the role of the USSR in the origins of the Second World War, have stimulated western scholars to reassess the topic as well. British historian Geoffrey Roberts has used the newly available Soviet documentation to reinforce and elaborate the position taken by Haslam and others, that collective security was genuinely the policy of the USSR in the 1930s.[45] In Roberts' view, Hitler's rejection of the Rapallo tradition and his implacable hostility to the USSR gave the Soviet leadership no choice but to seek an anti-German alliance with the western powers. Collective security was pursued with determination and patience by Moscow from December 1933 to August 1939. Of course, the Kremlin would have been happy to negotiate a rapprochement with Germany at any time during the decade, but only on terms which would have required a complete reversal of Hitler's aggressive foreign policy. Roberts argues powerfully that the Soviet Union sincerely pursued co-operation with Britain and France up to the time of the Munich conference in order to deter Nazi aggression. Munich convinced Stalin that war was now unavoidable, so thereafter the Soviet Union sought a full-scale war-fighting alliance with the western democracies. Only the collapse of these alliance negotiations in mid-August 1939, combined with tempting offers from Hitler, brought about the reversal of that policy and the signing of the Nazi–Soviet Pact.

The availability of recently published Soviet documents enables Roberts to analyze Russo-German relations in a much more sophisticated way. A revealing example concerns Aleksei Merekalov's memorandum of his meeting with Ernst Weizsäcker on April 17, 1939. This apparently pivotal meeting, known previously only through the German account, had led many western scholars to identify this as the point at which the Soviet government took the initiative in pursuing an agreement with Germany. However, Merekalov's report does not show any Soviet initiative for an improvement of political relations between Moscow and Berlin, and it indicates that it was the Germans who took the role of the pursuer in this courtship.[46] More broadly, after a number of contacts, Soviet diplomats reported to Moscow that their German counterparts took the lead in suggesting improved relations. The Soviets gained the impression from these gambits that there were important elements within the German diplomatic, industrial, and military elites who did not share the sharp antagonism of the Nazis toward the USSR. The Nazi regime, however, did not alter its anti-Soviet policies, so these hints of a possible rapprochement came to nothing.[47]

Roberts also departs from the common assumption that discipline, consistency, and overarching purposiveness typified Kremlin policy making. He characterizes Soviet foreign policy in the 1930s as often reactive, sometimes haphazard and accidental, and occasionally adrift. Whereas the formerly dominant totalitarian model portrayed the Soviet dictator as a bloodthirsty chess master, plotting his diabolical course many moves in advance, Roberts sees Stalin responding with increasing desperation to the uncontrollable rush of events. Thus, in his view, the Nazi–Soviet Pact did not inevitably lead to the invasion of eastern Poland, the Winter War with Finland, or the absorption of the Baltic republics. Instead, an initial policy of genuine neutrality gave way to one of expansion and quasi-alliance with Germany only under the pressure of events.[48]

The publication of new documents and the partial opening of Soviet archives have forced scholars to reexamine the question of whether the USSR would have come to the aid of Czechoslovakia against German aggression at the time of the Munich crisis, at least had France done so as well. Hochman and Igor Lukes have argued strongly that Stalin had no intention of honoring his treaty obligation to assist the Czechs.[49] Lukes has even gone so far as to suggest that Stalin was the only "winner" in the outcome of the Czech crisis since, he argues, it made war between Germany and the western powers almost inevitable.[50] Opposing the views of Hochman and Lukes, Hugh Ragsdale and Geoff Jukes demonstrate that there is evidence suggesting that Stalin would have fought for Czechoslovakia. Jukes uses the memoirs of Marshal M. V. Zakharov to show that, at the height of the Munich crisis, the Kiev Special Military District was ordered to mobilize and deploy a large proportion of its forces along its western boundary. The Belorussian Special Military District received similar instructions. In total the Red army may have deployed as many as 330,000 men along the central portion of its east-European frontier.[51] Critics have disputed the veracity of Zakharov's testimony, but Ragsdale has confirmed the accuracy of the marshal's account (and of documents subsequently published by the Soviet authorities) through his research in the records of Politburo meetings contained in the archives of the Communist Party. Ragsdale has found the original telegram transmitting the order for mobilization to the Kiev Special Military District.[52] It is, of course, impossible to prove definitively a hypothetical statement about what Stalin would have done had France honored its pledges to Czechoslovakia and had the whole crisis not been resolved so dishonorably at Munich. However, the evidence uncovered by Ragsdale suggests strongly that the USSR would have honored its treaty obligations had conditions for doing so materialized.[53]

The most recent major contribution to the study of Russia's role in the origins of the Second World War was written by the late Aleksandr Nekrich, who emigrated from the USSR in 1976 after his path-breaking 1965 work *June 22, 1941* proved to be too revealing in the repressive environment after Khrushchev's fall. Nekrich argues that the Kremlin followed a dual policy throughout the 1930s, both trying to restore a cooperative Rapallo-style relationship with Germany and, failing that, pursuing a collective security arrangement with Britain and France against the menace of Nazi aggression. This dual policy was maintained well into 1939. He emphasizes contacts between Red Army commanders and Reichswehr officers, as well as Kandelaki's approaches to Hjalmar Schacht as Soviet attempts to court non-Nazi German elites (the officer corps and big business). At least in the mid-1930s Stalin mistakenly thought these forces might be able to redirect German foreign policy away from its anti-Soviet course.[54] This line of analysis supports the work of Ingeborg Fleischhauer, discussed above.

In contrast to Haslam, Raymond, and Kulish, however, Nekrich assumes that Stalin dominated all foreign policy decision-making. In his account there are no debates or factions. Nekrich also argues that the dismissal of Litvinov as foreign commissar marked a new stage in Stalin's foreign policy. From this point on, he argues, territorial expansion became a significant goal.[55] This conclusion contrasts sharply with the work of Roberts, who sees the territorial gains of 1939–40 as defensive reactions to a rapidly deteriorating international situation.[56]

The last decade also has seen renewed interest in the life and work of the main apostle of collective security, Maksim Litvinov. Zinovy Sheinis, a Russian journalist, produced a substantial biography of the Soviet foreign commissar in

1988. The manuscript was completed in 1966, but only a few excerpts from it could be published before the *glasnost* era. Analytically, this book adds little to the works by Haslam, Roberts, and Nekrich, but it does supply many previously unknown details about Litvinov's activities.[57] The description of Litvinov's dismissal as foreign minister and the purge of the Soviet foreign commissariat is especially interesting. Hugh Phillips, an American academic, also has published a biography of Litvinov which focuses on his diplomatic career. For the 1930s, Phillips concentrates on the failure of collective security, though he blames the western leaders and Litvinov's Kremlin masters, rather than the foreign commissar himself.[58] Phillips suggests that after 1936 Litvinov was increasingly excluded by Stalin and Molotov from the foreign policy making process. Thus, Litvinov's dismissal in May 1939 is an anti-climax, inevitable given the western powers' failure to cooperate with the USSR and the foreign commissar's declining influence in the Kremlin. This view contrasts sharply with the suggestion by Geoff Roberts that Litvinov was fired so that Stalin and Molotov could finally gain complete control of Soviet foreign policy in order to intensify efforts to create a new Triple Entente.[59] Phillips' view of an increasingly marginalized Litvinov is contested by Haslam, who argues that "Litvinov's influence rested in part on the fact that Stalin – at least until 1939 and intermittently thereafter – was content to take advice on the conduct of foreign policy and delegate operational control to others: a wise precaution considering his ignorance of such matters...".[60]

The course of Soviet diplomacy in the 1930s doubtless will remain a controversial issue among historians, especially since, at the time of this writing, various economic, logistical, and political obstacles still hinder scholars' full access to all Soviet archives. Fortunately, however, the dedication to dispassionate and rigorous scholarship of such investigators as Roberts, Haslam, Nekrich, and Weinberg has raised the level of western analysis of Soviet foreign policy in this period. Cold War rhetoric and partisanship no longer dominate the scene as they once did. A. J. P. Taylor, similarly, was striving to overcome the problems of doctrinal bias and political purpose when he wrote *Origins*, though he went too far in denying the influence of ideological conceptions on international affairs.[61] Moreover, the recent outpouring of studies on Soviet diplomacy in the 1930s has demonstrated the important role of the USSR in Europe's drift toward the conflagration. Future historians of the origins of the Second World War must pay more attention to the Kremlin than Taylor did more than thirty-five years ago.

Notes

1 See T. M. Mason, "Some origins of the Second World War," *Past & Present*, no. 29, 1964, pp. 67–87; and D. C. Watt, "Some aspects of A. J. P. Taylor's work as diplomatic historian," *Journal of Modern History*, vol. 49, 1977, pp. 19–33.

2 A. J. P. Taylor, *The Origins of the Second World War*, Greenwich, CT, 1965, p. 25 and throughout. The reference here and elsewhere in this chapter is to the American second edition which includes a new Preface for American readers as well as a postscript in which the author defends himself against some of his early critics.

3 On the importance of anti-communism and counter-revolution in the foreign policy of the western states, see A. J. Mayer, *Politics and Diplomacy of Peacemaking: Containment and Counterrevolution at Versailles*, New York, 1967; J. M. Thompson, *Russia, Bolshevism, and the Versailles Peace*, Princeton, NJ, 1966; and two works by R. K. Debo, *Revolution and Survival: The Foreign Policy of Soviet Russia, 1917–18*, Toronto, 1979, and *Survival and Consolidation: The Foreign Policy of Soviet Russia, 1918–1921*, Montreal, 1992.

4 For evidence of the Soviet regime's fundamental insecurity in the international arena, see T. J. Uldricks, "Russia and Europe: diplomacy, revolution, and economic development in the 1920s," *International History Review*, vol. 1, 1979, pp. 55–83; J. P. Sontag, "The Soviet war scare of 1926–27," *Russian Review*, vol. 34, 1975, pp. 66–77; J. Haslam, *Soviet Foreign Policy, 1930–33: The Impact of the Depression*, New York, 1983; and J. Jacobson, *When the Soviet Union Entered World Politics*, Berkeley, CA, 1994, esp. pp. 273–280.

5 Compare with C. Fink, *The Genoa Conference: European Diplomacy, 1921–1922*, Chapel Hill, NC, 1984, and, "The NEP in foreign policy: the Genoa conference and the Treaty of Rapallo," in G. Gorodetsky (ed.), *Soviet Foreign Policy, 1917–1991: A Retrospective*, London, 1994, pp. 11–20.

6 A. J. P. Taylor, "Accident prone, or what happened next," *Journal of Modern History*, vol. 49, 1977, p. 7. Borrowing a gardening term from Sir Lewis Namier, Taylor refers to his historical "intuition" as "green fingers": "Some may say that I have relied on my green fingers too much. I think that I have relied on them too little."

7 Compare with J. E. Dreifort, "The French Popular Front and the Franco-Soviet Pact, 1936–37: a dilemma in foreign policy," *Journal of Contemporary History*, vol. 11, 1976, pp. 217–36.

8 For a sophisticated discussion of the bases of British appeasement policy which takes the factor of anti-communism into account (though, perhaps, still not sufficiently), see M. Gilbert, *Roots of Appeasement*. Also useful are M. Thomas, *Britain, France and Appeasement*, Oxford, 1996, and N. Jordan, *The Popular Front and Central Europe*, Cambridge, 1992. Compare with G. Niedhart, "British attitudes and policies towards the Soviet Union and international Communism, 1933–9," in W. J. Mommsen and L. Kettenacker (eds), *The Fascist Challenge and the Policy of Appeasement*, London, 1983, pp. 286–96.

9 For western perceptions of Soviet military strength (or weaknesses), see R. R. Rader, "Anglo-French estimates of the Red army, 1936–1937," *Soviet Armed Forces Annual*, vol. 3, 1979, pp. 265–80; and J. H. Herndon, "British perceptions of Soviet military capability, 1935–9," in Mommsen and Kettenacker, *Fascist Challenge*, pp. 297–319.

10 Since Taylor developed this argument, the matter of western expectations of the nature of future wars has been studied in much greater detail. See A. Preston (ed.), *General Staffs and Diplomacy before the Second World War*, London, 1978; R. J. Young, *In Command of France: French Foreign Policy and Military Planning, 1933–1940*, Cambridge, 1978; and E. R. May (ed.), *Knowing One's Enemies: Intelligence and Assessment Before the Two World Wars*, Princeton, NJ, 1984. These more detailed studies tend to support Taylor's suggestion that differing strategic conceptions added to the gulf between London and Moscow.

11 For an alternative interpretation stressing the logical continuity of theory and practice in Nazi foreign policy see G. L. Weinberg, *The Foreign Policy of Hitler's Germany*, vol. 1, *Diplomatic Revolution in Europe, 1933–36*, Chicago, IL, 1970; and vol. 2, *Starting World War II, 1937–1939*, Chicago, IL, 1980.

12 B. Ponomaryov, A. Gromyko, and V. Khvostov (eds), *History of Soviet Foreign Policy, 1917–1945*, Moscow, 1969, pp. 337–8. For the orthodox Soviet view also see I. K. Koblyakov, *USSR: For Peace, Against Aggression, 1933–1941*, Moscow, 1976; I. F. Maksimychev, *Diplomatiia mira protiv diplomatii voiny*, Moscow, 1981; and A. L. Narochitskii (ed.), *SSSR v bor'be protiv fashistskoi agressi, 1933–1941*, Moscow, 1976.

13 Ponomaryov, *et al.*, *History of Soviet Foreign Policy*, pp. 381–6; and *Falsificators of History: An Historical Note*, Moscow, 1948. Also see T. J. Uldricks, "Evolving Soviet views of the

Nazi–Soviet Pact," in R. Frucht (ed.), *Labyrinth of Nationalism/Complexities of Diplomacy*, Columbus, OH, 1992, pp. 331–60; and L. Bezymensky, "The secret protocols of 1939 as a problem in Soviet historiography," in Gorodetsky (ed.), *Soviet Foreign Policy*, pp. 75–85.

14 F. Borkenau, *European Communism*, New York, 1953, pp. 117, 132–5 and 234–5; B. Nikolaevskii, "Stalin i ubiistvo Kirova," *Sotsialisticheskii vestnik*, no. 10, 1956, p. 186, and no. 12, 1956, pp. 239–40; W. G. Krivitsky, *I Was Stalin's Agent*, London, 1939, pp. 18–34, 37–40; and V. Petrov, "A missing page in Soviet historiography: the Nazi–Soviet partnership," *Orbis*, vol. 11, 1968, pp. 1,113–37.

15 R. C. Tucker, "The emergence of Stalin's foreign policy," *Slavic Review*, vol. 36, 1977, pp. 563–89, 604–7; and Tucker, *Stalin in Power: The Revolution from Above, 1928–1941*, New York, 1990, chs 3–4, 10–11, 14, 16, 18, and 21. Similar arguments are made by S. Allard, *Stalin und Hitler: Die Soujetrussische Aussenpolitik, 1930–1941*, Bern and Munich, 1974, and by Walter Post, *Unternehmen Barbarossa*, Hamburg, 1996. On Stalin's assumptions about the "outside world," also see L. Lih's introduction to *Stalin's Letters to Molotov*, New Haven, CT, 1995, pp. 27–36.

16 R. C. Raack, *Stalin's Drive to the West, 1938–1945: The Origins of the Cold War*, Stanford, CA, 1995, pp. 12–16 and throughout.

17 See T. J. Uldricks, "Stalin and Nazi Germany," *Slavic Review*, vol. 36, 1977, pp. 599–603; and Uldricks, "Soviet security policy in the 1930s," in Gorodetsky (ed.), *Soviet Foreign Policy*, pp. 65–74, for critiques of the logic of Tucker's argument.

18 R. C. Tucker, "Stalin, Bukharin and history as conspiracy," in R. C. Tucker and S. F. Cohen (eds), *The Great Purge Trial*, New York, 1965, p. xxxvi. Also see G. F. Kennan, *Russia and the West under Lenin and Stalin*, New York, 1961, pp. 288–91 and 296.

19 T. J. Uldricks, "The impact of the great purges on the people's commissariat of foreign affairs," *Slavic Review*, vol. 36, 1977, pp. 187–204.

20 Weinberg, *Diplomatic Revolution*, pp. 220–2, 310; and *Starting World War II*, p. 214. Compare with his earlier work, *Germany and the Soviet Union, 1939–1941*, Leyden, 1954. His subsequent work, *World in the Balance*, Hanover, N.H., 1981, p. 7, advances even more strongly the theory of Stalin's preference for an agreement with Germany over one with the democracies. Also see Weinberg, "The Nazi–Soviet pacts: a half-century later," *Foreign Affairs*, vol. 68, 1989, pp. 175–89. Similar interpretations of Stalin's foreign policy can be found in A. Ulam, *Expansion and Coexistence*, New York, 1974, pp. 183–279; and J. E. McSherry, *Stalin, Hitler, and Europe*, vol. 1, Cleveland, OH, 1968.

21 F. Claudin, *The Communist Movement: From Comintern to Cominform*, New York, 1975, pp. 174–82. See also K. McDermott and J. Agnew, *The Comintern: A History of International Communism from Lenin to Stalin*, New York, 1997, chs 4 and 6. For examples of the devastating impact of the Nazi–Soviet Pact on foreign communists, see W. Leonhard, *Betrayal: The Hitler–Stalin Pact of 1939*, New York, 1989.

22 Also see V. M. Falin, *et al.* (eds), *Soviet Peace Efforts on the Eve of World War II, (September 1938–August 1939: Documents and Records)*, Moscow, 1973, 2 vols. On the sometimes tendentious practices of the editors of *Dokumenty vneshnei politiki SSSR*, see A. Nekrich, *Otreshis' ot strakha: vospominaniia istorika*, London, 1979, pp. 139–40. Also see R. H. Johnson (ed.), *Soviet Foreign Policy, 1918–1945: A Guide to Research and Research Materials*, Wilmington, DE, 1991, pp. 89–101, for a discussion of all Soviet diplomatic document collections issued through the early Gorbachev years.

23 E. Gnedin, *Katastrofa i vtoroe rozhdenie: memuarnye zapiski*, Amsterdam, 1977. Gnedin's other writings which deal with Soviet foreign policy in the 1930s include *Iz istorii otnoshenii mezhdu SSSR i fashistskoi Germaniei: dokumenty i sovremennye komentarii*, New York, 1977; *Vykhod iz labirinta*, New York, 1982; and "V narkomindele, 1922–1933: Inter'viu s E. A. Gnedinym," *Pamiat, (istoricheskii sbornik)*, no. 5, 1981, pp. 357–93.

24 Gnedin's indictment of Molotov for undermining the collective security drive is echoed by another Soviet dissident: see R. Medvedev, *All Stalin's Men*, Garden City, NY, 1984, pp. 89–90.

25 I. Fleischhauer, *Der Pakt: Hitler, Stalin und die Initiative der deutschen Diplomatie, 1938–1939*, Frankfurt, 1990, pp. 10–19 and 406ff.

26 J. Hochman, *The Soviet Union and the Failure of Collective Security, 1934–1938*, Ithaca, NY, 1984.

27 M. Litvinov, (pseudonym for Grigorii Besedovskii?), *Notes for A Journal*, New York, 1955. Also see E. S. Danielson, "The elusive Litvinov memoirs," *Slavic Review*, vol. 48, 1989, pp. 477–83.

28 J. Haslam, *The Soviet Union and the Struggle for Collective Security in Europe, 1933–39*, New York, 1984.

29 Haslam, *Collective Security*, pp. 5, 7, 22–3, 30, 33, 154–6, 158, 201.

30 P. D. Raymond, "Conflict and consensus in Soviet foreign policy, 1933–1939," Pennsylvania State University doctoral dissertation, 1979. The Russian scholar Vitaly Kulish takes a similar position on policy debates within the Kremlin. See Kulish, "U poroga voiny," *Komsomolskaia pravda*, August 24, 1988, p. 3.

31 R. C. Nation, *Black Earth, Red Star: A History of Soviet Security Policy, 1917–1991*, Ithaca, NY, 1992, pp. 78 and 93–4.

32 M. J. Carley, "End of the 'low, dishonest decade': failure of the Anglo-Franco-Soviet alliance in 1939," *Europe–Asia Studies*, vol. 45, 1993, pp. 303–41; and Carley, "Five kopecks for five kopecks: Franco-Soviet trade negotiations, 1928–1939," *Cahiers du Monde Russe et Soviétique*, vol. 33, 1992, pp. 23–58.

33 On the importance of far eastern considerations, see J. Haslam, *The Soviet Union and the Threat from the East, 1933–41*, Pittsburgh, PA, 1992. Compare with R. Ahmann, "Soviet foreign policy and the Molotov–Ribbentrop Pact of 1939: an enigma reassessed," *Storia delle relazioni internazionali*, vol. 5, 1989, pp. 349–69.

34 Haslam, *Collective Security*, pp. 230–2.

35 Haslam, *Collective Security*, pp. 158–94. But compare with D. N. Lammers, "The May crisis of 1938: the Soviet view considered," *South Atlantic Quarterly*, vol. 69, 1970, pp. 480–503, who doubts Soviet resolution to support the Czechs; and M. L. Toepfer, "The Soviet role in the Munich crisis: a historiographical debate," *Diplomatic History*, vol. 1, 1977, pp. 341–57, whose work tends to support Haslam's position. Also see B. M. Cohen, "Moscow at Munich: did the Soviet Union offer unilateral aid to Czechoslovakia?", *East European Quarterly*, vol. 12, 1978, pp. 341–8.

36 Haslam, *Collective Security*, pp. 195–229. R. Manne reaches similar conclusions about the tragic failure of the Anglo-Soviet negotiations, though he is not as critical of the Chamberlain government as is Haslam; see "British decision," pp. 3–26, and "Some British light on the Nazi-Soviet pact," *European Studies Review*, vol. 11, 1981, pp. 83–102.

37 Haslam, *Collective Security*, p. 231. Also see "'Has the colonel made an error in translation?...' An eyewitness account of military talks between Britain, France, and the Soviet Union on the eve of World War II," *New Times*, no. 34, 1989, pp. 23–5.

38 Declaring the secret protocols to be authentic, Afanas'ev told a massive crowd at a 1988 protest meeting in Tallinn, Estonia, "In no other country has history been falsified to such a degree as in the Soviet Union." Quoted in Leonhard, *Betrayal*, p. xiv. M. Semiriaga, "23 avgust 1939 goda: Sovetsko-Germanskii dogovor o nenapadenii: Bila li alternativa?," *Literaturnaia gazeta*, October 5, 1988, p. 14. Also see M. I. Semiriaga, *Tainy stalinskoi diplomatii, 1939–1941*, Moscow, 1992; and "Kruglyi stol: vtoraia mirovaia voina–istoki i prichiny," *Voprosy istorii*, 1988, no. 12, pp. 3–46.

39 See, for example, A. E. Senn, "Perestroika in Lithuanian historiography: the Molotov–Ribbentrop Pact," *The Russian Review*, vol. 49, 1990, pp. 43–56; I. Vizulis, *The Molotov–Ribbentrop Pact of 1939: The Baltic Case*, New York, 1990; and H. Arumäe, "Eshche raz o Sovetsko-Germanskom pakte o nenapadenii," *Sovetskaia estoniia*, August 17–18, 1988.

40 D. Volkogonov, *Stalin: Triumph and Tragedy*, New York, 1988, chs 34 and 35. Also see D. A. Volkogonov, "Drama reshenii 1939 goda," *Novaia i noveishaia istoriia*, no. 4, 1989, pp. 3–27.

41 Ministerstvo Inostrannykh Del SSSR, *God krizisa, 1938–1939: Dokumenty i materialy,* vol. 1, *sentiabria 29, 1938 g–31 maia 1939 g*; and vol. 2, *2 iiuniia 1939 g–4 sentiabria 1939,* Moscow, 1990. Ministerstvo Inostrannykh Del Rossiiskoi Federatsii, *Dokumenty vneshnei politiki, 1939 god,* vol. 1, *1 ianvaria–31 avgusta 1939g.,* and vol. 2, *1 sentiabria–31 dekabria 1939g,* Moscow, 1992.

42 See Bezymensky, "Secret protocols of 1939," pp. 80–84. The Russian language original of the secret protocols, which were previously thought to have been destroyed at Molotov's order in 1946, were, in fact, discovered in 1992 in the Presidential Archive of the Russian Federation.

43 N. A. Abramov and L. A. Bezymenskii, "Osobaia missiia Davida Kandelaki," *Voprosy istorii,* nos 4–5, 1991, pp. 144–56. Compare with G. Roberts, "A Soviet bid for coexistence with Nazi Germany, 1935–1937: the Kandelaki affair," *The International History Review,* vol. 16, 1994, pp. 94–101.

44 F. Chuev, *Molotov Remembers: Inside Kremlin Politics – Conversations with Felix Chuev,* Chicago, IL, 1993, p. 13. A. Gromyko, *Memoirs,* New York, 1989. Subsequent research has shown that, despite his denials, Gromyko had copies of the secret protocols made from the archival original for his perusal in 1975 and 1979. Bezymensky, "Secret protocols," p. 84.

45 G. Roberts, *The Soviet Union and the Origins of the Second World War: Russo-German Relations and the Road to War, 1933–1939,* London, 1995; and Roberts, *The Unholy Alliance: Stalin's Pact with Hitler,* London, 1989. Also see G. Gorodetsky, "The impact of the Ribbentrop–Molotov pact on the course of Soviet foreign policy," *Cahiers du Monde Russe et Soviétique,* vol. 31, 1990, pp. 27–42, for a similar analysis.

46 G. Roberts, "Infamous encounter? The Merekalov–Weizsäcker meeting of 17 April 1939," *The Historical Journal,* vol. 35, 1992, pp. 921–6. Also see *God krizisa,* vol. 1, p. 389.

47 Roberts, *Soviet Union,* pp. 63–84.

48 Roberts, *Soviet Union,* pp. 8, 83, 89 and 149.

49 Hochman, *Failure of Collective Security,* ch. 7; and I. Lukes, *Czechoslovakia Between Stalin and Hitler,* New York, 1996, ch. 7.

50 Lukes, *Stalin and Hitler,* pp. 260–63.

51 G. Jukes, "The Red Army and the Munich crisis," *Journal of Contemporary History,* vol. 26, 1991, pp. 195–214; and M. V. Zakharov, *General'nyi shtab v predvoennye gody,* Moscow, 1989.

52 H. Ragsdale, "The Munich crisis and the issue of Red Army transit across Romania," *The Russian Review,* vol. 57, 1998, pp. 614–17; and "Soviet Military Preparations and Policy in the Munich Crisis," *Jahrbücher für Geschichte Osteuropas,* forthcoming.

53 The evidence suggests that the USSR probably would not have come unilaterally to the aid of Czechoslovakia. See "Notes on events in Czechoslovakia in late September and early October 1938," *International Affairs,* Moscow, December 1988, pp. 125–32.

54 A. M. Nekrich, *Pariahs, Partners, Predators: German–Soviet Relations, 1922–1941,* New York, 1997, pp. 78 and 90–1. Note: though published in 1997, the manuscript of this work was completed in 1993, shortly before the author's death. Nekrich had access to the Foreign Ministry archives and some other government archives.

55 Nekrich, *Pariahs,* p. 110.

56 Roberts, *Soviet Union,* ch. 7.

57 Z. Sheinis, *Maxim Litvinov,* Moscow, 1990, English edition.

58 H. D. Phillips, *Between the Revolution and the West: A Political Biography of Maxim M. Litvinov,* Boulder, CO, 1992. Also see the comments on Phillips' interpretations in M. J. Carley, "Down a blind-alley: Anglo-Franco-Soviet relations, 1920–39," *Canadian Journal of History,* vol. 29, 1994, pp. 147–72.

59 G. Roberts, "The fall of Litvinov: a revisionist view," *Journal of Contemporary History*, vol. 27, 1992, pp. 639–57.

60 J. Haslam, "Litvinov, Stalin and the road not taken," in Gorodetsky, *Soviet Foreign Policy*, p. 57.

61 See A. Cassels, *Ideology and International Relations in the Modern World*, London, 1997, for a discussion of the important role that ideology has played in foreign policy.

9 Japan at war

History-writing on the crisis of the 1930s

Louise Young

On September 18, 1931, Japan's Kwantung Army initiated the military conquest of northeast China now known as the Manchurian Incident. With the occupation of Manchuria, Japanese imperialism entered a new and critical period. During this phase of empire building, Japan moved aggressively to expand its overseas territories, occupying first China and then south-east Asia, and initiating a succession of military conflicts against the nationalist and communist forces in China, the Soviet Union, the United States, and the British empire. During the rapid military expansion of the 1930s and 1940s, what Japanese officials called "autonomous diplomacy" signified two departures from past practice. First, it meant liberating imperial interests in Asia from a consideration of relations with the west. In the past, fearing diplomatic isolation, Japanese policy makers took careful stock of how a potential move in Asia was likely to be received in the west, and interventions were preceded by cautious multilateral negotiations. After 1931, however, the "Manchurian problem," the "China question," and the "advance south" were each decided unilaterally and in the face of western opposition. Second, autonomy signaled a new independence for Japan's colonial armies. In the wake of the Manchurian Incident, military *fait accomplis* followed one upon another, as aggressive field officers took their lead from the success of the Manchurian occupation. Since the 1890s, imperial expansion had begun with military conquest. But by the 1930s, the imperial garrisons had multiplied and the institutional complexity of the armed services had opened new possibilities for subimperialists. The trigger-happy proclivity of the garrison armies turned the boundaries of the empire into a rolling frontier.

In the conventional chronologies of modern Japanese history, the Manchurian Incident ushered in a new era in Japanese politics and foreign policy. It marked the beginning of a period of militarism, fascism, and war, characterized by repression and mobilization at home and aggressive expansion in Asia and the Pacific. The chain of events set off by the Manchurian Incident is thus viewed as the onset of a regional crisis and the first step on the road to the Second World War in Asia. Although most historians would agree with a chronology that identified the Manchurian Incident as some sort of turning-point, there is little consensus on the causes and nature of the crisis of the 1930s.

This essay examines the literature on wartime Japan and highlights the main lines of interpretation and the key debates that have animated historians' writings on this period. It is a subject that casts a long shadow over the image of modern Japan. The sheer numbers of books on the 1930s overwhelm those on other periods, and the war has a way of creeping into the conclusions of studies of seemingly unrelated topics. Most modern-history courses are enclosed within the bookends of the Meiji Restoration[1] and the Second World War; the postwar period is only beginning to be treated as a legitimate historical subject, and even then it takes as its starting-point the denouement of the Second World War. In short, Japan's modern history has been hijacked by the teleology of the Second World War. In the space of one essay I cannot do justice to the complexities of this historiography, but will focus on four dimensions of wartime Japan that have preoccupied historians: the domestic impact of the war; the question of Japanese fascism; the military history of the war; and the goals of Japanese foreign policy.[2]

Domestically, the Manchurian Incident marked a turning-point from the era christened "Taishô democracy," (*Taishô demokurashii*) to what Japanese called the "national emergency" (*hijôji*) of the early Shôwa period.[3] Many currents flowed together to produce the sea-change of the early 1930s. Politically, this period marked the end of party-run cabinets, and the dying gasp of the organized Left. The war set off a rapid military build-up and the foundation of what was called the quasi-wartime economy. The war fever that gripped Japan during the Manchurian Incident promoted the militarization of popular culture and encouraged the proliferation of social organizations for total war. In these ways the Manchurian Incident set in motion a chain reaction at home, culminating in the rise of army influence over the institutions of government and the formation of a popular consensus behind Japan's turn to "go-fast imperialism."[4]

Popular Japanese stereotypes of the 1930s explain the transformation of these years as the product of a militaristic police state which exercised unlimited powers of political repression to coerce an unwilling but helpless populace into cooperating with the army's expansionist designs. Historians have picked up on the popular narrative to reinforce the idea that the Japanese public were more victims than agents of the turn to militarism and war in the 1930s. For example, studies by Richard Mitchell, Kazuko Tsurumi, Gregory Kasza and others on the question of "thought control" have stressed the extensive powers of the state in the formation of ideological conformity.[5] Tsurumi's work focuses on what Japanese call the ideology of the emperor-system. According to this formulation, Japanese were "socialized for death" through the moral education they received in the schools and the army. There, they were inculcated with the belief that all Japanese were related by blood in a unique form of state known as the *kokutai*. The *kokutai* also signified the absolute authority of a divine emperor to whom they owed unquestioning obedience, and for whom they must be willing to die. Kasza and Mitchell look at the thought-control system from a different angle, focusing not on propaganda and indoctrination but rather on the apparatus of censorship. Mitchell's analysis takes the reader through the dense web of censorship laws, providing a draconian portrait of the Japanese state and its control over freedom of expression. Kasza's description of the relationship between the state and the mass media allows for more autonomy on the part of journalists and editors, suggesting that the state censorship apparatus, though it grew in the 1930s, was less than comprehensive.

One of the shortcomings of the literature on thought control is the tendency to minimize the genuinely popular support that existed for many of the government initiatives of the 1930s. The problem emerges in part from the concept of "thought control," which renders the Japanese public as passive, robot-like, consumers of an ideology of war produced by government propaganda and indoctrination. In my own work I have tried to call attention to the ways that consumers and producers of mass culture, in and out of government, collectively produced a new vision of empire that ennobled the military aggression of these years. This was particularly true during the Manchurian Incident's war fever of the early 1930s, when the Japanese public became eager consumers of war mongering and China bashing in the mass media. After the story broke of the military clash between Chinese and Japanese troops on September 18, 1931, the news of the latest action on the China continent commanded the headlines for months. War songs set the fashion in popular music and battlefield dramas filled the stage and screen. Such media sensationalism flooded popular consciousness with images of war and empire. Marketing militarism, the mass media became, in effect, unofficial propagandists, helping to mobilize popular support for the army's policy of military aggression against China.[6]

Leading the crusade were Japan's major dailies, the *Asahi* and the *Mainichi* newspapers. Both papers responded to the outbreak of hostilities by deploying recently purchased fleets of airplanes and cars, and mobilizing the latest printing and photo-telegraphic machinery in a drive to use the Manchurian Incident to expand their hold on the national news' market. The newspaper companies used airplanes to shuttle teams of correspondents and equipment back and forth between Japan and Manchuria, keeping the home front abreast of the daily progress of the occupation through morning and evening editions saturated with news from the front, plus additional photograph-filled Manchurian Incident "extras" hawked by bell-ringing newsboys throughout the day.

The press supplemented more conventional news presentation with reporting in the form of a public spectacle: newspaper-sponsored newsreel screenings, traveling lecture series, and exhibits of military paraphernalia. All of these were enormously popular, public enthusiasm driving the newspaper companies to new heights in their sensationalizing of the Manchurian Incident. *Asahi* and *Mainichi* newsreels that tracked the occupation of Manchuria, stage by victorious stage, filled public halls and packed city parks. Although both newspaper and film companies had made sporadic attempts at producing regular film news during the 1920s, newspaper company footage of the Manchurian Incident brought newsreels into widespread use for the first time. As fast as new film canisters could be flown in from Manchuria, the *Asahi* and *Mainichi* screened the newsreels in city parks in Osaka, Kobe, Kyoto, and Tokyo, and circulated the films for additional showings in department stores, elementary schools, and elsewhere throughout the country. In Osaka, for example, the first installment, "The military clash between the Japanese and Chinese armies," opened on September 21 – just three days after the clash began – and required several showings a night to accommodate the crowds. An account of the onset of the campaign for northern Manchuria, "The Nen River battle-front," proved to be the city's favorite for November, playing for 20,000 spectators on a single night. Five thousand stood outdoors on a chill January evening to watch marching columns of Japanese soldiers "entering Jinzhou." Since the free newsreels were a marketing tool, they were shown widely outside the urban areas, particularly in rural districts where the large dailies hoped to expand circulation.

An equally enthusiastic reception for traveling lecture series and exhibitions of military paraphernalia rewarded the big dailies with popular acclaim. On November 25, the Osaka *Asahi* touched off a lecture boom with a three-day lecture series on "Reports from the battlefield," with special correspondents lecturing to full houses in Osaka, Kobe, Kyoto, and Nagoya on their impressions of conditions at the front. A December 3 session drew a crowd of 6,000 in Osaka, and a report in Tokyo on the invasion of Jinzhou in January inspired standing ovations and three *banzais* for the *Asahi* from the enthusiastic crowd.

The large department stores offered space to both the *Mainichi* and *Asahi* newspaper companies for exhibitions, held in November and December, of military paraphernalia commemorating the Manchurian Incident. After opening in Tokyo, an exhibition of "Souvenirs of the fierce campaign to take the Fengtian Beitaying," sponsored by the Tokyo *Asahi*, went on to tour seventy locations to the north and the west. In Tokyo, exhibition-goers numbered 11,000 daily, while nation-wide a total of 600,000 saw the exhibition. The fusillade of Manchurian Incident "extras," the newsreel screenings, the lectures and exhibitions glorified military action, lionized the Kwantung army, and extolled the founding of Manchukuo. Such messages dovetailed beautifully with what the army wanted its public to hear about the Manchurian Incident. But the culture industries needed no arm-twisting to advertise the army's cause: they became unofficial propagandists because militarism was all the rage. Audiences flocked to watch the dramas of death in battle, and readers bought up the magazines commemorating the glories of the empire. From this perspective it was not the system of "thought control" that created popular support for the Manchurian Incident, but rather the operation of a commercial market for mass culture.

Another dimension of wartime ideology that has commanded the attention of historians is the problem of *tenkô*, the ideological conversions that devastated the ranks of communists, socialists, and liberals. Responding to new social and government pressures, scores of prominent intellectuals abandoned their public support for oppositional politics, effectively gutting the left-wing social movement in the 1930s. The literature on *tenkô*, while stressing the growth of state repression, also focuses on the agency of private individuals and organizations in the ideological shift of the 1930s, examining different motivations for erstwhile critics of the Japanese state to become its new supporters.[7] Intimately tied to the problem of *tenkō* are the issue of war responsibility and the question: Why were Japan's progressive intellectuals not a stronger voice against the militarism and ultranationalism of the 1930s? Tatsuo Arima, Victor Koschmann, and Matsumoto Sannosuke argue that, over the course of the modern period, Japanese intellectuals failed to carve out a position of individual autonomy from which they could develop a voice of genuine protest. This "failure of freedom," in Arima's words, fatally weakened the ability of intellectuals to stand against the state as it mobilized for war.[8] Others portray intellectuals in more forceful terms, quite capable of independent intervention to direct the course of culture and politics. The research of Miles Fletcher, for example, illustrates the active support given by many left-wing intellectuals to state goals in the 1930s. Drawn to fascist ideas of using the state as an agent of renovation, intellectuals helped shape the agenda for the wartime reconstruction of the economy and the New Order in Asia.[9]

Evidence tends to support the latter interpretation, particularly when one looks at the role played by progressive intellectuals in the expansion in China. Over the course of the 1930s, scholars and China experts flocked to Manchuria to take up research and planning posts in the rapidly expanding colonial state. The context for this mobilization of intellectual talent by Manchukuo was a transformation of the academic climate in Japan. Responding to a new assault on academic freedom in the academy by conservative bureaucrats and right-wing scholars, a series of university incidents brought scientific analysis of Japan's history, polity, and society increasingly under attack and purged from the academy liberal intellectuals like Takigawa Yukitoki and Minobe Tatsukichi. The increasing limitations on freedom of expression profoundly affected Japanese Sinologists, forcing them to maintain a show of public support for official government aims on the continent. At the same time, the expansion of the imperial project in Manchuria brought new pressures on Sinologists to co-operate, just as it opened up new opportunities for them. Depending on political convictions, scholars responded to these changes in diverse ways. In the last analysis, however, they had two options: mobilization or repression.

Numerous right-wing intellectuals, like Kyoto University professor Yano Jin'ichi, who had long advocated a larger Japanese presence in Manchuria, enthusiastically greeted the new situation. Immediately after the establishment of Manchukuo, Yano packed his bags for China, where he became a propagandist for the puppet state. For many left and liberal critics of Japanese expansion, however, to remain true to their beliefs meant the loss of a job or the threat of more serious punishment. Yanaihara Tadao, the liberal head of colonial studies at Tokyo University, was forced along with countless others to sit out the war years under intellectual house-arrest.

Although Yano Jin'ichi and Yanaihara Tadao took divergent paths in response to the suppression of the 1930s, both remained faithful to political beliefs that they had held in the 1920s. A whole segment of Japanese intellectuals, however, abandoned their former faiths, suddenly lending their support to a policy of imperial aggression in China that was in total violation of the anti-imperialist positions they had previously championed. Collectively these researchers and scholars made a great impact on the intellectual underpinnings of the empire. This impact was mediated through their participation in the state think-tanks like the South Manchurian Railway's research department, which became the locus of economic planning in Manchukuo during the 1930s.

While it might seem strange that the Manchukuo government hired leftists in such large numbers, it did so because of the enormous demand that the controlled economy placed on good research. The state needed social scientists with expertise in China, and a good percentage of Japan's trained Sinologists also happened to be left-wing in their political orientation. The viability of the bizarre partnership between the Kwantung army-controlled Manchukuo government and progressive researchers was based on an unspoken *quid pro quo*. In return for publicly supporting state goals and carrying out research and planning projects desired by the Kwantung army, intellectuals were permitted to do their own research as well. Army officers tolerated the Marxist debates which raged in the pages of research department publications. Thus Manchukuo provided one of the most stunning examples of the uneven application of political censorship in the 1930s, for while academics in Japanese universities at home were being jailed for seemingly mild critiques of the political system, Sinologists in Manchuria freely expressed unabashedly revolutionary sentiments toward the empire.[10]

While investigations of the contribution of intellectuals to the military expansion during the 1930s have focused on the processes of ideology and thought control, another group of books on the transformation of these years has taken up the ultranationalist movement, its role in the militarization of the state, and the rightward turn in Japanese politics. Thomas Havens and Ronald Dore have looked at right-wing radicalism in the countryside and the push from agrarian activists for a "totalitarian solution."[11] Others, like Richard Storry, George Wilson, and Ben-Ami Shillony, have focused on radicals in the military who initiated a series of terrorist incidents in the early 1930s, culminating in the failed coup attempt of 1936.[12]

What these books point to is the rise of new political groups which were profoundly alienated from existing political institutions, and which viewed the mainstream political parties as inaccessible and corrupt. In the 1910s and 1920s political activists on the left and the right began to use extra-parliamentary tactics to secure their demands. The left began to deploy a new politics of the crowd, using street demonstrations, urban riots, and other direct actions to exercise political influence. Such tactics often proved more effective than the voting-box in bringing down an offending cabinet. The extra-parliamentary tactics preferred by the right involved what one author characterized as "government by assassination."[13] In the 1930s, such tactics failed in their ultimate object to overturn the state, but they did nonetheless have a profound impact on the ability of the military to increase its control over the government. Since many of the terrorist incidents had originated from within the lower ranks of the army and navy officer corps, the high command was able to use the threat of military terrorism and insubordination to wrest control of the cabinet from Japan's political parties. In situation after situation, the high command promised to do its best to control the officer crops, insisting at the same time that unless some concessions to the demands of the young officers were made, this might prove impossible.

The wave of army conspiracies in 1931 and 1932 put teeth into such threats. In September and October 1931 officers in the Kwantung and Korea armies maneuvered against their superiors, acting without authorization to occupy the Manchurian city of Fengtian, to dispatch the Korea army across the border into Manchuria, to bomb Jinzhou, and to set up new political arrangements in the region. But probably more alarming to the army's opponents was a rash of domestic terrorism. In March 1931 plans for a coup d'etat by a group of officers fell apart at the last minute because of disunity, but their organization – the Cherry Society – drew up a second plan for October of the same year, again halted at the eleventh hour. The March plot called for the use of mock bombs to strike at party headquarters and the premier's residence, where the cabinet met; in the confusion that would follow, the conspirators planned to demand the resignation of the cabinet and install their own government. The October plot envisioned a larger operation, mobilizing twelve companies of troops and sixteen planes, and using real bombs to wipe out the cabinet during a meeting.

Close on the heels of the October incident, a series of assassinations also stunned the political world. In the spring of 1932, an organization of naval officers and civilian ultranationalists calling themselves the Blood Pledge League compiled an assassination list of political, business, and government leaders, killing former finance minister Inoue Junnosuke and the head of the Mitsui business conglomerate Dan Takuma before the main culprits were arrested. On May 15, the remnants of the Blood Pledge League joined army cadets in another attempted coup. This time, a plan for the assassination of prime minister Inukai Tsuyoshi, together with co-ordinated attacks on the Bank of Japan, the Metropolitan Police Office, Party headquarters, and other government buildings, were actually carried out. However, the army's failure to rise in sympathy scuttled the group's ambitions for a "Shôwa Restoration" of imperial power and the end of parliamentary government.

Although in all instances the conspirators failed to assume control of the government, military terrorism created an atmosphere of fear and uncertainty concerning the army, weakening the resolve to oppose demands of the high command. The ambiguity of the role played by senior officers certainly added to feelings of apprehension. A number were implicated by the inevitable rumors; whatever the extent of their actual involvement, army leaders showed extraordinary leniency in dealing with the conspirators. The March plotters, for example, were for several weeks placed under "house-arrest" at a luxurious inn, and, speaking publicly for the assassins of Inukai Tsuyoshi, the army minister, emphasized that "they acted neither for the sake of fame nor gain nor treason....They acted upon the genuine belief that this was for the interest of the Imperial country." When negotiating on the successor to Inukai, army leaders flatly refused to participate in a party cabinet. Civilian statesmen were told that young officers were "fundamentally in agreement with the principles held by [the assassins]. Should the cabinet again be handed over to a political party, second and third incidents would recur."[14]

In these ways army authorities made use of right-wing terrorism to exclude political parties from control of the cabinet and to assume much broader powers for themselves. The story of military radicalism, ably told by Wilson, Shillony, and others, looks at the growth of militarism at the level of high politics. An alternative approach to the problem of militarism in the 1930s is to focus on popular or grassroots militarism, as Richard Smethurst, Thomas Havens, and others have done. Both Smethurst and Havens frame their discussions in terms of wartime mobilization. Smethurst argues that the support of rural Japanese for the war effort and the turn to the right in the 1930s was mobilized through the army reservist associations and their affiliates: youth groups and the Women's Self-Defense Association. In this sense he sees the rise of militarism in the countryside as the product of an elaborate institution-building effort on the part of the army ministry and of the organizational genius of army bureaucrats like Tanaka Giichi.[15]

In addition to the historians cited earlier, Ben-Ami Shillony and Thomas Havens have also written on the subject of war and popular culture. Both frame their narratives in terms of mass control and mass mobilization, dealing with the variety of government campaigns that took place in the late 1930s and early 1940s: the campaign for spiritual mobilization through the mass media and state propaganda; the campaign against "extravagance" in household finance; social mobilization through the formation of an increasingly dense network of voluntary organizations that culminated in the creation of block associations. The story that Shillony and Havens tell, in other words, is about the ways in which the state sought to organize people into units for war.[16] Such an approach tends to depict "the people" in passive terms; the state becomes the agent of history and the people are merely its pawns. However, other writings on wartime mobilization challenge this picture of an all-powerful state. Gordon Berger's work on political parties in the 1930s suggests that the old-style political parties were never effectively absorbed into the totalitarian formation of the Imperial Rule Assistance Association. Richard Rice also stresses the imperfection of wartime controls, arguing that business interests managed to resist many provisions of the economic mobilization law.[17]

Whether they depict the wartime state in stronger or weaker terms, these writings highlight one of the important effects of the process of mobilization: the growth of a socially-interventionist state in the 1930s and a new, more intimate, relationship between state and society. A point that is sometimes lost in these discussions is that the forces reshaping the relationship between community and state did not emerge solely from the state itself. While government initiatives exerted new kinds of pressure on local communities, at the grassroots level the bureaucracy's operation of mobilization relied on the mediation of local elites. Ultimately, the extent to which the state was permitted into the local community was determined by these elites – the gatekeepers of local autonomy. In their desire to invite state intervention in what had been private affairs, elites were driven by different motivations – anxiety about an economy that appeared deadlocked by global depression, inability to handle the social devastation the Depression had wreaked on their communities, fears that social conflict over shrinking resources was spinning out of control. Whatever their motivations, actions by local elites to mobilize the state were as much responsible for the extension of state control over their lives as were the initiatives of bureaucrats in the central government.

In these ways, the literature on the war at home has taken up the question of "what happened" in the 1930s from diverse angles. Historians have given the transformations of these years a long list of labels, describing wartime Japan variously as ultranationalist, Japanist, militarist, corporatist, totalitarian, and fascist. Each label comes with its own interpretive framework, defining the character of state and society in the 1930s, and postulating the causes of Japan's turn to rapid military expansionism. Of all these labels, that of *fascism* has been the most frequently suggested and the most ardently contested. The "fascism debate," as it is known, began almost immediately after the end of the war and has been joined by historians on both sides of the Pacific.[18]

The opening round in the fascism debate was delivered by Japanese Marxist historians, who argued that the intensified military aggression abroad and political repression at home of the 1930s were the products of accumulated contradictions in the structures of Japan's political economy. For these historians, the roots of the 1930s' crisis went back to the Meiji reforms of the 1870s and 1880s, when the architects of Japanese modernization made "emperor-system absolutism" into the framework for the Japanese nation–state. As Herbert Bix has summarized it, the "emperor-system" represented a formula for rule that encompassed both an "ideology of absolutism, prompted by a regime in which the sovereign had virtually unlimited powers and was regarded as an object of popular veneration" and "a nationalism generated by periodic national crises." The emperor-system entered its fascist stage in the 1930s, when the absolutist political structures acquired fascist functions. When they proposed the concept of "emperor-system fascism," Japanese Marxists were underscoring the differences between fascism in Japan and fascism in Europe. While fascism in Japan and Europe emerged out of the same crisis in the capitalist system when it reached the stage of monopoly capitalism, the nature of imperial rule and the peculiar composition of the ruling class set Japan apart from its European counterparts. Thus their analysis stressed the pre-eminent position of the bureaucracy as the instrument of imperial absolutism, supported by a ruling class comprised of the military, landlords, and monopoly capitalists. In the 1930s, then, the bureaucracy became the prime agent of emperor-system fascism, "fascizing" the structures of the state in order to salvage Japanese monopoly capitalism.[19]

This interpretation was challenged by Maruyama Masao, in his enormously influential series of essays on Japanese politics, published in English under the title *Thought and Behavior in Modern Japanese Politics.*[20] Maruyama agreed with the

Marxists in labeling Japan fascist, but took issue with their exclusive focus on the structure of the state. Maruyama was interested in the superstructural dimensions of fascism, and approached it as a problem of thought and psychology. For Maruyama fascism was not the outcome of a ruling class attempt to save capitalism, but rather the product of a fascist movement, at first by ultranationalists outside of government ("fascism from below") then by figures within government, particularly the military ("fascism from above"). The turning-point in the transition from "fascism from below" to "fascism from above" was the incident of February 26, 1936. This attempted coup represented the culmination of efforts to inaugurate fascism from below, and its failure signaled the end of right-wing terrorism and the beginning of the fascization of the state from within. Like the Marxists, Maruyama analyzed the relationship between Japan's path to modernity and its turn to fascism in comparative terms. Japan stood apart from Germany and Italy where, led by criminals and misfits, mass movements effected the takeover of government. In Japan, however, it was the mainstream government leadership which became the engineer of fascism. Maruyama explained the susceptibility of Japanese leadership to the lure of fascist ideology, with its irrational atavistic elements, in terms of their lack of a modern consciousness. Outwardly, the structures of modernity had been put in place but, inwardly, a modern autonomous individuality had failed to take root.

Though the "emperor-system fascism" and "fascism-from-above" formulations differed in their explanations of Japanese fascism, both agreed that by the late 1930s Japan had a fascist state. This idea was first challenged in a sustained way in the Princeton University Press series on "Studies in the modernization of Japan." This series laid down a scheme of stages of economic development as an alternative to the Marxist teleology of capitalism. Like Maruyama, they focused on "attitude" as the agent of modernization. Here they employed a Weberian model as a counterfoil to Marxism, inverting the Marxist focus on structural elements in the economy and relations of production. Unlike Japanese scholars, who saw the roots of fascism in the Meiji Restoration and the creation of the absolutist state, the American group looked at the Meiji reforms in positive terms. In their analysis, the reforms of the 1870s and 1880s planted the seeds of political pluralism and the rule of law which flowered in the "Taishô democracy" of the 1920s. For them, Taishô was an era of internationalism, cosmopolitanism, and economic growth, of Wilsonian idealism in foreign policy and political pluralism at home. This picture contrasted sharply with Maruyama's depiction of Taishô as the first stage of the fascist movement and the focus, in Marxist literature, on economic concentration, the creation of cartels, and the rise of a radical left-wing movement implacably opposed to monopoly capitalism. Thus, while Japanese scholars stressed continuities in Japanese history and viewed the crisis of early Shôwa as the inevitable culmination of an incomplete modernity, for the modernization scholars the 1930s represented a sudden reversal of the dominant trends of the preceeding decade, when forces for democracy and parliamentarianism were thrust aside by militarists and noisy ultranationalists. Though they firmly rejected the explanatory concept of fascism, they were at something of a loss to explain "what went wrong" with a modernization that had previously been moving along so successfully. In the end they glossed over the problem by minimizing the importance of the 1930s as an aberration.[21]

The writings of the modernization school stimulated a new debate over the utility of the category of "fascism" to Japan in the 1970s. Most Japanese historians, while critiquing the earlier formulation of emperor-system fascism for its monolithic conceptualization of the Japanese ruling class, and "fascism from above" for neglecting the role of mass movements and support for fascism on the part of ordinary Japanese people, still upheld the propriety of "fascism" as a description of the 1930s. They attempted to salvage the concept by looking at fascism as the outgrowth of modernizing trends in the development of Japan's political and social system. For example, the newer literature on fascism focused on the pre-eminent role of the military in politics and postulated that for Japan fascism represented the product of a new political system designed to cope with total war.[22] Others, notably American historians such as Peter Duus, Daniel Okamoto, Ben-Ami Shillony, George Wilson, and Gordon Berger, followed the lead of the modernization scholars and questioned the use of "fascism" in the Japanese case. Approaching the problem with more analytical focus, these American scholars identified a number of key differences between Japanese and European fascism: Japan had no charismatic leader like Hitler or Mussolini, and unlike Italy and Germany the Japanese government was not taken over by a mass movement but remained in the hands of the old guard, the political elite. As Duus and Okamoto put it, though there may have been fascists in Japan there was nothing that could reasonably be defined as a fascist political system.[23]

In the place of the rejected paradigm of "fascism" its critics have offered a host of alternative rubrics: corporatism, totalitarianism, and militarism, among others. What is at stake in these labels? At the heart of the fascism debate is the question: Who are the villains of the debacle of the 1930s? What led Japan to war? Whether blame is placed on a government-manipulated system of thought control, or on an institutional structure peculiarly susceptible to military takeover, or on a form of late-capitalism which is driven by contradictions to repress at home and aggress abroad, historians in Japan and the United States have looked to domestic causes for the domestic crisis. Indeed, one of the striking aspects of the literature on wartime Japan is its tendency to segregate the domestic from the foreign context. In the works discussed thus far, problems in Japan's empire and in its relationship with the western powers are not considered as potential causes of the domestic turmoil of the 1930s, but only as its effects. The literature on the foreign crisis, to which I now turn, is characterized by a similar tendency to treat Japanese actions abroad in isolation from the profound transformations taking place in the domestic arena.

If the literature on the home front is prodigious, the literature on the foreign crisis is equally vast. Increasing the confusion is the fact that the Second World War in Asia was fought against many enemies and on many fronts: the war in China against the nationalists and the communists, the war along the Siberian border of Manchuria against the Soviet Union, the war against the European colonial powers in south-east Asia, and finally, the war in the Pacific against the United States. Even though these separate conflicts were ultimately connected in a single great war, they remained in many ways distinct from one another – distinct in their origins and chronology, in the nature of the conflict and the war aims of each side, and in the impact of their denouement on the postwar order. These distinctions are reflected in the literature and add to the complexity of the picture of the Second World War in Asia. Still, the question remains: How did these separate conflicts become connected? What were the steps that led the Japanese from a small war in Manchuria to the hell-fires of Hiroshima and Nagasaki?

The war in China began in Japan's sphere of influence in the northeast. The literature on the Manchurian Incident of 1931 focuses on two dimensions of the conflict. One set of studies looks at the diplomatic fall-out in the League of Nations and the escalating tensions between Japan and the western powers, including the American attempt to contain Japan through "moral diplomacy," the French and British attempts at appeasement, and the appointment of the Lytton Commission, whose critical report culminated in Japan's withdrawal from the League. Nish, Thorne, and others have debated the significance of Japan's withdrawal in terms of what it meant for international peacekeeping and whether it signified the evisceration of the League as an instrument for maintaining international order. A point they do not touch on is its significance in terms of Japanese diplomacy, for Japan's withdrawal signaled a profound departure from past practice. Since the forced opening of Japan in the nineteenth century, the overriding goal of foreign policy had been to join the great powers on terms of international equality. Choosing to stand against the western powers in the League in 1932–33, Japanese diplomats abandoned this goal in favor of "autonomous diplomacy." Of their own volition, Japanese statesmen withdrew from the great power club to which they had labored so long to gain entry. In the process, they ushered in an era of international isolation and entered on a collision course with rival imperialists.

The second set of studies on the Manchurian Incident focuses on the gathering conflict between Japan and its problematic ally in Manchuria, the warlord Zhang Xueliang. Documenting the series of events that led the army to act – the increasing intractability of Zhang Xueliang, the specter of the Chinese nationalist movement spreading to Manchuria, dissatisfaction with the civilian authorities' handling of the Manchurian question – these studies highlight the role of the Kwantung army, Japan's garrison force in Manchuria, and narrate the Manchurian Incident as military history.[24] What made the Kwantung army such a key player in the Manchurian Incident and in the military origins of the Second World War in Asia was its peculiar character as a rogue army. In this sense the fact that the Manchurian Incident was initiated by a Kwantung army conspiracy is of more than passing significance. On the evening of September 18, 1931, several Kwantung army officers secretly exploded a section of Japanese railway, blamed the explosion on Chinese agitators, and used this as the pretext to attack the forces of Zhang Xueliang. Such a modus operandi was nothing new; the Kwantung army had been a hotbed of intrigue for years and had been responsible for the assassination in 1928 of Zhang Zuolin, Xueliang's father and Japan's previous collaborator in the region. The conspirators of 1928 were not punished; nor were those of 1931. Instead, upon finding themselves in possession of a vastly expanded territory in northeast China, government authorities in Tokyo decided to endorse the Kwantung army's action as a *fait accompli* and ignore the insubordination of the officer corps of the most powerful of Japan's colonial garrisons.

While the Sino-Japanese conflict was temporarily resolved by the Tanggu truce of 1933, which recognized Japan's new position in Manchuria, tensions continued to simmer until they erupted again in 1937. Although the China Incident (as the undeclared China War was officially known) was a direct outgrowth of the Manchurian Incident, the Anglo-American literature treats it as a separate conflict. Books by John Boyle and Lincoln Li on the Japanese occupation look at the difficulties of maintaining effective control over local collaborators, but draw no comparisons with the Manchurian case.[25] Other works on the conflict focus on the military strategies employed by both sides, analyzing their respective successes and failures. On the Japanese side the most pressing question is: How did Japan become bogged down in what proved an unwinnable war? The answers are found in a series of tactical errors, minute missteps, and misjudgments. By beginning their narratives after 1933, these works suggest that the "success" of the Manchurian campaigns bore no relation to the failures of the China Incident.[26] And yet, the facility with which Japan occupied Manchuria nurtured the hubris of Japanese ambitions to crush the Nationalists in a quick and decisive strike, and fed mounting ambitions to absorb all of China's vast territories. Moreover, both incidents arose from the contradiction between Japanese imperialism and Chinese nationalism, and what Japanese military planners were blind to in both 1931 and 1937 was that the Nationalist movement could not be vanquished by military means. The occupation of Manchuria was an enormous stimulant to Chinese nationalism and steeled Chinese determination to resist Japan at all costs. As much as it reflected Japanese overconfidence, this determination to resist was the product also of the Manchurian Incident, and both attitudes helped precipitate the outbreak of fighting on the Marco Polo Bridge in 1937 and its escalation into all-out war.

Much like the analysis of the Manchurian and China Incidents, the histories of the other fronts in the Second World War in Asia are contained in separate literatures, each highlighting its distinctive origins and character.[27] The conflict with the Soviet Union that flared into the series of Manchukuo–Siberian border wars in 1937–39 was justified by a combination of Russophobia and anti-communism. Though fears of the "red peril" emerged powerfully in the wake of the Russian Revolution and the failure of Japan's military efforts to contain communism in the Siberian Expedition of 1918–22, Russophobia had deeper roots, going back to the competition over Korea and Manchuria that culminated in the Russo-Japanese War of 1904–5. When the Japanese occupied the Russian sphere of influence in north Manchuria in the early 1930s, they destroyed the geopolitical balance of power that had been laid down in 1905 and had lasted for twenty-five years. Both sides began preparations for war.

On another front, the Japanese sweep through south-east Asia was launched in the name of Asian liberation and to drive the "white peril" out of Asia. In the face of the Japanese assault, the European colonial edifice fell like a house of cards, and the Japanese took credit for exposing the hollow core of European racial arrogance. Although the ideology of white peril had long-term rhetorical roots, the decision to strike south was the product of an increasingly acute need for war resources (particularly the oil fields of the Dutch East Indies) and the desire to cut off China's supply routes through south-east Asia. These came to a head in the late 1930s, just when the outbreak of war in Europe diverted attention from Asia and weakened the defenses of the colonial powers.

In the meantime, along yet another front a naval war had broken out with the United States. Like the conflicts with China, the Soviet Union, and the European colonial empires, Japan's tensions with the United States had deep roots. The two had begun to jockey for strategic domination of the Pacific before the turn of the century, when a rivalry over Hawaii precipitated a war scare and ended in the American decision to annex. The two powers fought over who would inherit the German-held Pacific islands after the First World War; they prepared war plans and built up their navies against one another. Tensions rose in the 1930s with Japanese aggression in China and a new naval arms' race, but America did not take concrete action to stop Japan until it felt its position in the Philippines threatened by Japan's southward advance.

Clearly, the military conflicts between Japan and its many enemies in the Second World War were in fundamental ways quite distinct from one another. Yet the question remains: What, if anything, tied them together into a single great war? The analytic isolation of these different conflicts in the Anglo-American literature tends to minimize the connections. Conservative historians in Japan echo this position, arguing in particular that a line be drawn between the Manchurian and China incidents. The implication is that had the army stopped in Manchuria, Japan might well have avoided being drawn into the Second World War. Progressive Japanese historians have objected strongly to this argument, and many use the rubric "fifteen-year war" to stress the origins of the Second World War in the Manchurian Incident. As the historian who coined the term explained: "The term 'Fifteen-year War' is used in order to imply that the various military incidents which occurred between 1931 and 1945 were in fact a continuous undeclared war."[28] The point is that the Manchurian Incident set in motion a process of military expansion that became difficult to contain.

There were many reasons for this, not the least of which concerned the "shoot first, ask questions later" approach to empire-building inaugurated by the army in Manchuria. Again, one cannot underscore too heavily the ways the new military imperialism linked the Manchurian Incident to the later wars of the decade. Unlike subsequent conflicts, the Manchurian Incident was a success, in the sense that Japan's war aims were achieved. Yet "autonomous diplomacy" worked, in this instance, because Japan's diplomatic partners were too preoccupied to mount an effective resistance.[29] China and the Soviet Union, for example, responded initially to Japanese bellicosity with concessions. In the early 1930s, the nationalists were too busy fighting the communists to resist the takeover of Manchuria. Stalin, preoccupied with agricultural collectivization, the five-year plans and purging the party, decided to sell off the Chinese Eastern Railway in 1935 and retreat before Japan's advance into north Manchuria. But after the formation of a united Chinese communist–nationalist front in 1936 and the Soviet fortifications of the Manchurian–Soviet border, both China and the Soviet Union began to stand their ground. War broke out with China in 1937, and with the Soviet Union in 1938 and 1939.

Similarly, American and European interests in Asia were initially consumed with domestic economic problems and the dissolution of the international financial system. The day before the Manchurian Incident, Great Britain went off the gold standard, so there was little attention to spare for the far east. Although after 1937 the United States opposed Japan indirectly by supplying Jiang Jieshi with war materials, only in 1940, after the outbreak of war in Europe and the Japanese advance into Indochina, did the United States begin embargoes on strategic materials to Japan. The tightening of the economic screws led the Japanese to the decision, once again, to attack, and from December 1941 Japan was fighting a war against Britain and the United States, and the boundaries of the empire became an endless war front. In the process, the empire and the war grew indistinguishable. From a small war in Manchuria to the titanic naval battles of the Pacific, the hallmark of the new imperialism of the 1930s was a state of perpetual war.

Following the model pioneered in Manchukuo, the autonomous phase of empire also denoted a new kind of colonial rule. This was signaled initially in official rhetoric which sought to depict the Japanese colonial state as the ally of anti-colonial nationalism. First, Manchuria was "liberated" from China by a movement for independence; later, the Japanese set up an administration in south-east Asia under the slogan "Asia for the Asiatics." As vacuous and self-serving as these declarations seem in retrospect, at the time they were effective in initially mobilizing support both among Japanese at home and among the Asians who helped Japan create the new colonial institutions.

The organizational structure of the puppet state which was developed in Manchuria subsequently became the prototype for the creation of a string of collaborationist regimes in occupied China. In south-east Asia, the picture was more complex. With the support of local nationalist movements, Japan drove out western colonial rulers, establishing two types of administration. In Thailand (the sole independent country at the time of Japanese occupation) and, after January 1943, in Burma and the Philippines, alliances gave Japan the power of indirect rule. In Indonesia and Malaya, the occupying forces governed through a military administration. With the exception of French Indochina, where Japan ruled in collaboration with the French authorities and was opposed by Ho Chi Minh's newly organized Vietminh, south-east Asian nationalists cooperated with Japanese colonial rule, especially in its initial phase.

Strategies of mobilization were part of the Manchurian formula. Military, political, economic, and cultural institutions were created or reshaped to organize new communities of support for Japanese rule. Ambitious young Chinese found the Manchukuo army and military academy a route of advancement, as did their counterparts throughout the empire. Military institutions formed in the late colonial period in Burma, Korea, and elsewhere became the training grounds for postcolonial elites. Similarly, the Japanese established mass parties such as the Putera in Indonesia and the Kalibapi in the Philippines, patterned on Manchukuo's Kyôwakai. Throughout the empire, the Japanese created joint ventures with local capital. Sometimes this was a mask for Japanese control, sometimes a cover for appropriation of native capital, and sometimes, as in Korea, a means of cultivating a collaborative elite and splitting the nationalist movement. Assimilationist cultural policies were widely applied over the course of the 1930s and 1940s, in an attempt to create an elite cadre of youth loyal to Japanese rule. These policies went furthest in Taiwan and Korea, where the *kôminka*, (imperialization) movement sought to erase native cultural traditions, replacing them with the Japanese religious practices of shrine Shinto, the use of the Japanese language, and the Japanization of given names.

It was not only colonial state institutions, but also the experiment with economic autarky in Manchukuo that became the guiding spirit of the wartime Japanese empire. The integrated industrial and trading unit formed with the Japan–Manchuria bloc economy was extended first to include north China, then the rest of China, and finally south-east Asia in a self-sufficient yen bloc. In Korea, Taiwan, and north China this involved industrialization and heavy investment, as it did in Manchukuo. The lessons of economic management learned in Manchukuo, including currency reunification, production targets, semi-public development companies, and other tools of state control, were applied also in these new economies.

In all these ways the experiment in Manchukuo marked the beginning of a new imperialism, made necessary by the upsurge of revolutionary nationalist movements throughout the empires of Asia. European powers responded to the rise of Asian nationalism with a policy of appeasement, attempting to shore up the crumbling colonial edifice through political concessions in the middle east and India. The Japanese dealt with the same challenge by claiming a unity with Asian nationalism. They tried to co-opt the anti-colonial movement by declaring the Japanese colonial state to be the agent of nationalist liberation.

While this question of continuity between the various military incidents of the 1930s has constituted one of the interpretive divides in the literature on the foreign crisis, another division of opinion emerged over the issue of Japan's war responsibility. Stripped to its bare bones, the basic point of contention in the latter debate is whether the foreign crisis was the result of belligerent, extremist, and ultimately irrational Japanese policies, or whether those same policies represented a reasonable and realistic response to external pressures and provocations. In other words: Did Japan create the crisis in Asia, or was it merely drawn into a crisis of another's making?[30]

The former position is articulated in the argument that in the 1930s a cabal of reckless ultra-nationalist extremists in the army seized the reigns of government from civilian moderates and, reversing the course of foreign policy, led Japan down the path to war. This interpretation owes its origins to the "Japan crowd" in the US State Department, and especially to Joseph Grew, ambassador to Japan for much of the 1930s. Grew subscribed to a "pendulum theory" of Japanese history, arguing that the nation alternated between periods of intense nationalism and anti-foreign sentiment, followed by periods of internationalism and cooperation. Grew's view was that the Japanese government was divided into two hostile factions, the extremist nationalists and the moderate internationalists, and that American policy needed to co-operate with and encourage the latter at all costs.[31]

In postwar history books, this interpretation re-emerged in a "civilian–military split" thesis: the idea that liberal civilian moderates in government were thrust aside in the 1930s by military extremists. This was the position taken by the prosecution in the Tokyo War Crimes' Trial, officially known as the International Military Tribunal for the Far East. The IMTFE indicted Japanese militarism, embodied in the persons of twenty-eight defendants, for the crime of conspiracy to wage aggressive war. The hearings of the Tokyo trial involved a long excursion into Japanese history, and traced to its origins a putative Japanese plan to conquer the world, put into action through the series of military incidents that began in Manchuria.[32] Robert Butow's 1961 biography of wartime leader Tojo Hideki drew heavily on trial records and enshrined the judgments of the tribunal as academic orthodoxy. Echoing the Tokyo trial's verdict that a "militaristic clique" took hold of the government, Butow dated the military seizure of power and the first step on the road to Pearl Harbor from the Kwantung army's adventurism in the "neighbor's garden" of Manchuria.[33]

This viewpoint is given a slightly different inflection in the seven-volume series *The Road to the Pacific War* (*Taiheiyō sensō e no michi: kaisen gaikōshi*), published by the Japan Association of International Relations (*Nihon kokusai seiji gakkai*) in 1962–63 and translated more recently into English. This work aimed to criticize the structural arguments of Japanese Marxists. Eschewing any notion of a ruling class unified behind emperor-system fascism, the volumes in this series focused narrowly on the military as an organization. Unlike the Marxist historians, these researchers were given privileged access to the archives of the self-defense forces. Later they published many of the materials they discovered in a documentary supplement to the series.

The thrust of this scholarship is twofold. First, it takes issue with the "fifteen-year war" approach, choosing rather to treat the conflicts of the Second World War as isolated military incidents. Second, it looks for the causes of the various military conflicts in the minute day-to-day decisions of Japanese officers on-the-spot. Consequently, the Japanese military, and in particular its officer corps, bears the main burden of war responsibility: given its single-minded pursuit of military security to the exclusion of all other considerations, escalation of military conflict was inevitable, as was the eventual clash with the United States.

Diplomats are secondary figures in this narrative: they appear after the fact, attempting ineffectually to repair the damage done by precipitate and irresponsible military officers. In this analysis the explanation for war becomes, again, a military that has run amok. Yet while Butow's argument stresses the military seizure of power at the center, *The Road to the Pacific War* asserts the importance of military autonomy at the periphery of the Japanese empire.[34]

The military-conspiracy thesis is echoed in many ways in the work of progressive Japanese historians like Ienaga Saburô. Ienaga's book on the Pacific War, written in the mid-1960s, was part of a broader attempt to educate the Japanese population and to "stimulate reflection and self-criticism about the war." The book is concerned with the issue of responsibility, and examines the choices made during the war by ordinary citizens like Ienaga himself. In some ways his book follows from the line of interpretation of Japanese Marxist historians who located responsibility for war more broadly in the power structure of prewar Japan, that is to say the entire ruling class of landlords, monopoly capitalists, and state bureaucrats, of which the military was one part. Yet, though Ienaga acknowledges the importance of support given by other elements of the ruling class, the principal blame for the war falls on the army. The peculiar autonomy granted the military under the prewar constitution permitted this "authoritarian and irrational" institution the leeway to mobilize people for war, inculcating in them racist and hateful attitudes toward other Asians, promoting mass conformity and blind obedience to authority, and driving them into a frenzy of self-destruction for an unwinnable war.[35]

In contrast to such depictions of Japanese foreign policy in the 1930s driven by an irrational and out-of-control military, other historians have analyzed these same policies as the rational and realistic response to a crisis in the international system. In this literature, the key decision-makers appear not as ultra-nationalist extremists or trigger-happy colonial officers determined to overturn the world order but as sober and experienced bureaucrats laboring as responsible government officials to secure Japan's legitimate economic and political interests in the face of a increasingly unstable world situation.

This was the thrust of writing by American New-Left historians and critics of American imperialism such as Noam Chomsky. Placing the blame for the Pacific War squarely on the shoulders of the United States, Chomsky argued that Japanese foreign policy in the 1930s was a defensive response to American imperialism in Asia. Echoing the case made by Japanese statesmen in the 1930s, Chomsky wrote that American claims to have protected China from Japanese aggression were hypocritical and self-interested. Using economic strangulation to block Japanese access to China, America was guilty of a gross double-standard – denying Japan a guaranteed market in Asia like that possessed by America in Latin America and by Britain in its colonial territories throughout the world. American Asian policy was motivated not by paternalism toward China but rather by the interest of American capitalists in the China market. And since China was necessary for Japan's survival, US pressure to end its occupation propelled Japan to fight in self-defense. What Chomsky was suggesting, in other words, was that while American activities in Asia were aggressive and imperialistic, Japanese activities were driven by a legitimate desire for economic survival.[36] Guilty of falling prey to his own double-standard, Chomsky's vindication of Japanese aggression in Asia ironically echoed the views of reactionary Japanese historians like Hayashi Fusao. In his notorious apologia, Hayashi defended Japanese wartime policies as the but latest skirmish in a "hundred years war" to liberate Asia from the imperialist aggression of the west.[37]

Other American historians such as James Crowley, while eschewing any condemnation of US policy, tried to show the essential rationality of Japanese foreign policy in the 1930s. As Louis Morton points out,

> Crowley challenged two of the hallowed generalizations of the traditional interpretation of the origins of the Pacific War: that the basic cause of the war was Japan's aggressive foreign policy after 1931; and that this policy was the work of a military clique that seized political power after 1931 through a program of terror, political assassinations, and conspiracies.[38]

Crowley looked at the interaction between military leaders on the ground in China and the cabinet in Tokyo. He argued that the actions of the Kwantung army were not independent initiatives of insubordinate military extremists, but were fully consistent with national policy formulated by responsible civilian and military leadership in Tokyo. To Crowley, the use of military measures to secure Japan's position in Manchuria and the willingness to risk diplomatic confrontation to defend those actions constituted a rational policy response to the economic and military security dilemmas facing Japan in Asia in these years.[39]

Crowley's attack on the "civilian–military split" thesis has been reinforced more recently by Michael Barnhart. In Barnhart's view, foreign policy in the 1930s was guided by a drive for economic security and the need to prepare for total war, both of which factors became priorities in military planning after the First World War. Though in hindsight it became clear that military self-sufficiency was in fact unattainable for resource-poor Japan, in pursuit of this goal planners steered Japan down the "road to ruin" in China and into the great gamble at Pearl Harbor. Barnhart's work concentrates heavily on the role of military planners in the policy decisions of the 1930s and highlights how a ruinous rivalry between army and navy factions led to some very damaging decisions. In his narrative, the military, although a key player, acts in concert with civilian government officials, and Barnhart is careful to show how the drive for autarky in the military converged with the drive for domestic reform among other government factions.[40]

Whether arguing that the machinery of government was seized by a group of extremists, or that the policy decisions of the 1930s were a rational response to a difficult set of circumstances, the literature on the foreign crisis has tended to overlook the fact that government officials were not in sole control of the policy-making process. Indeed, to understand the success of military officials in promoting their policy agenda, one must look beyond the realm of bureaucratic politics to see how the decision to embark on the new military imperialism played out on social and political battlefields far from the centers of government power. As in Europe, the democratization of politics and the growth of mass organizations in the late nineteenth and early twentieth centuries changed the process of imperial policy-making in Japan. Using new vehicles of mass mobilization such as political parties, labor unions, and voluntary associations, government officials tried to enlist popular political forces in support of their course of action. At the same time, political organizations used the imperialist cause to appeal to a mass following. When imperialism became a tool of domestic politics for both government officials and private citizens, it spelled the end of a government monopoly over imperial policy; henceforth policy decisions would be made collectively. Thus, whether army officers are to be held accountable for an irrational war or commended for trying to make the best of a bad set of choices, they must share either the censure or the accolades with the wide variety of interest groups that helped mobilize popular support for the advance into China and south-east Asia. This included the mass media as well as academic institutions, women's and youth groups, chambers of commerce, the tourist industry, the film and entertainment industry, and a host of other institutions.

The concentration of historical attention on wartime Japan reflects widespread consensus that the Second World War constituted an epochal event in modern Japanese history. Although the literature on the war is prodigious, many questions are still unanswered. In conclusion, I would like to suggest two new avenues of research which I believe will open up fresh interpretations in the future. The first is the question of popular agency. Thus far, the story of the Showa crisis gives a sense of how the war affected "the people," but has had little to say on the reverse process. Stimulated by trends in social and cultural history, new research will, I believe, focus increasingly on popular initiatives and pressures from below that helped precipitate the crisis of the 1930s. Second, new research is likely to deal more explicitly with the ways that the domestic and foreign crises interlock, or to borrow Jon Halliday's phrase – to look at "the dialectic of the internal and the external."[41] The connection between foreign aggression and domestic repression – defining features of the 1930s – has been assumed, but not analyzed. Such an analysis might take up the question of how new military initiatives in the empire were directly tied to the army's quest for power at home, it could explore the relationship between the domestic economic crisis and the breakdown in the global trading and financial system; or it could look at the ways that a social movement aiming at domestic reform became transformed into a social imperialist project.

Notes

1 In the Meiji Restoration of 1868 the feudal state was overthrown and a series of modernizing reforms inaugurated, culminating in the creation of a constitutional monarchy.

2 In addition to the items discussed here, see also works listed in E. R May and J. C. Thomson, Jr, *American–East Asian Relations: A Survey*, Cambridge, MA, 1972. See the essays in W. I. Cohen (ed.), *New Frontiers in American–East Asian Relations: Essays Presented*

to Dorothy Borg, New York, 1983; A. Iriye, "The Asian factor," in G. Martel (ed.), *The Origins of the Second World War Reconsidered: The A. J. P. Taylor Debate After Twenty-five Years*, Boston, MA, 1986, pp. 227–43; J. W. Dower with T. S. George, *Japanese History and Culture From Ancient to Modern Times: Seven Basic Bibliographies*, 2nd edn, Princeton, NJ, 1995; and S. Asada (ed.), *Japan and the World, 1853–1952: A Bibliographic Guide to Japanese Scholarship in Foreign Relations*, New York, 1989. The Dower bibliography will be especially useful for students seeking to do more specialized reading on a particular topic. For students who read Japanese, the Asada volume provides an excellent overview of the Japanese academic debates together with an extensive bibliography of primary and secondary materials. Within the text of this essay Japanese names are written in Japanese order: family name first, personal name second. In citations of English-language translations of Japanese authors, names are written as published.

3 The *Meiji*, (1868–1912), *Taishô*, (1912–1926), and *Shôwa*, (1926–1989) eras demarcate imperial reigns.

4 J. W. Dower (*Empire and Aftermath: Yoshida Shigeru and the Japanese Experience, 1878–1954*, Cambridge, MA, 1979, p. 85) uses this phrase to stress the continuity of Japanese expansionist policies from the 1920s to the 1930s:

> The common ground of both diplomacies was Japan's inextricable entanglement in the coils of imperialism, and the difference between the so-called "soft" and "hard" or "liberal" and "militarist" approaches was essentially one of timing…the difference, as it were, between go slow imperialism and go fast imperialism…

For further discussion of the sea-change of the early 1930s, see L. Young, *Japan's Total Empire: Manchuria and the Culture of Wartime Imperialism*, Berkeley, CA, 1998, pp. 55–182.

5 R. H. Mitchell, *Thought Control in Prewar Japan*, Ithaca, NY, 1966, and *Censorship in Imperial Japan*, Princeton, NJ, 1984; Kazuko Tsurumi, "The army: the emperor system in microcosm," and "Socialization for death: moral education at school and in the army," both in her *Social Change and the Individual: Japan before and after Defeat in World War II*, Princeton, NJ, 1966, G. J. Kasza, *The State and the Mass Media in Japan, 1918–1945*, Berkeley, CA, 1988.

6 The discussion which follows on the mass media and the Manchurian Incident is drawn from Young, *Japan's Total Empire*, pp. 62–7.

7 Shunsuke Tsurumi, *An Intellectual History of Wartime Japan, 1931–1945*, London, 1986; P. G. Steinhoff, "Tenkô and thought control," in G. L. Bernstein and Harahiro Fukui, (eds), *Japan and the World: Essays on Japanese History and Politics in Honour of Ishida Takeshi*, London, 1988, pp. 78–94; P. G. Steinhoff, *Tenkô: Ideology and Social Integration in Prewar Japan*, New York, 1991; Kazuko Tsurumi, "Six types of change in personality: case studies of ideological conversion in the 1930s," in her *Social Change and the Individual*, Princeton, NJ, 1966; I. Neary, "Tenkô of an organization: the Suiheisha in the late 1930s," *Proceedings of the British Association for Japanese Studies*, vol. 2, 1977, pp. 64–76.

8 Tatsuo Arima, *The Failure of Freedom: A Portrait of Modern Japanese Intellectuals*, Cambridge, MA, 1969; J. V. Koschmann, "Introduction: Soft rule and expressive protest," and Matsumoto Sannosuke, "Special introductory essay: The roots of political disillusionment: 'public' and 'private' in Japan," both in J. V. Koschmann (ed.), *Authority and the Individual in Japan*, Tokyo, 1978, pp. 1–53.

9 W. M. Fletcher, *The Search for a New Order: Intellectuals and Fascism in Prewar Japan*, Chapel Hill, NC, 1982; and "Intellectuals and fascism in early Shôwa Japan," *Journal of Asian Studies*, vol. 39, 1979, pp. 39–63. Other discussions of intellectuals and the New Order include: B.-A. Shillony, "Japanese intellectuals during the Pacific War," *Proceedings of the British Association for Japanese Studies*, vol. 2, 1977, pp. 90–9; James B. Crowley, "A New Asian Order: some notes on prewar Japanese nationalism," in B. S. and H. D. Harootunian (eds), *Japan in Crisis*, Princeton NJ, 1974, pp. 270–98; J. B.

Crowley, "Intellectuals as Visionaries of the New Asian Order," in J. Morley (ed.), *Dilemmas of Growth in Prewar Japan*, Princeton, NJ, 1971, pp. 319–73; Donald Keene, "Tenkô literature: the writings of ex-communists," in his *Dawn to the West: Japanese Literature in the Modern Era*, New York, 1984, pp.846–905.

10 For a more elaborated version of this discussion, see Young, *Japan's Total Empire*, pp. 268–82.

11 See the chapters "The totalitarian solution' and "Tenancy and aggression' in R. P. Dore, *Land Reform in Japan*, New York, 1985 (1959), pp. 86–114, 115–25; T. R. H. Havens, *Farm and Nation in Modern Japan; Agrarian Nationalism, 1870–1940*, Princeton, NJ, 1974.

12 B.-A. Shillony, *Revolt in Japan: The Young Officers and the February 26, 1936 Incident*, Princeton, NJ, 1972; G.M. Wilson, *Radical Nationalist in Japan: Kita Ikki, 1883–1937*, Cambridge, MA, 1969; R. Storry, *The Double Patriots: A Study of Japanese Nationalism*, NY, 1957.

13 H. Byas, *Government by Assassination*, New York, 1942.

14 This discussion is drawn from Young, *Japan's Total Empire*, pp. 127–128.

15 R. Smethurst, *A Social Basis for Prewar Japanese Militarism: The Army and the Rural Community*, Berkeley, CA, 1974.

16 T. R. H. Havens, *Valley of Darkness; The Japanese People and World War Two*, Lanham, MD, 1986; B.-A. Shillony, *Politics and Culture in Wartime Japan*, Oxford, 1981.

17 G. Berger, "Politics and mobilization in Japan, 1931–1945," in P. Duus (ed.), *Cambridge History of Japan*, vol. 6: *The Twentieth Century*, Cambridge, MA, 1988, pp. 97–153; G. M. Berger, *Parties Out of Power in Japan, 1931–1941*, Princeton, NJ, 1977; R. Rice, "Economic mobilization in wartime Japan: business, bureaucracy, and military in conflict," *Journal of Asian Studies*, vol. 38, 1979, pp. 689–706.

18 For a sampling of the debate, see G. Kasza, "Fascism from below? A comparative perspective on the Japanese Right, 1931–1936," *Journal of Contemporary History*, vol. 19, 1984, pp. 607–30; I. Morris (ed.), *Japan 1931–1945: Militarism, Fascism, Japanism?*, Boston, MA, 1963; Fletcher, "Intellectuals and fascism," pp. 39–63; G. McCormack, "Nineteen-thirties' Japan: fascism?', *Bulletin of Concerned Asian Scholars*, vol. 14, 1982, pp. 20–33; P. Duus and D. I. Okimoto, "Fascism and the history of pre-war Japan: the failure of a concept," *Journal of Asian Studies*, vol. 39, 1979, 65–76, H. P. Bix, "Rethinking 'emperor-system fascism': ruptures and continuities in modern Japanese history," *Bulletin of Concerned Asian Scholars*, vol. 14, 1982, 2–19; G. M. Wilson, "A new look at the problem of 'Japanese fascism,' ' *Comparative Studies in Society and History*, vol. 10, 1968, 401–12; R. Dore and Tsutomu Ôuchi, "Rural origins of Japanese fascism," in Morley (ed.), *Dilemmas of Growth*, pp. 181–209.

19 The "emperor-system fascism" thesis is restated in Bix, "Ruptures and continuities," pp. 3–5, the quoted statement from p. 4. For a discussion of the Marxist position, see G. A. Hosten, *Marxism and the Crisis of Development in Prewar Japan*, Princeton, NJ, 1986, pp. 256–63, and McCormack, "Nineteen-thirties' Japan," pp. 30–1.

20 I. Morris (ed.), *Thought and Behavior in Modern Japanese Politics*, Oxford, 1963.

21 The volumes in this series include: M. Jansen (ed.), *Changing Japanese Attitudes toward Modernization*, 1965; W. E. Lockwood (ed.), *The State and Economic Enterprise in Japan*, 1965; R. P. Dore (ed.), *Aspects of Social Change in Modern Japan*, 1971; R. E. Ward (ed.), *Political Development in Modern Japan*, 1971; D. Shively (ed.), *Tradition and Modernization in Japanese Culture*, 1971; and Morley (ed.), *Dilemmas of Growth*. For critical evaluation of this series, see J. W. Dower, "E. H. Norman, Japan and the uses of history," in Dower (ed.), *Origins of the Modern Japanese State. Selected Writings of E. H. Norman*, New York, 1975, pp. 31–65.

22 For a discussion of this literature, see Hatano Sumio, "Japan's foreign policy, 1931–1945: historiography," in Sadao Asada, *Japan and the World, 1853–1952: A Bibliographic Guide to Japanese Scholarship in Foreign Relations*, New York, 1989, pp. 218–33.

23 Duus and Okimoto, "Failure of a concept," p. 67.

24 On the diplomacy of the Manchurian Incident, see C. Thorne, *The Limits of Foreign Policy: The West, the League, and the Far Eastern Crisis of 1931–1933*, London, 1972; I. H. Nish, *Japan's Struggle with Internationalism: Japan, China, and the League of Nations, 1931–1933*, New York, 1993. On the military dimension: S. N. Ogata, *Defiance in Manchuria:*

The Making of Japanese Foreign Policy, 1931–1932, Berkeley, CA, 1964; Takehiko Yoshi-hashi, *Conspiracy at Mukden: The Rise of the Japanese Military*, New Haven, CT, 1963; J. Crowley, *Japan's Quest for Autonomy: National Security and Foreign Policy, 1930–38*, Princeton, NJ, 1966; M. Peattie, *Ishiwara Kanji and Japan's Confrontation with the West*, Princeton, NJ, 1975; J. Morley (ed.), *Japan Erupts: The London Naval Conference and the Manchurian Incident, 1928–1932*, New York, 1984.

25 J. H. Boyle, *China and Japan at War, 1937–1945: The Politics of Collaboration*, Stanford, CA, 1972; L. Li, *The Japanese Army in North China, July 1937–December 1941: Problems of Political and Economic Control*, New York, 1975.

26 J. Morley (ed.), *The China Quagmire: Japan's Expansion on the Asian Continent, 1933–1941*, New York, 1983; D. Wilson, *When Tigers Fight: The Story of the Sino-Japanese War, 1937–1945*, New York, 1982.

27 For bibliography on these separate conflicts, see book lists on Japanese foreign relations by country in Dower and George, *Seven Basic Bibliographies*, pp. 249–346.

28 Shunsuke Tsurumi, *An Intellectual History of Wartime Japan, 1931–1945*, London, 1986, p. 124n. For a summary of the "fifteen-year war" debate, see Hatano, "Japan's foreign policy," pp. 217–25.

29 This discussion of "autonomous diplomacy" and the new phase of empire building is drawn from Young, *Japan's Total Empire*, pp. 47–50.

30 The basic contours of this debate are laid out in Section X, "Japan's foreign policy in the 1930s: search for autonomy, or naked aggression?", in H. Wray and H. Conroy (eds), *Japan Examined: Perspectives on Modern Japanese History*, Honolulu, HI, 1983, pp. 291–330.

31 Dower, *Empire and Aftermath*, pp. 108–9.

32 R. Minear, *Victor's Justice: The Tokyo War Crimes Trial*, Princeton, NJ, 1971; Chihiro Hosoya, Nisuke Andô, Yasuaki Ônuma and R. H. Minear (eds), *The Tokyo War Crimes Trial: An International Symposium*, New York, 1986.

33 R. J. C. Butow, *Tojo and the Coming of the War*, Princeton, NJ, 1961.

34 Five volumes of the English-language version have been published by Columbia University Press (New York) under the general editorship of J. W. Morley: *Japan Erupts*; *China Quagmire*; *Deterrent Diplomacy: Japan, Germany, and the USSR, 1935–1940* (1984); *The Fateful Choice: Japan's Advance Into Southeast Asia, 1939–1941* (1980); Japan's Road to the Pacific War; Japan's Negotiation with the United States (1994).

35 Saburô Ienaga, *The Pacific War, 1931–1945*, New York, 1978. This is based on series of lectures written in 1964 and translated into English by Frank Baldwin. For Ienaga's arguments about racist attitudes toward Asia, thought control, and the military, see Baldwin's introductory "Note," pp. vii–x; Ienaga's Preface, pp. xi–xvi, and Part I, "Why was the war not prevented?"

36 N. Chomsky, "The revolutionary pacifism of A. J. Muste," in his *American Power and the New Mandarins*, New York, 1969, pp. 159–220.

37 Hatano, "Historiography," p. 223.

38 Morton, "1937–1941," in *American–East Asian Relations* p. 282.

39 J. B. Crowley, *Japan's Quest for Autonomy: National Security and Foreign Policy, 1930–1938*, Princeton, NJ, 1968.

40 M. A. Barnhart, *Japan Prepares for Total War; The Search for Economic Security, 1919–1941*, Ithaca, NY, 1987.

41 J. Halliday, *A Political History of Japanese Capitalism*, New York, 1975, p. 14.

10 More than meets the eye

The Ethiopian War and the origins of the Second World War

Brian R. Sullivan

"No concrete 'interest' was at stake in Abyssinia – not even for Italy: Mussolini was concerned to show off Italy's strength, not to acquire the practical gains (if any such exist) of Empire.... But Italy still stood condemned as an aggressor; and the two Western Powers could not bring themselves to recognize the King of Italy as Emperor of Abyssinia. The Stresa front was gone beyond recall, Mussolini forced on to the German side. This outcome was unwelcome to him. In attacking Abyssinia, Mussolini had intended to exploit the international tension on th eRhine, not to opt for Germany. Instead he had lost his freedom of choice."

A.J.P. Taylor, Origins, pp. 96, 106–7.

The influence on the origins of the Second World War of the crisis provoked by the Ethiopian War appears clear from a glance at the evidence. Prior to the Italian invasion of Ethiopia, Mussolini had made military agreements with the French and formed a coalition with the British and the French to prevent German aggression in Europe. Following the Ethiopian War, Fascist Italy and Nazi Germany moved from providing joint military aid to the Nationalists in the Spanish Civil War, to formal alliance in May 1939, to waging war together on France and Britain in June 1940.

The argument explicating this sequence of events goes as follows. British attempts to prevent the Italian conquest of Ethiopia created deep bitterness within the Fascist regime and among the great majority of the Italian people. Hoping to save the anti-German coalition, the French had tried to mediate the British–Italian quarrel. After that attempt failed, the French reluctantly selected the British as the superior partner. This choice struck Fascist leaders as betrayal. Considering that the British were thus revealed as hostile and the French as treacherous, Mussolini began a détente with the Germans in January 1936, to escape diplomatic isolation.[1]

There remained many sources of friction between Italy and Germany, particularly Italian protection of Austria and German penetration of the Balkans. However, common ideology and compatible goals, as well as Hitler's skillful wooing of Mussolini, drew the two regimes closer over the next three years. This relationship helped Hitler to remilitarize the Rhineland, annex Austria, extort the Sudetenland, and seize Bohemia–Moravia and Memel. But these events pushed Italy into a position of increasing inferiority to Germany. Seeking to right the balance of power in the Balkans, Mussolini invaded Albania in April 1939. As a consequence of Axis aggression in March–April 1939, London and Paris gave guarantees to other East European states, dividing Western Europe into two hostile camps.[2]

In turn, Italy and Germany formed an offensive military alliance, the Pact of Steel, in May. Strengthened on one flank, Hitler reached comprehensive agreement with Stalin in August without consulting Mussolini. This granted Hitler security to the east. Two weeks later, Germany invaded Poland and precipitated war with France and Britain – an action that initially infuriated Mussolini. But over the fall and winter, the Duce concluded that the Germans were strong enough to defeat the British and French. While Mussolini knew his forces were unprepared for a lengthy conflict, in March 1940 he promised Hitler he would enter the fighting as soon as possible. German victory in Norway, followed by the astonishing success of their campaign against France, convinced Mussolini to intervene immediately. The Duce declared war on a near-prostrate France and a desperately isolated Britain on June 10, 1940.[3]

The cause-and-effect relationship between the events of 1935–36 and of 1939–40 appears obvious. Through a series of miscalculations and inept diplomacy, the British and French had alienated Mussolini. They had inadvertently pushed him first into association, then into alliance, with Hitler. Moreover, a closer examination of two eighteen-month periods, one on either side of the Ethiopian War, seems to confirm this interpretation. In April 1934, following the signature of the Rome protocols by the governments of Italy, Austria, and Hungary to coordinate opposition to German expansion in the Danube basin, Mussolini agreed to confer with Hitler. Meanwhile, the anti-German diplomats, Fulvio Suvich and Pompeo Aloisi, who ran the Italian foreign ministry attempted to gain Polish, Yugoslav, and Romanian adherence to the protocols.

The German and Italian dictators met near Venice that June. Mussolini demanded respect for Austrian independence. Hitler agreed. Afterwards, Mussolini told his aides that he had found the German repellent. The next month, Austrian Nazis attempted a *putsch* in Vienna and murdered Dollfuss, the Austrian chancellor. Hitler had approved the coup, had ordered arms be given to the Austrian Nazis in Bavaria, and allowed them passage into Austria. But Mussolini rapidly deployed several divisions and air squadrons to the Brenner Pass. He warned that a German move against Austria would provoke war. Dollfuss had been Mussolini's friend, and his wife and children were vacationing at the Duce's country home at the time of the assassination. It fell to Mussolini himself to inform Frau Dollfuss of her husband's fate, and he remained extremely bitter over the murder.[4]

In reply, Mussolini ordered new attempts to settle differences with France, efforts spurned by the French in July 1932. This time, Italian and French diplomats arrived at a negotiated resolution of most of the differences dividing their two countries throughout the summer and fall of 1934. These discussions led to agreements between Mussolini and Laval in Rome in January 1935. Laval granted Italy a "free hand" in Ethiopia. Mussolini pledged co-operation to prevent German remilitarization of the Rhineland, or an *Anschluss*. Over the following six months, Italian–French staff talks worked out the details. In April 1935, the Italian, French, and British heads of government met at Stresa and reaffirmed their Locarno treaty obligations to preserve the German western frontiers established in 1919.[5]

Thereafter, British–Italian relations worsened. Mussolini had begun sending large forces to the Italian colonies bordering Ethiopia. At Stresa, mid-level British diplomats had made clear to their Italian counterparts that Britain would oppose an attack on Ethiopia. When Anthony Eden, minister for League of Nations' affairs, and Mussolini discussed the issue in Rome in late June 1935, they could not agree. Mussolini politely but firmly insisted that Italy would acquire a protectorate over Ethiopia. Several weeks earlier, London and Berlin had announced British acceptance of German naval and air rearmament – in violation of the Versailles treaty. Many Italians saw the British countenancing expansion of German power in Europe while denying Italians their "place in the sun" in East Africa. Eden had told Mussolini that one aspect of the Versailles treaty, the authority of the League of Nations to prevent aggression, must be respected. Nonetheless, the British had given the Germans freedom to ignore a major Versailles restriction on their ability to conduct aggression. This hypocrisy produced outrage within the Fascist leadership.[6]

Yet the naval agreement pleased the Duce. The British violation of one clause of the treaty of Versailles provided him with the excuse to violate another: the prohibition on use of force to settle international disputes. The accord also allowed an increase in German sea power to the disadvantage of France, adding pressure on Paris to maintain its new security relationship with Rome. Further-more, the naval agreement indicated that the Royal Navy might reduce forces in the Mediterranean to bolster defenses in the North Sea. This increased the odds in Italy's favor in case of a clash with Britain over Ethiopia.[7]

The crisis between London and Rome did expand from diplomatic quarrels to actions close to war over the summer of 1935. Mussolini sent three divisions to Libya, threatening Egypt and also British control of the Suez Canal. In late August, the British Mediterranean Fleet deployed from its vulnerable base at Malta to Alexandria. Simultaneously, London ordered the reinforcement of the Mediterranean by sending warships from the Home Fleet to Gibraltar. Nonethe-less, at maneuvers held close to the Austrian–Italian border that same month, Mussolini demonstrated his continued opposition to German expansion, even at the cost of war. This show of continued Italian adherence to the anti-German front formed at Stresa, however, did not prevent increasing friction between Rome and London. British–Italian relations grew very tense in mid-September after Royal Navy battle squadrons blocked both exits from the Mediterranean. Mussolini was not deterred, however. Italian forces invaded Ethiopia on October 3, 1935.[8]

Despite other war scares between December 1935 and April 1936 arising from Italian concerns that the League might impose oil sanctions on Italy or that Britain might shut the Suez Canal, the conquest of Ethiopia proceeded. In early May 1936 Italian forces entered Addis Ababa, while emperor Haile Selassie fled into exile. From his balcony overlooking the Piazza Venezia, the Duce announced the establishment of a Fascist Roman *Impero* in East Africa. Still, most of Ethiopia remained unconquered.[9]

Yet another possibility of war flared in early June 1936. Mussolini worried about even harsher League sanctions on Italy as retaliation for the erosion of Ethiopian independence. In that case, he was prepared to invade Yugoslavia in concert with the Hungarians, to seize the rich natural resources of Croatia and Serbia. Over the following weeks, however, Mussolini grew ever more certain that the League would end the economic blockade of Italy. Under strong British and French pressure the League revoked sanctions against Italy in July 1936. For a few weeks Europe returned to tranquillity.[10]

The eighteen months prior to the Italian attack on Ethiopia provide a distinct contrast with the eighteen months following Mussolini's proclamation in May 1936 of Vittorio Emanuele III as emperor of Ethiopia. In early June, Mussolini advised Kurt von Schuschnigg, Dollfuss' successor, to settle his differences with Hitler. A few days later, Mussolini dismissed Suvich and Aloisi, and made his pro-German son-in-law Galeazzo Ciano foreign minister. In late July, Italian and German air crews began cooperating to transport General Francisco Franco's rebel Army of Africa from Morocco to Spain. Over the next few weeks, Mussolini and Hitler agreed to coordinate their aid to the Nationalists in the Spanish Civil War. That October, Ciano visited Germany, concluding his trip with friendly conversations with Hitler. Speaking in Milan on November 1, 1936, Mussolini described the new ties between Rome and Berlin as "an axis around which may cooperate all European states...".[11] The following month the Italians and Germans agreed to pursue coordinated diplomatic and economic policies in the Danubian region.

Hermann Goering visited Rome in January 1937. He and Mussolini agreed that Italy should predominate in Axis assistance to the Spanish Nationalists. While Mussolini responded coldly to the suggestion that an *Anschluss* was inevitable, he stressed his enthusiasm for co-operation with Hitler. Afterwards, Ciano hinted to Goering that Italy might eventually acquiesce to German annexation of Austria. In May, Mussolini accepted Hitler's invitation to visit Germany, and his September tour proved a triumph of Nazi propaganda. Mussolini returned deeply impressed with German power. In November 1937 Italy adhered to the Anti-Comintern Pact between Germany and Japan. As Ciano noted, the agreement was "anti-Communist in theory but in fact [was] unmistakably anti-British."[12] The previous day, Hitler had said that he expected Mussolini to attack Britain and France, possibly that coming summer, and that Germany would supply Italy with raw materials but would seize the opportunity to annex Austria and Czechoslovakia. The Führer expected the Duce to accept this with good grace.[13]

Judged by these events, the A. J. P. Taylor thesis that French and British in-flexibility in 1935–36 drove an unwilling Mussolini into an alliance of necessity with Hitler appears unexceptionable.[14] But his contention that British opposition to and French inconsistency over the Italian conquest of Ethiopia proved instrumental in creating the Axis reflects *post hoc ergo propter hoc* reasoning: logic undermines Taylor's argument, as does evidence available to him at the time he was writing *Origins*.

Mussolini's statements and actions from May 1936 to June 1940 make it easy to distinguish the degrees of his hostility toward Germany, Britain, and France. Toward Germany, Mussolini moved from proclaiming the Rome–Berlin Axis, in November 1936, to paying a state visit to Hitler in September 1937, to acceptance of the *Anschluss* in March 1938, to receiving Hitler in Italy in May 1938, to willingness to join Germany in war in September 1938, to a formal Italian–German alliance in May 1939, to a summit conference with Hitler in March 1940 where he pledged intervention on Germany's side, and, finally, to partnership in a war against France and Britain in June 1940.

With Britain, Mussolini proved willing to make diplomatic settlements: the "Gentlemen's Agreement" (January 1937), the Nyon patrol arrangements (October 1937) and the Easter Accords (April 1938). In September 1938 Mussolini and Chamberlain hurriedly worked out a proposal for the Munich conference; they conducted private discussions during the meetings, and Mussolini received the British head of government in Rome in January 1939. Finally, throughout the second half of August 1939, Mussolini allowed Ciano to attempt an Italian–British mediation to prevent the German invasion of Poland. Only in the period January–March 1940 did the Italian–British diplomatic relationship crumble, due to Mussolini's refusal to sell Britain arms and the British blockade of sea-borne deliveries of German coal to Italy.[15]

Toward France Mussolini directed rage and contempt from 1936 to 1940. Neither the Duce nor Léon Blum hid their disdain for one another after the latter became premier of France in June 1936. Two months later, they became engaged in a bitter proxy war in Spain, where they were almost drawn into fighting one another, particularly when the Italian-led Nationalist offensive approached the Pyrenees. Another potential conflict arose from French fears that the Italians would establish permanent bases on Majorca. Because of their refusal to recognize the King of Italy as Emperor of Ethiopia, the French had no ambassador in Rome between October 1936 and November 1938. In October 1937 Mussolini withdrew his ambassador from Paris. In March 1937, with the Italian–Yugoslav accord, Mussolini effectively detached Yugoslavia from its alliance with France. A year later, Mussolini rejected French attempts to join the Easter Accords.

In May 1938, following Hitler's visit to Italy, Mussolini insisted that his country and France were enemies, fighting "on opposite sides of the barricade" dividing Spain, and that the spirit of the Stresa conference was "dead and buried." After the French government finally appointed a duly-accredited ambassador to Rome in November 1938, the Fascist regime replied with a stinging diplomatic insult to Paris. Eleven days following the new French envoy's arrival, a pre-arranged demonstration took place in the Chamber of Fasces and Corporations. Italian deputies responded to a reference by Ciano to the "aspirations of the Italian people" with shouts of "Tunisia, Jibuti, Corsica, Nice, Savoy!" These demands were followed by Mussolini's denunciation of the 1935 agreements with Laval. The French responded to Italian troop movements in Africa by sending reinforcements to Tunisia and French Somaliland.[16]

These events immediately preceded Neville Chamberlain's calm three-day visit to Rome in mid-January 1939, indicating Mussolini's hopes of separating Britain from France. Surprisingly, the French proved willing to consider Italian demands for colonial concessions. But the dispatch of a special emissary to Rome in early February served only to convince the Fascists of French weakness. Between then and the Italian declaration of war on France sixteen months later, other diplomatic feelers were extended from both Paris and Rome. But the Italians seemed to seek only bribes for temporary good behavior and interpreted French initiatives as signs of cowardice.[17]

A. J. P. Taylor erred in asserting that the British and French drove Mussolini into alliance with Hitler. Ironically, Mussolini responded to Germany, Britain, and France in inverse proportion to their degree of dishonesty and their threat to Italy: Germany, which consistently treated Italy worse than did the other two countries, was rewarded with Mussolini's friendship; France, which generally offered Italy the highest level of co-operation and true partnership, was rewarded with rebuffs and abuse. British policy, and Mussolini's reaction to it, fell between these extremes.[18]

The Nazis treated Mussolini's regime so badly that the formation of the Axis and the Pact of Steel is inexplicable without reference to information largely unknown in the 1930s. True, Hitler and his lieutenants had flattered the Duce and Fascism in public statements from the mid-1920s until the Nazis took power in January 1933. This praise continued until mid-1934. But Hitler's actions belied Nazi words.[19]

Mussolini received only a day's warning of German withdrawal from the League of Nations in October 1933. This surprise wrecked the Duce's cherished Four Power Pact, which he had formulated to remove the restrictions on Germany that had been imposed by the treaty of Versailles while maintaining European stability. Mussolini believed Italy could determine the balance of power during and after German rearmament. Following their June 1934 meetings, Mussolini announced that the Führer had promised to respect Austrian sovereignty. But the next month, the Nazis attempted to seize power in Vienna in a manner which indicated that they had acted with Hitler's approval. Following large-scale Italian troop movements to East Africa, it became public knowledge that Germany was supplying the Ethiopians with arms. Hitler also offered weaponry to the British for use against Mussolini's forces, while rejecting Italian requests to purchase German rifles. These actions marked the nadir of relations between Mussolini and Hitler.[20]

The Italian and German governments moved toward reconciliation in early 1936. In December 1935–January 1936 Italy's defeat in Ethiopia seemed possible, while it faced diplomatic isolation in Europe. That January, Mussolini told the German ambassador that he was willing to end Italian protection of Austria in return for German diplomatic support. Starting late that month, the able Italian ambassador in Berlin, Bernardo Attolico, began warning the Duce of impending German remilitarization of the Rhineland. Through his diplomats, Hitler strongly suggested to Mussolini in late February that this action was imminent and asked for his cooperation. Mussolini agreed. He refused to back the British and French in any forceful response after German troops marched across the Rhine on 7 March.[21]

Six months later, following the outbreak of the Spanish Civil War, both Mussolini and Hitler decided to support the Nationalists. In late 1936, their governments began coordinating diplomatic, economic, and military aid to their Spanish allies. Mussolini watched these developments closely. In public, renewed Nazi–Fascist friendship was signaled by Mussolini's proclamation of the Axis in November. Yet Mussolini harbored deep suspicions about German foreign policy, particularly toward Austria and Hungary. Indeed Hitler's actions toward the Fascist regime displayed perfidy and disdain.[22]

Throughout the 1930s, the Nazis insisted that they respected Italy's aspirations for hegemony in the Mediterranean–Danubian–Balkan region – so long as the Italian government accepted eventual German domination of Austria.[23] But Berlin's promises proved false. By mid-1934 the drain on hard currency and gold reserves of all-out German rearmament efforts had placed the economy under unbearable strain. This led to the adoption of the "New Plan," by which the costs of German imports would be offset by credits for purchases of German goods. Two months after the failed *putsch* in Vienna, the Germans began a sustained effort at economic expansion into southeast Europe. Under the circumstances of late 1934, Hitler disregarded Italian anger over the invasion of their markets.[24]

The Ethiopian War created new economic opportunities for Germany. Yugoslavia, Romania, Bulgaria, Greece, and Turkey respected the League sanctions imposed on Italy, and Germany filled the vacuum, particularly in arms' sales throughout the region. Even without sanctions, the demands of the war effort in East Africa would have prevented Italy from competing with Germany, whose armaments' deals soon brought Berlin significant political advantages at Italian expense. In December 1936, after the radical improvement in Italian–German relations over the previous eleven months, the two governments agreed to economic collaboration in the Danubian Basin. But the imbalance in economic strength of the two countries, which grew ever-more favorable to Germany, made the protocol of little value to Italy. By early 1938, many Italian diplomats believed that the Germans were seeking to dominate the Balkans, and even the Mediterranean, by economic penetration followed by political influence. A year later, the Italian economy itself had become subservient to the German.[25]

The Germans became a major supplier of weapons to Spain in 1935. They took advantage of the Civil War to increase their economic penetration of Nationalist territory. Despite numerous statements that Italian interests took priority, in July 1937 Berlin extracted concessions from the Salamanca government giving Germany economic preponderance. When Spain's war ended in March 1939, the Italians had outspent the Germans nearly two-to-one in aiding the Nationalists. But German economic superiority in the Spanish market had become unshakeable.[26]

German territorial expansion in 1938–39 greatly facilitated Berlin's penetration of the Danube–Balkan region. Hungary, which had been allied with Italy since 1928, began receiving clandestine Italian arms' shipments in the late 1920s and served Mussolini as a bulwark against German influence in 1933–36. But growing German dominance of the Hungarian economy, combined with Berlin's acquiescence to Budapest's annexation of former-Czechoslovak territories, weakened Italian influence. Still, the Italians supplied Hungary with warplanes when the expansion of the Luftwaffe limited the number of aircraft Germany was willing to sell; the 640 Italian military airplanes eventually delivered to Hungary (or built there under license) allowed Mussolini to maintain some influence, as did his Munich conference advocacy of Hungarian claims to southern Slovakia. Still, by mid-1939, Hungary was, in effect, a German satellite.[27]

Hitler's government also reduced Romania to subjugation. Mussolini's support of Hungarian and Bulgarian irredentism meant that Italy had relatively little influence in Bucharest in the 1920s and early 1930s. Still, the Italians depended heavily on Romanian petroleum. By 1940, Romania was supplying about 40 percent of Italy's needs. But the Romanian–German economic treaty of March 1939 gave Berlin near-control of the Ploesti oilfields. This made the Italian economy even more subservient to the German. Italian firms had sold the Romanian air force about eighty aircraft from the mid-1920s to the late 1930s, and the Romanians had manufactured about another 200 under license. These orders were significant for the small Italian aircraft industry. But the Romanian army had depended on Czechoslovak arms until 1939. The German seizure of Bohemia–Moravia forced Bucharest to turn to Berlin for military equipment. Thereafter, the German grip tightened, and during the spring of 1940 Romania was forced into political, military, and diplomatic dependence on Germany.[28]

In mid-1936, Mussolini suspended his efforts to dismember Yugoslavia through support of Croatian terrorism and Albanian nationalism. In the aftermath of League sanctions, and with the possibility of an *Anschluss* increasing, he wished to secure trade with resource-rich Yugoslavia and create a new barrier against Germany's south-eastward advance. These considerations, added to general concerns about German economic advances in the Balkans, had come to worry him considerably by August 1936. He authorized negotiations with Belgrade, leading to an economic agreement in September 1936 and a friendship pact in March 1937. In effect, the Yugoslavs exchanged French protection for Italian, while the Italians attempted to replace Austria with Yugoslavia as an ally against Germany. However, by 1937 Germany's trade with Yugoslavia surpassed Italy's, and by 1939 Germany all but controlled the Yugoslav economy. German eradication of Czecho-Slovakia that March opened the way to greater political influence over Belgrade, and Hitler stopped short of outright domination only because he wished to avoid totally alienating Mussolini and to preserve a neutral Yugoslavia as a source of minerals in case of war. Even so, to Fascist consternation, the Croatian national terrorist organization the *Ustaše* moved from the Italian into the German orbit in early 1939.[29]

Under these circumstances, the Italian invasion of Albania in April 1939 is understandable. Mussolini enjoyed the respect shown to him by the Greek dictator Metaxas, who regarded Fascist Italy with admiration and fear. Mussolini's annexation of Albania reinforced this by placing Greece inside a box formed by Epirus, Cyrenaica, and the Dodecanese. The Duce's annexation of Albania also granted Italy enough geographical proximity to Bulgaria to regain some influence there. Various Bulgarian governments had, since the 1920s, followed Mussolini's lead in foreign policy, a relationship symbolized by the marriage of Boris, King of Bulgaria, to a daughter of Vittorio Emanuele III. But Bulgarian hopes to gain Yugoslav, Romanian, and Greek territory with Italian aid had proved futile. Ties between Rome and Sofia had slackened after Mussolini focused his attention on Africa and the Mediterranean. Despite Boris' determination to preserve his freedom of action, Germany had become Bulgaria's economic master by the late 1930s. By 1939, 70 percent of Bulgarian exports went to Germany, compared with only 6 percent to Italy. After Greece, Yugoslavia, Romania, and Turkey agreed to Bulgarian rearmament in July 1938, Germany became the major supplier of weapons to Boris' army. With Italian arsenals drained by Ethiopian and Spanish wars, Mussolini could not compete. It also became clear that Bulgaria's acquisition of Macedonia, Thrace, and Southern Dobrudja depended on German, and possibly Soviet, support. Boris would have preferred the less-domineering Italians as his patrons, but this gave small comfort to the Duce. Furthermore, that only Albania and Greece – the poorest countries in eastern Europe – had been temporarily granted by Hitler as sops to Mussolini clearly indicated the nature of the Italian–German relationship by the summer of 1939.[30]

But Italian sensibilities were most deeply wounded by the lies, surprises, and pretensions that characterized Nazi diplomacy between March 1938 and August 1939. The German seizure of Austria following only eight hours' warning to Mussolini; Hitler's message to Mussolini, on September 25, 1938, that he intended to attack Czechoslovakia six days later (at a time when the Italian armed forces were not prepared for war); the treacherous German backing of the Czecho-Slovaks, while the Italians supported Hungarian claims to southern Slovakia, nearly provoking a German–Italian proxy war in late November 1938; the German sabotage of Italian attempts to gain concessions from France between November 1938 and February 1939; Hitler's sudden destruction of Mussolini's "masterpiece," the Munich treaty, by his occupation of Bohemia–Moravia in mid-March 1939; Hitler's false assurances, on May 21, 1939 (immediately prior to the signing of the Pact of Steel), that he would avoid war for at least three years; Hitler's decision to attack Poland, despite Mussolini's strong objections; Ribbentrop's giving one-day's notice, on August 21, that he would depart for Moscow to sign the Nazi–Soviet Pact; Hitler's outright rejection of Mussolini's frenzied efforts to settle the Polish crisis – all these shocks, betrayals, and insults describe Italian–German relations in the eighteen months preceding Hitler's initiation of the Second World War.[31]

Nazi abuse of Fascist interests had begun with their 1933 withdrawal from the League. But, as the balance of power tipped ever more in Germany's favor, such insults to Italian pride increased in frequency and intensity. The cause-and-effect relationship between Italian exertions in the period 1935–37 and the ability of Nazi Germany to dominate central Europe over the following two years is what provides the Ethiopian War with its real significance for the origins of the Second World War.

The price paid for the invasion and pacification of Ethiopia was far higher than the Fascist regime ever admitted. Mussolini's government stated officially that the conquest had taken the lives of 2,800 Italian and 1,600 colonial troops. Precise figures are unknown, but lie in the range of 12,000 Italians and 4,000–5,000 Libyans, Eritreans, and Somalis. Contrary to Fascist claims, large portions of Ethiopia remained rebellious, with the result that another 12,000 Italians died in East Africa from May 1936 to June 1940. Deaths of colonial troops are estimated as between 30,000 and 35,000.[32]

Over 4,000 Italian soldiers, sailors, and airmen fell fighting for the Nationalists in the Spanish Civil War. Thus, Mussolini sent 28,000 of his countrymen to their deaths in East Africa and Spain from October 1935 to June 1940. For a country of 42.9 million (according to the 1936 census), these were fairly heavy losses (twice as high, proportionately, as American casualties in Vietnam in mid-1965–mid-1970) though light compared with Italian dead in the world wars.[33] Although the losses in manpower did not seriously diminish Italy's strength, the billions of lire squandered on its wars in Africa and Spain did.

Prior to invading Ethiopia, Mussolini had calculated that it would cost 4–6 billion lire to conquer the country. This proved a gross underestimate. While the Italian government later placed the cost of the Ethiopian War at 12.1 billion lire, the true figure was 33.5 billion. This drain on finances forced the Fascist regime to devalue the lire by 40 percent in October 1936. Mussolini poured another 24.1 billion lire into the pacification and development of his East African empire from 1936 to 1940. The cost to Italy of intervention in Spain remains uncertain, but may be approximated as 12–14 billion lire. This included equipment for 15–20 infantry divisions and over 700 combat aircraft. In total, Mussolini's 1935–40 military and colonial adventures devoured at least 70 billion lire. As a result, between the beginning of the Ethiopian War and Italian entry of the Second World War, government expenditures exceeded revenues by 73.4 billion lire. The combined Italian national budgets for 1933, 1934, and 1935 had totalled only 69.5 billion lire.

To put this in perspective, all Italian military expenditures from mid-1935 to mid-1940 totaled about 108 billion lire. Italy's budget for 1938–39 amounted to 39.9 billion lire; and its gross national product in 1938 to 153 billion. The impoverished Italians struggled to pay such costs, but the figure represented only 27 percent of German military expenditure during this period. Rendered in American dollars of the time, Italian military budgets and the cost of maintaining the Fascist militia for the fiscal years 1935/36–1938/39, as well armed forces' spending hidden in colonial budgets, amounted to some $5 billion. From January 1935 to December 1938 the *Wehrmacht* received the equivalent of $18.4 billion.[34]

Huge military expenditures made Nazi Germany much stronger, while they made Fascist Italy comparatively weak. This arose from differences in their expenditures: Germany's were concentrated in the Reich; Italy's were dispersed abroad. As his military power grew at home, Hitler used it as a powerful adjunct to diplomacy to annex Austria, the Sudetenland, Bohemia–Moravia, and Memel; in 1933 he ruled 66 million Germans; by 1939 he directly controlled 87 million people. The number of males under German domination aged 20–39 had increased from 11.2 million to 14.3 million. Furthermore, Nazi Germany gained riches from its bloodless conquests. Not only did it acquire the armaments and resources of two central European countries but it captured their gold and foreign exchange reserves. Confident in the economic potential of the expanded Reich, Hitler's new subjects retrieved monies they had stashed abroad. All in all, the Nazi regime laid its hands on bullion and hard currency worth the equivalent of 13.4 billion Italian lire in the seventeen months following the *Anschluss*. By the spring of 1939, the industrial production of the Greater German Reich equaled that of the United States. Its economy was annually producing goods and services four times higher than the value of Germany's gross national product when Hitler had taken over the country six years before.[35]

Italian demographics and economics developed much less favorably. With the conquest of Ethiopia and the seizure of Albania, Mussolini added 10–11 million Africans and 1.1 million Europeans to his empire. Yet in the invasion and pacification of Ethiopia Italian forces slaughtered hundreds of thousands of Ethiopians, perhaps as many as 7 percent of the population. In the process, the Italian colonial forces also suffered: at least 125,000 Eritreans and Somalis were killed or disabled. As a result, Mussolini enjoyed only minor demographic advantages from his conquests. In 1931, Italy had a population of 41.2 million, with a further 2.3 million in its colonial empire. By 1940, the Italian population amounted to 44.5 million and that of the colonies and Albania to 15 million. But, of the latter, all but the populations of Albania, Libya and the Dodecanese Islands – about 2.1 million – were cut off from Italy after it entered the Second World War. Mussolini had hoped to form a "Black Army" of 1 million men in Ethiopia, to coerce the population into subjugation for slave labor and then to undertake a march of conquest across the Sudan and Egypt to the Suez Canal. Instead, by 1940, his East African colonial troops numbered only 200,000, and could do little more than hold the roads and towns of an *Impero* ablaze in rebellion.

Furthermore, Italian East Africa had drained Italy of the 250,000 soldiers and the mostly male settlers there by June 1940. Throughout the Mediterranean at this time Mussolini commanded only 6.7 million male Italians, and about 180,000 Albanians and Libyans, in the 20–39 age bracket, less than half the German and Czech manpower available to Hitler. The Fascist regime's pronatalist efforts had been heavily offset by its colonial policy. As a result, it had gained only 500,000 more men of military age in Europe and North Africa than it had commanded in 1933. During the same period, Nazi Germany had acquired 3.1 million more men fit for war service or heavy labor.[36]

Albania contained significant unexploited mineral wealth, and Ethiopia possessed huge agricultural potential. Mussolini believed his East African empire also contained great deposits of iron, copper, coal, gold, platinum and steel alloys. He anticipated establishing a vast network of mines, foundries and armaments' manufacturing plants there, certainly a practical gain of empire to his way of thinking. But the geological riches the Italians hoped to find never materialized, and the ongoing insurgency prevented introduction of large-scale mechanized farming. The Italians did increase Albanian oil, copper, chrome, and bitumen extraction in 1939–40. But petroleum production remained less than 7 percent of Italian imports in 1939. The Italians needed more time and investments to realize significant output from their Balkan colony. Both Albania and East Africa probably would have yielded major profits eventually to Italy. But between 1936 and 1940, they only absorbed Italian capital – vast amounts in the case of the *Impero*. Between 1936 and 1938, Italy's exports to East Africa were valued at 5.3 billion lire, her imports at only 477 million.[37]

Italy's economy did expand from 1933 to 1939: industrial production rose by about 40 percent in those years, mostly due to armaments' output. But this was much less than German production and without the rich additions the Reich derived from the factories, farms, and mines of Austria and Bohemia–Moravia. In early 1933, Italy's gross national product was about half of Germany's; by mid-1939 it had been reduced to 18 percent. Per capita income for middle-class Italians rose perhaps 5–6 percent between 1930 and 1940; for workers and farm laborers it actually dropped by about 10 percent. For all levels of German society, average income doubled during the same time. Small wonder that the Italians had lost out to the Germans in their economic competition in Spain and south-east Europe.[38]

The costs of the Ethiopian War, the East African pacification campaigns, and involvement in Spain combined to gravely weaken Italy's economy and military. Of the $5 billion the Italians spent on their armed forces between mid-1935 and mid-1939, $2.9 billion went into the conquest and pacification of Ethiopia. With another $700 million expended on intervention in Spain, this meant that only 28 percent of Italian military outlays between 1935 and 1939 – some $1.4 billion – was used to strengthen the armed forces in Italy, Libya, and Albania. The allocation of 34.8 billion lire ($1.8 billion) to the armed forces in 1939–40 – of which 2.1 billion lire ($110 million) was spent on the military in East Africa – could not suddenly make up for the previous four years of profligacy. Meanwhile, the Germans were rearming at an all-out pace, followed belatedly by the French and the British.

The result was a rapid decline in Italian strength from a high point in 1934–35, when Mussolini could have prevented the *Anschluss* and defied Britain in the Mediterranean, to a position of near-impotence in 1938–39. Mussolini could not halt the spread of Nazi power throughout central Europe and the Balkans, nor restrain Hitler's attack on Poland, nor extract territorial concessions from the

French, nor even risk joining the Germans in war against the western Allies. Yet over the winter of 1939–40 he decided that Italy had become so vulnerable that it could not remain neutral. Whichever belligerent won the ongoing conflict would punish the Italians for perfidy – however defined – at the war's end. Furthermore, an unprecedented historical opportunity had arisen. The territorial aims of the Fascist regime indicated intervention on the German side. It was as easy for Hitler to promise Mussolini the Mediterranean, Middle Eastern, and African possessions of the French and British empires, as it was difficult – even impossible – for Paris and London to concede them. However, the Nazis had treated Fascist Italy so poorly in the 1933–39 period, when Hitler had needed Mussolini's support, that an obvious question arose: how would a victorious Third Reich, the master of a prostrate Europe, deal with its far weaker Italian ally after they had together defeated the western powers? The fluid European relationships of 1933–36 had solidified considerably by early 1940. Nonetheless, Mussolini still faced alternatives: he was not compelled to enter Hitler's war against the western Allies.[39]

Although the full consequences of the Ethiopian War were not yet clear to Mussolini in mid-1936, he knew that he had miscalculated. He understood that the East African conflict had sapped Italy's strength far more than anticipated. But this does not explain his decision to tie Fascist Italy so closely to Nazi Germany later that year. Mussolini had agreed to something like an Italian–German condominium in Austria when, the previous January, he had desperately needed Hitler's support. But there were no practical reasons why he had to honor this agreement: he lied habitually when he considered it advantageous to do so. Furthermore, Hitler had broken several promises to Mussolini, notably in July 1934 and again over his shipments of arms to Ethiopia. Well into 1937, Hitler himself suspected that Mussolini was deceiving him by avowing a new Austrian policy. The Germans enjoyed no greater influence in Austria immediately after the Ethiopian War than before. Thus, they could not bring any greater pressure on Rome or Vienna. But, from June 1936, Mussolini urged Schuschnigg to reach a *modus vivendi* with Hitler. Mussolini sometimes refused to admit the consequences to others – occasionally even to himself – but he knew the July 1936 agreement marked a major step toward an *Anschluss*.[40]

That Mussolini chose to ally with Hitler, rather than being forced, is indicated by the approaches made to Rome by the French and the British throughout 1936. For their part, the French repeatedly made clear their wish to reinvigorate the Stresa Front and maintain the Mussolini–Laval pact of 1935. France's leaders displayed an almost humiliating determination to retain Italy as an ally. This is remarkable. The remilitarization of the Rhineland had ended Mussolini's obligation to aid France against such a German action. Yet the French were offering unilateral assistance to Italy to prevent an *Anschluss*. The French also guaranteed that they would help end League sanctions against Italy, which they did.[41]

But Mussolini despised the leftist Popular Front government that came to power in Paris in early June 1936, considering it another sign of French decadence. This undermined his willingness to maintain an alliance with France. He ignored Premier Blum's appeals – seconded by both the French and Italian high commands – to set aside their differences to prevent German hegemony over Europe. But the failure of the previous French government to respond with force to the German move into the Rhineland made him doubt that he could count on the French to help stop a similar move into Austria. He considered the new Popular Front government even weaker. Certainly, Blum's decision to aid the Spanish Republicans and Mussolini's to aid the Nationalists in late July made further cooperation between their two governments very unlikely. By late August 1936, the Fascists and Nazis were coordinating their military efforts in Spain, and the possibility of reviving the Italian–French anti-German partnership had evaporated. However, Mussolini made his decision to intervene in Spain slowly and deliberately. He was not forced into a proxy war alongside Germany against France: he had acted freely.[42]

The British made similar appeals to Mussolini immediately before, during, and after the Ethiopian War. In September 1935, the Baldwin government had confidentially informed Mussolini that Royal Navy movements in the Mediterranean were meant only to bolster public opinion. Britain would not take military action against Italy, nor would it close the Suez Canal. Even before the Italians invaded Ethiopia, British representatives had assured Mussolini that their government's supposed pro-League position was only a sham to satisfy the British public. British diplomats insisted that London wanted to maintain the closest possible relations with Rome.[43]

By February 1936, after Italian victories in Ethiopia had made Mussolini's adventure appear successful, members of the governing Conservative Party began assuring Grandi, the Italian ambassador, that they considered war with Italy out of the question, that they opposed sanctions, and that they considered the League a troublesome nuisance. Behind many of these pleas to restore Italian–British amity lay exhortations from the Admiralty which was concerned about the vulnerability of imperial communications through the Mediterranean. The strongest proponents of regaining the cooperation of Mussolini were Neville Chamberlain and, most of all, Winston Churchill, who had long admired Mussolini and who now praised him to Grandi as the greatest statesman in Europe.[44] With an Italian triumph in East Africa a *fait accompli*, Churchill and Chamberlain hoped to regain Mussolini as an ally – against Hitler. Baldwin, they insisted, had been misguided in his pro-League policies, encouraged by that unbalanced Italian-hater and fool, Anthony Eden.

Through Grandi, Mussolini encouraged his English friends. Together with the French, the British had removed League sanctions in July 1936. And, like the French, their longing for Italian friendship and their obvious fear of Germany had convinced Mussolini that they too were scared and weak. Italian aggression had been rewarded not only with a great empire in East Africa but with demonstrations of enhanced respect from Paris and London. The Stresa Front was hardly gone beyond recall. In the spring and summer of 1936 London and Paris begged Mussolini to revive it. They did not condemn Italy as an aggressor, except in the most formal sense. The French and British were hailing Mussolini as the potential savior of Europe from Hitler. Unfortunately for them, such importuning raised a fatal question in Mussolini's mind: What might Italy achieve if it pressed its advantage, especially in concert with Hitler's new Germany?[45]

British appeasement, which had steadily intensified by mid-1936, was applied more toward Fascist Italy than Nazi Germany. This emphasis increased after Mussolini intervened in the Spanish Civil War. Britain and France must remain neutral in that conflict, Churchill insisted to the Italian *chargé d'affaires* Leonardo Vitetti in August. But Italy, he argued, had to join in the fighting to prevent the spread of communism in western Europe – and many British officials privately agreed. Churchill himself worried that the Popular Front government presaged a communist France. Mussolini must not let that happen in Spain as well, he warned. A few days earlier, Laval had said almost the same to the Italian ambassador in Paris about the Duce's intervention in Spain. Two months later Robert Vansittart, the British permanent under-secretary of state for foreign affairs, delivered a similar message to Grandi, although in more guarded terms. Mussolini ordered intelligence reports showing the wide extent of French and Soviet military aid to the Spanish Republicans to be circulated in London. This produced dismay among British leaders. Only a few, notably Vansittart and Churchill, eventually realized that the Fascists were playing them for dupes. But, in Churchill's case, illusions about Mussolini lasted far longer than he later would admit.

The British Conservatives continued to believe that stopping the spread of communism in Spain and reaching a lasting understanding with Britain were Mussolini's principal goals. Among those taken in by Mussolini's lies, Chamberlain stood out. Seven months after he became prime minister in May 1937, Chamberlain shunted aside Vansittart in favor of the more optimistic Alexander Cadogan. A few months later Eden, in protest over Chamberlain's relentless appeasement of Italy, was forced to resign. What conclusions could Mussolini draw from such short-sightedness, other than that the French and British were divided, each hopelessly in moral decline? In early 1938 it certainly appeared that Fascist Italy's best course was to align itself with dynamic Nazi Germany.[46]

Yet even after the *Anschluss*, when German expansion to Italy's northern frontier seemed to have locked Mussolini permanently into the Axis, Hitler himself remained unsure of the future course of Italian foreign policy. In April 1938 Hitler remarked to his adjutant that Mussolini might be satiated, having conquered Ethiopia and gained British recognition of its annexation through the Easter Accords. In that case, he mused, further German territorial aggrandizement would occur only in the "distant future."[47]

Despite Hitler's worry over Mussolini's support, the Nazi treatment of Italy most likely to alienate the Duce took place from March 1938 to August 1939. Any one of the incidents previously mentioned presented Mussolini with an excellent reason to break with Hitler. Even after the signing of the Pact of Steel, Hitler's broken promises to avoid a major war for three or four years and to consult prior to any major foreign policy initiative, as well as the shock of the Nazi–Soviet Pact, offered sufficient grounds to renounce the Axis. As late as December 1939, this struck many well-informed observers as a distinct possibility. Certainly it was Ciano's preferred option. Mussolini recommitted himself to Hitler in March 1940, well before German victories in Scandinavia and the west. The explanation lies in Mussolini's foreign policy and ideology, both set years before the Nazis came to power.

Mussolini had proclaimed himself an imperialist as early as 1920. In 1922 he declared that Italy must dominate the Mediterranean, recreate the Roman empire and destroy that of Britain. Mussolini also sought to end French power in the Mediterranean. In February 1923, he ordered his war ministry to instigate an insurrection on Corsica. After the army leadership refused, Mussolini assigned the Fascist Party the task. Six months later he prepared to fight Britain for Corfu, backing down only when his admirals convinced him that to do so would prove suicidal. Shortly after he became dictator in January 1925, he adopted a long-term program of expansion. He planned to conquer Ethiopia, but as a step toward joining "the two shores of the Mediterranean and of the Indian Ocean into a single Italian territory."[48] This required the acquisition of territory from Tunisia to Kenya. In late 1926, Mussolini explained his plans to the army general staff: "A nation which does not have free access to the sea cannot be considered a free country. A nation which does not have free access to the oceans cannot be considered a great power. Italy must become a great power."[49]

Escaping the "Mediteranean prison" became the focus of Mussolini's foreign policy. Secure passage to the oceans, however, required war with France or Britain, or their surrender. Conquering Ethiopia strengthened Italian control of Somalia's coast and facilitated any offensive to link Libya to the *Impero*. But these were only steps toward the goal. Thereafter, Mussolini's actions – especially intervention in Spain – and his words openly indicated his geographic aims. When declaring war on June 10, 1940 Mussolini was explicit. The Italian people, he insisted, wanted "to break the bars which suffocate them in *mare nostrum*, because a people…is not truly free if they do not have free access to the ocean."[50]

However, the Corfu crisis and an appreciation of the balance of power taught Mussolini harsh truths. Italy was too weak to threaten the French or British empires. After studying the demographics, he concluded that prospects would improve after 1934, when the impact of losses in the First World War would begin to reduce British and, especially French, military manpower. This largely explains Fascist pro-natalist policies. The Duce wanted large armies for war with the West. However, even with growing manpower advantages, Mussolini decided he needed allies for a successful struggle. Countries like Hungary and Bulgaria could assist in conflicts against lesser states, such as Yugoslavia. But to defeat the imperial powers, Italy needed major partners. In Europe, only Germany and the Soviet Union met his specifications. He flirted with Moscow in 1933–34, in case playing the French and Germans off against each other went wrong. But given his ardent anti-Bolshevism, from 1924–25

Mussolini's preferred co-conspirator to overthrow the Versailles order had been Germany. [51]

Weimar Germany's leaders had rebuffed Mussolini's approaches, but Hitler extended offers of cooperation for years before coming to power and by 1932 Mussolini had decided to respond positively. However, a possible coalition with Hitler upset some Fascist leaders, notably the foreign minister Dino Grandi and the air minister Italo Balbo, who had come to distrust the Nazis. While he discussed an alternative French alliance to placate these leaders, the Duce clearly preferred one with a Nazi Germany. Mussolini exiled Grandi to London as ambassador in July 1932. After the Nazis came to power, Balbo agreed to assist the still-clandestine Luftwaffe and begin joint war planning against France. But Balbo opposed a true Fascist–Nazi alliance. In late 1933, Mussolini isolated him as governor of Libya. By then, the Duce had been actively preparing an attack on Ethiopia for over a year. [52]

In the Duce's grand design, the period of German animosity between 1934 and 1936 was an aberration, as was the reconciliation with France and the co-operation with Britain. The January 1936 Italian–German understanding marked Mussolini's return to his preferred policy and explains the strengthening of the Axis thereafter, despite the shocks Hitler administered to his pride in 1938–39.

How clear was this to the British and French after 1936? Not very, although the view from Paris was more focused than that from London. While both states attempted to appease Mussolini, the British retained their illusions about separating the Fascists and Nazis far longer than did the French. The friction between Paris and Rome from 1926 to 1934 had given the French a more realistic understanding of Fascist foreign policy and they took Mussolini far more seriously than did the British. For example, after the demonstration demanding French territory in the Chamber in November 1938, the Daladier government rushed reinforcements to Tunisia and Jibuti. In contrast, when informed in April 1939 that the Italians had invaded Albania, Chamberlain replied with incredulity: "I feel sure Mussolini has not decided to go against us." [53]

Yet since 1922 Mussolini had sought to destroy the British empire. Moreover, this was known in London: in May 1923 the British Secret Intelligence Service supplied a detailed report on this to the foreign office. SIS passed on "first-hand information from a highly reliable agent" who had met Mussolini with an Indian revolutionary group in late February and early May. Mussolini stated that he intended to expel the British from the Mediterranean. He gave "full assurance of help" in ridding India of British rule. "It will be the happiest day of my life when India becomes independent," he insisted. He added that until the British empire was destroyed Italy could not gain full prosperity and power. A cover sheet to the report noted that it had been "to some extent confirmed by [an] annexed telegram from M. Mussolini." This suggested that British code breakers had been reading Italian diplomatic traffic for some time, gaining other information on covert Fascist activities. But marginal comments on the report by British officials described it as "little more than the vast imaginings of an imperial mind"; "the schemes cannot be taken at their face value"; and "I doubt whether all details are really true."[54]

In August 1923, two weeks before the Corfu incident, another SIS report reached the foreign office. The Indians had met Mussolini again. He had promised them financial support. However, the nationalists had grown suspicious and began to wonder if Mussolini's intentions were to expel the British only to impose Italian rule on India. Once again, however, British official reactions were dismissive: "It is all very vague and intangible....I take all such reports with a considerable amount of reserve"; and " *'Cum grano salis'* applies to all these reports." Among those who had annotated the SIS documents were Lord Curzon, Eyre Crowe, Harold Nicolson, Miles Lampson, Robert Vansittart, and Alexander Cadogan.[55]

French intelligence on Mussolini's intentions to attack France in the 1920s is less certain. But, like the British, the French had broken some Italian codes. Italian planning for conflict with France arose from plans to destroy Yugoslavia. In November 1927 the French and Yugoslav governments signed a pact of amity and understanding. Sixteen months later, Mussolini ordered his high command to plan an attack on France simultaneously with an offensive against Yugoslavia. Studies continued until at least late 1931. Evidence strongly indicates that the Deuxième Bureau gained knowledge of such plans. In July 1932, Mussolini contacted Kurt von Schleicher, the German chancellor, about Italy and Germany waging war together against France; Schleicher replied favorably, but added that Germany needed time to rearm. Later that month Mussolini ordered that plans be drawn up for an invasion of Corsica. He also authorized *Ustaše* landings in Dalmatia to spark a Croat revolt, although the uprising was crushed that fall. In January 1933 he proposed to invade Yugoslavia that summer, and to instigate another Croat uprising. Next, he considered using his army's August maneuvers to cover a surprise attack on France. He believed that France, politically unstable since mid-1932, was nearing collapse.[56]

However, the Deuxième Bureau discovered Mussolini's intentions. General Weygand urged a preventive attack on both Italy and Germany, guaranteeing Italian defeat in a few months. His confidence indicates that the French general staff had acquired a thorough picture of Italian military dispositions and planning. Soon after, Italian military intelligence learned that the French had uncovered Italian plans and were making their own war preparations. Mussolini postponed invasion of Ethiopia and delayed his proposed attack on France. He preferred to wait, to join the Germans in crushing the French in 1934. Meanwhile, the Austrian question had begun to hinder Nazi–Fascist co-operation. Furthermore, Hitler stated that Germany would remain unready for a major war for several years. Mussolini's advisers persuaded him that these circumstances made conflict with France a folly, and he reluctantly agreed. His thoughts returned to Ethiopia and the need of an agreement with France to render practical his East African conquest under the prevailing European conditions. Nonetheless, Italian military planning since 1927 indicates that

Mussolini's post-Ethiopian War hostility to France was of long duration, not a reaction to the crisis of 1935–36.[57]

In May 1934 Mussolini and the Italian high command marked Britain as Italy's main European enemy. In discussing the impending attack on Ethiopia, Marshal Pietro Badoglio, chief of the supreme general staff, advised deploying three divisions to Libya. At a second conference he ordered: "Absolute silence with the governments of France and Great Britain regarding these military preparations." These meetings led to sending forces to Cyrenaica in September 1935 to threaten the Suez Canal. By April 1935, before either the Stresa conference or the fateful June meeting between Eden and Mussolini, the Duce had ordered preparation of Mediterranean aero-naval operations against the British, anticipating their opposition to his invasion of Ethiopia. In late 1936, when Italian war planning resumed following the Ethiopian conflict, intervention in Spain and the proclamation of the Axis, Badoglio announced that preparations would be aimed only at British territory. Planning for conflict with France and Yugoslavia resumed only in December 1937. Friendly Italian diplomacy toward London in 1936–40 represented only camouflage for the anti-British aggression Mussolini had advocated since 1922.[58]

While Nazi foreign policy complemented Fascist imperial aims, the ideological similarity of the two regimes made their alliance almost inevitable. In February 1923 Mussolini described the links between his ideology and foreign policy, presaging the Nazi–Fascist partnership. Speaking to the aforementioned Indian nationalists, Mussolini explained his willingness to work with Britain:

> When I came into power I found an empty treasury, a country economically and industrially ruined, and dominated economically by England and America. In these circumstances what more was it possible for me to do? I have two great aims in view, firstly to get rid of the economic domination of foreign countries and reorganize and develop Italian industries, and secondly to change the social laws and systems of government...
>
> But this advance cannot be achieved in a day. I and my party are trying to enlist gradually the sympathy of the masses to destroy the power of all other political parties. Whatever we may appear to be doing with England, I tell you frankly as Duce of the Fascist Party, we are doing it in order to get rid of the economic domination of that country. You must know quite well what my views are on the subject of English imperialism. I mean to stick to these views through thick and thin, so as ultimately to drive the English out of the Mediterranean. I am fully aware that until such time as the countries on the Mediterranean are freed from English control, and until such time as India is independent, it is impossible for Italy to be prosperous and powerful.[59]

Twelve years later Mussolini explained his reasons for invading Ethiopia to the Hungarian military attaché in similar terms:

For the past thirteen years I have been asking, begging, threatening so that the Italian people get their own place within lawful boundaries. I want the Italians to be able to earn their own bread and to be liberated from having to work for starvation wages at the arbitrary wishes of foreign powers. I want these poor masses to have enough in order to eat sufficiently at least once a day, because at this moment they eat no more than once a day. But even so, they are eating very poorly. What I could achieve on Italian soil by improving this earth, I have already done. This cannot be forced any further...

Even if we sacrificed billions on our existing colonies, the first crops from olive trees would be ripe no sooner than in fifteen to twenty years. We need territories, otherwise we shall explode. Thus, when I gained a free hand from Laval, I myself have "exploded." There is no stopping here....We shall do everything in our power, we shall sacrifice everything we must, but we shall not surrender our aims![60]

Mussolini believed Fascism gave Italy the power to solve its domestic problems through war. But he also calculated that military victory would strengthen his regime's grip on Italian society. Furthermore, both Duce and Führer believed their systems provided revolutionary solutions to the crisis afflicting Europe. Their alliance would smash the "pluto-democracies" of the west, then bend all mankind to their will. As Hitler remarked to an Italian diplomat in early 1933: "Fascism is a force which must be imposed on the world. This common ideal will make us constantly stronger and more united."[61] Before the Nazi takeover and during his regime's first year, Hitler flattered Mussolini, calling himself the Duce's disciple. As he gained confidence, the Führer preferred to refer to the Duce as his equal. In any case, both agreed that they had nothing in common with the "capons" and "worms" who governed Britain and France.[62]

Although Hitler's words were meant to manipulate Mussolini, he was sincere. He viewed Fascist institutions as models he intended to emulate. Equally important, while Nazi Germany remained weak Hitler needed Fascist Italy for support. The Führer's personal daring, unshakable beliefs and the nature of Nazism led him to the failed *Anschluss* of July 1934. Although the coup infuriated Mussolini, Hitler did not reciprocate that hostility. He was certain fate and faith linked Nazism and Fascism indissolubly. The Duce's reckless courage in defying Britain and the League during the Ethiopian War deeply impressed Hitler. He also recognized the danger to Mussolini's survival. That is why Hitler ended German arms' shipments to Ethiopia in late 1935 and also explains his welcome of Mussolini's January 1936 rapprochement. True, the Führer used Italian difficulties to advance his plans for Austria and, more immediately, to move forces across the Rhine. But Hitler hardly wanted the Duce to succumb to economic sanctions or military defeat.[63]

Mussolini also concluded that the survival of the two regimes was linked. As father of radical-right totalitarianism, both pride and lust for power motivated him to seek the expansion of Fascism and Nazism. On the tenth anniversary of the March on Rome, Mussolini had proclaimed: "the 20th century will be the century of Fascism, will be the century of Italian power, will be the century during which Italy will return for the third time as the director of human civilization....Within a decade all Europe will be Fascist or fascistized."[64]

By late 1937, Mussolini had come to the painful recognition that the goal lay beyond his power. He disliked Hitler but needed Nazi power to fulfill his historic mission. In September 1938, when Mussolini feared general war due to Hitler's demands on Czechoslovakia, he pledged solidarity with Germany. He knew the parlous state of Italian armaments and the grave dangers in joining a conflict with the West; he believed, however, that Hitler could not win such a war alone and, if Nazi Germany fell, that Fascist Italy would become the target of British and French revenge.[65]

A year later, Mussolini still had not entered the war started by Hitler, though he longed to do so. Under a barrage of arguments from his advisers, he agreed that his armed forces were too weak – the result of his profligate use of resources since 1935. But he estimated that Germany had grown so powerful, and the Western leaders so timid, that the Nazi regime could survive fighting Britain and France on its own. As soon as possible, however, Mussolini intended to intervene on Hitler's side. Neutrality negated the meaning of Fascism. It also meant missing the opportunity to gain all that he had been seeking since 1922. When the opportunity presented itself again in the spring of 1940, Mussolini seized it in order to achieve his dream of re-establishing the Roman empire.[66]

But Mussolini's decision was carefully and consciously made; British and French policies had not forced him on to Hitler's side. Instead, in a manner no one then realized, the Ethiopian crisis had exposed vulnerabilities and created opportunities that he seized to realize his imperial vision. He had long believed Italy could gain world-power status through conquest of an empire stretching from the Strait of Gibraltar to the Strait of Hormuz. In June 1940 he acted on that faith and in the hope that he had nurtured for two decades. Over the next five years, he and all Italians would pay dearly for that fatal mistake.

Notes

1   The better studies – including the works they cite – of European diplomacy during the Ethiopian crisis are: P. M. H. Bell, *The Origins of the Second World War in Europe*, London, 1986; Hans-Jürgen Döscher, *Das Auswärtige Amt im Dritten Reich: Diplomatie im Schatten der Endlösung*, Berlin, 1986; A. R. Peters, *Anthony Eden at the Foreign Office, 1931– 1938*, New York, 1986, pp. 114–206; Harold G. Marcus, *Haile Selassie I. The Formative Years, 1892–1936*, Berkeley, CA, 1987, pp. 124–80; Arianna Arisi Rosa, *La diplomazia del ventennio. Storia di una politica estera*, Milan, 1990, pp. 73–130; Alan Cassels (ed.), *Italian Foreign Policy, 1918–1945*, revised edn, Wilmington, DE, 1991; Patrick Finney (ed.), *The Origins of the Second World War*, London, 1997.
2   In addition to the books previously mentioned, among the better works dealing with European international relations for 1936–40 are: Wolfgang Michalka, *Ribbentrop und die deutsche Weltpolitik, 1933–1940*, Munich, 1980; Brunello Vigezzi, *L'Italia unita e le sfide della politica estera. Dal Risorgimento alla Repubblica*, Milan, 1997, pp. 177–259.
3   Mussolini's policies, August 1939–June 1940, are brilliantly analyzed in MacGregor Knox, *Mussolini Unleashed, 1939–1941. Politics and Strategy in Fascist Italy's Last War*, New York, 1982. For a view of Mussolini's diplomacy incorporating the Taylor thesis, with

documentation unavailable in 1961, see Richard Lamb, *Mussolini and the British*, London, 1997.

4 *Documents on German Foreign Policy, 1918–1945* [henceforth, *DGFP*], series C, vol. 2, nos 332, 354, 377; vol. 3, nos 5–7, 127–8, 152, 266; vol. 4, no. 61; *I documenti diplomatici italiani, Settanta Serie: 1922–1935* [henceforth *DDI*], vol. 15, nos 411, 419; Reinhard Spitzy, *How We Squandered the Reich*, Norwich, 1997, pp. 36–47; Lamb, *Mussolini*, p. 106; Renzo De Felice, *Mussolini il duce*; vol. 1: *Gli anni del consenso, 1929–1936*, Turin, 1974, pp. 484–506.

5 Enrico Serra, "Dalle trattive sul confine meridionale della Libia al baratto sull' Ethiopia," *Nuova Antologia*, no. 542, 1980, pp. 164–74; *Documents Diplomatiques Français* [henceforth *DDF*], 1re série, tome 8, nos 12, 88, 97, 100, 163, 182, 190, 247, 261–63, 267, 326, 332, 345, 348, 365, 368, 372, 414–15; tome 10, nos 4, 63, 404; tome 11, no. 179; Pompeo Aloisi, *Journal, 25 juillet 1932–14 juin 1936*, Paris, 1957, pp. 235–66; D. C. Watt, "The secret Laval–Mussolini agreement of 1935 on Ethiopia," *The Middle East Journal*, vol. 15, 1961, pp. 69–78; Salvatore Minardi, "Mussolini, Laval e il désistement della Francia in Etiopia," *Clio*, vol. 22, 1986, pp. 77–107, and "L accordo militare segreto Badoglio–Gamelin del 1935," *Clio*, vol. 23, 1987, pp. 271–300; Nicole Jordan, "Maurice Gamelin, Italy and the eastern alliances," *Journal of Strategic Studies*, vol. 14, 1991, pp. 431–3; Martin S. Alexander, *The Republic in Danger. General Maurice Gamelin and the Politics of French Defence, 1933–1940*, New York, 1992, pp. 51–3, 216, 255–6; *Documents on British Foreign Policy, 1919–1939* [henceforth *DBFP*], series 2, vol. 12, nos 681, 691, 707, 722; G. W. Baer, *The Coming of the Italian–Ethiopian War*, Cambridge, MA, 1967, pp. 62–129; De Felice, *Mussolini il duce*, vol. 1, pp. 506–33, 643–62.

6 *DBFP*, series 2, vol. 12, no. 722; vol. 14, nos 230, 232, 320, 325–7; Baer, *Coming*, pp. 183–201; A. R. Peters, *Eden*, pp. 118–23.

7 Reynolds Salerno, "Multilateral strategy and diplomacy: the Anglo-German naval agreement and the Mediterranean crisis, 1935–1936," *Journal of Strategic Studies*, vol. 17, 1994, pp. 56–63.

8 Baer, *Coming*, pp. 211–374; De Felice, *Mussolini il duce*, vol. 1, pp. 671–93; Peters, *Eden*, pp. 123–34; *DBFP*, series 2, vol. 15, no. 480.

9 *Documents on Canadian External Relations*; vol. 5: *1931–1935*, nos 472, 478; vol. 6: *1936–1939*, no. 686; G. W. Baer, *Test Case: Italy, Ethiopia, and the League of Nations*, Stanford, CA, 1976; De Felice, *Mussolini il duce*, vol. 1, pp. 693–746.

10 Hungarian National Archives, K100, Foreign Ministry Archives, László Szabó Military Attaché Papers [hereafter SP]; 1936, file 7: "Talks with Pariani on June 8"; file 11: "Memorandum about the talks with the Duce on June 12, 1936."

11 *Opera Omnia di Benito Mussolini* [henceforth *OO*], Edoardo and Duilio Susmel (eds), 37 vols, Florence, 1951–1962, vol. 28, pp. 69–70.

12 Galeazzo Ciano, *Diario 1937–1943*, Milan, 1980, p. 52.

13 *DGFP*, series D, vol. 1, nos 17–19; *Ciano's Diplomatic Papers*, Malcolm Muggeridge (ed.), London, 1948, pp. 138–46; Renzo De Felice, *Mussolini il duce*; vol. 2: *Lo Stato totalitario*, Turin, 1981, pp. 338–449; Arisi Rota, *La diplomazia*, pp. 124–40.

14 A. J. P. Taylor, *The Origins of the Second World War*, 2nd edn, New York, 1965, esp. pp. 96, 106–7.

15 *DBFP*, 2nd series, vol. 12, nos 426, 440–2, 445, 447, 451, 456, 460–1, 482–3, 499, 500, 502, 508–9, 514, 522, 526–30; vol. 19, nos 196, 210, 214, 279, 484, 490, 497–98, 532, 538, 543, 556, 573, 556, 575, 620–7; 3rd Series, vol. 2, nos 1125, 1159, 1161, 1165–8, 1190, 1192, 1223–4, 1227, 1231; vol. 3, 456, 461, 463–4, 467–78, 480, 482, 485, 488; vol. 7, nos 31, 47, 51, 59, 62, 71, 72, 79, 85, 86, 101, 120, 133, 166, 190, 192, 222, 261, 296, 319, 324, 327, 361–3, 369, 375–6, 378, 383–4, 389, 392, 409, 422, 425, 427, 432–4, 440, 446, 449, 452–3, 462, 465, 476, 480–1, 488, 500, 506–07, 511, 513, 518, 531, 567, 585, 595, 610, 621, 646–47, 653, 659, 660, 670; *DGFP*, series D, vol. 1, no. 578; *Ciano's Diplomatic Papers*, pp. 157–99; Peters, *Eden*, pp. 235–9, 291–3, 337–50; Dino Grandi, *Il mio paese. Ricordi autobiografici*, Bologna, 1985, pp. 419–38; Knox, *Mussolini Unleashed*, pp. 69–86.

16 *DDF*, 2e série: *1936–1939*, tome 2, nos 275, 482; tome 3, nos 46, 104, 106, 341, 502, 509; tome 9, nos 335, 339, 355, 360, 372; tome 12, nos 288, 433; tome 13, nos 1, 9, 15, 17, 26, 53, 166, 193–4, 270, 313, 354, 377, 426, 448, 459; tome 14, nos 6, 82, 121, 138, 176, 237; tome 15, nos 212, 286, 510; *DGFP*, series D, vol. 1, nos 736–41, 746, 751, 766, 799; vol. 4, no. 412; *OO*, vol. 29, pp. 99–102, Mussolini quotations, pp. 100, 101; Ciano, *Diario*, pp. 123, 212, 217–28, 234–7; *Ciano's Diplomatic Papers*, pp. 247–53; William Shorrock, *From Ally to Enemy: The Enigma of Fascist Italy in French Diplomacy, 1920–1940*, Kent, OH, 1988, pp. 181–251.

17 Ciano, *Diario*, pp. 238–40, 244, 246–7, 254, 275, 289, 291, 311, 329, 396, 421–2, 434–5; *Ciano's Diplomatic Papers*, pp. 257–66; *DBFP*, series 3, vol. 3, nos 500–2; *DDF*, 2e série, tome 14, nos 11, 26, 46, 112, 131, 281; *DGFP*, series D, vol. 4, nos 447, 452; Shorrock, *From Ally*, pp. 252–86.

18 Contemporary knowledge of events, 1933–40, can be obtained from the relevant volumes of *Survey of International Affairs*, London, 1934–58.

19 Brian R. Sullivan, "From little brother to senior partner: Fascist Italian perceptions of the Nazis and of Hitler's regime, 1930–1936," *Intelligence and National Security*, vol. 13, 1998, pp. 90–6.

20 *DDI*, series 8: *1935–1939*, vol. 3, nos 124, 261, 275, 322, 396, 433, 466; *DGFP*, series C, vol. 4, nos 212, 485, 575, 579, 592, 598; Manfred Funke, *Sanktionen und Kanonen: Hitler, Mussolini and der internationale Abessinienkonflikt, 1934–1936*, Düsseldorf, 1970, pp. 43–5, 59 n. 70, 68–9; James Thomas Emmerson, *The Rhineland Crisis, 7 March 1936. A Study in Multilateral Diplomacy*, London, 1977, pp. 75–103, 152–4, 202–3.

21 *DDI*, series 8, vol. 4, nos 715, 787, 800, 819; vol 5, nos 46, 95, 140, 305, 316, 397, 425, 429, 520, 531, 546, 598, 605, 614, 627, 630, 644, 648, 649, 680, 691; *DGFP*, series D, vol. 3, nos 30, 47, 84; De Felice, *Mussolini il duce*, vol. 2, pp. 368–84.

22 For examples of such statements, see *DGFP*, series C, vol. 1,no 14 [Feb. 7, 1933]; no.166 [June 24, 1935]; *DDI*, series 8,vol. 5, no. 277, p. 317 [Oct. 24, 1936]; vol. 6,no.60 [Jan.15, 1937]; *DGFP*, series D,vol. 1, no. 769 [May 20, 1938]; Ciano, *Diario*, p. 299 [May23, 1939].

23 *DGFP*, series C, vol. 3, nos 13, 18, 169, 175, 207, 250, 316; vol. 4, nos 22, 110, 209, 307; Hjalmar Schacht, *My First Seventy-Six Years*, London, 1955, pp. 327–34.

24 *DGFP*, series C, vol. 4, nos 283, 310, 312, 369, 434, 446, 459, 481, 539, 557; vol. 6, nos 86, 368; series D, vol. 1, nos 84, 745; vol. 4, nos 399, 414, 427–9, 438, 445–6, 448, 457; *DDI*, series 8, vol. 5, no. 567.

25 *DGFP*, series C, vol. 4, nos 303, 330, 445, 450; John F. Coverdale, *Italian Intervention in the Spanish Civil War*, Princeton, NJ, 1975; Alberto Rovighi and Filippo Stefani, *La partecipazione italiana alla guerra civile spagnola, 1936–1939*, 2 vols, Rome, 1992–93; vol. 2: *Dall autunno 1937 all estate del 1939. Testo*, pp. 505–6.

26 *DGFP*, series D, vol. 1, no. 795; vol. 2, nos 198, 248, 284, 296, 390, 395, 402, 541, 554–5, 557, 577; vol. 4, nos 163, 165, 167, 179–83, 198–9, 214, 217, 237, 243; Maria Ormos, "L'opinione del conte Stefano Bethlen sui rapporti italo – ungheresi, 1927–1931," *Storia contemporanea*, vol. 2, 1971, pp. 283–314; Alfredo Breccia, "La politica estera italiana e l Ungheria, 1922–1933," *Rivista di studi politici internazionali*, vol. 47, 1980, pp. 93–112; C. A. Macartney, *October Fifteenth. A History of Modern Hungary, 1929–1945*, Edinburgh, 1956, part 1, pp. 330–63; Thomas Sakmyster, *Hungary, the Great Powers, and the Danubian Crisis, 1936–1939*, Athens, GA, 1980, pp. 223–7, and *Hungary's Admiral on Horseback. Miklós Horthy, 1918–1944*, New York, 1994, p. 234; George Punka, *Hungarian Air Force*, Carrollton, TX, 1994; Jörg K. Hoensch, *A History of Modern Hungary, 1867–1994*, New York, 1996, pp. 132, 143–5.

27 Dov B. Lungu, *Romania and the Great Powers, 1933–1940*, Durham, NC, 1989, pp. 140, 153–237; Keith Hitchins, *Romania, 1866–1947*, Oxford, 1994, pp. 441–50; Mark Axworthy, Cornel Scafe, and Cristian Craciunoiu, *Third Axis, Fourth Ally. Romanian Armed Forces in the European War*, London, 1995, pp. 17–30, 266–76; Angela Raspin, *The Italian War Economy 1940–43*, London, 1986, p. 410.

28 *DDI*, series 8, vol. 4, nos 53, 99, 248, 293, 371, 555, 558, 782; vol. 5, nos 329, 458, 459; vol. 6, nos 118, 211, 340; *DGFP*, series C, vol. 6, nos 20, 27, 254, 565; series D, vol. 4, no. 411; vol. 6, nos 15, 45, 55; *Ciano's Diplomatic Papers*, pp. 276–81; J. B. Hoptner, *Yugoslavia in Crisis, 1934–1941*, New York, 1962, pp. 31–161.

29 *DDI*, series 8, vol. 5, no. 251; vol. 6, nos 29, 348; vol. 12, nos 10, 100, 214, 300, 419, 467, 510, 559, 792; vol. 13, nos 165, 240, 413; Ciano, *Diario*, pp. 206–7, 243, 245, 262–88; *DGFP*, series D, vol. 4, nos 449, 450; Marshall Lee Miller, *Bulgaria During the Second World War*, Stanford, CA, 1975, pp. 5–23; R. J. Crampton, *A Concise History of Bulgaria*, Cambridge, 1997, pp. 168–70.

30 Ciano, *Diario*, pp. 108–14, 183–6, 214–23, 244–9, 262–71, 299–300, 325–42, 374–5; *Ciano's Diplomatic Papers*, pp. 282–8, 296–304; *DGFP*, series D, vol. 1, nos 152, 155, 160–1, 207–8, 348–50, 352, 361, 399; vol. 2, nos 610, 627, 661, 662; vol. 4, nos 43, 57–65, 68, 74–80, 84–98, 105, 118–34, 139, 365–76, 382, 384, 408, 412, 447, 463; vol. 6, nos 86, 87, 140; *DDI*, series 8, vol. 13; *DBFP*, series 3, vol. 7, no. 679; *DDF*, 2e série, vol. 13, nos 87, 93, 202, 348, 351, 428, 456; Gerhard L. Weinberg, *The Foreign Policy of Hitler's Germany*, 2 vols, Chicago, 1970 and 1980; vol. 2: *Starting World War Two, 1937–1939*; Watt, *How War Came*; De Felice, *Mussolini il duce*, vol. 2, pp. 467–674.

31 Alberto Sbacchi, "The price of empire: toward an enumeration of Italian casualties in Ethiopia, 1935–40," in Alberto Sbacchi (ed.), *Legacy of Bitterness. Ethiopia and Fascist Italy, 1935–1941*, Lawrenceville, NJ, 1997; Brian R. Sullivan, "The Italian–Ethiopian War, October 1935–November 1941: causes, conduct, and consequences," in A. Hamish Ion and E. J. Errington (eds), *Great Powers and Little Wars. The Limits of Power*, Westport, CT, 1993, pp. 185–94.

32 Brian R. Sullivan, "Fascist Italian involvement in the Spanish Civil War," *The Journal of Military History*, vol. 59, 1995, p. 713; Virgilio Ilari, *Storia del servizio militare in Italia*, 4 vols, Rome, 1989–91; vol. 4: *Soldati e partigiani, 1943–1945*, pp. 23, 28; B. R. Mitchell, *International Historical Statistics. Europe, 1750–1988*, London, 1992, p. 6.

33 Ministero del Tesoro, Ragioneria Generale dello Stato, *Il Bilancio dello Stato negli esercizi finanziari dal 1930–31 al 1941–42*, Rome, 1951, pp. 203, 205, 257, 373, 403, 407; Francesco A. Répaci, "Le spese delle guerre condotte dall Italia nel ultimo quarantac-inquennio, 1913–14 – 1957–58," *Rivista di politica economica*, vol. 50, 1960, pp. 695–713; Sullivan, "Italian–Ethiopian War," p. 185; Maurice F. Neufeld, *Italy: School for Awakening Countries*, Ithaca, NY, 1961, pp. 401, 411; Vera Zamagni, "Un analisi macro-economica," in Zamagni, ed., Come perdere la guerra e vincere la pace, Bologna, 1997, p. 46; Alberto Sbacchi, "Italian mandate or protectorate over Ethiopia, 1935–36," *Rivista di studi politici internazionali*, vol. 42, 1975, p. 588; Raspin, *Italian War Economy*, pp. 434–6; Virgilio Ilari and Antonio Sema, *Marte in Orbace. Guerra, esercito e milizia nella concezione fascista della nazione*, Ancona, 1988, p. 261; Sullivan, "Fascist Italian involvement," pp. 711, 723; Knox, *Mussolini Unleashed*, pp. 292–6; Mitchell, *Statistics*, pp. 800, 895; *The World Almanac & Book of Facts for 1942*, New York, 1942, p. 515.

34 *DGFP*, series D, vol. 4, nos 170, 201; Williamson Murray, *The Change in the European Balance of Power, 1938–1939. The Path to Ruin*, Princeton, NJ, 1984, pp. 149–53, 290–2; Mitchell, *Statistics*, pp. 3, 4, 13, 16, 22, 892, 894.

35 Giorgio Rochat, *Il colonialismo italiano*, Turin, 1973, pp. 28, 103, 146, 187; Mitchell, *Statistics*, pp. 3, 6, 12, 28; Sullivan, "Italian–Ethiopian War," pp. 191, 193; Aloisi, *Journal*, p. 382; Ferdinando Quaranta, *Ethiopia: An Empire in the Making*, London, 1939, pp. 95–6; SP, 1936, file 11: "Memorandum about the talks with the Duce on June 12, 1936," p. 2.

36 Aloisi, *Journal*, p. 382; Sbacchi, "Italian colonization in Ethiopia: promises, plans and projects, 1936–1940," *Legacy*, pp. 103–22; James C. McCann, *People of the Plow. An Agricultural History of Ethiopia, 1800–1990*, Madison, WI, 1990; Renato Mori, "Delle cause dell impresa etiopica mussoliniana," *Storia e politica*, vol. 17, 1978, pp. 689–706; Quaranta, *Ethiopia*, pp. vii, 19–110; Derek Hall, *Albania and the Albanians*, London, 1994, pp. 22–4, 102–5; Ciano, *Diario*, pp. 330–1, Raspin, *Italian War Economy*, p. 407.

37 Mitchell, *Statistics*, pp. 894–5; *The World Almanac 1942*, p. 515; Raspin, *Italian War Economy*, pp. 11–51, 62–104; Neufeld, *Italy*, pp. 530, 538, 540.

38 Vigezzi, *L'Italia unita*, pp. 199–204, 243–59; Salerno, "Multilateral strategy," pp. 66–70; Brian R. Sullivan, "The Impatient Cat: Assessments of Military Power in Fascist Italy, 1936–1940," in Williamson Murray and Allan R. Millett (eds), *Calculations. Net Assessment and the Coming of World War II*, New York, 1992, pp. 112–35.

39 *DGFP*, series C, vol. 4, nos 486, 506, 525, 545, 569; series D, vol. 1, nos 152, 155, 207–8; *DDI*, series 8,vol. 4, nos 192, 448, 489, 496, 499; vol. 6, no. 330; De Felice, *Mussolini il duce*, vol. 1, pp. 755–6.

40 Anthony Adamthwaite, *France and the Coming of the Second World War, 1936–1939*, London, 1977, pp. 32–6; Robert J. Young, *In Command of France: French Foreign Policy and Military Planning, 1933–1940*, Cambridge, MA, 1978, pp. 110–14; Jean-Baptiste Duroselle, *La Décadence, 1932–1939*, Paris, 1979, pp. 147–57.

41 *DDF*, 2e série, vol. 2, nos 248, 275, 374, 454, 482; vol. 3, no. 114; *DDI*, series 8, vol. 4, nos 190, 223, 227, 294, 326, 383, 490, 589, 598, 601, 677, 684, 685, 738, 819; Jordan, "Maurice Gamelin," pp. 434–5.

42 *DBFP*, series 2, vol. 14, nos 591, 603–4, 611, 620, 630, 662, 663; *DDI*, series 8, vol. 2, nos 166, 181, 189, 209, 236; Baer, *Coming*, pp. 323–66.

43 *DBFP*, series 2, vol. 15, nos 98, 154, 175, 198, 317, 427.

44 "Mr Churchill on Fascism," *The Times*, Jan. 21, 1927; Grandi, *Il mio paese*, p. 234; Yvon De Begnac, *Taccuini mussoliniani*, Bologna, 1990, p. 352; De Felice, *Mussolini il duce*, vol. 1, p. 553.

45 *DDI*, series 8, vol. 3, nos 251, 491, 808, 815, 846; vol. 4, nos 94, 236, 242, 251, 262, 283, 286, 338; Alberto Pirelli, *Taccuini 1922/1943*, Bologna, 1984, pp. 170–7; Peters, *Eden*, pp. 196–206; Salerno, "Multilateral strategy," pp. 65–6; Daniel Waley, *British Public Opinion and the Abyssinian War, 1935–6*, London, 1975, pp. 77–88, 117–35.

46 *DDI*, series 8, vol. 4, nos 678, 686, 701, 708; vol. 5, nos 182, 368; vol. 6, nos 144, 425; Winston Churchill, *The Gathering Storm*, New York, 1948, pp. 220–2, 240–67; *The Diaries of Sir Alexander Cadogan, 1938–1945*, David Dilks (ed.), New York, 1972, pp. 27–51; Peters, *Eden*, pp. 321–51; M. L. Roi, "From the Stresa Front to the Triple Entente: Sir Robert Vansittart, the Abyssinian crisis and the containment of Germany," *Diplomacy & Statecraft*, vol. 6, 1995, pp. 61–90.

47 *DGFP*, series D, vol. 2, no. 132.

48 *OO*, vol. 12, p. 323; vol. 18, pp. 160–1, 439, 535–6; G. A. Chiurco, *Storia della rivoluzione fascista*, 2 vols, Florence, 1929, vol. 1, p. 270; *DDI*, series 7, vol. 1, nos 427, 548, 705, 742; vol. 3, no. 604; vol. 4, nos 420, 460; Ezio Ferrante, "Un rischio calcolato? Mussolini e gli ammiragli nella gestione della crisi di Corfù," *Storia delle relazioni internazionali*, vol. 5, 1989, pp. 231–39; *DBFP*, series 1, vol. 24, nos 664, 704; Pirelli, *Taccuini*, pp. 54, 123–4; Gustavo Pesenti, *Fronte Kenya*, Borgo San Dalmazzo, 1953, p. 12, quotation; MacGregor Knox, "The Fascist regime, its foreign policy and its wars: an 'anti-anti-Fascist' orthodoxy?', in Finney (ed.), *Origins*, p.162; Archivio Centrale dello Stato, Carte Badoglio, busta 4, fascicolo 6, nos 1, 2; Philip Morgan, *Italian Fascism, 1919–1945*, London, 1995, pp. 131–40.

49 Emilio Canevari, *La guerra italiana*, 2 vols, Rome, 1948, vol. 1, pp. 211–12.

50 National Archives [hereafter NA], microfilm series T586, reel 405, frames 39–46; *DDI*, series 9, vol. 3, no. 669; *OO*, vol. 29, p. 404, quotation; MacGregor Knox, "Il fascismo e la politica estera italiana," in R. J. B. Bosworth and Sergio Romano (eds), *La politica estera italiana (1860–1985)*, Bologna, 1991, pp. 296–302.

51 Papers of General Pietro Gazzera, [henceforth GP], supplied to author by Renzo De Felice. Meetings with Mussolini, Aug. 7, 1929, Jan. 27, 1931; *OO*, vol. 22, p. 386; vol. 23, p. 177; Enrico Caviglia, *Diario*, Rome, 1952, p. 60; Augusto Turati, *Fuori dell'ombra della mia vita. Dieci anni nel solco del fascismo*, Brescia, 1973, p. 21; J. Calvitt Clarke, *Russia and Italy Against Hitler. The Bolshevik–Fascist Rapprochement of the 1930s*, New York, 1991; De Felice, *Mussolini l'alleato*, vol. 1, p. 59; Knox, "The Fascist regime," pp. 160–1.

52 Jens Petersen, *Hitler e Mussolini. La difficile alleanza*, Bari, 1975, pp. 11–173; Knox, "The Fascist regime," pp. 160–1; GP, meeting with Mussolini, Jan. 27, 1931; NA, record group 331, reel 476A, extract no. 11: "Address by Mussolini to the Fascist

Grand Council – 7 April 1932," pp. 11–13, 18–19; Grandi, *Il mio paese*, 315–16, 341–2, 352–3, 359–60; *DDI*, series 7, vol. 12, nos 38, 393, 449, 460, 534; vol. 13, nos 305, 406; Gregory Alegi, "Balbo e il riarmo clandestino tedesco. Un episodio segreto della collaborazione italo-tedesco," *Storia contemporanea*, vol. 23, 1992, pp. 305–17.

53 Alan Cassels, "Deux empires face à face: la chimère d'un rapprochement anglo-italien (1936–1940)," *Revue d'histoire de la deuxiéme guerres mondiales et conflits contemporains*, vol. 41, 1991, pp. 67–96; Romain Rainero, *La rivendicazione fascista sulla Tunisia*, Milan, 1978; Juliette Bessis, *La mediterranée fasciste. L'Italie mussolinienne et la Tunisie*, Paris, 1980; Shorrock, *From Ally*, pp. 49–84, 240–51; René Albrecht-Carrié, *Italy at the Paris Peace Conference*, New York, 1938; Brian R. Sullivan, "The strategy of the decisive weight: Italy, 1882–1922," in Williamson Murray, MacGregor Knox, and Alvin Bernstein (eds), *The making of strategy. rulers, states, and war*, New York, 1994, pp. 343–51; R.A. Butler, *The Art of the Possible*, London, 1971, p. 79, Chamberlain quotation.

54 PRO, FO 371/8889 C9802, June 5, 1923; PRO HW 12/40.

55 PRO, FO 371/8889 C13963 August 14, 1923.

56 Antonello Biagini and Alessandro Gionfrida (eds), *Lo Stato Maggiore Generale tra le due guerre. (Verbali delle riunioni presiedute da Badoglio dal 1925 al 1937)*, Rome, 1997, pp. 93–292; GP, meetings with Mussolini, Mar. 16, Nov. 18, Dec. 27, 1929; May 30, June 30, July 14, Nov. 6, Dec. 23, 1930; May 5, July 22, 1931, July 22, Aug. 11, 1932; Jan. 4, Jan. 8, 1933; *DDI*, series 7, vol. 10, no. 174; vol. 11, nos 147, 155, 169; *DDF*, 1e série, tome 2, nos 140, 154, 182, 201, 236, 242, 365, 419; *DGFP*, series C, vol. 1, nos 83, 122; Sergio Pelagalli, "Il generale Pietro Gàzzera al ministero della guerra (1928–1933)," *Storia contemporanea*, vol. 20, 1989, pp. 1,038–44; Hoptner, *Yugoslavia*, pp. 12–14; Douglas Porch, *The French Secret Services. From the Dreyfus Affair to the Gulf War*, New York, 1995, p. 141; Salvatore Loi, *Le operazioni delle unità italiane in Jugoslavia (1941–1943)*, Rome, 1978, pp. 15–17; Aloisi, *Journal*, pp. 39–40, 45–50, 60–1; Alexander, *Republic*, pp. 211–15; Fortunato Minniti, "L'ipotesi più sfavorevole. Una pianificazione operativa italiana tra strategia militare e politica estera (1927–1933)," *Nuova Rivista Storica*, vol. 79, 1995, pp. 613–50; Knox, "Il fascismo," pp. 302–8, 314–17; William A. Shirer, *The Collapse of the Third Republic. An Inquiry into the Fall of France in 1940*, New York, 1969, pp. 170, 194–6.

57 GP, meetings with Mussolini, Jan. 8, Feb. 4, Feb. 14, March 14, April 21, May 5, 1933; meeting with Vittorio Emanuele III, Jan. 9, 1933; meeting of council of ministers, May 27, 1933; Emilio Faldella, *L'Italia nella seconda guerra mondiale. Revisione di giudizi*, Rocca San Casciano, 1959, pp. 16–17; "Le guerre segrete di Mussolini," *La Stampa*, Jan. 9, 1982; Pelagalli, "Il generale Pietro Gàzzera," pp. 1,045–9; Knox, "Il fascismo," pp. 317–19, and "The Fascist regime," pp. 160–1.

58 *Lo Stato Maggiore Generale tra le due guerre*, pp. 293–5, 311–27, 373–82, 420, quotations, pp. 295, 373; Fortunato Minniti, " 'Il nemico vero.' Gli obiettivi dei piani di operazione contro la Gran Bretagna nel contesto etiopico (maggio 1935–maggio 1936)," *Storia contemporanea*, vol. 26, 1995, pp. 580–1.

59 PRO FO 371/8889 C9802, p. 126.

60 SP,1935,Szabótoarmychief of staff,Oct.11,1935,"AudiencewiththeDuce,"Oct.3,1935.

61 *DDI*, series 7, vol. 13, no. 69.

62 MacGregor Knox, "Conquest, foreign and domestic, in Fascist Italy and Nazi Germany," *Journal of Modern History*, vol. 56, 1984, pp. 1–57; De Felice, *Mussolini il duce*, vol. 1, pp. 32–53, 177–322, 544–87, and *Mussolini il duce*, vol. 2, pp. 265–330; Sullivan, "From little brother," pp. 95–6; *The Empire at Bay. The Leo Amery Diaries, 1929–1945*, London, 1988, p. 406; Ciano, *Diario*, pp. 130, 238; *DGFP*, series D, vol. 7, no. 171.

63 Petersen, *Hitler e Mussolini*, pp. 383–428; Funke, *Sanktionen*, pp. 43–5, 59, 68–9.

64 *OO*, vol. 25, pp. 147–50.

65 *OO*, vol. 29, pp. 144–65; *DGFP*, series D, vol. 2, nos 494, 565; Ciano, *Diario*, pp. 179–85; De Felice, *Mussolini il duce*,vol. 2, pp. 515–18; Jens Petersen, "L'Italia fascista tra impegno e neutralismo. I rapporti italo-tedeschi, 1938–1940, *Qualestoria*, vol. 13, 1990.

66 De Felice, *Mussolini il duce*,vol. 2, pp. 677–793; Knox, *Mussolini Unleashed*, pp. 42–112, and "The Fascist regime," p. 164; Sullivan, "The Impatient Cat," pp. 114–35.

11 The Spanish Civil War and the origins of the Second World War

Mary Habeck

In his treatment of the Spanish Civil War, as with so much else in his seminal work on the origins of the Second World War, A. J. P. Taylor managed to delineate the causes, course, and consequences of a complex international crisis in a most succinct and skillful way. Using less than fifteen pages, Taylor showed the profound impact that the nationalist rebellion had on great power politics. He argued effectively that this war, perhaps more than any other crisis before the general conflict began, prevented the unification of Great Britain and France against the dictators, alienated the Soviet Union from the western democracies, and distracted attention from far greater perils. Scholars since Taylor have added greatly to our knowledge of the facts surrounding the Civil War, but have not bettered his interpretation of its significance.

Yet the conflict continues to exert a strong fascination. One of the reasons for this interest is the enduring perception that Taylor was right: this war was important both for how it affected Spain and in terms of broader events taking place concurrently in other parts of Europe. Although the war stemmed from fissures within Spanish society itself, the struggle between Nationalists and Republicans soon became caught up in the wider ideological and great power conflicts of the time. Within days of the uprising both sides had appealed for aid from those nations that they knew shared their views of government and society. Weeks later military assistance had begun to arrive, and would continue to pour in for the next two-and-a-half years. Volunteers, some there truly of their own free will and others "volunteered" by their governments, swiftly came to help their ideological brothers in the struggle. Less than two weeks after the rebellion began, policy makers in Britain, France, Germany, and the Soviet Union recognized the possibility that the war might spread to other nations and start a general European conflict. This realization, and other considerations, led every major European country but one to seek to limit interference in Spain – in effect to quarantine the Civil War until it died of its own accord. True believers at either end of the ideological spectrum refused to accept this decision and worked either directly, by volunteering, or indirectly, through publicizing and glorifying the conflict, to aid their chosen comrades.

The result was that some observers of the war shifted their focus from its Spanish roots, perceiving it to be an extension of the larger struggles occurring elsewhere at the time, a sort of preview of the much greater conflict that would shortly play itself out on the battlefields of the world. This was, they argued, the first clash between despotism and democracy, between Fascism and liberalism, that later erupted into the more intense flames of the Second World War. It was no wonder, then, that Claude Bowers, the American ambassador to Spain and a fervent supporter of the Republicans, would sub-title the reminiscences of his time spent in that country "Watching the rehearsal for World War II."[1] In a more radical version of this same opinion, the Spanish Civil War became part of a great "master plan" designed by Hitler and Mussolini to dominate first Europe and then the world. No one stated this viewpoint better than José Alvarez del Vayo, the former president of the Spanish Republic, who argued in 1940 that the Spanish Civil War was preceded and followed by a series of aggressions – in Manchuria, the Rhineland, Abyssinia, Austria, Czechoslovakia, Albania – but it was in Spain that the battle against totalitarian barbarism had been fought with the greatest intensity; in Spain that there had been a chance to stop the aggressor powers; and in Spain that these powers had, instead, been helped to victory and given encouragement for further advances which have since become history.[2]

As with other supposed examples of a Hitlerian master plan, Taylor decisively rejected this view of the Civil War. He argued that, while the conflict played an important role in shaping great power politics and the origins of the Second World War, it had begun for purely internal reasons. With the exception of a few scholars, such as Pierre Broué and Emile Témime, who continued to see the war as little more than another aspect of the struggle between the great powers of Europe, historians over the last thirty years have generally agreed with Taylor's view of the conflict.[3] Scholars today emphasize the deep indigenous roots of the war, discussing the ways that great wealth clashed with dire poverty, conservative traditions with anarchism and other radical views, even deeply-felt Catholicism with liberal, (or socialist) anti-clericalism, to produce smoldering resentments that needed only the slightest provocation to burst into flame. The problems of land wealth were immense. In 1931, just 2 percent of the people held 65 percent of the land while about 75 percent owned less than 5 percent.[4] This meant that incomes were also wildly skewed, with 1 percent of the landlords averaging 30,000 pesetas a year and the "bottom" 95 percent averaging about 200 pesetas. Even worse, the majority of this latter group averaged only twenty-four pesetas a year.[5] A radical anarchism found fertile soil in the discontent created by these inequities, while Spanish liberalism was more extreme than in other European nations. On the other side was a conservative backlash that sought to counter this extremism by emphasizing native Spanish traditions and Nationalism. As Burnett Bolloten has written, the social tensions of the time meant that "no foreign intervention was necessary to ignite the tinder of civil strife."[6]

Yet intervene foreign countries did, and soon the war had become entangled in great-power politics. There is thus truth to the assertion that this conflict was more than just civil war. In fact it could be argued that the conflict in Spain, though by no means part of some sinister plot by Hitler or Mussolini, did, as Taylor suggests, significantly influence the origins and even course of the Second

World War. Perhaps most important was the fact that the uprising forced each of the great powers to decide on the principles for which they were willing to risk a general war. All but one of the European nations came to the same decision: that they were prepared to limit their own actions, even working against strategic interests and deep ideological beliefs, in order to secure peace on the continent. Once the great powers had made this difficult decision, there were additional reasons either to remain involved or to disengage, and these say something about how nations viewed the international situation. The war also profoundly influenced the two major alliances of the interwar period: that between Italy and Germany on the one hand and between Britain and France on the other. Through the events in Spain, ties between Germany and Italy became closer than ever, with Hitler able to use the crisis to begin to assert his primacy in the relationship. The French likewise found themselves bound more tightly to their British allies, and Chamberlain's ideal of appeasement became, slowly but surely, their own policy as well. Finally, Germany was able to benefit economically from involvement in Spain, squeezing Franco at his time of greatest need for the raw materials that helped Hitler to build the war machine that would begin the Second World War.

Perhaps the most significant way in which the Spanish Civil War affected the origins of the Second World War was in clarifying when European powers would be willing to go to war. This conflict was the first clash within western Europe after the First World War, and therefore acted, in some ways, as a test case for the strength of the peace that had held for the previous eighteen years. On the surface of things there were many factors that militated against limiting the war to the Spanish peninsula. After all, the conflict involved a nation that had traditionally been the provoker of major wars. The great powers of Europe had several times fought over who was to control Spain, most recently in the Franco-Prussian War. The British, French, and Italians each had, in addition, good strategic reasons to desire a friendly nation on the Mediterranean. Since Spain was on its very borders, France had even more compelling interests in making certain that the rebels did not succeed in overthrowing the Republican government. Lastly, while Germany, Italy, and the Soviet Union had the best ideological grounds for intervening, there were strong currents within France and Britain that also pushed for aid to be sent to one side or the other. Yet, despite these historical, strategic, and ideological reasons for intervention, every one of these countries, except for Italy, chose to curtail their involvement in Spain. The war in fact showed that most of the powers were willing to go to great lengths to preserve peace, while those who desired to push the boundaries were unwilling, at least at this point, to commit themselves.

The decision that European powers faced in the summer of 1936 was an extremely complex one. Elections held earlier that year in Spain had returned a majority of candidates from liberal and leftist parties to the Cortes, where they had formed a Popular Front government, modeled after the French example. The new administration immediately set about trying to right some of the social injustices that they perceived within Spanish society. Thus encouraged, peasants, workers, and anarchists began to demand more extensive changes, holding strikes, staging demonstrations, seizing land, and attacking churches when they thought that the government was moving too slowly. The problem was that, due to the way that voting was weighed in the elections, the Right had actually received several hundred thousand more votes than had the left-of-center parties.[7] Conservatives and other critics of the Left thought that the elections had been "stolen" or that, at the very least, the Popular Front regime had no mandate to impose on them its vision of a just society. As the summer began, the unrest initiated by the Left, and answered by the Right, escalated, until there was an increasing number of violent exchanges and assassinations. On July 18, 1936 Spanish military forces, led by generals Franco and Sanjurjo, tried to carry out a coup d'etat against what they perceived as a communist conspiracy to set up a "Soviet dictatorship."[8] Their failure to immediately topple the Popular Front government set the stage for the next two-and-a-half years of war.

Almost immediately both the Republicans and the Nationalists turned to the great powers for military support, the former appealing to France and the Soviet Union and the latter to Italy and Germany. On July 19, José Giral, the Spanish Prime Minister, sent a telegram to Léon Blum, the leader of the French Popular Front government, requesting aircraft to put down the uprising. Blum met with several members of his cabinet two days later, and all agreed that they should aid the rightful government of Spain in its attempts to suppress the rebellion. The primary reason that Blum gave for helping Spain was that a Franco victory would mean German and Italian bases in the Canaries and Balearics.[9] Besides this strategically sound reason for agreeing to the request, the French had a 1935 commercial treaty with Spain that allowed for the purchase of matériel, and there was some feeling that the two Popular Front governments ought to support each other whenever possible. Yet within four days the Blum cabinet reversed its decision and announced that France would not send the aircraft to its supposedly ideological brothers in Spain. Shortly afterward the French would propose and then strongly promote a policy of non-interference in Spanish affairs. By early August Blum's cabinet had developed a plan to quarantine the war that included a non-intervention agreement and the creation of a non-intervention committee (NIC) to oversee the agreement.

The abrupt nature of this about-face has provoked intense speculation over Blum's motives. Many scholars, most prominently Jill Edwards, Antony Beevor, and John Dreifort, have argued that Blum was persuaded to back away from supporting the Republicans by British opposition to his plans; France in any case wished to avoid upsetting its closest partner.[10] On July 22, Blum had traveled to London for meetings with English officials to discuss an unrelated matter. It was just after he had returned from Britain that the French government announced the decision not to ship the aircraft to the Republicans, leading many people to the obvious conclusion that the British had discouraged French involvement in the developing war.

As will be outlined below, the British government did indeed have motives for keeping its ally out of the conflict.[11] Nevertheless, it was apparent even at the time that there was more to the French decision than simply doing whatever the British suggested. Almost as soon as Blum's administration had determined to support the Republicans, its intentions were leaked to the public by a pro-Franco supporter at the Spanish embassy in Paris.[12] This created a huge furor both in the press and among conservatives in the senate.[13] When the cabinet met to discuss the problem on July 25, the rightist campaign against supporting the Republicans and opposition from conservative senators, as well as British attitudes, were high on its list of concerns.[14] Members of the cabinet were worried also about the conflict spreading to other countries, or even turning into another general European war.[15] It was this combination of factors rather than British pressure alone that dampened the original enthusiasm of Blum and his cabinet for aiding the Republicans.[16] The French now consulted the other great powers on a non-intervention pact, an initiative that received general approval.[17] Here was a policy that could replace individual interference in the war, please the British, and avoid the risks of a large-scale conflict. After initially sending some aircraft – while publicly denying that he was doing so – Blum repudiated any military support for the Republicans, and worked hard over the next several months to keep the war from spreading beyond the Spanish borders.[18]

The change of heart by the Popular Front government showed that France would not chance a great war without the full support of its people and of Britain. Although the Blum administration felt a profound ideological closeness to the Republicans, and knew that there was a strong possibility that the conflict would result in a regime favorable to enemies directly on France's borders, neither strategic nor ideological arguments were strong enough to convince the French. Throughout the rest of 1936, Blum and Delbos would continue to express their fears that the war might spill over into a larger conflict. In December Blum would claim that it was "a miracle" that the war had so far been confined to Spain alone.[19] He would also tell Alvarez del Vayo that "the crux of the matter was in London," and that the British had to be convinced to abandon non-intervention if any help was to come to Spain.[20] These were not the words of a man who felt that France could afford to risk entering a war on its own, regardless of the incentives to do so.

At about the same time, José Giral wrote the Soviet ambassador in Paris and asked the Soviet Union to supply the Republicans with arms for their struggle against the rebels.[21] Despite numerous reports from agents in Spain that the war was going badly for the government, Stalin would not decide to send military aid to the Republicans until early September.[22] The causes for the delay are still not clear, although there has been much speculation about what he had in mind.[23] It is clear, however, that the Soviet Union, like France, had as much to lose as to gain from intervening in the Civil War.[24] The only good reason for helping Spain was ideological: as the world's first socialist nation, the Soviet Union was seen as the natural protector of the Republicans. Stalin was soon faced with demands from European socialists and communists that he save Spain's embattled Popular Front government.[25] Unfortunately, to do so too openly or too decisively would certainly frighten all of the other great powers of Europe.[26] At a time when

Stalin was seeking to work with France and Britain against Fascism and Nazism, he could hardly afford to alienate them.

The danger associated with intervening in Spain, and the fact that the Soviet Union had little to gain, explains why Stalin at first supported the non-intervention agreement and the NIC.[27] Yet, just a few weeks later, he too changed his mind and decided to provide arms to Spain and to encourage the formation of international brigades that would fight for the Republican cause. A detailed description of Soviet armaments sent to Spain shows that there were four groups of equipment shipped by the end of October 1936 and a fifth group planned for early November.[28] The timing of the shipments provides evidence of the reasoning that led Stalin to begin aiding the Republicans: by September it was clear that Germany and Italy were supporting the Nationalists, and that their matériel was giving Franco the edge that he needed to defeat the Republicans. This may have convinced Stalin that he could now safely intervene in the war, since it was possible to argue that other powers were blatantly violating the terms of the non-intervention agreement. On October 23, the USSR issued a statement at the NIC that it would no longer feel obligated to follow the agreement to any greater degree than were other participants.[29] At the same time, volunteers from all over Europe and the Americas had been arriving in Spain to help the Republicans in their fight. Throughout the autumn André Marty, the head of the French Communist Party, organized these men into international brigades with the direct aid and supervision of the Soviet Union.[30] The presence of these volunteers made it easier for Stalin to claim that the workers of Europe had spontaneously decided to aid the Republic and to slip in additional assistance from the Soviet Union. There was also an economic incentive for helping the Spanish government. In late August, just as Stalin was deciding whether or not to intervene, three officials of the Republic came to the Soviet Union to buy war supplies, offering in exchange huge sums of Spanish gold.[31] In the end the majority of Spain's gold supply would be transferred to Moscow in return for arms, allowing Stalin to help the Republic, win propaganda points in the ideological struggle with Germany and Italy, and yet pay no economic costs.

It is important to note that the Soviet leadership did not intend to risk a widening of the conflict: it was simply answering an intervention begun by Italy and Germany. Among other things this meant that the Soviets were not firmly committed to helping the Republicans to win if to do so would force the conflict to spread beyond the Spanish borders or damage the new Soviet relationship with the western powers.[32] In a revealing conversation with the American ambassador in Moscow, Maxim Litvinov commented that from the point of view of European peace the Republicans had done "almost too well": he feared that the reversals suffered by the Italians would compel Mussolini to send more men into Spain in order to save face, and that this might have the effect of widening the war.[33] The Soviet Union did not, in fact, provide the Republicans with anything like the manpower or matériel that Germany and Italy gave the Nationalists, and Stalin told the few hundred Soviet advisors to "stay out of range of the artillery fire" when he sent them off to the war.[34] After the summer of 1937 the amount of arms and number of men sent to Spain tapered off sharply, as Stalin and the Politburo decided that it would be more advantageous to have the war drag on as long as possible in order to keep Hitler tied up in a low-intensity conflict.[35]

There was, in fact, little desire in Germany to escalate the conflict. Although Hitler invested more in Spain in terms of men, matériel and money than did Stalin, he also wanted to avoid a general war. At the same time, he had more reason than either France or the Soviet Union to become involved in the Civil War, and he was willing to take more chances. Hitler, like Stalin, saw himself as reacting to provocation rather than initiating any interference in Spanish affairs. As early as July 23, the Germans knew that the French were contemplating sending matériel to the Republicans. Johannes Welczeck, the German ambassador to France, informed his superiors that supplying the amount and sorts of weaponry that he had heard of would cause Franco's situation to deteriorate decisively.[36] Two Germans in Spain, both Nazis and one an agent of the Auslandsorganisation (AO), a kind of Nazi Party foreign office, may have had similar fears. The rebellion had stalled in southern Spain for lack of reinforcements from Franco's troops, which were stranded in Africa, and needed only this sort of aid to the Republic to fail completely. When Franco asked the two Germans to act as his emissaries, they left for Berlin almost immediately with a letter for Hitler requesting military aid.[37]

In their meeting with top Nazi officials, it became clear that Hitler was alone in supporting some sort of intervention in the war. Werner von Blomberg, the head of the Wehrmacht, was, as usual, extremely cautious, as was Göring.[38] Even the foreign office was not asked to participate in the decision-making process, but later statements from the heads of that ministry would show their fears that the war could expand into a more general conflict.[39] Despite this lack of support from his advisors, Hitler decided to provide the aircraft necessary to airlift Franco's forces from Africa to Spain. Over the next two months, though Hitler would sign the non-intervention agreement, he gradually expanded his involvement in the war, providing 5,000 German troops and hundreds of millions of marks in military equipment.[40]

At the various stages of his involvement in the Civil War, Hitler proved willing to face the risks attending intervention. However, each time he decided to make a greater commitment to Franco's cause, he did so in a way which guaranteed that the war would not spread beyond Spain's borders. The supplies he first sent to the Nationalists were limited in scope and were almost directly proportional to those that the French were about to send to the Republicans. The initial German involvement thus did not pose much danger, since it was simply a response to the French initiative, and could have very great returns, in the form of a regime friendly to Germany installed on France's southern border.

Increasing the aid to Franco would have seemed a different matter, since the chances for provoking retaliation were higher, but once again Hitler had good reason to believe that there would be no serious consequence. He chose to increase his involvement in the war at the end of October – after both Italy and the Soviet Union had already tested the international climate and found that France and Britain were unwilling to go to war over Spain. The decision was not, therefore, as risky as it might seem. But Hitler also had good ideological and economic reasons for supporting the Nationalists. As many historians have pointed out, Hitler and Göring frequently talked about the dangers of a communist Spain and the need to aid Franco, a fellow anti-communist, in his struggles with the common enemy.[41] Although other scholars, such as Glenn Harper, believe that this was mere rhetoric used by Hitler to sell his policy to the Nazi "true believers," it is difficult to ignore the influence of ideology in Hitler's policies.[42] It is significant that the German foreign office, which expressed the greatest concern about the war spreading, was prevented from taking part in the decision-making process over Spain. Instead, it was the ideologically oriented Nazi AO which at several critical junctures took the lead, urging Hitler toward greater commitments to save the Nationalist movement.[43] In addition to ideology, there were sound economic grounds for becoming more involved in Spain. Germany had a desperate need for raw materials to fuel its rearmament drive. Even before the Civil War, Spain had provided much-needed iron ores for German manufacturers, and once the conflict broke out both German businessmen and policy makers were quick to seize the opportunity to benefit at the expense of their only serious competitors, the British.[44] In a speech in June 1937 Hitler boldly declared: "Germany needs ore. That is why we want a Nationalist Government in Spain – to be able to buy Spanish ore."[45] The Germans conducted intensive negotiations with Franco to ensure a reliable supply of raw materials once the conflict had ended.

Once Hitler had sent large numbers of troops into the war, additional strategic and military reasons emerged for remaining in Spain, but again he kept his involvement within strict bounds. Strategically, it would be very helpful to keep British and French attention focused on Spain and away from Hitler's more important interests in central Europe.[46] As Mussolini became ever more deeply drawn into the Spanish conflict, Hitler saw the usefulness of keeping the Italians occupied there so that he would have a free hand in Austria and elsewhere.[47] Göring and other military leaders argued that Spain was a good arena in which to test the new air and tank forces. As new branches of the German armed forces, the Luftwaffe and Panzer forces had yet to develop either a role or a doctrine for fighting in the next large conflict. Spain provided the Wehrmacht with a convenient proving ground to decide both of these questions. It is highly unlikely that Hitler decided to intervene in the Civil War to test his new forces but, once involved, he was more than willing to send large contingents of pilots and other troops to please Göring and the generals, and to try out his military machine in action.[48] At the same time, Hitler was unwilling to go too far, agreeing for instance with Blomberg and Neurath that Germany should not send a complete infantry division to Spain, and stating in late 1937 that he was not really interested in allowing Franco a quick victory.[49]

In contrast to the relative restraint shown by Hitler, Mussolini's intervention in the Civil War was massive from the very beginning, and was aimed at the complete victory of the Nationalist forces. This policy was not clear at the beginning of the rebellion. When representatives from Franco flew to Italy to ask for aid at the same time as the German emissaries were approaching Hitler, Mussolini hesitated for several days, and twice refused to send military assistance before finally agreeing, on 28 July, to begin helping the Nationalists.[50] Once he had made the decision, however, he threw all of his energy into ensuring that the Nationalists would defeat the Republicans. Over the next two-and-a-half years he sent tens of thousands of regular soldiers from the Italian infantry, tank, and air forces, and invested billions of lire in Spain.

Why did Mussolini change his mind? Robert Whealey has pointed out the many reasons that Mussolini had for not becoming involved in the conflict: opposition from his military and policy advisors; the expense of such an operation; and, most importantly, the international complications that were sure to arise, especially after Italy' recent experience in Abyssinia.[51] As with Germany and the Soviet Union, however, there were factors that limited the risks of intervention and explain why Italy desired a Nationalist victory. The French decision to send aircraft to Spain, so decisive in shaping policy for Hitler, also affected Mussolini. It was only after Blum had determined that he could provide the Republicans with aid, while publicly denying that he was doing so, that Mussolini changed his mind about intervening in the war. Blum's later change of heart and support for non-intervention had no effect for, once in Spain, a complete victory by the Nationalists became a matter of national pride and prestige for Italy, especially after Mussolini recognized the Franco regime in November 1936.[52] Mussolini also became convinced that the Spanish arena was a good place to create a more warlike spirit in the Italian people. "When Spain is finished," Mussolini declared in November 1937, "I will think of something else. The character of the Italian people must be molded by fighting."[53]

Two additional factors convinced Mussolini to interfere in the Civil War. Italy had powerful strategic interests for wanting a friendly Spain: the new Roman empire that the Fascists hoped to build depended on control, either direct or indirect, of the Mediterranean. If the Republicans won the war Spain, which had been friendly toward Italy in the recent past, might turn to France for support. The interest that Mussolini showed in the Balearic Islands during the Civil War confirmed this ambition.[54] Like the Germans and the Soviets, the Italians also had ideological motives for aiding the Nationalists. In a conversation early on in the war, Ciano tried to convince the Germans that their struggle against the common enemy – communism – made it their duty to help Franco by supplying not only matériel but men.[55] A more comprehensive description of Italian fears came in statements to the United States made by the Italian ambassador, who painted a picture of the danger that communism constituted to western civilization. He added that Italy could not tolerate the establishment of a communist regime in Spain since "it would soon spread to France and to the very borders of Fascist Italy. Such a development…would place Italy in grave peril in view of the fact that she [was] faced on the East by Slav peoples racially affiliated with the Russians and who might in time fall victim to Communism and thus close Italy in on two sides."[56] Fascist concerns about communism were not limited to fears of foreign countries falling to its abhorrent ideology: as a German observer pointed out, Italian officials also saw that a Republican victory might encourage the spread of communism to Italy itself.[57]

Prompted by these apprehensions, the Italians went further than any of the great powers in their attempts to control the outcome of the Civil War. While other countries were careful to restrict their aid sufficiently to prevent the war spreading abroad, Italy took more risks. The reasons for this were twofold: the perception of Nationalist victory as tied to Italian prestige; and the desire to make up for the economic costs of the war. Once Italy had invested so many men in the war, recognized Franco's regime, and made themselves publicly into the firmest supporters of the Nationalists, there was little chance that the Fascist regime could see Franco defeated without enormous domestic and international repercussions to itself.[58] On a more practical note, Italy put so much money into the war that it could ill-afford to withdraw before making up for its investment. By October 1937 Mussolini declared that the war in Spain had to be won at all costs, and that he would persevere until it was successfully concluded. He had already spent 3 billion lire by this point, and he intended to get his money back, which he believed to be possible because of Spain's richness in raw materials.[59] Mussolini's determination to win in Spain served to encourage both the Germans and the Soviets to invest more there than they might otherwise have done; it served also to heighten tensions throughout Europe, and so push the world to the brink of war.

In the end, however, Mussolini's adventures did not widen the conflict into the European conflagration that so many feared, primarily because Britain was willing to compromise almost everything in order to avoid a general war. In comparison to French agonizing, the British apparently had no difficulty in deciding to avoid a conflict by not involving themselves in the Civil War. The main reason for the difference was quite simple: the British saw no reason to wish success for either side in the conflict. The Conservatives thought that the Republicans were nothing more than communists in disguise, but they had no desire to see the Nationalists win either.[60] In his diary entry for August 8, 1936, Harold Nicolson expressed perfectly the attitude of many British officials:

The Spanish situation is hell. Philip Noel-Baker writes in *The Times* pretending that the Madrid Government is one which should command the support of all democratic liberals. In fact, of course, it is a mere Kerensky Government at the mercy of an armed proletariat. On the other hand, Franco and his Moors are no better. The Germans are fussing outside Barcelona with their pocket-battleships "making themselves felt". It is serious in that it emphasizes the division of Europe between left and right. Which way do we go? The pro-German and anti-Russian tendencies of the Tories will be fortified and increased.[61]

His concern that pro-Right tendencies would be strengthened were well-founded, since British strategic and economic interests favored the Nationalists, if anyone. Businessmen feared that a "red" success might mean the confiscation of the large British holdings in the country, while Chamberlain and others in the government thought that reaching agreements with Italy and Germany was more important than the outcome of the war in Spain. The British also had a more sophisticated understanding of Franco's designs for postwar Spain than did any of the other European powers. In a conversation with an American official, Anthony Eden, the British foreign secretary, stated that Franco's whole purpose "was an Iberian policy…with Spaniards in control in Spain and all German and Italian influence eliminated."[62] A Nationalist Spain was therefore not a strategic threat, as France believed. Perhaps the best statement of British policy on the war was provided by the American chargé in London, who informed Cordell Hull in 1937 that

> though Great Britain dislikes the prospect of a dictatorship in Spain friendly to Germany and Italy, the British government has to consider whether it is not time to start cultivating Franco's friendship. British public opinion, and the Press, are of course influenced by their taste for the Left or the Right in Spanish politics. But it is unlikely that these feelings have any important influence on Great Britain's policy, in Spain or anywhere else, which is simply aimed at serving strategic and other interests of Great Britain and the Empire regardless.…I have no desire, in making these remarks, to minimize in any way what I believe has been, from the beginning of the Spanish conflict, the sincere and open desire on the part of the British, paramount among various considerations, to keep the fighting strictly confined to the Spanish peninsula with a view to preserving European peace.[63]

With this slight bias toward the Nationalists, it should come as no surprise that early on in the crisis Stanley Baldwin, then prime minister, gave Eden explicit instructions that "on no account, French or other, must he bring us into the fight on the side of the Russians."[64]

Given the absence of a real desire to see either side win, the succeeding British administrations were determined to support any policy that would keep the war confined to the Spanish borders. After giving their French allies no encouragement in July to implement Blum's plans for intervention, British officials were pleased to be approached about a non-interference pact the next month. Over the course of the war, the British would be the most enthusiastic supporters of the NIC and its agreement, even when it was obvious that three of the great powers were blatantly violating its terms. Despite its problems, non-intervention suited all of the British thinking about the Civil War,[65] and even those members of parliament who were most critical of the government's other foreign policies found good reason to support this imperfect pact rather than taking sides and risking a European war.[66]

Non-intervention also fitted well into Neville Chamberlain's policy of appeasement by allowing him to contain the war and ignore most of its unpleasant implications. After he became prime minister, decisions over Spain were left up to the foreign office.[67] Chamberlain focused his energy and attention on appeasing Germany and Italy, and viewed events in Spain mainly in terms of how they would affect this more important goal.[68] The "Gentleman's Agreement" with Italy, which he hoped would relax tensions between the two nations and encourage Mussolini to break with Hitler, illustrated his thinking on Spain. Unfortunately for his plan, the agreement was long delayed by Italy's flagrant violations of the non-intervention pact and by Eden's increasing unwillingness to ignore them. Pressed by Eden and others, Chamberlain pledged to tie talks with Mussolini to the withdrawal of Italian volunteers from Spain, a promise he would later regret.[69] Throughout the war Mussolini continually broke his word on withdrawing troops from Spain, and Eden worked hard to keep Chamberlain from overlooking these breaches in good faith. Only after Eden resigned in protest was the prime minister able to press ahead with an accord, choosing to ignore the clear signs that Mussolini did not keep to the terms of treaties.[70]

In fact Britain was unwilling to risk a war, or even to endanger a potential agreement, over Spain, regardless of the actions taken by the Italians and Germans. In the spring of 1937 Cordell Hull instructed the US ambassador in London to inquire about British attitudes toward a hypothetical full-scale intervention by the Italians.[71] The ambassador replied that the British would try to maintain their original policy of stalemate or peace without victory, "but certainly without resort to armed intervention."[72] If total Italian involvement in Spain would not induce the British to go to war, then "minor" violations by Mussolini would certainly not persuade them to change their policy.

That the Americans would wish to know British opinions on the Spanish conflict was indicative of US policies toward the war: first was the need to keep to the neutrality laws that had been overwhelmingly passed by congress and were firmly supported by the majority of Americans. The second was to follow the lead established by the great powers of Europe which were more nearly concerned with the war and its possible spread.[73] Together these policies meant that, even compared with Britain, the US was the great power least likely to risk involvement in a war over Spain. The ambassador to France, William Bullitt, felt it his duty to warn Delbos early in the conflict "not to base his foreign policy or any part of it on an expectation that the United States would ever again send troops or warships or floods of munitions and money to Europe."[74] In keeping with these sentiments, the US began a "moral embargo" of Spain that soon became a legal one, and otherwise completely followed British and French policies.[75] Although Hull firmly backed neutrality, not all American officials supported the decision.[76] The US ambassador to Spain, for instance, was a vociferous supporter of the Republicans, while some cabinet members, such as Harold Ickes, also thought that the US had chosen the wrong path.[77] Their voices were marginalized, however, and Roosevelt continued to defend his policy until it became clear that the Civil War had been won by the Nationalists.[78]

The differing decisions over intervention or non-intervention helped to clarify the conditions under which the great powers were willing to go to war, but they also deeply affected the two great alliances on the continent: those between Britain and France, on the one hand, and between Germany and Italy, on the other. With regard to the former, events in Spain showed that France was becoming much more dependent on Britain. Troubled by internal dissent and political instability, France was unable to come to the aid of an ideological friend located on its very borders without the firm support of Britain. Once the French had conceded that their foreign policy was so closely tied to that of the British, there was little chance that they could recover their freedom of action. There was but one hopeful sign for the alliance and the cause of peace during the course of the war – when Britain and France successfully worked together to deter Mussolini. Any benefit accruing from this single success did not last, and soon France found itself again following the lead of its ally. Blum and other French leaders protested violations of the non-intervention agreement and sought to have them halted, but nothing was done unless the British agreed to help.

Only once during the war were the French able to strike out on their own to counter German and Italian intervention. In March 1938 Blum came to power the second time determined to do something to aid the Republicans. The Spanish government had just suffered a serious defeat on the Aragon front and was pleading for aid from the French. Unlike the cautious Delbos, Joseph Paul-Boncour, the new foreign minister, told the British that if they would not agree to mediate the French would be forced to open the frontier and intervene on the side of the Spanish. The British may not have taken this very seriously, since they expected the Blum government to fall shortly.[79] They were right, but Blum had decided to act while he could, and therefore ordered the borders opened fully for the passage of arms to the Spanish government. Edouard Daladier, who shortly replaced him, continued and even expanded this policy, telling Bullitt that he had allowed the Soviets to send 300 airplanes to the Republicans through France, even though he had had to "cut down many miles of trees along the sides of roads in order that the large bombers might pass."[80] This burst of independence was short-lived, ending most probably for the same reasons that the French had declined to intervene in 1936: British resistance, and French reluctance to continue a risky policy on their own.[81] Along with this independent French action, there was also one example of French and British co-operation that served the interests of both while also deterring a dictator. In the summer of 1937 the Italians began covertly using submarines and aircraft to harass the Republican navy and to sink ships from any country that was trading with the Spanish government. Both the British and the French complained about this obvious escalation in the war, but the British were unwilling to support any action until it became apparent that their trade was being affected. Not only did the Italians sink merchantmen supplying the Republicans with arms, but they were rather indiscriminate in their targeting and began destroying ships carrying ore back to Britain.[82] When Delbos approached the British about a meeting to discuss the problem, Chamberlain agreed. The result – the Nyon conference of September 1937 – ended in almost complete success. The participating powers agreed with Britain and France to begin patrolling the Mediterranean with warships that were empowered to counterattack any ships that tried to sink neutral vessels. Although there were some loopholes in the agreement, such as granting the Italians a stretch of the sea to patrol which allowed them to continue supplying the Nationalists, submarine attacks did cease.[83] Nyon showed that determined firmness by Britain and France could alter the aggressive actions of dictators, but it was a lesson that was either misunderstood or soon forgotten. Rarely after 1937 could the two muster the political will to risk a war by standing up to either Hitler or Mussolini.

However successful it may have been in the short term, the Nyon conference, along with the French decision to open their borders, also showed the serious limitations on autonomous French action. Just twice during the entire Spanish crisis were they able to assert themselves, and then only for short periods or when the British had strong interests of their own at stake. To A. J. P. Taylor and other students of the origins of the Second World War this was all very familiar, for the Spanish Civil War strengthened and even introduced patterns of behavior in the alliance that would lead to the agreement at Munich.

The relationship between Germany and Italy was even more greatly affected by the events surrounding the Spanish conflict. On one level, through their joint interests in Spain Hitler and Mussolini were drawn together into closer association. As the German ambassador to Italy pointed out, Germany had every reason to encourage Italy in its Spanish adventure, since it clearly revealed the conflicting interests that Italy had with France and Britain, and also demonstrated to Italy the advisability of confronting the western powers "shoulder to shoulder" with Germany.[84] This was very much what happened during the course of the war.

Italy would decide to join Japan in signing the Anti-Comintern Pact with Germany in November 1937.[85] Unlike distant Japan, with whom no concrete military plans were developed, entering the Axis meant that Italy would certainly be drawn into any wars in which Germany became involved, while Hitler would now feel himself obliged to come to the aid of Mussolini if the Italians asked for assistance. Even before Mussolini signed the pact with Hitler it was clear that the two felt they had more in common since the Spanish conflict had begun. At the NIC, many of the positions that Germany and Italy took had obviously been worked out in advance, thereby strengthening their hand over issues on which they disagreed with Britain, France, or the Soviet Union. By insisting together, for instance, that they would only agree to ban volunteers in Spain once an effective system of control had been worked out, Germany and Italy were able to put off for as long as they wished any attempts to get their troops out of Spain.[86] The decision to intervene may even have been made jointly although, as we have seen, each had differing motives for intervention.[87]

The war also created new tensions between Italy and Germany and a new sense of who was to lead the alliance. Italy's commitment to Franco's victory clashed with Germany's desire to have the war last as long as possible, while German economic interests at times forced Mussolini to change his plans for the benefit of Germany.[88] Even more important was the rise of Hitler at the expense of Mussolini, especially after the defeats suffered by Italian forces at Guadalajara in early 1937. Before the war, Hitler saw Mussolini as a role model and a great man, whose wishes had to be respected. The more established Mussolini had greater international prestige than Hitler and acted as the leading statesman in the cause of radical nationalism. This relationship changed during the Civil War, as Hitler was gradually able to assert his will to achieve the ends that he wanted, sometimes at the expense of Italian interests. By the time the conflict ended, Hitler had completely eclipsed Mussolini in the Axis alliance. Although there were other reasons for this transformation, the Italian commitment to the Nationalists' victory played a vital role in the gradual decline of Mussolini's power and influence. Because he had less at stake in Spain Hitler could further his own interests at the expense of a Mussolini absorbed in his Spanish troubles. Hitler recognized this, commenting during Mussolini's state visit in September 1937: "Italy was sinking deeper in the mire of the civil war in Spain, leaving Germany free to move forward in the east."[89] As Mussolini saw his influence fading, he became obsessed with having Franco win as a way to shore up both his personal prestige and that of Italy, thus fulfilling Hitler's wish to prolong the war.[90]

Mussolini's new – lowered – status in the Axis in turn affected two significant milestones on the way to the Second World War: the *Anschluss* and the Anglo-Italian accord. There were, of course, other causes for these events, but Italy's involvement in the Civil War was an important factor in both. Before the war Mussolini had expressed his sharp disapproval of Hitler's plans for Austria. As Italy became more deeply drawn into the conflict, his concern over a German–Austrian union, and his ability to prevent such a union, lessened. Schuschnigg was told early on in the war that Italy could no longer supply Austria with arms because of her commitments in Spain.[91] By 1938 Hitler's dominance in the Axis, fed by Mussolini's distraction over Spain, was so well-established that it was clear that he could not stop Germany from taking Austria even had he desired to do so. At almost the same moment as he saw himself becoming the junior partner in the alliance Mussolini decided to re-open negotiations with Britain, resulting in the accord signed that April.[92] The agreement did little to halt the precipitous decline of Italy's influence in the alliance with Germany. By the time the Nationalists had defeated the Republicans in early 1939, Germany and Italy were bound more tightly than ever, but Hitler was now firmly in control of the Axis.

If events in Spain added greatly to Hitler's power and prestige, it also made a difference in German economic strength. As mentioned above, Germany hoped to use the war to secure the raw materials necessary to equip the army with modern armaments. In November 1936 Hitler was already ordering general Wilhelm von Faupel, the new chargé to the Nationalist government, to concern himself with improving commercial relations between the two countries. The opportunity afforded by the war would keep Britain from taking away the market at a later stage and secure for Germany a permanent supply of iron for Hitler's

Four-Year Plan.[93] Negotiations with Franco to cement these economic ties took up a great deal of time, but ended with agreements that Hitler prized more than any friendship treaty with Franco.[94] By 1937, Germany had managed to obtain 1.6 million tons of iron ore and 956,000 tons of pyrites without spending any foreign currency.[95] As in other matters, Hitler was not averse to using under-handed means to secure the iron that Germany desperately needed. When Nationalist forces ran into difficulties in the summer of 1938 and Franco was compelled to beg for help, Hitler agreed to send additional troops, but at a price: the Spanish leader was told that his partners had a "justifiable interest" in a co-operative attitude on Spain's part to guarantee Germany's ore supply.[96] Franco must have acquiesced, for it was shortly afterward that the most important of the accords over economic ties was signed between the two powers. While Germany was able to obtain iron from other countries, such as Sweden, Spain provided a cheaper source of this and other ores essential to German war industries.

As the example of economic benefits shows, the Spanish Civil War was a vital stepping-stone on the way to world war, but not in the way that people at the time understood it. Although Fascists and Nazis would battle communists and liberals, the war, as Taylor argued, was less a preview of the next conflict than it was another in a series of crises that exposed the underlying weaknesses in the international system. As with other events in the Rhineland, Abyssinia, Austria, and Munich, the war in Spain showed that Britain, France, and the United States could not risk war in order to deter the dictators; that Hitler and Mussolini were willing to take calculated risks to achieve their ideological, strategic, and economic interests; and that the Soviet Union, while trying to avoid alienating the western democracies, would follow its own course. The war also confirmed that the alliance between Britain and France, dominated by a Britain that was firmly committed to appeasement, could not keep the two revisionist powers from doing almost all that they wished. Meanwhile, Hitler used the conflict in Spain, as he would other crises, to gain the upper hand in the Axis and to move toward his ultimate goal of living-space in the east, taking as he did so the raw materials that he needed for any further steps. Perhaps even more significant for later events, successes in Spain encouraged Hitler, and Mussolini to believe that they could employ their armies on the European continent without fear of retaliation, as long as they did so step-by-step, while the non-intervention agreement was one of the first that Hitler signed and yet broke with impunity, laying the groundwork for his later unkept promises.

Notes

1 See also his description of what was at stake in the war in Claude G. Bowers, *My Mission to Spain. Watching the Rehearsal for World War II*, New York, 1954, p. 272.

2 J. Alvarez del Vayo, *Freedom's Battle*, New York, 1971 [1940], p. xix. See also Ivan Maisky, *Spanish Notebooks*, London, 1966, p. 9; Bowers to Roosevelt, August 11, 1937, *Foreign Relations of the United States* [henceforth *FRUS*], 1937, vol. 1:*General*, Washington, 1954, p. 372; and Richard Griffiths, *Fellow Travellers of the Right. British Enthusiasts for Nazi Germany, 1933–9*, London, 1980, p. 261.

3   Pierre Broué and Emile Témime, *The Revolution and the Civil War in Spain*, Cambridge, MA, 1970.

4   Dante A. Puzzo, *Spain and the Great Powers, 1936–1941*, Freeport, CT, 1962, p. 5.

5   Alvarez del Vayo, *Freedom's Battle*, p. 142.

6   Burnett Bolloten, *The Spanish Civil War. Revolution and Counterrevolution*, Chapel Hill, NC, 1991, p. 21. The best treatment of the numerous underlying causes for conflict in Spain during the early part of this century can be found in Gerald Brenan, *The Spanish Labyrinth. An Account of the Social and Political Background of the Civil War*, Cambridge, 1967.

7   See Anthony Rhodes, *The Vatican in the Age of the Dictators, 1922–1945*, London, 1973, p. 122, for this little-noted fact.

8   See Franco's declaration to the Germans that the uprising was necessary "to anticipate a Soviet dictatorship, which was already prepared." Wegener [Tetuán consulate] to foreign ministry, July 24, 1936, *Documents on German Foreign Policy, 1918–1945* [henceforth *DGFP*], series D, 1937–45, vol. 3, p. 8.

9   Michael Alpert, *A New International History of the Spanish Civil War*, London, 1994, p. 14.

10   Among those scholars who have emphasized the role that the British had in discouraging the French from supporting the Republicans are Jill Edwards, *The British Government and the Spanish Civil War, 1936–1939*, London, 1979, pp. 25–30; Antony Beevor, *The Spanish Civil War*, London, 1982, pp. 109–10; John E. Dreifort, *Yvon Delbos at the Quai D'Orsay. French Foreign Policy during the Popular Front, 1936–1938*, Lawrence, KS, 1973, pp. 50, 54; Robert H. Whealey, *Hitler and Spain. The Nazi Role in the Spanish Civil War, 1936–1939*, Lexington, KY, 1989, p. 15; William E. Watters, *An International Affair. Non-Intervention in the Spanish Civil War, 1936–1939*, New York, 1971, p. 38; Broué and Témime, *Revolution and the Civil War*, pp. 328–9; Puzzo, *Spain and the Great Powers*, 82–8; Pierre Cot, *Triumph of Treason*, Chicago, IL, 1944, pp. 94, 344–6.

11   And at least one British official, the ambassador to France, warned the French against helping out the Republicans, although he said that he was speaking "personally" and not officially. See Dreifort, *Delbos*, pp. 46–7.

12   Cot, *Triumph of Treason*, p. 338.

13   Cot, *Triumph of Treason*, pp. 344–6; Alpert, *New International History*, pp. 14, 21–2; Dreifort, *Delbos*, p. 35.

14   Dreifort, *Delbos*, p. 40.

15   Anthony Adamthwaite, *France and the Coming of the Second World War, 1936–1939*, London, 1977, p. 42. Throughout the rest of 1936 Blum and Delbos would continue to talk about their fears that the war would widen into a greater conflict, showing the strength that this held in their decision to support non-intervention. Telegram from Bullitt to acting-secretary of state, November 28, 1936, *FRUS*, 1936, vol. 2: *Europe*, pp. 578–80; Welczeck to the foreign ministry, December 15, 1936, *DGFP*, series D, vol. 3, 167–8.

16   Most recent scholars have recognized that it was all of these ingredients working together that militated against French involvement in the war. Even those who believe that it was primarily British warnings that convinced the French to back down are careful to list the other reasons for Blum's change of mind. See Puzzo, *Spain and the Great Powers*, pp. 82–8; Broué and Témime, *Revolution and the Civil War*, pp. 328–9; Dreifort, *Delbos*, p. 53.

17   Anthony Eden, *Facing the Dictators. The Memoirs of Anthony Eden, Earl of Avon*, Boston, MA, 1962, p. 455. Delbos was among those most enthusiastic about the policy of non-intervention. Cot, *Triumph of Treason*, p. 339; Dreifort, *Delbos*, pp. 39–40, 43.

18   Cot, *Triumph of Treason*, pp. 339–42; Alpert, *New International History*, pp. 22–3.

19   Welczeck to the foreign ministry, December 15, 1936, *DGFP*, series D, vol. 3, pp. 167–8.

20   Julio Alvarez del Vayo, *Give Me Combat*, Boston, MA, 1973, pp. 159–60.

21 Letter from Giral to Soviet ambassador in Paris, July 25, 1936. *Russian State Military Archive* [hereafter *RGVA*], f. 33987, op. 3, d. 991, pp. 56–9. The timing of the letter is important because it refutes those historians who have argued that the abandonment of the Republic by the western democracies threw it into the arms of the Soviet Union and thus gave substance to the association of the Republican cause with communism. See e.g. Paul Preston, "The creation of the Popular Front in Spain," in Helen Graham and Paul Preston (eds), *The Popular Front in Europe*, London, 1987, p. 84.

22 See e.g. "Information on military situation in Spain," September 8, 1936, and September 19, 1936, *RGVA*, f. 33987, op. 3, d. 845, vol. 2, pp. 20–3, 46–8.

23 See Bolloten, *Spanish Civil War*, p. 110.

24 David T. Cattell, *Communism and the Spanish Civil War*, Berkeley, CA, 1955, pp. 162–3.

25 Broué and Témime, *Revolution and the Civil War*, pp. 367–9.

26 For Baldwin's attitude toward the Republicans, see Edwards, *British Government*, p. 18.

27 Carr believes that the Soviets agreed to non-intervention because they wanted to keep in step with Britain and France and because they lacked the capacity to send military supplies to Spain on any scale matching those of Germany and Italy. E. H. Carr, *The Comintern and the Spanish Civil War*, New York, 1984, pp. 17–18.

28 List of the cost of all ABT material sent to Spain from the ABTU to Langov, dated November 1, 1936, *RGVA*, f. 33987, op. 3, d. 832, pp. 272–5.

29 Ivan Maisky, *Spanish Notebooks*, London, 1966, p. 49.

30 Memorandum from Manuil'skii to Stalin, November 1936, *RGVA*, f. 33987, op. 3, d. 832, p. 309.

31 W. G. Krivitsky, *In Stalin's Secret Service*, New York, 1939, p. 80.

32 See R. H. Haigh, D. S. Morris, and A. R. Peters, *Soviet Foreign Policy, the League of Nations and Europe, 1917–1939*, Totowa, NJ, 1986, pp. 62–3.

33 Davies (ambassador in the Soviet Union) to Hull, March 26, 1937, *FRUS*, 1937, pp. 263–5.

34 Krivitsky, *Secret Service*, p. 77.

35 Alexander Orlov, *The Secret History of Stalin's Crimes*, New York, 1953, p. 238.

36 Telegram from Welczeck to the foreign ministry, July 23, 1936, *DGFP*, series D, vol. 3, p. 4.

37 Manfred Merkes, *Die deutsche Politik gegenüber dem spanischen Bürgerkrieg, 1936–1939*, Bonn, 1961, p. 19; Alpert, *New International History*, p. 24; William Carr, *Arms, Autarky, and Aggression. A Study in German Foreign Policy, 1933–1939*, New York, 1972, p. 69.

38 For the attitudes expressed at this meeting see André Brissaud, *Canaris*, London, 1973, p. 37; Alpert, *New International History*, pp. 27, 30.

39 See Memorandum by Neurath, August 4, 1936, *DGFP*, series D, vol. 3, p. 29; Memorandum by Weizsacker, director of the political department, July 4, 1937, *DGFP*, series D, vol. 3, p. 391.

40 Hans-Henning Abendroth, *Hitler in der spanischen Arena*, Paderborn, 1973, pp. 63–4; Whealey, *Hitler and Spain*, p. 8; Raymond L. Proctor, *Hitler's Luftwaffe in the Spanish Civil War*, Westport, CT, 1983, p. 253.

41 See e.g. Abendroth, *spanischen Arena*, pp. 30, 34–8; Merkes, *deutsche Politik*, p. 25; Carr, *Arms*, p. 69; Gerhard L. Weinberg, *The Foreign Policy of Hitler's Germany. Diplomatic Revolution in Europe, 1933–36*, Chicago, IL, 288–9.

42 Glenn T. Harper, *German Economic Policy in Spain during the Spanish Civil War, 1936–1939*, The Hague, 1967, pp. 16–17.

43 See e.g. Memorandum from the foreign ministry to the war ministry, July 24, 1936, *DGFP*, series D, vol. 3, p. 7; Memorandum by Dieckhoff, director of the political department, July 25, 1936, *DGFP*, series D, vol. 3, pp. 10–11 and Ernst von Weizsäcker, *Erinnerungen*, München, 1950, p. 129. For secondary source discussions of this, see Harper, *German Economic Policy*, pp. 13–14, 40; Merkes, *deutsche Politik*, pp. 20–1.

44 Almost every student of Germany's part in the war has mentioned the German desire for raw materials as a primary reason for further involvement in the war. See e.g. Broué and Témime, *Revolution and the Civil War*, pp. 359–60, 364; Carr, *Arms*, p. 69; Harper, *German Economic Policy*, pp. 16–17, 40–1; Weinberg, *Diplomatic Revolution in Europe*, pp. 288–9.

45 Quoted in Harper, *German Economic Policy*, p. 65.

46 For one statement of this argument see Harper, *German Economic Policy*, pp. 16–17.

47 Carr, *Arms*, pp. 75–6; Memorandum [hereafter The Hossbach Memorandum], November 10, 1937, *DGFP*, series D, vol. 1, pp. 36–7. For a fuller discussion of the effects that Spain had on the relationship between Italy and Germany see below.

48 One historian who doubts this interpretation is Abendroth; see *spanischen Arena*, pp. 30, 34–8.

49 Neurath to Blomberg, December 15, 1936, *DGFP*, series D, vol. 3, p. 168; Telegram from Hassell (ambassador in Italy) to foreign ministry, December 17, 1936, *DGFP*, series D, vol. 3, p. 169; Memorandum by Neurath, January 13, 1937, *DGFP*, series D, vol. 3, p. 222; The Hossbach Memorandum, p. 37. See also Weinberg, *Diplomatic Revolution in Europe*, pp. 297–8.

50 See Alpert, *New International History*, pp. 35–8 for a complete discussion of Mussolini's decision.

51 Whealey, *Hitler and Spain*, p. 12.

52 *Ciano's Diary, 1937–1938*, London, 1952, pp. 50–1.

53 *Ciano's Diary, 1937–1938*, p. 32. See also p. 26 for Ciano's attitude toward this issue.

54 For an excellent discussion of this factor in determining Italian policy, see John F. Coverdale, *Italian Intervention in the Spanish Civil War*, Princeton, NJ, 1975, pp. 75–6, 127ff.

55 Merkes, *deutsche Politik*, p. 31.

56 Memorandum by Murray (chief of the division of near-eastern affairs), November 2, 1936, *FRUS*, 1936, p. 549.

57 Plessen (chargé d'affaires in Rome) to foreign ministry, August 14, 1936, *DGFP*, series D, vol. 3, pp. 38–9.

58 Gerhard L. Weinberg, *The Foreign Policy of Hitler's Germany. Starting World War II, 1937–1939*, Chicago IL, 1980, pp. 144, 149

59 Memorandum from von Bülow-Schwantz (protocol department, German foreign ministry) to Neurath, October 2, 1937, *DGFP*, series D, vol. 1, pp. 4–5.

60 Edwards, *British Government*, pp. 35–7.

61 Stanley Olson (ed.), *Harold Nicolson. Diaries and Letters, 1930–1964*, London, 1980, p. 101.

62 Telegram from Bingham to Hull, July 6, 1937, *FRUS*, 1937, pp. 353–4.

63 Letter from Johnson (chargé in London) to Hull, August 23, 1937, *FRUS*, 1937, pp. 375–6.

64 Quoted in Edwards, *British Government*, p. 18.

65 Edwards gives reasons other than the fit non-intervention with British policies, including the fact that it would obey a chief of staff dictum to remain on good terms with whichever side won, prevent France from going "red," maintain a veneer of impartiality to quieten the British Left, and impede the growing alienation of Italy and Germany from the rest of Europe. See Edwards, *British Government*, p. 61.

66 For a sophisticated discussion of how Conservative critics in particular were convinced to support Chamberlain's policies, see Neville Thompson, *The Anti-Appeasers. Conservative Opposition to Appeasement in the 1930s*, Oxford, 1971, pp. 116–19. For Eden's attitude see Eden, *Facing the Dictators*, p. 451.

67 Eden, *Facing the Dictators*, p. 454; Larry William Fuchser, *Neville Chamberlain and Appeasement. A Study in the Politics of History*, New York, 1982, pp. 61–2.

68 Keith Middlemas, *The Strategy of Appeasement. The British Government and Germany, 1937–39*, Chicago, IL, 1972, p. 42; Ian Colvin, *The Chamberlain Cabinet*, London, 1971, p. 45.

69 Eden and other cabinet members thought this a good first step, but wanted to go even further, making the war inseparable from events in Czechoslovakia. See e.g. Middlemas, *Strategy of Appeasement*, pp. 183–4.

70 Thompson, *Anti-Appeasers*, pp. 41, 143.

71 Hull to Bingham (ambassador in London), March 27, 1937, *FRUS*, 1937, p. 268.

72 Bingham to Hull, March 31, 1937, *FRUS*, 1937, pp. 270–2.

73 See e.g. Memorandum by Welles (undersecretary of state), October 18, 1937, *FRUS*, 1937, pp. 425–7.

74 Telegram, Bullitt to acting-secretary of state, November 28, 1936, *FRUS*, 1936, pp. 578–80.

75 For complete discussions of US policy during the war, see Richard P. Traina, *American Diplomacy and the Spanish Civil War*, Bloomington, IN, 1968; Alpert, *New International History*, pp. 109–11; C. A. MacDonald, *The United States, Britain and Appeasement, 1936–1939*, London, 1981, p. 1. Little argues that the US and Britain were motivated by fears of a communist state in Spain to adopt a "malevolent neutrality" in the war. See Douglas Little, *Malevolent Neutrality. The United States, Great Britain, and the Origins of the Spanish Civil War*, Ithaca, NY, 1985.

76 Cordell Hull, *The Memoirs of Cordell Hull*, vol 1, New York, 1948, p. 477.

77 Letter from Bowers to Roosevelt, August 11, 1937, *FRUS*, 1937, p. 372; Bowers, *Mission to Spain*; Harold L. Ickes, *The Secret Diary of Harold L. Ickes*, vol 2: *The Inside Struggle, 1936–1939*, New York, 1954, pp. 93, 424–5.

78 At which point he seems to have regretted his choice of policy. See Ickes, *Secret Diary*, vol. 2, p. 569.

79 John Harvey (ed.), *The Diplomatic Diaries of Oliver Harvey, 1937–1940*, London, 1970, p. 118.

80 Telegram from Bullitt to Hull, May 9, 1938, *FRUS*, 1938, p. 192.

81 See Oliver Harvey's note in his diaries: "The French are getting increasingly restive as a result of having closed their frontier as a result of our urging," in Harvey (ed.), *Diplomatic Diaries*, p. 157.

82 Hugh Thomas, *The Spanish Civil War*, New York, 1986, pp. 740–1 has this interpretation of the British decision to support the French.

83 Dreifort, *Delbos*, pp. 76–7.

84 Report from Hassell to the foreign ministry, December 18, 1936, *DGFP*, series D, vol. 3, pp. 170–2.

85 Coverdale, *Italian Intervention*, pp. 110–13.

86 See e.g. Telegram from Neurath to the embassy in Italy, January 12, 1937, *DGFP*, series D, vol. 3, p. 220; Telegram from Hassell to the foreign ministry, January 13, 1937, *DGFP*, series D, vol. 3, p. 221.

87 Whealey, *Hitler and Spain*, pp. 12–13.

88 Weinberg, *Starting World War II*, pp. 144, 149; Memorandum from von Bülow-Schwantz to Neurath, October 2, 1937, *DGFP*, series D, vol. 1, pp. 4–5; The Hossbach Memorandum, p. 37.

89 Carr, *Arms*, pp. 75–6.

90 C. J. Lowe and F. Marzari, *Italian Foreign Policy, 1870–1940*, London, 1975, p. 298.

91 Lowe and Marzari, *Italian Foreign Policy*, p. 298.

92 Coverdale, *Italian Intervention*, pp. 352–3.

93 Minute by Sabath (economic policy department), November 27, 1936, *DGFP*, series D, vol. 3, p. 142.

94 Von Ribbentrop actually drew up a "treaty of friendship" between Spain and Germany, but Hitler thought that a commercial treaty was better than something like this, which had "little value." See Memorandum from Ribbentrop to Hitler (1938),

DGFP, series D, vol. 3, pp. 631–4; Memorandum from Spitzy (foreign minister's secretariat) to Ribbentrop, *DGFP*, series D, vol. 3, pp. 634–5.

95 Carr, *Arms*, p. 69.

96 Stohrer (ambassador in Madrid) to foreign ministry, July 6, 1938, *DGFP*, series D, vol. 3, p. 716.

12 The phantom crisis

Danzig, 1939

Sean Greenwood

Taylor provides us with a striking passage on the atmosphere surrounding the final dispute which was to lead to the Second World War.[1] "In strange contrast to earlier crises," he notes, "there were no negotiations over Danzig, no attempts to discover a solution; not even attempts to screw up the tension." It exhibited "none of the manoeuvres and bargaining which had marked the Czechoslovak crisis." While this is a pertinent observation on the extraordinary reluctance of the powers to seek a resolution to what seemed to divide them, Taylor is right but for the wrong reasons. In his view, the Danzig crisis was "formulated in the last days of March when Germany made demands concerning Danzig and the Corridor and the Poles rejected them." It is quite possible, however, to omit almost all reference to increasing German pressure on the Poles between October 1938 and March 1939 for a settlement of the Danzig and "Polish Corridor" questions without obscuring our understanding of the events of 1939. Taylor's interpretation of the advent of war is founded on the proposition that possession of the Free City was what Hitler truly wanted and that a deal, in which the British were prepared to collude, might have been arranged to give it to him, but that time ran out. In reality, the central issues were the wider ambitions of Hitler, their implications for the future of Poland, and the distribution of power in Europe.

The relative inactivity on which Taylor remarks existed precisely because Danzig was always a sub-plot, though admittedly one which, because of tensions in the Free City, threatened to become the plot itself. The demands made upon Warsaw by Berlin, although giving a dangerous edge to German–Polish relations, did not mark the beginning of a new Hitler crisis. This was to be provided by the Anglo-French guarantee to Poland of March 31 which was offered largely in ignorance of recent German–Polish discussions and certainly without knowledge of their collapse three days before the guarantee was given. In fact, the guarantee was prompted by fears of a general attack on Poland, not merely a Nazi coup in Danzig. Once in place, it unintentionally collided with the simmering Danzig question, became entangled with that issue, and began the spiral toward war. The guarantee appeared publicly to commit the British over Danzig. Also, unknown to London it impelled Hitler toward a military solution. The sure-footedness for which the führer was notorious and which should have been a major asset in his dealings over what Taylor calls "the most justified of German grievances" (p. 265) was already creaking under the weight of impatience, and now was overwhelmed by spite. Taylor does hint that the Danzig issue was essentially peripheral: at one point he concedes that the crisis was only "ostensibly" about Danzig. He notes that at the height of the tension the Poles hung back so that action would be forced on them – "and in Danzig it never was." Even so, Taylor continues to emphasize Danzig because it is central to his thesis that the thwarting of a legitimate and limited objective, through a process of human error, thrust Europe into war.

Personal frailty is no more acutely in evidence, so far as Taylor is concerned, than in Warsaw. His depiction of Poland and, more specifically the Polish foreign minister Józef Beck, is far from flattering. Poland is a state with deluded pretensions to "Great Power" status, prepared to act as the "jackal to Germany in the east" and with designs on the Soviet Ukraine. Beck, in Taylor's eyes, is an arrogant manipulative lightweight who "always possessed complete self-confidence, though not much else" (p. 111). It was Beck's overconfident decision not to play Hitler's game, but to keep the Danzig issue between the two states in order to avoid more general co-operation with Germany, which would destroy Poland's policy of balance between Germany and Russia: "It did not cross his mind that this might cause a fatal breach" (see pp. 241–3).

Beck, a man who "apparently possessed some genius for making people distrust him," was indeed regarded with suspicion by many of his own countrymen and by his French allies, and was condemned in the British Foreign Office as "a menace, perhaps only second to Herr von Ribbentrop."[2] It seems that even Hitler did not trust Beck.[3] Under Beck, Poland had pursued an incautious policy of sniping at the League of Nations and disputing the frontiers of northern and southern neighbors, though the legitimacy of these derived from the 1919 peace settlement, on which Polish rights in Danzig also hinged. Evidence for Polish aspirations to the east points both ways, though since the founding of the state the Poles' predatory actions against Russia, Lithuania, and, more recently, Czechoslovakia, do not suggest an absence of territorial ambition. Beck's dream of constructing a Polish-dominated "Third Europe" from the Baltic to the Balkans had fallen apart in the face of Berlin's economic penetration of central and south-eastern Europe, which revealed the weakness of Poland's position. Arguably, as Taylor implies, the Poles should now have come to terms with the reality of German power. Many thought that they had. Poland's behavior since her non-aggression pact with Germany in 1934 was sufficient to feed suspicions in Paris and London that Poland was in Berlin's pocket, and Beck possibly in Hitler's pay. Taylor is surely right to suggest that Hitler's overtures at the end of 1938 rested on a recognition that Poland "had stretched the Non-Aggression Pact far in Germany's interest" (p. 240), and that his hints of joint German–Polish activity in the east were viewed as part of a tempting package to get the Poles further into his camp. Put another way: "Poland's foreign policy was discredited in Paris and London, and Beck himself suspected of collusion with

Hitler. He was more than unpopular in Moscow. And now, confronted with Nazi demands, Poland was alone."[4]

Nevertheless, if Danzig, which was regarded in Warsaw as the barometer of German–Polish relations, seemed set to stormy at the beginning of 1939, the Poles were not unduly alarmed. Beck and his two close associates Józef Lipski, the Polish ambassador in Berlin, and Jan Szembek, the Polish deputy minister for foreign affairs, were convinced that the demand for the return of Danzig was merely a temporary phase in German foreign policy and that Hitler's long-term aspirations in the east meant that Poland would be a necessary ally to Germany.[5] Though Beck decided to stand firm in the face of what was judged to be German bluster, it is not quite the case, as Taylor would have it, that he kept the issue in the way or that the Poles "were determined not to yield an inch" (p. 242). Over Polish rights in Danzig itself, Warsaw was adamant. However, Beck was not averse to some form of compromise over communications across the Corridor which might appease Hitler without turning Poland into a German satellite. His confidence that Hitler's demands were a bluff, and that Polish military strength was sufficient to deal with any aggression which might arise, survived until war broke out, supporting Taylor's image of Poland as a state with a "false pride as a Great Power" (p. 241).[6]

The vital issue as the crisis enfolded, however, was not Danzig. Nor was it simply the future of Poland. It was the scope of Hitler's ambitions. This, of course, is the central problem with Taylor's account. Why the Hitler of Taylor's construction – who supposedly spent his time after his "dazzling success" at Munich "drawing dream-plans for the rebuilding of Linz, the Austrian town where he went to school" (p. 238), and who had no desire for "theatrical displays of glory" (p. 239) but sought a steady extension of German power at which he would arrive through his usual process of letting others do his work for him – should now have bothered to put his sketches aside in order to raise the future of Danzig presents a problem which Taylor attempts to resolve by resorting to equivocation. He presents the issue as having materialized spontaneously: it was principally a matter of selling a partnership with Poland to a German public which bitterly resented the loss of the Polish Corridor in 1919 but would be appeased by the restoration of Danzig to Germany. The objective of this German–Polish association would be to allow the two to "act together in the Ukraine" (p. 242). But Taylor doubts that Hitler was interested in territorial gains in the east. If, on the other hand, he "really aspired to reach the Ukraine he must go through Poland" (p. 240).

It may be, though Taylor does not mention this, that Hitler was indeed stirred into action by the Poles themselves, when they raised the Danzig question in the midst of the Czechoslovak crisis in the hope of fixing the status quo.[7] This would provide some support for Taylor's general thesis that Hitler's foreign policy was fueled by the initiatives of others, and the Polish approach may have drawn attention to Poland's vulnerability. Hitler could hardly have failed to recognize that Polish hostility toward Prague during and immediately after the Czechoslovak crisis had, by tilting Warsaw towards Berlin, further compromised their ideal of preserving a balance between Germany and Russia. Also, as von Ribbentrop noted, Poland's position had been weakened by "the evident chill in Poland's relations with the western powers."[8] Perhaps there was sufficient here to stimulate the imagination of a musing dictator. Maybe it was not outsiders at all but members of Hitler's own entourage who manipulated events so as to prompt him to bring Poland further into the German embrace.[9] But the Hitler of *The Origins of the Second World War* is, as is now generally accepted, Taylor's particular fabrication, and the irrational, tortured, vindictive individual, consumed by a neuralgic impulse to act before his own early death – the Hitler who so many sources assure us existed – is absent. Yet, despite all his efforts to banish him, Hitler the man of ambition and purpose has survived the daydreaming Chaplinesque creation of Taylor. Weinberg, for example, is convinced that after Munich Hitler continued to pursue his long-term goal of securing living-space in the east. More specifically, he "wanted to be able to concentrate all his forces in the west without having to worry about trouble with Poland on his eastern border, and he therefore tried by persuasion and pressure to convert that country into a satellite."[10] Donald Watt provides us with a similar picture: a Hitler who, even before the crisis over Czechoslovakia had reached its climax, had begun to prepare for war against Britain and needed Poland to be negotiated onto his side as one of the preliminaries for this.[11] His is an angry, brooding, subtly semi-Taylorian Hitler, one lacking the psychological capacity to follow through long-held goals, letting events take their course, and trusting to instinct. His decision, around 1937, to take a more pro-active course merely complicated matters and destroyed his earlier sureness of touch. This is not a passive, not even a barely patient, dictator. After Munich, for perfectly sound reasons, Poland was expected to be compliant. Tension began to boil over when it was discovered in Berlin that, against the odds, the Poles refused to be submissive.

By the time von Ribbentrop raised Danzig with the Poles for the fourth time on March 21, post-Munich Czecho-Slovakia had already disappeared and the process of coercing Lithuania, which would lead to the annexation of Memel on the March 23, had started. This deteriorating climate had its impact on German–Polish relations, but had much more momentous repercussions in London. If, as Taylor surmises, the German pounce on Memel – a question which otherwise, apparently, "exploded of itself" (p. 258) – held an implicit warning to the Poles to be co-operative, it had the opposite effect, making opinion in Warsaw "indignant, alarmed and at the same time defiant."[12] On March 28 Beck informed the German ambassador to Poland that any attempt by Germany to alter unilaterally the status of Danzig would be viewed as an act of war. "Until this moment," Taylor says, "everything had gone on in secret, with no public hint of German–Polish estrangement. Now it blazed into the open" (p. 258). Here certainly was the kindling for a crisis, but as both Berlin and Warsaw continued to be publicly evasive over the significance of their discussions on Danzig the issue continued to flicker rather than to flare. Ignition came because of shifting British perceptions of Hitler's intentions, subsuming Danzig within the wider questions of Britain's power and security.

The ambiguity in British policy following the occupation of Prague on March 15, provides us with one of Taylor's more convincing passages. Hitler's destruction of the Munich settlement increased the esteem of the "prophets of woe" in Britain, and the appeasers were now "on the defensive." To the British government, however, "the change was not final or decisive. There was still a hope of conciliating Hitler under the determination to resist him, just as previously there had been an inclination to resist under the top layer of appeasement" (p. 252). Appeasement was not sunk. It had merely turned turtle. Chamberlain's firm statement, in a speech given at Birmingham on March 17, was in some ways misleadingly assertive, for, although it was "the turning point in British policy," Taylor says, "[i]t was not meant as such," being rather a "change of emphasis, not a change of direction" (p. 253). The Prime Minister's "challenge," as he liked to call it, at Birmingham was not a decision for war, and it ruled out new commitments.

The consensus is with Taylor. This is the view that "a general settlement with Hitler remained the British object" and that if war were to be avoided "Hitler must be 'deterred': he must not be 'provoked' " (p. 254). R. A. C. Parker, for instance, follows Taylor closely in his observation that for Chamberlain one lesson of March 1939 was that he "became more ready to warn Hitler. However, he remained anxious not to provoke him."[13] We now have a fuller picture than Taylor was able to provide of post-Prague Chamberlain – disappointed, resentful, more suspicious of Hitler, but with his determination to preserve peace intact.[14] Even so, Taylor's version stands. He is, however, peculiarly puzzled by the roots of this change. He finds the leap of respect for the opponents of appeasement "impossible to define," and its effect on Chamberlain a mystery that "the historian cannot pin down." It seems that "somehow, somewhere, it was brought home to him that he must respond more forcefully to Hitler's occupation of Prague' (pp. 252–3). But this is a problem only if Taylor's depiction of Hitler as a semi-detached participant in these events was also the image held by contemporaries *and* if we assume additionally that the turn of events in Prague" was the sole source of a shift in policy in London. Neither was the case. As Halifax, the foreign secretary, stated in cabinet, this was the first time that "Germany had applied her shock tactic to the domination of non-Germans," and this was "completely inconsistent with the Munich Agreement."[15] Not even "the symbol of appeasement," Nevile Henderson in Berlin, was able to persuade himself that Hitler had been compelled by events to break the promises made at Munich or that any definition of justice could be stretched to include what Germany had done.[16]

Moreover, the British cabinet was already steeped in mistrust of Hitler. Taylor, a pioneer of the view that change in British policy after Prague was relative rather than revolutionary, has little to say of the changes taking place before March 15. In the wake of Munich, the British had, as he says, "talked themselves into a condition of extreme anxiety." Fears, in the early weeks of 1939, of a German attack in the west, on Holland or on Switzerland, we now know were "nightmares without substance" (p. 247–8), probably manufactured by various anti-Nazi informers with the intention of stiffening British policy. If this was so, these German opponents of Hitler were successful. Indeed, the very readiness of the British to believe these false alarms "shows how little confidence anyone in British government circles had in Hitler's good intentions."[17] And rumor also generated action: the resolve to treat an attack on Holland as a *casus belli*, overtures for staff talks with the French, and the preparation of a British field force to fight on the continent.[18] True, by the beginning of March, optimism had reasserted itself. But the occupation of Prague could hardly be dismissed as an hallucination, and it lent credibility to the continuing flow of ominous intelligence reports, even among those who earlier had been inclined to doubt them. Prague also demonstrated, and Memel was to reinforce this, that Hitler's victims were now succumbing with an alarming lack of determination. The groping attempts, earlier in the year, to construct impediments to German advances now became more purposeful and took the form of supporting the will to resist of those who appeared most immediately threatened.

At this point, another important player entered the stage. The presence of German troops in Bohemia and Moravia made an alarm sounded by Tilea, the Rumanian minister in London, only two days after the Prague coup, that his country was about to become Germany's next victim, seem fearfully likely. Probably, the scare over Rumania made a specific contribution to the hardening of Chamberlain's public response to events between the occupation of Prague on March 15 and his Birmingham speech two days later. It certainly gave a wider vista to British policy. On March 21 Halifax told the French foreign minister: "His Majesty's Government thought it was now a question of checking German aggression, whether against France or Great Britain, or Holland, or Switzerland, or Romania, or Poland, or Yugoslavia, or whoever it might be. They saw no escape from this."[19] Taylor gives us the basic ingredients of what was taking place, but the nuance of the transformation in British thinking, in the fortnight between the Birmingham speech and the guarantee to Poland, is missing. Over the Tilea incident, British ministers "swallowed the alarm; and dismissed its denial," deciding in some vague way that "something must be done at once as a demonstration against further German advance" (p. 255). Settling on Poland as the fulcrum of this display, he implies, almost random. In his view, the initial notion of a quadripartite security arrangement, to include Britain, France, the Soviet Union, and Poland, fell foul of Russian apprehensions over the intentions of the western powers and Polish suspicions of Russia. "Relieved not to be associated with Bolshevik Russia; and to have hit on a substitute" (p. 256), the British chose Poland. This fits in with Taylor's earlier assertion that the British were now "more pushed along by events and less in control of them than they liked to think or than they made out later" (p. 254). While it is true that they did not know where the next blow from Hitler might fall – even after Bucharest backtracked over Tilea's warnings it was impossible to ignore that a threat to Rumania's freedom of action continued to exist – or precisely how they might cope with it, that the British were embarking upon an essentially haphazard attempt to regain the initiative lost to them over the last half dozen years is much more open to question.

British policy now acquired a harder edge, and was rather more systematic and purposeful than Taylor allows. The two weeks between Tilea's *démarche* and the guarantee to Poland was a period of intense activity which saw the British consciously reviving and developing the concept of a barrier to Hitler that they had begun to stumble towards back in January. Taylor's abbreviated account provides only a half-glimpse at what was taking place. In *Origins* the start of this process was a proposal for a declaration of support for any state threatened by Germany in which the French, Soviet, and Polish governments were also asked to participate. The initial draft was Chamberlain's own, though it had to be firmed-up by the French to include action as well as consultation. Its intention was, as Taylor says, "geared to the supposed threat to Rumania" (p. 255). But the British, Taylor implies, were diverted, even gulled, from this purpose by Beck's refusal to associate Poland with Russia and his insistence upon a simple Anglo-Polish declaration.

In fact, the Four-Power Declaration was not Chamberlain's invention but a proposal made on the morning of March 18 by the chiefs of staff. Understandably, given the Tilea episode and their ignorance of the details of German–Polish discussions on Danzig, their focus of concern was Rumania. It continued for a while to be so. Ten days after the Tilea scare Halifax still thought Rumania "may be the State primarily menaced by Germany's plans for Eastern expansion."[20] Rumania was crucial to the British because of her oil and grain: Britain's ability to wage economic warfare against Germany would be seriously diminished if Hitler controlled these.[21] The chiefs of staff advised that an immediate diplomatic initiative to forge an alliance with Russia and Poland might deter Germany from action against Rumania. An earlier and wider request for reactions to the Rumanian scare, which Taylor ignores, had already been made in Paris, Warsaw, and Moscow as well as in Bucharest, Athens, Ankara, and Belgrade. The inspiration for this was probably Tilea himself.[22] Chamberlain has been criticized for abandoning this larger scheme for the more modest proposal of the chiefs of staff.[23] But this was forced upon him because the responses from the eastern-European states approached were an unsatisfactory mix of suspicions of British firmness of purpose and resistance to an alignment with the Soviet Union, such that there was little substantial on which to work. Chamberlain dismissed the foreign office as "pretty barren of suggestions" and, encouraged by the chiefs of staff, came up with his own solution.[24] This moved British policy forward from a vague intention of simply supporting what others might do in the event of further German aggression toward the more precise construction of an east-European bloc to hem Hitler in – though the intention remained that this should be achieved by warnings rather than by specific new British obligations.

The British needed to associate Poland with the Four-Power Declaration not out of their worries for Polish security but because of their fears for Rumania. This involved two specific factors: Poland's ability to provide assistance if

Rumania became the victim of a German attack; and her value as a participant in a bloc which would send a signal to Berlin that in any future conflict (which at this juncture seemed most likely to arise through German aggression on Rumania) Germany might have to fight a war on two fronts. This was a logical approach, attempting to embrace Chamberlain's developing suspicion of Hitler, his desire to marginalize the growing critics of appeasement, his continuing determination to try to avoid war, and his reluctance to break with the tradition of avoiding commitments in eastern Europe. The idea of an eastern front had the support of the war office and, in the opinion of the British military attaché in Berlin, such a construction would create, for the next two or three years at least, conditions unfavorable to Germany's success in a European war.[25] In fixing on the Poles, therefore, the British were certainly not seeking to commit themselves to protecting Poland. When Warsaw was first approached by the British there seemed to be no immediate threat to Poland. London had some knowledge of the recent conversations over Danzig between the Germans and Poles, though Beck continued to mislead the British about their precise content for some time and the foreign office only "succeeded in worming them out of the Poles" at the beginning of May, after the guarantee to Poland had been given.[26] Again, there was the impression that Poland was on the verge of being lost to Germany. Indeed, as Taylor suggests, the less the Poles disclosed about the Polish–German negotiations the more anxious the British were of them falling in with some deal which would pull Warsaw into the orbit of Berlin and away from participation in a bloc against Germany (p. 256). All the more reason to get the Poles quickly into an eastern front.[27]

The British were less the dupes of a slippery Polish foreign minister than Taylor insinuates. Indeed, Chamberlain's suggestion of a Four-Power Declaration came at an awkward time for Beck. As we have seen, it coincided with a more serious phase in German demands over Danzig. Despite British suspicions, Beck had no intention of caving in to these requests. But neither was he keen to inject a potentially provocative association with Britain into a war of nerves with Hitler which he still believed Poland could win. Moreover, if the British leaders were mistrustful of Russian communism their counterparts in Warsaw were both traditionally suspicious of the Russians and ideologically repelled by communism. This made Polish refusal to co-operate in a declaration which associated them with the Soviet Union all-but a foregone conclusion. The Poles were also fearful that an arrangement with Russia would wreck their so-called policy of balance and perhaps influence for the worse their delicate relations with Germany.

But the enthusiasm of the British for bringing in the Soviets was also superficial. Prejudice played its part here, too, but so did calculation. The military experts in the British embassies at Moscow and Warsaw tended to be pessimistic about the value of the Russians and optimistic about the Poles.[28] And if, as Taylor says, Britain exaggerated the fighting capacity of Poland, so did the Poles themselves. The British did not, as he asserts, arrive at their assessment "without enquiry" (p. 256). When Chamberlain sought the guidance of the chiefs of staff on the most effective partner for an eastern front, their responses also favored the Poles. They advised that Russia would be a more useful ally against Germany than would Poland – but only marginally so. Should there be a simultaneous strike from Germany, Italy, and Japan, even an Anglo-Russian alliance, they believed, would be of limited value. Added to this, there was evidence to suggest that a British arrangement with the Russians would alienate a range of potential support and might even tip the balance in pushing Italy and Japan toward closer partnership with Germany. If a choice had to be made, then choosing Poland seemed less complicated. What was at stake, in any case, was not a decision between peace and war but a policy of restraint through the construction of an eastern front. At the same time, account had to be taken of the possibility that deterrence might not work, and, if Britain had to fight, the estimation was that she would do better with Poland than the Soviet Union on her side.

As Taylor puts it, "the British hardly reflected that, by choosing Poland, they might lose Russia" (p. 256). Whilst bowing to the reservations of both the Rumanians and the Poles to any association with Russia, the British worked on the assumption that once Poland was embraced by "the organization which we were trying to build up for the defence of Roumania" the Poles would then accept "indirect Soviet assistance."[29] Here is Taylor's image of Russian assistance being "turned on and off at will like a tap" (p. 278). The Russian complication was, however, instrumental in maneuvering the British away from the Four-Power Declaration and toward a more restricted and committed agreement with the Poles. The spur continued to be to protect Rumania. On March 22 Halifax pondered that, "in order to persuade Poland to commit herself to support Roumania, Great Britain and France would have to give Poland a private undertaking that, if Poland came in, they would both come in also."[30] An approach from Beck on March 24 accelerated the idea of a possible bilateral understanding. But developments did not go entirely Beck's way. Confident of being able to deal with Germany alone and "terrified" of anything more overt for fear of antagonizing Hitler, he pressed for a secret arrangement with Britain.[31] In this way, between March 17 and 24 the number of states to be associated with Britain and France in an eastern bloc was on the point of being reduced from three to one – yet the intention remained to construct the larger edifice. The outline of the British guarantee to Poland is thus already discernible – though, as it turned out, Beck was to get more publicity than he had hoped for. The process was to be completed when a new war scare switched the spotlight from Rumania to Poland.

By the end of March the rumor factory in Whitehall had resumed full production with warnings of threatening moves by Germany toward France and Belgium, and of possible air raids on London. Poland, viewed initially as not much more than an element in the construction of an eastern security bloc, at this point entered the eye of the storm with the warning from Ian Colvin, the Berlin correspondent of the *News Chronicle*, that "an attack on the Polish Republic" was imminent.[32] Colvin's warnings of a general threat to Poland were presented to Chamberlain shortly after the cabinet had agreed to opt for reciprocal guarantees with Poland and Rumania. Once again, this information was false, having been planted by the German opposition to Hitler. Whether, as Taylor argues, "after the occupation of Prague and the supposed threat to Rumania, the British were ready to believe anything" (p. 260), or whether, as some have more recently suggested, Halifax simply manipulated the incident to press for action, everything now changed. Reciprocity was ignored, Rumania was temporarily forgotten and, on March 31, a unilateral guarantee was offered to Poland.

Few would dispute Taylor's view that the guarantee was "a revolutionary event in international affairs" (p. 264). Unintended by and unknown to the British, it also marked the beginning of the process which would lead to war. Incensed at the "ingratitude of the Poles" and at what he regarded as a process of encirclement by the British, Hitler reversed his policy by withdrawing his recent proposals to Poland, revoking the non-aggression pact of 1934 and also the Anglo-German naval agreement.[33] Prior to this, on April 3 he ordered preparations for a possible attack on Poland to mature by September 1. That Britain now "plunged into alliance with a country far in Eastern Europe, and one which, until almost the day before, had been not worth the bones of a British grenadier" (p. 264), is Taylorian hyperbole. The undoubted scramble surrounding the issuing of the guarantee – not yet an alliance – is deceptive. As we have seen, British thinking was already shifting towards the idea of some direct assurance to Poland, and "Colvin's warning precipitated the public announcement of a policy already being formulated."[34] To Taylor, the British were now "committed to resistance" (p. 263), though he also has them simultaneously "faced with the choice between resistance and conciliation." Anyhow, they "preferred the second course" (p. 264), and appeasement was to be continued. But in their haste to provide "some vague and generous gesture to moderate the speed of Germany's advance," Taylor argues, the British found that they had given all the aces to Beck. "The assurance was unconditional. The Poles alone were to judge whether it should be called upon. The British could no longer press for concessions over Danzig; equally they could no longer urge Poland to cooperate with Soviet Russia" (p. 260).

Taylor has significant support here. Geoffrey Roberts accepts that the guarantee constricted British and French freedom of maneuver, "tying them into an inherently dangerous situation."[35] More specific is Watt's assertion that "[i]f the Poles took up arms then Britain fought too. The decision, war or peace, had been voluntarily surrendered by Chamberlain and his cabinet into the nervous hands of Colonel Beck and his junta comrades-in-arms."[36] Anna Cienciala makes a rather different point, arguing that the guarantee served the double purpose of persuading Hitler to abandon aggression while allowing Britain and France to press the Poles into giving Hitler what he apparently wanted. To her, "A. J. P. Taylor was closest to the mark in viewing the guarantee as a continuation of appeasement because it envisaged further territorial revision in Eastern Europe."[37] But Chamberlain did not believe he had overplayed his hand with the Poles and, whereas adjustments to preserve the peace remained on the cards –

over Danzig, for instance – the guarantee had drawn a line beyond which Hitler must not go. With Strang's view that the guarantee meant that "Britain had committed itself to fight for Polish independence, and had allowed the decision on war or peace largely to pass out of its hands" we get closer to the nub of the issue.[38] The key word here is *independence*. The guarantee was not envisaged as a "blank cheque" to the Poles. It was certainly not regarded by the British as a provocation, a "deliberate challenge," and a stimulant to Polish intransigence which increased the probability of war.[39] Beck admitted at the time that the attitude of the Poles was not altered by the guarantee.[40] They had already made up their minds to resist Hitler if necessary. An arrangement over Danzig was still a possibility so far as the British were concerned. There was no written commitment on their part to underwrite the existing situation. Nor did Chamberlain intend one. As Taylor admits, Danzig did not seem to be an urgent issue at the end of March. Poland's integrity did. Fears were for a weekend fall on Poland, not on the Free City. Press comment within hours of the declaration, probably government-inspired, sought to remove any implication of a commitment to Danzig.[41] Chamberlain still hoped, if it remained a possiblity, to remove grievances which might be the cause of war, and these might well include Danzig. As he privately stated, "what we are concerned with is not the boundaries of states but attacks upon their independence. And it is we who will judge whether this independence is threatened or not."[42] Halifax also made it clear to Warsaw that continuance of the guarantee was dependent upon the creation of reciprocal guarantees between Britain, France, Poland and Rumania.[43] Only in this particular sense does Taylor's view that "the British were no sooner committed than they realized the flaws in what they had done" (p. 261) and were determined to remedy them have pertinence.

The principal purpose of the guarantee was to defer war by restraining Hitler. It was premature to argue that the guarantee marked "a retreat from the initial comprehensive British proposal towards central and southeastern Europe which had been considered in the wake of German action in Prague" or that with it "the possibility of an eastern front against Germany was lost."[44] This is to echo Taylor's opinion that once negotiations with Beck were under way the "peace front" and collective security vanished from the scene." This may have been the outcome. It was not the intention. The objective of the Four-Power Declaration to provide what Halifax called a "rallying point" to other Balkan states survived.[45] When apprised of the need for a guarantee to Poland, the cabinet and the House of Commons were told of its "interim" nature to meet the possibility of a sudden move by Germany. It was envisaged as part of an interconnecting east-European web. As Halifax pointed out to the cabinet, "if Poland was over-run, there would be no hope of saving Roumania."[46] And if, as Taylor says, it was the case that the British could now no longer urge the Poles to include the Soviet Union in this future arrangement, their inclination to do so, as we have seen, had always been wafer-thin.

Taylor, along with others, has pointed out that there was no practical way for Britain to fulfill the guarantee.[47] But, as he also indicates, "the British government were striving to preserve the peace of Europe, not to win a war" (p. 278). Arrangements were to proceed to build a wider security front to contain Germany. Although these were focused on eastern Europe, the possibility of an attack in the west could not be ruled out. Should the dam in the east fail to deter, the calculation seems to have been, it would nevertheless provide an additional capability for Britain to conduct a war with some expectation of success. The fact that the guarantee was not followed up with military or financial support to Poland – that, as Taylor remarks, "no credit had passed by the time war broke out; no British bomb or rifle went to Poland" (p. 271) – is not an indication of an empty policy of bluff or panic. Rather, it was the strategically rational, if cynical, extension of a perceived need to harbor all resources for a long war. It might not have been possible to assist Poland were an attack to be made. Yet the very process of her defeat would stretch German resources, and victory over Poland would require significant manpower to defend the new German–Soviet frontier.[48] This point was made emphatically in cabinet by Lord Chatfield, the minister for co-ordination of defence, on the day before the Polish guarantee was issued.[49] This may cast some doubt on Taylor's view that British policy "was determined by morality, not by strategical calculations" (p. 278).

The crucial failure of the British lay less in their neglect to provide material support for the Poles than in the collapse of their attempts to build a solid "eastern front." By mid-May guarantees had been extended to Rumania, Greece and Turkey – a somewhat disparate and erratically constructed "rallying point," admittedly, but close to the original design of mid-March. The real prize, the Soviet Union, eluded them. Soviet intentions during the summer of 1939 are examined elsewhere in this volume. The vain hope of Russian assistance without strings for any neighbors of the USSR faced with aggression – turning the Russian tap on and off at will – was dashed by Moscow's refusal to play along. The British reluctance to enter into anything more formal produced fatal hesitation. Taylor seems uncertain whether to blame this dilatoriness on incompetence or on a calculated attempt to avoid being dragged by the French into an unwelcome arrangement with Russia. Chamberlain's profound reluctance and its ideological overtones are undeniable. Yet condemning British scruples to avoid over-riding the attitude of the lesser states as "the narrow moralism of the reformed drunkard" (p. 277) is to miss the point. The proposed front might collapse if Poland and Rumania were lost at the expense of the Soviets. Moreover, Soviet insistence upon a full alliance implied a military, rather than a diplomatic, slant to the scheme which perhaps would further excite German fears of encirclement. These were not mere rationalizations but real concerns which Halifax, most of the cabinet, and the foreign office initially shared with Chamberlain.[50] By the end of May, pressure from the French, from public and parliamentary opinion, plus a change of mind by the chiefs of staff and the recurrent worry that the Russians might do a deal with the Germans, had isolated Chamberlain from the majority of his colleagues on this issue. Taylor's charge that the British were not interested in an alliance with the Soviets is overstated, though without access to cabinet records it was an easy assumption to make. The Soviets, of course, eventually drew the same conclusion. The signs are that, once it had dawned that the Russians would settle for nothing less than a full-blown alliance, the British did reluctantly move forward, but did so with such evident distaste as to drive the Russians into the arms of the Nazis, thus burying the possibility of an eastern deterrent of any substance.

Chamberlain's culpability for the failure to reach agreement with the Soviets was considerable, but the burden should not be uniquely his. Though he was its keenest advocate, Chamberlain was not the sole vessel of appeasement. Taylor, however, has very little to say about Chamberlain's colleagues. Indeed, his account of the events of 1939 is largely a two-man show, a kind of disembodied dialogue between Hitler and Chamberlain. The same might be said of his image of Nazi Germany, with hardly a nod being made to the so-called "polycratic" nature of the Nazi system. In Taylor's drama Halifax, the foreign secretary, is a relatively minor character, "coached by the foreign office," or helping shake Chamberlain's confidence after the Prague coup on hearing "the call of conscience in the watches of the night" (pp. 243, 253). Halifax's stock has risen since the publication of *Origins*, and his impact in redefining the direction of British policy and in urging and manipulating an increasingly isolated Prime Minister into taking it has been emphasized.[51] Though the evidence for this remains inconclusive, it does provide some of the depth that is lacking in Taylor's rather flat canvas.

It is possible to see Halifax, ever since Hitler's upping of his demands against the Czechs at Godesberg, nursing a developing, if not unswerving, pessimism about German objectives. This increasingly put him out of step with the Prime Minister – for example, over the need to widen the base of the government after Munich, the need to set up a ministry of supply and over the appropriate response to the extinction of Czechoslovakia. Vindicated by the seizure of Prague, Halifax now possessed the confidence to press his opinions on Chamberlain. This line of argument is not without its problems. The government was not broadened until after war broke out. The ministry of supply, half-heartedly set up in April, was as much the product of pressure from others as from Halifax. It has been suggested that without Halifax's presence "Chamberlain would have been able to view Prague as a setback instead of being forced to see it as a major reversal."[52] This may be so, though it is difficult to believe that Chamberlain's obstinacy would have been sufficiently dented had he not himself also been shaken by the starkness of what had now happened and at the end of an extended period of nerve-wracking rumors. The ease with which the tough-minded Chamberlain was purportedly persuaded or finessed is a hurdle which the supporters of Halifax do not always effectively clear. Maybe Halifax "inserted a passage into the Birmingham speech" envisaging war as preferable to dishonor, but those who say so are not explicit about their sources.[53] We might, just as reasonably, take Chamberlain's own explanation for the "very restrained and cautious exposition" in the Commons on March 15, which he put down to having had "no time to digest" the news of the Prague coup, "much less to form a considered opinion of it." His intention two days later at Birmingham was "to correct that mistake."[54] Halifax's supposed manipulation of the Tilea and Colvin episodes to stiffen British policy is also circumstantial and not proven.

The Polish guarantee provides an awkward problem for protagonists of the apparent development of Halifax's political machismo. If it really was the case that "it was Halifax and his Foreign Office advisers who created the policy," then this first tangible outcome of his ascendant influence might be judged a scarcely propitious one. The guarantee is, after all, as an overly-sympathetic biographer of Halifax admits, open to "many valid criticisms." Furthermore, the desire for concessions continued.[55] It does seem to be the case that the notion of a bilateral agreement with Poland was strengthened by Halifax and his officials on March 25 in Chamberlain's absence. But there is nothing significant in this: it was their job, and the Prime Minister's previous acquiescence is quite clear.[56] Close examination of cabinet discussions in the period between the Prague coup and the guarantee reveals Chamberlain and Halifax as the joint principals in leading their colleagues toward increasingly narrow and more specific commitments in eastern Europe.[57] Moreover, the draft of the guarantee was Chamberlain's own, and had been completed without assistance.[58] The Prime Minister and his foreign secretary were not identical in their views. Halifax perhaps came earlier to the conclusion that force might have to be used than did Chamberlain. But the differences in their points of view were fewer than has been suggested and they remained, until war was declared, partners on the same tandem.[59] It was a vehicle which, with Halifax firmly astride it, was to develop a pronounced wobble after the attack on Poland.

Like Chamberlain, Halifax viewed aspects of the Polish question, particularly Danzig, as negotiable. It is certainly not the case that "by March 19th he had decided that Britain would have to fight for Danzig."[60] His mantra to the Poles, to the Russians, and to the French was that a negotiated settlement of the Danzig issue was desirable, but that "if the Danzig question should develop in such a way as to involve a threat to Polish independence, then this would be a matter of the gravest concern to ourselves." What this might amount to was made plain to the Polish ambassador on March 21 in the context of German pressure on Lithuania. This time Halifax followed his usual form of words with the comfortless view that "in the same way it might well be that the Lithuanian Government might be constrained to surrender Memel; but if Lithuanian independence were placed in jeopardy, this was a matter which would affect us all."[61] Forty-eight hours later Memel (like Danzig a German city) was surrendered to Hitler with little protest from London. Two months after the guarantee Halifax's views remained unchanged.[62] It seems clear that, "from the beginning, Halifax envisaged the return of Danzig to Germany."[63] Taylor may not have had much to say about Chamberlain's foreign secretary, but his implication that over Danzig he was not averse to another Munich is close to the truth. The real point that is being made here, however, concerns neither who was directing British policy at this stage nor to what extent former appeasers were now ready to retract, but rather the one-dimensional rendition that Taylor provides.

The Danzig crisis had, as Taylor indicates, a feel very different from that over Czechoslovakia the year before. Compared to the tensions and diplomatic activity surrounding the Sudeten issue it was a more subdued, understated, muted affair; hardly a crisis at all but a series of flickering, fizzling scares throughout the summer, and with no direct diplomatic exchanges between Hitler and the Poles before the outbreak of war or with the British until the middle of August. Each of the participants "shrank from raising the question of Danzig," giving it the quality of a phantom crisis – "Danzig was not there; and if all the Powers wished hard enough it would go away" (p. 307). Taylor's explanation for this is that the Poles felt they could only lose by entering negotiations, as the western powers would force conciliation upon them. Hitler pursued his usual stratagem of waiting for events to take their course. The west, meanwhile, did nothing, because it recognized that the intransigence of both Berlin and Warsaw might result in war if the Danzig question were raised: tension in the free city and its surrounding territory meant that it was always highly combustible. But, as Taylor says, it was a crisis that never broke. Hitler was indeed playing a characteristic game, though not the one which Taylor suggests. Once more, Hitler was claiming the moral high ground in order to divide his opponents. But, as he frequently stated to his entourage, Danzig was not the issue. His reticence to discuss it was not because he waited for others to force the Poles to give it to him, but because he was apprehensive that if he stated his terms some unwelcome form of conciliation would be foisted upon him by the west. Similarly, as Taylor states, the motive of the Poles was to avoid pressure from the west for a new version of the Runciman mission – mingled with a suspicion, which he only partly acknowledges, that behind German pressure was a threat to the existence of Poland. Fears of a third party conjuring up a deal were not unrealistic. To the British, as well as to the French and Italians, Danzig was not worth a war. Though they were not entirely convinced that a settlement over Danzig would end Hitler's belligerence, neither could they be certain that it would not. They were torn between a recognition of the logic of the German case over Danzig and a perception that it was another pretext hiding Hitler's real objectives. This gave a "dual nature" to British policy, making it "as much concerned to moderate the Poles as to restrain Hitler," and, though this is overstated, "ready, even eager, to give way over Danzig" (pp. 270, 272). Nonetheless, there was no intention to backpedal over the promise to support Poland's independence. Co-existing with the view that Danzig was "a bad wicket on which to make a stand," and that "if an impartial Martian were to act as arbitrator...he would give judgment...more or less in accordance with Hitler's offer," was the tart assessment that "if Danzig were to be restored to Germany in virtue of the right of self-determination, Hitler should be required to evacuate Prague."[64] The problem remained one of deciding where legitimacy ended and an unacceptable extension of German power began. Because their judgment as to Hitler's more likely purpose inclined toward the latter, the British played down Danzig from fear that the issue might run out of control.

The British held to the illusion that they could be the ones who decided whether Polish independence was at risk, not the unstable Hitler nor the unreliable Beck. In the attempt to avoid a provocative action either from Berlin or from Warsaw the British, while attempting to avoid undercutting the resolution of the Poles to stand up to Germany or to allow Hitler to cry "encirclement," hoped – in a rather indolent way – that a solution which just might draw the fire from the Danzig question would turn up. The problem was that this raised the politically unacceptable vision of a new Munich. In Taylor's words, "the British government were trapped not so much by their guarantee to Poland, as by their previous relations with Czechoslovakia. With her they had imposed concession; towards her they had failed to honour their guarantee. They could not go back on their word again, if they were to keep any respect in the world or with their own people" (p. 263). The quandary in which the British found themselves did not mean that they were "in effect, leaving the decision on war or peace to Colonel Beck."[65] Nor was it the case that Danzig had become some kind of symbol of Polish independence. Indications suggest that had a crisis erupted over Danzig alone the British would have found excuses for backing off. In the high summer of 1939 Halifax pointed out to the cabinet that although there was an assumption that Britain was committed to fight for Danzig, the reality was that "Danzig of itself should not be regarded as providing a *casus belli*. If, however, a threat to Polish independence arose from Danzig, then this country would clearly become involved."[66] In the end, this was never put to the test, for Danzig never came under isolated attack. On September 1, fifty-two divisions of the Wehrmacht smashed into Poland along four fronts.

The culmination of Taylor's argument is that war broke out in September 1939 because of "a mistake, the result on both sides of diplomatic blunders" (p. 269); or, more famously, because of Hitler's "launching on 29 August a diplomatic manoeuvre which he ought to have launched on 28 August" (p. 336). Only in this sense should we see it as "Hitler's war." This is no longer controversial. It is simply wrong. To explain the actions of his singular version of Hitler, a complex but coherent series of events is strained to breaking-point. It appears beyond much doubt that by the end of April in Hitler's mind the military destruction of Poland had replaced the intention of drawing the Poles into the German ambit. Convinced that the Poles would not play his game and that they had been encouraged in this attitude by the British guarantee, this was viewed as the prelude to an eventual conflict with the west. On August 12 Hitler's generals were instructed to bring forward the September 1 timing and to prepare themselves for an attack on Poland in a fortnight's time – on 26 August. Hitler's conviction of his own historic mission to lead Germany in a war of domination, his frustration at being cheated out of war in September 1938, pressed him forward. At a meeting on August 22, and with von Ribbentrop now in Moscow dealing directly with Stalin, his commanders were told that a war with the western democracies was inevitable. Poland, which had failed to respond to his offers of "an acceptable relationship," must be neutralized first. Neither Britain nor France were expected to intervene.[67]

If the consistency of his thesis is to be maintained, Taylor cannot allow Hitler to take this kind of initiative. So when, during late spring and summer, Hitler spoke of his aggressive intentions toward Poland, he had "talked for effect" or it was merely "a rigmarole." It was, anyway, "not a serious directive for action." Danzig remained his central concern, and Hitler's intention was to "score another Munich." The "premature offensive" of the August 26 was "a 'try-on,'" mere "play-acting to impress the generals and through them the Western Powers" (pp. 320–27). The objective, in other words, was to put pressure on his opponents in order to achieve a diplomatic victory. War preparations were necessary anyway to support his threats, and would be used only if matters got out of hand in Danzig. Even so, it seems he had a deadline for military action – September 1, a date decided on by "sticking a pin in the calendar" (p. 307). The frenetic urgency to get von Ribbentrop to Moscow before the August 26 has little to do with Hitler's military planning, as he was "aiming at another 'Munich,' not at war" (p. 316), and attempting to break the nerve of his opponents. August 26 was so peripheral to Hitler that in the hurly-burly of diplomatic activity he forgot his new timetable. Remembering it, he then canceled it because it was not intended seriously.

It was more straightforward than this. There seems little doubt that Hitler called off his detailed, if inelegantly executed, plan of attack because of Italian backsliding and the announcement of the Anglo-Polish alliance, which suggested that more time was needed for negotiation. Taylor's judgment of the British in 1939, "trying to strike a balance between firmness and conciliation; and, being what they were, inevitably [striking] the wrong one," is generally correct. But British actions sometimes did have an impact on Hitler, and their confirmation of the alliance with Poland was one such occasion. This looked like firmness, as indeed it was. The shock of the Nazi–Soviet pact had not dislodged British intention. This was to fight to preserve Polish independence. Danzig continued to be another matter. A secret protocol to the alliance accepted for the first time that an attack on the free city would be a threat to this independence. Even so, the British continued to have reservations about giving *carte blanche* to the Poles.[68] As late as August 28 Chamberlain was telling the leader of the Liberal Party that "negotiations might conceivably cover such questions as a cession to Germany of a narrow strip across the Corridor to link East Prussia with the main block of Germany; the disappearance of the League of Nations' High Commissioner; the recognition of Danzig as a German town, with German citizenship for its citizens but with full preservation of Polish rights and interests," though Poland was not to be forced to yield what she considered to be essential to her independence.[69] Here again is the essential dissonance in Taylor's thesis. Hitler did bank on room for maneuver between August 26 and September 1. But this was to isolate the Poles from the west, not to precipitate what to him was an irrelevant settlement of the Danzig question. The indications are that the British, for their part, could have been separated from the Poles and were quite ready to settle Danzig over Polish heads if they thought it would do any good. But they could not let Poland itself fall under Germany's sway. The kind of settlement sought was one which would include a German guarantee for Poland into which the Poles should enter freely. Lack of trust in Hitler's word meant that there was no attempt to coerce the Poles into this, as there had been with the Czechs a year earlier. This was the legacy of Prague. No close contingency of view existed between London and Berlin. Hitler did not leave himself short of a crucial twenty-four hours of negotiating time (such precise measurement for such an imprecise activity!), on the last day of August, which would have opened the breach between the Poles and the west if only he had timed things right.

There were obvious failings on the British side. Both the hiatus between the guarantee and the Anglo-Polish alliance and indications that they were prepared for a deal on Danzig no doubt fed Hitler's belief that, in the last resort, the British would betray the Poles, just as they had abandoned the Czechs. The shuttling of Dahlerus and the intervention of other semi-official intermediaries may, as Taylor suggests, have added to this belief. But if the British took such jockeying seriously, and there are good indications that they did not, it was just as easy for them to interpret these as a mark of Hitler's failure of nerve.[70] Possibly this, and the clear evidence available to them that Hitler had indeed backed down on the August 26, filled some in London with undue optimism that an acceptable solution to German–Polish antagonism might yet be found.[71] Essentially, however, the purpose of British negotiations at this stage was to ensure that every possible avenue to preserve peace which did not violate the assurances given to protect Poland had been tried. Impatience had impelled Hitler to act on the August 26. It did so again on September 1, even though the diplomatic situation had not altered in Germany's favor. There is even an indication that his timetable for action could have been stretched to September 2, but rather than waiting to the last moment he attacked before it was technically necessary to do so. As Weinberg trenchantly insists, "there is…no sensible person who today disputes the fact that the Third Reich initiated World War II."[72]

The avalanche of evidential material which has emerged since *Origins* was first published over thirty years ago has inevitably added sophistication to our understanding of why war came in 1939. That Taylor's assessment would have been substantially different, had this material been available to him, is, however, questionable. Certainly he did not demonstrate much inclination to recant in his later references to *Origins*.[73] His notorious rejection or manipulation of documentation inconvenient to what he admitted was an "academic exercise" (p. 266) would likely have survived. As would his Namierite view of history, in which ideologies and impersonal structures are considerably less important forces in human activity than are the fallible attempts of individuals to pursue what were perceived to be traditional national interests within the parameters of a 100-year-old European state system. Indeed, while what seemed most shocking thirty years ago, his interpretation of Hitler and the accidental nature of the outbreak of war, continues to be the most inadmissible, many of Taylor's general conclusions have endured in the face of more recent approaches and fresh source material.

Taylor dismisses as crude Marxist dogma the view that economic crisis propelled Hitler's action in 1939. Despite the heat which has sometimes been generated by this debate, it remains an unsettled question. There is little in what has emerged from it which would have caused Taylor to rethink his position. Indeed, his conclusion that "the economic argument ran against war, not in its favour," probably still represents majority thinking on this.[74] On the other hand, Taylor's relegation of the economic dimension to an afterthought leaves a layer of gauze across our understanding. As has already been suggested, economic considerations played some part in the British attitude to backing Poland. A German–Polish conflict, provided resources were not wasted on the Poles, would enhance Britain's chances of victory in a long war. Some indication of this was available to Taylor, though a whole range of economic, political, and military intelligence material, of course, was not. His account, one may cautiously surmise, would not have varied much in its interpretation had he been able to work from intelligence records. It is far from clear that such evidence has made any significant difference to our understanding of these events, and its impact on those who received it appears to have been indecisive. It tended to reinforce, rather than alter, predominant inclinations. The economic intelligence available to the Chamberlain cabinet was inaccurate, contradictory, and therefore confusing. Reports at the end of 1938 that the German economy was in good shape and ready for war tended to produce the glum response that Britain could only match this performance if "totalitarian" methods were adopted. More optimistic analyses, such as that of the chiefs of staff in February 1939 induced complacency and the belief that a war postponed could only increase Britain's advantage over Germany.[75] Their opinion that the British economy was better placed than the German for a long war was contested five months later by the treasury.[76] The failure of British political intelligence between the wars is widely accepted. The British had accurate warning before Germany pounced on Bohemia, but they failed to act. Secret reports revealing the true nature and ambitions of the Nazi regime between November 1938 and March 1939 may have played their part in propelling the British government toward resistance to Hitler on moral grounds.[77] But this underplays the shock of the reality of events in Prague and Memel. After all, public opinion responded with moral indignation to what happened there without being privy to secret intelligence reports. By the same token, though military and economic forecasts might, after Munich, have given some comfort to the British cabinet, there is room for doubt that this was sufficient to encourage any coolly calculated decision on the optimum time for Britain to go to war. In the end it was public revulsion against Nazi ambitions as much as any careful estimate of the current status of the balance of forces which pressed the British government forward, though optimistic predictions would naturally give a fillip to this more basic impetus. Faced with a mixture of the same weary view at which the French had also arrived, that there must be an end to this, and a recognition that, as Taylor points out, a failure to act decisively would mean the collapse of the government, accounts for the final decision.

Origins remains a monument to Taylor's passion for argument. Despite its clear signs of age, its insights still have the capacity to impress largely because of the verve and audacity of the author's style. Yet it is often this very stylistic impudence, with its arrogant over-assertions, which grate to the extent of detracting from much of its acuity. Sometimes it seems more one of Taylor's televisual *tours de force* than it does a work of scholarship. His treatments of Polish policy and the transformation of appeasement after Prague still have something valuable to tell us. His insistence upon Danzig as itself the pivotal issue is against the evidence, while the immediate circumstances which produced war are simply perverse. Integral to this is his idiosyncratic picture of Hitler. It is this flaw that, like a kind of academic metal fatigue, brings the intricate structure falling to its destruction – though some parts have survived the impact. *Origins* has stimulated the work of a generation of historians. But its reign of influence is over. The debts to it have been fully acknowledged, and there is, frankly, no reason to resort to it now other than as a piece of historiography. To paraphrase the final sentence of the book: *The Origins of the Second World War* has become a matter of historical curiosity.

Notes

1 A. J. P Taylor, *The Origins of the Second World War*, Harmondsworth, 1964, pp. 302–3. Page numbers in the text are from this edition.

2 J. Karski, *The Great Powers and Poland, 1919–1945: From Versailles to Yalta*, Lanham, MD, 1985, p. 324. Public Record Office, Kew, PRO, FO 371, 21569, C11867/2319/12. October 4, 1938.

3 *Documents on British Foreign Policy* (henceforth *DBFP*), 3rd series, vol. 5, no. 268.

4 Karski, *Great Powers*, p. 261.

5 A. Prazmowska, *Britain, Poland and the Eastern Front, 1939*, Cambridge, 1987, pp. 31 and 33.

6 J. Lipski, *Diplomat in Berlin, 1933–1939*, New York, 1968, pp. 503–4 and 566.

7 G. L. Weinberg, *The Foreign Policy of Hitler's Germany: Starting World War II, 1937–1939*, Chicago, IL, 1980, p. 480.

8 Quoted in A. J. Prazmowska, "Poland's foreign policy: September 1938–September 1939," *Historical Journal*, vol. 29, 1986, p. 858.

9 D. C. Watt, *How War Came: The Immediate Origins of the Second World War, 1938–1939*, London, 1989, p. 67; *DBFP*, vol. 5, no. 274.

10 Weinberg, *Hitler's Germany*, p. 465 and pp. 503–4.

11 Watt, *How War Came*, pp. 38–45.

12 *DBFP*, vol. 4, no. 515; Kennard to Halifax, March 25, 1939.

13 R. A. C. Parker, *Chamberlain and Appeasement*, London, 1993, p. 205.

14 See e.g. J. Charmley *Chamberlain and the Lost Peace*, London, 1989, pp. 164 and 167; Parker, *Chamberlain*, p. 203–5.

15 PRO, CAB 23/98 11(39), March 18, 1939.

16 J. Harvey (ed.), *The Diplomatic Diaries of Oliver Harvey, 1937–1940*, London, 1970, p. 433. The phrase is Harvey's.

17 Watt, *How War Came*, pp. 103–8.

18 Watt, *How War Came*, p. 108.

19 *DBFP*, vol. 4, no. 458.

20 *DBFP*, vol. 4, no. 551, Halifax to Lindsay, Washington, March 28, 1939.

21 S. Newman, *March 1939: The British Guarantee to Poland*, Oxford, 1976, p. 129; Prazmowska, *Eastern Front*, p. 51.

22 *DBFP*, vol. 4, no. 395, Halifax to Hoare, Bucharest, March 17, 1939.

23 C. Hill, *Cabinet Decisions on Foreign Policy: The British Experience, October 1938–June 1941*, Cambridge, 1991, pp. 27–8.

24 D. Dilks (ed.), *The Diaries of Sir Alexander Cadogan, 1938–45*, London, 1971, p. 157 (diary entry of March 16, 1939); Chamberlain statement quoted from Hill, *Cabinet Decisions*, p. 27.

25 W. K. Wark, *The Ultimate Enemy: British Intelligence and Nazi Germany, 1933–1939*, London, 1985, pp. 116–20; *DBFP*, vol. 4, no. 522.

26 *DBFP*, vol. 5, no. 361, foreign office memorandum, May 4, 1939.

27 *DBFP*, vol. 4, no. 523.

28 Newman, *British Guarantee*, p. 139.

29 *DBFP*, vol. 4, no. 523.

30 *DBFP*, vol. 4, no. 523.

31 *DBFP*, vol. 4, no. 518; Harvey, *Diaries*, p. 267 (diary entry of March 25, 1939).

32 I. Colvin, *Vansittart in Office*, London, 1965, p. 305.

33 *DBFP*, vol. 5, no. 281.

34 Weinberg, *Hitler's Germany*, p. 555.

35 A. Roberts, *"The Holy Fox": A Biography of Lord Halifax*, London, 1991, p. 148.

36 Watt, *How War Came*, pp. 185–6.

37 A. M. Cienciala, "Poland in British and French policy in 1939: determination to fight – or avoid war?", in P. Finney (ed.), *The Origins of the Second World War*, London, 1997, p. 429.

38 G. Bruce Strang, "Once more unto the breach: Britain's guarantee to Poland, March 1939," *Journal of Contemporary History*, vol. 31, 1996, p. 724.

39 Newman, *British Guarantee*, pp. 196 and 219.

40 *DBFP*, vol. 5, no. 274.

41 A. J. Foster, "An unequivocal guarantee? Fleet Street and the British guarantee to Poland, 31 March 1939," *Journal of Contemporary History*, vol. 26, 1991, pp. 33–48.

42 Quoted in Foster "Unequivocal guarantee?", p. 43.

43 *DBFP*, vol. 4, no. 584.

44 Prazmowska, *Eastern Front*, pp. 56–7.

45 *DBFP*, vol. 4, no. 458.

46 PRO, CAB 23/98, 16(39), meeting of March 30, 1939. See also *DBFP*, vol. 4, no. 584.

47 See W. K. Wark, "Something very stern: British political intelligence, moralism and grand strategy in 1939," *Intelligence and National Security*, vol. 5, 1990, pp. 163–4.

48 Strang, "Britain's guarantee," p. 743.

49 PRO, CAB 23/98, 16(39), meeting of March 30, 1939.

50 C. Hill, *Cabinet Decisions*, ch. 3; Parker, *Chamberlain*, pp. 229–31.

51 Halifax's influential role during this period is described in: Watt, *How War Came*; Charmley, *Lost Peace*; Parker, *Chamberlain*; R. J. Q. Adams, *British Politics and Foreign Policy in the Age of Appeasement, 1935–39*, London, 1993; Roberts, *Halifax*; and Strang, "Britain's guarantee."

52 Roberts, *Halifax*, p. 143.

53 Charmley, *Lost Peace*, p. 167; Adams, *Age of Appeasement*, p. 140; Watt, *How War Came*, p. 167. Roberts states that Halifax "inserted a passage into the Birmingham speech" envisaging war as preferable to dishonor, but provides no evidence for such direct intervention on the part of the foreign secretary; *Halifax*, p. 144. Also Hill, *Cabinet Decisions*, p. 22.

54 Cmd 6106, p. 5.

55 The quotation is from Strang, "Britain's guarantee." Roberts and Charmley take the same view. Roberts, *Halifax*, p. 148. Charmley's assessment of the guarantee is uncharacteristically muted. Strang sees it as flawed but logical.

56 Newman, *British Guarantee*, pp. 144–5.

57 Hill, *Cabinet Decisions*, pp. 30–6.

58 Foster, "Unequivocal guarantee?", p. 42.

59 D. Dilks, " 'We must hope for the best and prepare for the worst": the prime minister, the cabinet and Hitler's Germany, 1937–1939," in Patrick Finney (ed.), *The Origins of the Second World War*, London, 1997, p. 56.

60 Newman, *British Guarantee*, p. 169.

61 *DBFP*, vol. 4, no. 471.

62 *DBFP*, vol. 5, no. 636, Halifax to Kennard, Warsaw, May 26, 1939.

63 Cienciala, "British and French policy," p. 418.

64 *DBFP*, vol. 5, nos 340, 364 and 631.

65 Charmley, *Lost Peace*, p. 187.

66 PRO, CAB 23/100, 40 (39), August 2, 1939. See also *DBFP*, vol. 7, nos 309, 326, 543 and 632.

67 Watt, *How War Came*, pp. 441 and 445. Weinberg, *Hitler's Germany*, pp. 559 and 610–11.

68 Prazmowska, *Eastern Front*, p. 165.

69 J. Vincent, "Chamberlain, the Liberals and the outbreak of war, 1939," *English Historical Review*, vol. 113, 1998, p. 371.

70 Watt, *How War Came*, p. 499 ; Charmley, *Lost Peace*, p. 202; Parker, *Chamberlain*, p. 334.

71 Parker, *Chamberlain*, p. 336.

72 G. L. Weinberg, *Germany, Hitler and World War II*, Cambridge, 1995, p. 146.

73 See e.g. Taylor's contribution to R. Douglas (ed.), *1939: A Retrospective Forty Years After*, London, 1983.

74 See e.g. D. Kaiser, T. Mason, and R. J. Overy, "Debate: Germany, 'domestic crisis' and War in 1939," *Past & Present*, vol. 122, 1989, pp. 205–40, and A. J. Crozier, *The Causes of the Second World War*, Oxford, 1997, pp. 229–31.

75 W. K. Wark, "British military and economic intelligence: assessments of Nazi Germany before the Second World War," in C. M. Andrews and D. Dilks (eds), *The Missing Dimension: Governments and Intelligence Communities in the Twentieth Century*, London, 1984. pp. 97–9; S. Greenwood, "Sir Thomas Inskip as minister for the co-ordination of defence. 1936–39," *Government and the Armed Forces in Britain, 1856–1990*, London, 1996. pp. 187–8.

76 F. H. Hinsley, *British Intelligence in the Second World War*, London, 1979, vol. 1, pp. 69–70.

77 W. K. Wark, "Something very stern", pp. 153–7.

Bibliography

Abendroth, Hans-Henning, *Hitler in der spanischen Arena*, Paderborn, 1973.

Adams, R. J. Q., *British Politics and Foreign Policy in the Age of Appeasement, 1935–39*, London, 1993.

Adamthwaite, Anthony, *France and the Coming of the Second World War, 1936–1939*, London, 1977.

——*The Lost Peace: International Relations in Europe, 1918–1939*, New York, 1981.

——*Grandeur and Misery. France's Bid for Power in Europe, 1914–1940*, London, 1995.

Aigner, D., *Das Ringen um England: das deutsch–britische Verhältnis*, Munich, 1969.

Aldcroft, Derek H., *From Versailles to Wall Street, 1919–1929*, Berkeley, CA, 1977.

Alexander, Martin S., *The Republic in Danger. General Maurice Gamelin and the Politics of French Defense, 1933–1940*, New York, 1992.

Allard, Sven, *Stalin und Hitler: Die Sowjetrussische Aussenpolitik, 1930–1941*, Bern and Munich, 1974.

Alpert, Michael, *A New International History of the Spanish Civil War*, London, 1994.

Andrews, C. M. and D. Dilks (eds), *The Missing Dimension: Governments and Intelligence Communities in the Twentieth Century*, London, 1984.

Angress, W. T., *Stillborn Revolution*, Princeton, NJ, 1963.

Artaud, Denise, *La Question des dettes interalliées et la reconstruction de l'Europe, 1917–1929*, 2 vols, Lille, 1978.

Axworthy, Mark, Cornel Scafe, and Cristian Craciunoiu, *Third Axis, Fourth Ally. Romanian Armed Forces in the European War*, London, 1995.

Baechler, Christian, *Gustave Stresemann*, Strasbourg, 1996.

—— and Carole Fink (eds), *The Establishment of European Frontiers after the Two World Wars*, Bern, 1996.

Baer, G. W., *Test Case: Italy, Ethiopia, and the League of Nations*, Stanford, CA, 1976.

——*The Coming of the Italian–Ethiopian War*, Cambridge, MA, 1967.

Bagel-Bohlan, A., *Hitlers industrielle Kriegsvorbereitung, 1936 bis 1939*, Koblenz, 1975.

Ball, Stuart, *Baldwin and the Conservative Party: The Crisis of 1929–1931*, New Haven, CT, 1988.

Bariéty, Jacques, *Les Relations franco-allemandes après la première guerre mondiale*, Paris, 1977.

Barnett, Corelli, *The Collapse of British Power*, London and New York, 1972.

——*The Audit of War: The Illusion and Reality of Britain as a Great Power*, London, 1996.

Barnhart, Michael A., *Japan Prepares for Total War; The Search for Economic Security, 1919–1941*, Ithaca, NY, 1987.

Barrot, Olivier, and Pascal Ory (eds), *Entre deux guerres. La création entre 1919 et 1939*, Paris, 1990.

Beevor, Antony, *The Spanish Civil War*, London, 1982.

Bell, P. M. H., *The Origins of the Second World War in Europe*, London, 1986.

——*France and Britain, 1900–1940: Entente and Estrangement*, London, 1996.

Beloff, Max, *Imperial Sunset*; vol. 2: *Dream of Commonwealth, 1921–42*, London, 1989.

Bennett, E. W., *Germany and the Diplomacy of the Financial Crisis*, 1931, Cambridge, MA, 1962.

——*German Rearmament and the West, 1932–1933*, Princeton, NJ, 1979.

Benz, Wolfgang and H. Graml (eds), *Sommer 1939. Die Grossmächte und der Europäische Krieg*, Stuttgart, 1979.

Berger, Gordon M., *Parties Out of Power in Japan, 1931–1941*, Princeton, NJ, 1977.

Bernstein, Gail Lee, and Harahiro Fukui, (eds), *Japan and the World: Essays on Japanese History and Politics in Honour of Ishida Takeshi*, New York, 1988.

Berstein, Serge, *La France des années 30*, Paris, 1988.

Bessis, Juliette, *La mediterranée fasciste. L'Italie mussolinienne et la Tunisie*, Paris, 1980.

Bialer, U., *The Shadow of the Bomber: The Fear of Air Attack and British Politics 1932–1939*, London, 1980.

Birn, D. S., *The League of Nations' Union 1918–1945*, London, 1981.

Bischof, E., *Rheinischer Separatismus, 1918–1924*, Bern, 1969.

Blackbourn, David and G. Eley, *The Peculiarities of German History*, Oxford, 1984.

Bloch, M., *Von Ribbentrop*, London, 1992.

Boemeke, Manfred F., Gerald D. Feldman, and Elisabeth Glaser-Schmidt (eds), *The Treaty of Versailles: A Reassessment after Seventy-Five Years*, Cambridge, 1998.

Bolech Cecchi, D., *L'accordo di due imperi: L'accordo italo-inglese del 16 aprile 1938*, Milan,1977.

Bolloten, Burnett, *The Spanish Civil War. Revolution and Counterrevolution*, Chapel Hill, NC, 1991.

Bond, B., *British Military Policy Between the Two World Wars*, Oxford, 1980.

Borchardt, K., *Wachstum, Krisen, Handelsspielräume der Wirtschaftspolitik*, Göttingen, 1982.

Bosworth, R. J. B., and G. Rizzo (eds), *Altro Polo: Intellectuals and Their Ideas in Contemporary Italy*, Sydney, 1983.

—— and Sergio Romano (eds), *La politica estera italiana (1860–1985)*, Bologna, 1991

——*Explaining Auschwitz and Hiroshima: History Writing and the Second World War, 1945–1990*, London, 1993.

——*Italy and the Wider World, 1860–1960*, London, 1996.

Boyce, Robert and Esmonde M. Robertson (eds), *Paths to War: New Essays on the Origins of the Second World War*, London, 1989.

Boyle, John H., *China and Japan at War, 1937–1945: The Politics of Collaboration*, Stanford, CA, 1972.

Braunthal, J., *History of the International*; vol. 2: *1914–1943*, New York, 1967.

Brenan, Gerald, *The Spanish Labyrinth. An Account of the Social and Political Background of the Civil War*, Cambridge, 1967.

Broué, Pierre and Emile Témime, *The Revolution and the Civil War in Spain*, Cambridge, MA, 1970.

Browning, Christopher, *Ordinary Men: Reserve Battalion 101 and the Final Solution in Poland*, New York, 1992.

Brundu Olla, P., *L'equilibrio difficile: Gran Bretagna, Italia e Francia nel Mediterraneo*, Milan, 1980.

Burgwyn, H. James, *Il revisionismo fascista: La sfida di Mussolini alle grande potenze nei Balcani e sul Danubio, 1925–1933*, Milan, 1979.

——*The Legend of the Mutilated Victory: Italy, the Great War, and the Paris Peace Conference, 1915–1919*, Westport, CT, 1993.

——*Italian Foreign Policy in the Interwar Period, 1918–1940*, Westport, CT, 1997.

Burk, K., *Britain, America and the Sinews of War, 1914–1918*, London, 1985.

Burleigh, M., *Germany Turns Eastwards*, Cambridge, 1988.

Burleigh, M. and Wolfgang Wippermann, *The Racial State: Germany, 1933–1945*, Cambridge, 1991.

Butow, Robert J. C., *Tojo and the Coming of the War*, Princeton, NJ, 1961.

Buxton, N. K., and D. H. Aldcroft (eds), *British Industry Between the Wars*, London, 1979.

Calleo, D., *The German Problem Reconsidered*, Cambridge, 1978.

Campbell, F. G., *Confrontation in Central Europe*, Chicago, IL, 1975.

Carley, Michael, *Revolution and Intervention: The French Government and the Russian Civil War, 1917–1919*, Kingston, ONT, 1983.

Carls, Stephen D., *Louis Loucheur and the Shaping of Modern France, 1916–1931*, Baton Rouge, LA, 1993.

Carlton, D., *MacDonald versus Henderson: The Foreign Policy of the Second Labour Government*, London, 1970.

——*Anthony Eden*, London, 1981.

Carr, E. H., *Twilight of the Comintern, 1930–1935*, New York, 1982.

——*The Comintern and the Spanish Civil War*, New York, 1984.

Carr, William, *Arms, Autarky, and Aggression. A Study in German Foreign Policy, 1933–1939*, New York, 1972.

Cassels, Alan, *Mussolini's Early Diplomacy*, Princeton, NJ, 1970.

——*Ideology and International Relations in the Modern World*, London, 1997.

Ceadel, M., *Pacifism in Britain, 1914–1945*, Oxford, 1980.

Chabod, F., *Italian Foreign Policy: The Statecraft of the Founders*, Princeton, NJ, 1996.

Chandler, A. D., Jr, *Scale and Scope*, London, 1990.

Charmley, John, *Chamberlain and the Lost Peace*, London, 1989.

Chihiro Hosoya, Msuke Andô, Yasuaki Ônuma and Richard H. Minear (eds), *The Tokyo War Crimes Trial: An International Symposium*, New York, 1986.

Clark, M., *Modern Italy*, 2nd edn, London, 1996.

Clarke, J. Calvitt, *Russia and Italy Against Hitler. The Bolshevik–Fascist Rapprochement of the 1930s*, New York, 1991.

Clarke, S. V. O., *Central Bank Cooperation, 1924–1931*, New York, 1967.

Claudin, Fernando, *The Communist Movement: From Comintern to Cominform*, New York, 1975.

Clough, S. B., *The Economic History of Modern Italy*, New York, 1964.

Cockett, Richard, *Twilight of Truth: Chamberlain, Appeasement, and the Manipulation of the Press*, London, 1989.

Cohen, Warren I. (ed.), *New Frontiers in American–East Asian Relations: Essays Presented to Dorothy Borg*, New York, 1983.

Cole, R., *A. J. P. Taylor: The Traitor Within the Gates*, London and New York, 1993.

Colvin, Ian, *The Chamberlain Cabinet*, London, 1971.

——*Vansittart in Office*, London, 1965.

Costigliola, F., *Awkward Dominion*, Ithaca, NY, 1985.

Coverdale, John F., *Italian Intervention in the Spanish Civil War*, Princeton, NJ, 1975.

Cowling, M., *The Impact of Hitler*, Cambridge, 1975.

Crampton, R. J., *A Concise History of Bulgaria*, Cambridge, 1997.

Crowley, James B., *Japan's Quest for Autonomy: National Security and Foreign Policy, 1930–1938*, Princeton, NJ, 1966.

Crozier, Andrew J., *The Causes of the Second World War*, Oxford, 1997.

——*Appeasement and Germany's Last Bid for Colonies*, London, 1988.

De Felice, Renzo, *Mussolini*, 8 vols, Turin, 1965–98.

——*Fascism: An Informal Introduction to its Theory and Practice*, New Brunswick, NJ, 1976.

——*D'Annunzio politico, 1918–1938*, Bari, 1978.

De Grand, A., *The Italian Nationalist Association and the Rise of Fascism in Italy*, Lincoln, NE, 1978.

Debicki, R., *The Foreign Policy of Poland, 1919–1939*, New York, 1962.

Debo, Richard K., *Revolution and Survival: The Foreign Policy of Soviet Russia, 1917–18*, Toronto, 1979.

——*Survival and Consolidation: The Foreign Policy of Soviet Russia, 1918–1921*, Montreal, 1992.

Deist, Wilhelm, *The Wehrmacht and German Rearmament*, London, 1981.

——*et al.*, *Germany and the Second World War*, vol. 1: *The Build-Up of German Aggression*, Oxford, 1990.

Del Boca, A. (ed.), *Adua: Le ragioni della sconfitta*, Rome, 1997.

Deutsch, H., *Hitler and His Generals: The Hidden Crisis, January–June 1938*, Minneapolis, MN, 1974.

Dilks, David (ed.), *Retreat from Power*, 2 vols, London, 1981.

——*Neville Chamberlain*, Cambridge, 1984, vol. 1.

Dingman, R., *Power in the Pacific*, Chicago, IL, 1976.

Dockrill, Michael L. and J. Douglas Goold, *Peace Without Promise: Britain and the Peace Conferences, 1919–1923*, Hamden, CT, 1981.

—— and Brian McKercher, *Diplomacy and World Power: Studies in British Foreign Policy, 1890–1950*, New York, 1996.

Döscher, Hans-Jürgen, *Das Auswärtige Amt im Dritten Reich: Diplomatie im Schatten der Endlösung*, Berlin, 1986.

Doughty, Robert A., *The Seeds of Disaster. The Development of French Army Doctrine, 1919–1939*, Hamden, CT, 1985.

——*The Breaking Point. Sedan and the Fall of France, 1940*, New York, 1990.

Douglas, R. (ed.), *1939: A Retrospective Forty Years After*, London, 1983.

Dower, J. W., *Empire and Aftermath: Yoshida Shigeru and the Japanese Experience, 1878–1954*, Cambridge, 1979.

Dreifort, John E., *Yvon Delbos at the Quai D'Orsay. French Foreign Policy During the Popular Front, 1936–1938*, Lawrence, KS, 1973.

——*Myopic Grandeur. The Ambivalence of French Foreign Policy Toward the Far East, 1919–1945*, Kent, OH, 1991.

Duroselle, J.-B., *La Décadence, 1932–1939*, Paris, 1979

Dutton, David, *Austen Chamberlain: Gentleman in Politics*, New Brunswick, NJ, 1985.

——*Simon: A Political Biography of Sir John Simon*, London, 1992.

——*Anthony Eden: A Life and Reputation*, New York, 1997.

Duus, Peter (ed.), *Cambridge History of Japan*; vol. 6: *The Twentieth Century*, Cambridge, 1988.

Edwards, Jill, *The British Government and the Spanish Civil War, 1936–1939*, London, 1979.

Eichengreen, B., *Golden Fetters*, New York, 1992.

Emmerson, James T., *The Rhineland Crisis, 7 March 1936. A Study in Multilateral Diplomacy*, London, 1977.

Endicott, S. L., *Diplomacy and Enterprise: British China Policy, 1933–1937*, Vancouver, BC, 1973.

Engel, G., *Heeresadjutant bei Hitler, 1938–1943; Aufzeichnungen des Majors Engel*, Stuttgart, 1974.

Enssle, Manfred J., *Stresemann's Territorial Revisionism*, Wiesbaden, 1980.

Erdmann, K. D., *Adenauer in der Rheinlandpolitik nach dem Ersten Weltkrieg*, Stuttgart, 1966.

Favez, J.-C., *Le Reich devant l'occupation franco-belge de la Ruhr en 1923*, Geneva, 1969.

Feldman, Gerald D., *Iron and Steel in the German Inflation, 1916–1923*, Princeton, NJ, 1977.

——*The Great Disorder: Politics, Economics and Society in the German Inflation, 1914–1924*, Oxford, 1993.

Felix, David, *Walther Rathenau and the Weimar Republic*, Baltimore, MD, 1971.

Ferris, John R., *Men, Money, and Diplomacy: The Evolution of British Strategic Foreign Policy, 1919–1926*, Ithaca, NY, 1989.

Fink, Carole, *The Genoa Conference: European Diplomacy, 1921–1922*, Chapel Hill, NC, 1984.

—— Isabel V. Hull, and MacGregor Knox, *German Nationalism and the European Response, 1890–1945*, Norman, OK, 1985.

——*et al.*, *Genoa, Rapallo, and European Reconstruction in 1922*, Washington, DC, 1991.

Finney, Patrick (ed.), *The Origins of the Second World War*, London, 1997.

Fischer, Fritz, *From Kaiserreich to Third Reich*, trans. Roger Fletcher, London, 1986.

Fleischhauer, Ingeborg, *Der Pakt: Hitler, Stalin und die Initiative der deutschen Diplomatie, 1938–1939*, Frankfurt, 1990.

Fletcher, William M., *The Search for a New Order: Intellectuals and Fascism in Prewar Japan*, Chapel Hill, NC, 1982.

Floto, Inga, *Colonel House in Paris*, Åarhus, 1973.

Foot, M. R. D. (ed.), *War and Society*, London, 1973

Fox, J., *Germany and the Far Eastern Crisis, 1931–1938: A Study in Diplomacy and Ideology*, Oxford, 1982.

Frankenstein, Robert, *Le prix du réarmement français, 1935–1939*, Paris, 1982.

Frei, N.and H. Kling (eds), *Der nationalsozialistische Krieg*, Frankfurt am Main, 1990.

Friedlander, Saul, *Nazi Germany and the Jews*, New York, 1997.

Frucht, Richard (ed.), *Labyrinth of Nationalism/Complexities of Diplomacy*, Columbus, OH, 1992.

Fry, M. G., *Illusion of Security*, Toronto, 1972.

Fuchser, L.W., *Neville Chamberlain and Appeasement. A Study in the Politics of History*, New York, 1982.

Funke, Manfred, *Sanktionen und Kanonen: Hitler, Mussolini und der Abessinienkonflikt, 1934–1936*, Düsseldorf, 1970.

Gannon, F. R., *The British Press and Germany, 1936–39*, Oxford, 1971.

Gates, Eleanor M., *End of the Affair: The Collapse of the Anglo-French Alliance, 1939–1940*, Berkeley, CA, 1980.

Gatzke, Hans W. (ed.), *European Diplomacy Between Two Wars, 1919–1939*, Chicago, IL, 1972.

Geyer, M., *Aufrüstung oder Sicherheit: Die Reichswehr in der Krise der Machtpolitik, 1924–1936*, Wiesbaden, 1980.

Gibbs, N., *Grand Strategy*, London, 1976, vol. 1.

Gilbert, Martin, *The Roots of Appeasement*, London and New York, 1966.

—— and R. Gott, *The Appeasers*, London, 1963.

Gillingham, John, *Coal, Steel and the Rebirth of Europe, 1945–1955: The Germans and French from Ruhr Conflict to Economic Community*, Cambridge, 1991.

Giordano, G., *Il Patto a Quattro nella politica estera di Mussolini*, Bologna, 1976.

Girault, René and Robert Frank (eds), *La Puissance en Europe, 1938–1940*, Paris, 1984.

Gnedin, Evgenii; *Vykhod iz labirinta*, New York, 1982.

Goldstein, Erik, *Winning the Peace: British Diplomatic Strategy, Peace Planning and the Paris Peace Conference, 1916–1920*, Oxford, 1991.

Gorodetsky, Gabriel (ed.), *Soviet Foreign Policy, 1917–1991: A Retrospective*, London, 1994.

Gordon, G. A. H., *British Seapower and Procurement Between the Wars: A Reappraisal of Rearmament*, London, 1988.

Graham, Helen and Paul Preston (eds), *The Popular Front in Europe*, London, 1987.

Griffiths, Richard, *Fellow Travellers of the Right. British Enthusiasts for Nazi Germany, 1933–9*, London, 1980.

Grundmann, K.-H., *Deutschtumpolitik zur Zeit der Weimarer Republik*, Hanover, 1977.

Gunsburg, Jeffery A., *Divided and Conquered: The French High Command and the Defeat of the West, 1940*, Westport, CT, 1979.

Haggie, P., *Britannia at Bay: The Defence of the British Empire Against Japan*, Oxford, 1981.

Haigh, R. H., Morris, D. S., and Peters, A. R., *Soviet Foreign Policy, the League of Nations, and Europe, 1917–1939*, Totowa, NJ, 1986.

Halliday, Jon, *A Political History of Japanese Capitalism*, New York, 1975.

Hannah, L., *The Rise of the Corporate Economy*, London, 1983.

Hansen, E. W., *Reichswehr und Industrie*, Boppard am Rhein, 1981.

Haraszti, E. H., *Treaty-Breakers or Realpolitiker? The Anglo-German Naval Agreement of June 1935*, Boppard am Rhein, 1973.

Hardie, F. M., *The Abyssinian Crisis*, London, 1974.

Harper, Glenn T., *German Economic Policy in Spain during the Spanish Civil War, 1936–1939*, The Hague, 1967.

Haslam, Jonathan, *Soviet Foreign Policy, 1930–33: The Impact of the Depression*, New York, 1983.

——*The Soviet Union and the Struggle for Collective Security in Europe, 1933–39*, New York, 1984.

——*The Soviet Union and the Threat from the East, 1933–41*, Pittsburgh, PA, 1992.

Havens, Thomas R. H., *Farm and Nation in Modern Japan; Agrarian Nationalism, 1870–1940*, Princeton, NJ, 1974.

——*Valley of Darkness; The Japanese People and World War Two*, Lanham, MD, 1986.

Heiber, Helmut, *The Weimar Republic*, trans. W. E. Yuill, Oxford, 1993.

Heinemann, J. L., *Hitler's First Foreign Minister*, Berkeley, CA, 1979.

Hiden, John, *Republican and Fascist Germany*, London, 1996.

Hilberg, Raul, *The Destruction of the European Jews*, New York, 1985 edn.

Hildebrand, K., *Vom Reich zum Weltreich*, Munich, 1969.

——*The Foreign Policy of the Third Reich*, London, 1973.

——J. Schmädeke and K. Zernack (eds), *1939: an der Schwelle zum Weltkrieg*, Berlin, 1990.

——*Das vergangene Reich: Deutsche Aussenpolitik von Bismarck bis Hitler, 1871–1945*, Stuttgart, 1995.

Hill, C., *Cabinet Decisions on Foreign Policy: The British Experience, October 1938–June 1941*, Cambridge, 1991.

Hinsley, F. H., *British Intelligence in the Second World War: Its Influence on Strategy and Operations*, London, 1979, vol. 1.

Hochman, Jiri, *The Soviet Union and the Failure of Collective Security, 1934–1938*, Ithaca, NY, 1984.

Hoensch, Jörg K., *A History of Modern Hungary, 1867–1994*, New York, 1996.

Hoepke, K.-P., *Die deutsche Rechte und der italienische Faschismus*, Düsseldorf, 1968.

Hogan, M. J., *Informal Entente*, Columbia, MO, 1977.

Hogenhuis-Seliverstoff, Anne, *Les relations franco-soviétiques, 1917–1924*, Paris, 1981.

Holtfrerich, Carl-Ludwig, *The German Inflation, 1914–1923: Causes and Effects in International Perspective*, trans. Theo Balderston, Berlin, 1986.

Hölzle, E. (ed.), *Die deutschen Ostgebiete zur Zeit der Weimarer Republik*, Cologne, 1966.

Hoptner, J. B., *Yugoslavia in Crisis, 1934–1941*, New York, 1962.

Hosten, Germaine A., *Marxism and the Crisis of Development in Prewar Japan*, Princeton, NJ, 1986.

Howard, Michael, *The Continental Commitment*, London, 1972.

Howson, S. and D. Winch, *The Economic Advisory Council, 1930–1939*, Cambridge, 1977.

Hughes, J. M., *To the Maginot Line*, Cambridge, MA, 1971.

Ilari, Virgilio and Antonio Sema, *Marte in Orbace. Guerra, esercito e milizia nella concezione fascista della nazione*, Ancona, 1988.

——*Storia del servizio militare in Italia*, 4 vols, Rome, 1989–91.

Ingram, Norman, *The Politics of Dissent: Pacifism in France, 1919–1939*, Oxford, 1991.

Ion, A. Hamish and E. J. Errington (eds), *Great Powers and Little Wars. The Limits of Power*, Westport, CT, 1993.

Iriye, A., *After Imperialism*, Cambridge, MA, 1965.

Jäckel, E., *Hitler's Weltanschauung: A Blueprint for Power*, Middletown, CT, 1972.

——*Hitler's World View*, Cambridge, MA, 1981.

Jacobsen, H.-A., *Nationalsozialistische Aussenpolitik, 1933–1938*, Frankfurt am Main, 1968.

Jacobson, J., *Locarno Diplomacy: Germany and the West, 1925–1929*, Princeton, NJ, 1972.

——*When the Soviet Union Entered World Politics*, Berkeley, CA, 1994.

Jaffe, Lorna S., *The Decision to Disarm Germany*, Boston, MA, 1985.

Jarausch, Konrad, *The Four Power Pact*, Madison, WI, 1965.

Jaworski, R., *Vorposten oder Minderheit?*, Stuttgart, 1977.

Jordan, Nicole, *The Popular Front and Central Europe: The Dilemmas of French Impotence, 1918–1940*, New York, 1992.

Karski, J., *The Great Powers and Poland, 1919–1945: From Versailles to Yalta*, Lanham, MD, 1985.

Kasza, Gregory James, *The State and the Mass Media in Japan, 1918–1945*, Berkeley, CA, 1988.

Kazuko Tsurumi, *Social Change and the Individual: Japan Before and After Defeat in World War II*, Princeton, NJ, 1966.

Keeton, E. D., *Briand's Locarno Policy*, New York, 1987.

Keiger, J. F. V., *Raymond Poincaré*, Oxford, 1997.

Kennan, George F., *Russia and the West under Lenin and Stalin*, New York, 1961.

Kennedy, M. D., *The Estrangement of Great Britain and Japan, 1917–1935*, Manchester, 1969.

Kent, Bruce, *The Spoils of War: The Politics, Economics and Diplomacy of Reparations, 1918–1932*, Oxford, 1989.

Kershaw, I., *The Nazi Dictatorship*, 3rd edn, London, 1993.

Keylor, William R. (ed.), *The Legacy of the Great War: The Peace Settlement of 1919 and its Consequences*, Boston, MA, 1997.

Kier, Elizabeth, *Imagining War. French and British Military Doctrine Between the Wars*, Princeton, NJ, 1997.

Kiesling, Eugenia C., *Arming Against Hitler. France and the Limits of Military Planning*, Lawrence, KA, 1996.

Kimmich, C. M., *The Free City*, New Haven, CT, 1968.

Kindermann, G.-K., *Hitler's Defeat in Austria, 1933–1934: Europe's First Containment of Nazi Expansionism*, Boulder, CO, 1988.

King, J. M., *Foch versus Clemenceau*, Cambridge, MA., 1960.

Kitchen, Martin, *Europe Between the Wars: A Political History*, London, 1988.

Kley, S., *Hitler, Von Ribbentrop und die Entfesse ung des Zweiten Weltkrieges*, Paderborn, 1996.

Klug, A., *The German Buybacks, 1932–1939*, Princeton, NJ, 1993.

Knipping, F., *Deutschland, Frankreich, and das Ende der Locarno-Ära 1928–1931*, Munich, 1987.

Knox, MacGregor, *Mussolini Unleashed 1939–1941. Politics and Strategy in Fascist Italy's Last War*, New York, 1982.

Koblyakov, I. K., *USSR: For Peace, Against Aggression, 1933–1941*, Moscow, 1976.

Köhler, H., *Novemberrevolution und Frankreich*, Düsseldorf, 1980.

——*Adenauer und die rheinische Republik*, Opladen, 1986.

Korbel, J., *Poland Between East and West*, Princeton, NJ, 1963.

Koschmann, J. Victor (ed.), *Authority and the Individual in Japan*, Tokyo, 1978.

Kottman, R. N., *Reciprocity and the North Atlantic Triangle, 1932–1938*, Ithaca, NY, 1968.

Krekeler, N., *Revisionsanspruch und geheime Ostopolitik der Weimarer Republik*, Stuttgart, 1973.

Krüger, Peter *Deutschland und die Reparationen, 1918/19*, Stuttgart, 1973.

——*Die Aussenpolitik der Republik von Weimar*, Darmstadt, 1985.

——*Versailles: deutsche Aussenpolitik zwischen Revisionismus und Friedenssicherung*, Munich, 1986.

Kube, A., *Pour le mérite und Hakenkreuz: Hermann Göring im Dritten Reich*, Munich, 1986.

Kuusisto, S., *Alfred Rosenberg in der nationalsozialistischen Aussenpolitik 1933–1939*, Helsinki, 1984.

Laffan, M. (ed.), *The Burden of German History, 1919–1945*, London, 1988.

Lamb, R. A., *Mussolini and the British*, London, 1997.

Lammers, D. N., *Explaining Munich: The Search for Motive in British Policy*, Stanford, CA, 1966.

Laqueur, Walter, *Russia and Germany*, Boston, MA, 1965.

Large, David C. (ed.), *Contending with Hitler: Varieties of Resistance in the Third Reich*, Washington, DC, 1991.

Ledeen, M., *Universal Fascism: Theory and Practice of the Fascist International, 1928–1934*, New York, 1972.

——*The First Duce: D'Annunzio at Fiume*, Baltimore, MD, 1977.

Lee, B. A., *Britain and the Sino-Japanese War, 1937–1939*, Stanford, CA, 1973.

Lee, Marshall and Wolfgang Michalka, *German Foreign Policy, 1917–1933*, Leamington Spa, 1987.

Leffler, Melvyn P., *The Elusive Quest*, Chapel Hill, NC, 1979.

Leitz, C., *Economic Relations between Nazi Germany and Franco's Spain 1936–1945*, Oxford, 1996.

Lentin, A., *Lloyd George, Woodrow Wilson, and the Guilt of Germany*, Baton Rouge, LA, 1985.

——*The Versailles Peace Settlement: Peacemaking with Germany*, London, 1991.

Leonhard, Wolfgang, *Betrayal: The Hitler–Stalin Pact of 1939*, New York, 1989.

Levillain, P. and R. Riemenschneider (eds), *La guerre de 1870/71 et ses conséquences*, Bonn, 1990.

Lewis, J., *The Left Book Club*, London, 1970.

Li, Lincoln, *The Japanese Army in North China, July 1937–December 1941: Problems of Political and Economic Control*, New York, 1975.

Link, W., *Die amerikanische Stabilisierungspolitik in Deutschland 1921–1932*, Düsseldorf, 1970.

Lipski, J. *Diplomat in Berlin, 1933–1939*, New York, 1968.

Little, Douglas, *Malevolent Neutrality. The United States, Great Britain, and the Origins of the Spanish Civil War*, Ithaca, NY, 1985.

Loi, Salvatore, *Le operazioni delle unità italiane in Jugoslavia (1941–1943)*, Rome, 1978.

Louis, W. R., *British Strategy in the Far East 1919–1929*, Oxford, 1971.

—— (ed.), *The Origins of the Second World War: A. J. P. Taylor and His Critics*, New York, 1972.

Low, A. D., *The Anschluss Movement 1918–1919 and the Paris Peace Conference*, Philadelphia, PA, 1974.

Lowe, C. J. and F. Marzari, *Italian Foreign Policy, 1870–1940*, London, 1975.

Lowe, P., *Great Britain and the Origins of the Pacific War, 1937–1941*, Oxford, 1977.

Lukes, Igor, *Czechoslovakia Between Stalin and Hitler*, New York, 1996.

Lundgreen-Nielsen, Kay, *The Polish Problem at the Paris Peace Conference*, Odense, 1979.

Lungu, Dov B., *Romania and the Great Powers, 1933–1940*, Durham, NC, 1989.

Lyttleton, A., *The Seizure of Power: Fascism in Italy, 1919–1929*, 2nd edn, Princeton, NJ, 1988.

Macartney, C. A., *October Fifteenth. A History of Modern Hungary 1929–1945*, Edinburgh, 1956.

MacDonald, C. A., *The United States, Britain, and Appeasement, 1936–1939*, New York, 1981.

Mack Smith, Denis, *Mussolini's Roman Empire*, New York, 1976.

Maier, Charles S., *Recasting Bourgeois Europe*, Princeton, NJ, 1975.

——*The Unmasterable Past: History, Holocaust, and German National Identity*, Cambridge, MA, 1988.

Maksimychev, I. F., *Diplomatiia mira protiv diplomatii voiny*, Moscow, 1981.

Marcus, Harold G., *Haile Sellassie I. The Formative Years, 1892–1936*, Berkeley, CA, 1987.

Marder, A. J., *Old Friends, New Enemies: the Royal Navy and the Imperial Japanese Navy*, Oxford, 1981.

Marks, Sally, *The Illusion of Peace: International Relations in Europe, 1918–1933*, London, 1976.

——*Innocent Abroad: Belgium at the Paris Peace Conference of 1919*, Chapel Hill, NC, 1981.

Marquand, David, *Ramsay MacDonald*, London, 1977.

Marrus, Michael, *The Holocaust in History*, Hanover, NH, 1987.

Martel, Gordon (ed.), *Modern Germany Reconsidered*, London, 1992.

Maurer, I. and U. Wengst, (eds), *Politik und Wirtschaft in der Krise: Quellen zur Ära Brüning*, 2 vols, Düsseldorf, 1980.

May, Ernest R. and James C. Thomson, Jr, *American–East Asian Relations: A Survey*, Cambridge, MA, 1972.

—— (ed.), *Knowing One's Enemies: Intelligence and Assessment Before the Two World Wars*, Princeton, NJ, 1984.

Mayer, Arno J., *Politics and Diplomacy of Peacemaking: Containment and Counterrevolution at Versailles*, New York, 1967.

McDermott, Kevin and Jeremy Agnew, *The Comintern: A History of International Communism from Lenin to Stalin*, New York, 1997.

McDougall, Walter A., *France's Rhineland Diplomacy, 1914–1924*, Princeton, NJ, 1978.

McIntyre, W. D., *The Rise and Fall of the Singapore Naval Base*, London, 1979.

McKercher, B. J. M., *The Second Baldwin Government and the United States, 1924–1929*, Cambridge, 1984.

—— (ed.), *Anglo-American Relations in the 1920s*, Edmonton, 1990.

McSherry, James E., *Stalin, Hitler, and Europe*, Cleveland, OH, 1968, vol. 1.

Medvedev, Roy, *All Stalin's Men*, Garden City, NY, 1984.

Megill, A., (ed.), *Rethinking Objectivity*, Durham, NC, 1994.

—— and R. J. Evans, *In Defence of History*, London, 1997.

Melchionni, M. G., *La vittoria mutilata*, Rome, 1981.

Meyers, R., *Britische Sicherheitspolitik, 1934–1938*, Düsseldorf, 1976.

Michaelis, Meir, *Mussolini and the Jews: German–Italian Relations and the Jewish Question in Italy, 1922–1945*, Oxford, 1978.

Michalka, W., *Ribbentrop und die deutsche Weltpolitik, 1933–1940*, Munich, 1980.

—— and M. M. Lee, (eds), *Gustav Stresemann*, Darmstadt, 1982.

Middelton, R., *Towards the Managed Economy: Keynes, the Treasury and the Fiscal Policy Debates in the 1930s*, London, 1985.

Middlemas, Keith, *Diplomacy of Illusion*, London, 1972.

——*The Strategy of Appeasement. The British Government and Germany, 1937–39*, Chicago, IL, 1972.

Miller, Marshall Lee, *Bulgaria During the Second World War*, Stanford, CA, 1975.

Miller, Michael B., *Shanghai on the Métro. Spies, Intrigue, and the French Between the Wars*, Berkeley, CA, 1994.

Millett, A. R. and W. Murray (eds), *Military Effectiveness*, 2 vols, Boston, MA, 1988

Milward, A. S., *War, Economy, and Society, 1939–1945*, Berkeley, CA, 1977.

Minear, Richard, *Victor's Justice: The Tokyo War Crimes Trial*, Princeton, NJ, 1971.

Mitchell, Richard H., *Thought Control in Prewar Japan*, Ithaca, NY, 1966.

——*Censorship in Imperial Japan*, Princeton, NJ 1984.

Mommsen, H., D. Petzina, and B. Weisbrod (eds), *Industrielles System und politische Entwicklung in der Weimarer Republik*, Düsseldorf, 1974.

Mommsen, Wolfgang J. and Lothar Kettenacker (eds), *The Fascist Challenge and the Policy of Appeasement*, London, 1983.

Montgomery Hyde, H. *British Air Policy Between the Wars*, London, 1976.

Morgan, P., *Italian Fascism, 1919–1945*, Basingstoke, 1995.

Mori, R., *Mussolini e la conqista dell'Etiopia*, Florence, 1978.

Morley, James (ed.), *Dilemmas of Growth in Prewar Japan*, Princeton, NJ, 1971

—— (ed.), *Deterrent Diplomacy: Japan, Germany, and the USSR, 1935–1940*, Princeton, NJ, 1976.

—— (ed.), *The Fateful Choice: Japan's Advance into Southeast Asia, 1939–1941*, New York, 1980.

—— (ed.), *The China Quagmire: Japan's Expansion on the Asian Continent, 1933–1941*, New York, 1983.

—— (ed.), *Japan Erupts: The London Naval Conference and the Manchurian Incident, 1928–1932*, New York, 1984.

Morris, Ivan (ed.), *Japan 1931–1945: Militarism, Fascism, Japanism?*, Boston, MA, 1963.

—— (ed.), *Thought and Behavior in Modern Japanese Politics*, Oxford, 1963.

Mosse, G., *The Crisis of German Ideology: Intellectual Origins of the Third Reich*, London, 1970.

Murray, Williamson, *The Change in the European Balance of Power, 1938–1939. The Path to Ruin*, Princeton, NJ, 1984.

—— and Allan R. Millett (eds), *Calculations. Net Assessment and the Coming of World War II*, New York, 1992.

—— MacGregor Knox, and Alvin Bernstein (eds), *The Making of Strategy: Rulers, States, and War*, New York, 1994.

Nadler, H. E., *The Rhenish Separatist Movements in the Early Weimar Republic*, New York, 1987.

Narochitskii, A. L. (ed.), *SSSR v bor be protiv fashistskoi agressi, 1933–1941*, Moscow, 1976.

Nation, R. Craig, *Black Earth, Red Star: A History of Soviet Security Policy, 1917–1991*, Ithaca, NY, 1992.

Naylor, J. F., *Labour's International Policy*, London, 1969.

Neidpath, J., *The Singapore Naval Base and the Defence of Britain's Eastern Empire, 1919–1941*, Oxford, 1981.

Nekrich, Aleksandr, *Otreshis' ot strakha: vospominaniia istorika*, London, 1979.

——*Pariahs, Partners, Predators: German–Soviet Relations, 1922–1941*, New York, 1997.

Nello, P., *Dino Grandi: Un fedele disubbidiente*, Bologna, 1993.

Nelson, Harold I., *Land and Power: British and Allied Policy on Germany's Frontiers, 1916–19*, Toronto, 1963.

Nelson, Keith, L. *Victors Divided*, Berkeley, CA, 1975.

—— and Spencer C. Olin, Jr, *Why War? Ideology, Theory, and History*, Berkeley, CA, 1979.

Neufeld, Maurice F., *Italy: School for Awakening Countries*, Ithaca, NY, 1961.

Newman, Simon, *March 1939: The British Guarantee to Poland*, Oxford, 1976.

Niedhart, G., *Grossbritannien und die Sowjetunion, 1934–1939*, Munich, 1972.

Nish, Ian. H., *Alliance in Decline*, London, 1972.

——*Japan's Struggle with Internationalism: Japan, China, and the League of Nations, 1931–1933*, New York, 1993.

Noel-Baker, P., *The First World Disarmament Conference, 1932–1933, and Why It Failed*, New York, 1979.

Ogata, Sadako N., *Defiance in Manchuria: The Making of Japanese Foreign Policy, 1931–1932*, Berkeley, CA, 1964.

Orde, Anne, *Britain and International Security, 1920–1926*, London, 1978.

——*British Policy and European Reconstruction After the First World War*, Cambridge, 1990.

Ovendale, Russia., *Appeasement and the English-Speaking World*, Cardiff, 1975.

Overy, R. J., *Goering: The "Iron Man,"* London, 1984.

——*War and Economy in the Third Reich*, Oxford, 1994.

Parker, R. A. C., *Chamberlain and Appeasement. British Policy and the Coming of the Second World War*, London and New York, 1993.

Parrini, C., *Heir to Empire*, Pittsburgh, PA, 1969.

Payne, Stanley, *A History of Fascism, 1914–1945*, Madison, WI, 1995.

Peattie, Mark, *Ishiwara Kanji and Japan's Confrontation with the West*, Princeton, NJ, 1975.

Peden, G. C., *British Rearmament and the Treasury, 1932–1939*, Edinburgh, 1979.

Pereboom, Maarten L., *Democracies at the Turning Point: Britain, France and the End of the Postwar Order, 1928–1933*, New York, 1995.

Peters, A. R., *Anthony Eden at the Foreign Office, 1931–1938*, New York, 1986.

Petersen, Jens, *Hitler e Mussolini. La difficile alleanza*, Bari, 1975.

Petricioli, Marta (ed.), *A Missed Opportunity? 1922: The Reconstruction of Europe*, Bern, 1995.

Phillips, Hugh D., *Between the Revolution and the West: A Political Biography of Maxim M. Litvinov*, Boulder, CO, 1992.

Pimlott, Ben, *Labour and the Left in the 1930s*, Cambridge, 1977.

——*Hugh Dalton*, London, 1985.

Pipes, R., *The Bolshevik Regime*, New York, 1994.

——*The Unknown Lenin*, New Haven, CT, 1996.

Pitts, V. J., *France and the German Problem, 1924–1929*, New York, 1987.

Pohl, K.-H., *Weimars Wirtschaft und die Aussenpolitik der Republik, 1924–1926*, Düsseldorf, 1979.

Poidevin, R. and J. Bariéty, *Les relations franco-allemands, 1815–1975*, Paris, 1977.

Pollard, S., *The Development of the British Economy, 1914–1967*, London, 1969.

Ponomaryov, B., A. Gromyko, and V. Khvostov (eds), *History of Soviet Foreign Policy, 1917–1945*, Moscow, 1969.

Porch, Douglas, *The French Secret Services. From the Dreyfus Affair to the Gulf War*, New York, 1995.

Post, Gaines, Jr, *The Civil–Military Fabric of Weimar Foreign Policy*, Princeton, NJ, 1973.

——*Dilemmas of Appeasement: British Deterrence and Defense, 1934–1937*, Ithaca, NY, 1993.

Pratt, P. R., *East of Malta, West of Suez: Britain's Mediterranean Crisis, 1936–1939*, Cambridge, 1975.

Prazmowska, A. *Britain, Poland and the Eastern Front, 1939*, Cambridge, 1987.

Preston, Adrian (ed.), *General Staffs and Diplomacy Before the Second World War*, London, 1974.

Proctor, Raymond L., *Hitler's Luftwaffe in the Spanish Civil War*, Westport, CT, 1983.

Punka, George, *Hungarian Air Force*, Carrolton, TX, 1994.

Puzzo, Dante A., *Spain and the Great Powers, 1936–1941*, Freeport, CT, 1962.

Quartararo, R., *Roma tra Londra e Berlino: Politica estera fascista dal 1930 al 1940*, Rome, 1980.

Raack, R. C., *Stalin's Drive to the West, 1938–1945: The Origins of the Cold War*, Stanford, CA, 1995.

Radice, L., *Prelude to Appeasement: East European Central Diplomacy in the Early 1930s*, Boulder, CO, 1981.

Rainero, Romain, *La rivendicazione fascista sulla Tunisia*, Milan, 1978.

Raspin, Angela, *The Italian War Economy, 1940–43*, London, 1986.

Réau, Elisabeth du, *Edouard Daladier, 1884–1970*, Paris, 1993.

Reynolds, D., *The Creation of the Anglo-American Alliance, 1937–1941*, Chapel Hill, NC, 1981.

Rhodes, Anthony, *The Vatican in the Age of the Dictators, 1922–1945*, London, 1973.

Rhodes James, Robert, *Anthony Eden*, London, 1987.

Rich, N., *Hitler's War Aims*, New York, 1973, vol. 1.

Roberts, Andrew, *"The Holy Fox": A Biography of Lord Halifax*, London, 1991.

Roberts, Geoffrey, *The Unholy Alliance: Stalin's Pact with Hitler*, London, 1989.

——*The Soviet Union and the Origins of the Second World War: Russo–German Relations and the Road to War, 1933–1939*, London, 1995.

Robertson, E. M. (ed.), *The Origins of the Second World War: Historical Interpretations*, London, 1971.

Rochat, Giorgio, *Il colonialismo italiano*, Turin, 1973.

Rodder, A., *Stresemanns Erbe: Julius Curtius und die deutsche Aussenpolitik 1929–1931*, Paderborn, 1996.

Rohwer, Jürgen and Eberhard Jäckel (eds), *Kriegswende, Dezember 1941*, Frankfurt-am-Main, 1984.

Rosa, Arianna Arisi, *La diplomazia del ventennio. Storia di una politica estera*, Milan, 1990.

Rosenbaum, Kurt, *Community of Fate: German–Soviet Diplomatic Relations, 1922–1928*, Syracuse, NY, 1965.

Roskill, S., *Naval Policy Between the Wars*, 2 vols, London, 1968 and 1976.

Rothwell, V. H., *British War Aims and Peace Diplomacy, 1914–1918*, Oxford, 1971.

Rovighi, Alberto and Filippo Stefani, *La partecipazione italiana alla guerra civile spagnola, 1936–1939*, 2 vols, Rome, 1992–93.

Rowland, B. M., *Commercial Conflict and Foreign Policy*, New York, 1987.

Rupieper, Hermann J., *The Cuno Government and Reparations, 1922–1923*, The Hague, 1979.

Rusinow, D. J., *Italy's Austrian Heritage, 1919–1946*, New York, 1969.

Saburô Ienaga *The Pacific War, 1931–1945*, New York, 1978.

Sadkovich, J. J., *Italian Support for Croatian Separatism, 1927–1937*, New York, 1987.

Sakmyster, Thomas, *Hungary, the Great Powers, and the Danubian Crisis 1936–1939*, Athens, GA, 1980.

——*Hungary's Admiral on Horseback. Miklós Horthy, 1918–1944*, New York, 1994.

Salewski, M., *Entwaffnung und Militärkontrolle in Deutschland, 1919–1927*, Munich, 1966.

——*Die deutsche Seekriegsleitung, 1939–1945*, 2 vols, Frankfurt am Main, 1970.

Sbacchi, Alberto (ed.), *Legacy of Bitterness. Ethiopia, and Fascist Italy, 1935–1941*, Lawrenceville, NJ, 1997

Schmidt, G. (ed.), *Konstellationen internationaler Politik, 1924–1932*, Bochum, 1983.

Schmidt, Royal J., *Versailles and the Ruhr*, The Hague, 1968.

Schmitz, D. F., *The United States and Fascist Italy, 1922–1940*, Chapel Hill, NC, 1988.

Schmokel, W. W., *Dream of Empire: German Colonialism, 1919–1945*, New Haven, CT, 1964.

Schröder, H.-J. (ed.), *Confrontation and Cooperation*, Providence, RI, 1993.

Schuker, Stephen A., *The End of French Predominance in Europe*, Chapel Hill, NC, 1976.

——*American "Reparations" to Germany, 1919–33*, Princeton, NJ, 1988.

Schwabe, Klaus, *Woodrow Wilson, Revolutionary Germany, and Peacemaking, 1918–1919: Missionary Diplomacy and the Realities of Power*, trans. Rita and Robert Kimber, Chapel Hill, NC, 1985.

Schwerin von Krosigk, L., *Staatsbankrott: Finanzpolitik des Deutschen Reichs 1920–1945*, Stuttgart, 1974.

Segrè, C., *Fourth Shore: The Italian Colonization of Libya*, Chicago, IL, 1974.

Semiriaga, M. I., *Tainy stalinskoi diplomatii, 1939–1941*, Moscow, 1992.

Shai, A., *Origins of the War in the East: Britain, China, and Japan, 1937–41*, London, 1976.

Sharp, Alan, *The Versailles Settlement: Peacemaking in Paris, 1919*, New York, 1991.

Shay, R. P., Jr, *British Rearmament in the Thirties: Politics and Profits*, Princeton, NJ, 1977.

Sheinis, Zinovy, *Maxim Litvinov*, Moscow, 1990.

Shillony, Ben-Ami, *Revolt in Japan: The Young Officers and the February 26, 1936 Incident*, Princeton, NJ, 1972.

——*Politics and Culture in Wartime Japan*, Oxford, 1981.

Shorrock, W. I., *From Ally to Enemy: The Enigma of Fascist Italy in French Diplomacy, 1920–1940*, Kent, OH, 1988.

Shunsuke Tsurumi, *An Intellectual History of Wartime Japan, 1931–1945*, London, 1986.

Silberman, Bernard, and H. D. Harootunian (eds), *Japan in Crisis*, Princeton, NJ, 1974.

Silverman, Dan P., *Reconstructing Europe after the Great War*, Cambridge, MA, 1982.

Sisman, Adam, *A. J. P. Taylor: A Biography*, London, 1994.

Skidelsky, Robert, *John Maynard Keynes*, London, 1983.

Smethurst, Richard, *A Social Basis for Prewar Japanese Militarism: The Army and the Rural Community*, Berkeley, CA, 1974.

Smith, M., *British Air Strategy Between the Wars*, Oxford, 1984.

Smith, W. D., *The Ideological Origins of Nazi Imperialism*, Oxford, 1986.

Soutou, G., *L'Or et le sang*, Paris, 1989.

Spitzy, Reinhard, *How We Squandered the Reich*, Norwich, 1997.

Steinhoff, Patricia G., *Tenkō: Ideology and Social Integration in Prewar Japan*, New York, 1991.

Steinmeyer, G., *Die Grundlagen der französischen Rheinlandpolitik 1917–1919*, Stuttgart, 1979.

Stern, F., *The Politics of Cultural Despair: A Study in the Rise of the German Ideology*, Berkeley, CA, 1961.

Stevenson, D., *French War Aims Against Germany, 1914–1919*, Oxford, 1982.

——*The First World War and International Politics*, Oxford, 1988.

Stoakes, G., *Hitler and the Quest for World Dominion*, Oxford, 1986.

Stürmer, M. (ed.), *Die Weimarer Republik*, Königstein, 1980.

Suval, S., *The Anschluss Question in the Weimar Era*, Baltimore, MD, 1974.

Takehiko Yoshihashi, *Conspiracy at Mukden: The Rise of the Japanese Military*, New Haven, CT, 1963.

Tatsuo Arima, *The Failure of Freedom: A Portrait of Modern Japanese Intellectuals*, Cambridge, MA, 1969.

Taylor, T., *Munich: The Price of Peace*, London, 1979.

Thomas, Hugh, *The Spanish Civil War*, New York, 1986.

Thomas, Martin, *Britain, France and Appeasement*, Oxford, 1996.

Thompson, John M., *Russia, Bolshevism, and the Versailles Peace*, Princeton, NJ, 1966.

Thompson, Neville, *The Anti-Appeasers. Conservative Opposition to Appeasement in the 1930s*, Oxford, 1971.

Thorne, Christopher, *The Limits of Foreign Policy: The West, the League and the Far Eastern Crisis of 1931–1933*, London, 1972.

——*Allies of a Kind*, Oxford, 1978.

Tillman, Seth P., *Anglo-American Relations at the Paris Peace Conference of 1919*, Princeton, NJ, 1961.

Toscano, M., *The Origins of the Pact of Steel*, Baltimore, MD, 1967.

——*Designs in Diplomacy*, Baltimore, MD, 1970.

Trachtenberg, Marc, *Reparation in World Politics*, New York, 1980.

Traina, Richard P., *American Diplomacy and the Spanish Civil War*, Bloomington, IN, 1968.

Treue, Wolfgang and Jürgen Schmädeke (eds), *Deutschland 1933*, Berlin, 1984.

Troebst, S., *Mussolini, Macedonien und die Mächte, 1922–1930*, Cologne, 1987.

Trotter, A., *Britain and East Asia, 1933–1937*, Cambridge, 1975.

Tucker, Robert C., *Stalin in Power: The Revolution from Above, 1928–1941*, New York, 1990.

—— and Stephen F. Cohen (eds), *The Great Purge Trial*, New York, 1965.

Ulam, A. B., *Expansion and Coexistence*, rev. edn, New York, 1974.

Vaïsse, Maurice, *Sécurité d'Abord. La politique française en matière de désarmament, 9 décembre 1930–17 avril 1934*, Paris, 1981.

Vigezzi, Brunello, *L'Italia unita e le sfide della politica estera. Dal Risorgimento alla Repubblica*, Milan, 1997.

Vincent, C. Paul, *The Politics of Hunger: The Allied Blockage of Germany, 1915–1919*, Athens, OH, 1985.

Vinen, Richard, *The Politics of French Business, 1936–1945*, Cambridge, 1991.

Vizulis, Izidors, *The Molotov–Ribbentrop Pact of 1939: The Baltic Case*, New York, 1990.

Vogelsang, T., *Reichswehr, Staat und NSDAP*, Stuttgart, 1962.

Volkogonov, Dmitri, *Stalin: Triumph and Tragedy*, New York, 1988.

Waite, Robert G. L., *Vanguard of Nazism*, New York, 1969 edn.

Waley, Daniel, *British Public Opinion and the Abyssinian War, 1935–36*, London, 1975.

Walworth, Arthur, *Wilson and his Peacemakers*, New York, 1986.

Wandel, E., *Die Bedeutung der Vereinigten Staaten von Amerika für das deutsche Reparationsproblem, 1924–1929*, Tübingen, 1971

Wandycz, Piotr S., *France and Her Eastern Allies, 1919–1925*, Minneapolis, MN, 1962.

——*The Twilight of French Eastern Alliances, 1926–1936*, Princeton, NJ, 1988.

Wark, Wesley K., *The Ultimate Enemy: British Intelligence and Nazi Germany, 1933–1939*, Ithaca, NY, 1985.

Watkins, K. W., *Britain Divided: The Effect of the Spanish Civil War on British Public Opinion*, London, 1963.

Watt, D. C., *How War Came: The Immediate Origins of the Second World War, 1938–1939*, London, 1989.

Watters, William E., *An International Affair. Non-Intervention in the Spanish Civil War, 1936–1939*, New York, 1971.

Weber, Eugen, *The Hollow Years: France in the 1930s*, New York, 1994.

Weidenfeld, W., *Die Englandpolitik Gustav Stresemanns*, Mainz, 1972.

Weinberg, Gerhard L., *The Foreign Policy of Hitler's Germany*, 2 vols, Chicago, IL, 1970 and 1980.

——*World in the Balance*, Hanover, 1981.

——*Germany, Hitler and World War II*, Cambridge, 1995.

Weisbrod, B., *Schwerindustrie in der Weimarer Republik*, Wuppertal, 1978.

Wendt, B.-J., *Grossdeutschland: Aussenpolitik und Kriegsvorbereitung des Hitler-Regimes*, Munich, 1987.

Whealey, Robert H., *Hitler and Spain. The Nazi Role in the Spanish Civil War, 1936–1939*, Lexington, KY, 1989.

White, Christine A., *British and American Commercial Relations with Soviet Russia, 1918–1924*, Chapel Hill, NC, 1992.

Williams, Andrew J., *Trading with the Bolsheviks*, Manchester, 1992.

Wilson, Dick, *When Tigers Fight: The Story of the Sino-Japanese War, 1937–1945*, New York, 1982.

Wilson, George M., *Radical Nationalist in Japan: Kita Ikki, 1883–1937*, Cambridge, MA, 1969.

Winkler, H., *Paths Not taken: British Labour and International Policy in the 1920s*, Chapel Hill, NC, 1994.

Wray, Harry and Hilary Conroy (eds), *Japan Examined: Perspectives on Modern Japanese History*, Honolulu, HI, 1983.

Wurm, C. A., *Die französische Sicherheitspolitik in der Phase der Umorientierung, 1924–1926*, Frankfurt, 1979.

Young, Louise, *Japan's Total Empire: Manchuria and the Culture of Wartime Imperialism*, Berkeley, CA, 1998.

Young, Robert J., *In Command of France: French Foreign Policy and Military Planning, 1933–1940*, Cambridge, 1978.

——*Power and Pleasure: Louis Barthou and the Third French Republic*, Montreal, 1991.

——*France and the Origins of the Second World War*, New York, 1996.

Zakharov, M. V., *General'nyi shtab v predvoennye gody*, Moscow, 1989.

ARTICLES AND ESSAYS

Abramov, N. A. and L. A. Bezymenskii, "Osobaia missiia Davida Kandelaki," *Voprosy istorii*, no. 4/5, 1991, pp. 144–56.

Adamthwaite, A., "The British government and the media," *Journal of Contemporary History*, vol. 18, 1983, pp. 281–97.

Ahmann, Rolf, "Soviet foreign policy and the Molotov–Ribbentrop Pact of 1939: an enigma reassessed," *Storia delle relazioni internazionali*, vol. 5, 1989, pp. 349–69.

Aigner, Dietrich, "Hitler's war aims – a program of world dominion?", in H. W. Koch (ed.), *Aspects of the Third Reich*, London, 1985, pp. 251–66.

Alegi, Gregory, "Balbo e il riarmo clandestino tedesco. Un episodio segreto della collaborazione italo-tedesco," *Storia contemporanea*, vol. 23, 1992, pp. 305–17.

Alexander, Martin S., "The fall of France, 1940," *Journal of Strategic Studies*, vol. 13, 1990, pp. 12–21.

—— "Did the Deuxième Bureau work? The role of intelligence in French defence policy and strategy, 1919–1939," *Intelligence and National Security*, vol. 6, April 1991, pp. 293–333.

Aster, Sidney, " 'Guilty men': The case of Neville Chamberlain," in Robert Boyce and Esmonde M. Robertson (eds), *Paths to War: New Essays on the Origins of the Second World War*, London, 1989, pp. 233–68.

Azzi, S. C., "The historiography of Fascist Italy," *Historical Journal*, vol. 36, 1993, pp. 187–203.

Bariéty, J., "Le Rôle de la minette dans la sidérurgie allemande et la restructuration de la sidérurgie allemande après le traité de Versailles," *Centre de Recherches Relations Internationales de l'Université de Metz*, vol. 3, 1975, pp. 233–77.

—— "Das Zustandekommen der Internationalen Rohstahlgemeinschaft als Alternative zum misslungenen 'Schwerindustriellen Projekt' des Versailler Vertrages," in H. Mommsen, D. Petzina, and B. Weisbrod (eds), *Industrielles System und politische Entwicklung in der Weimarer Republik*, Düsseldorf, 1974, pp. 552–68.

Bauer, Y., "Antisemitismus und Krieg," in N. Frei and H. Kling (eds), *Der nationalsozialistische Krieg*, Frankfurt am Main, 1990, pp. 146–61.

Berger, Gordon, "Politics and mobilization in Japan, 1931–1945," in Peter Duus (ed.), *Cambridge History of Japan*; vol. 6: *The Twentieth Century*, Cambridge, 1988, pp. 97–153.

Bezymensky, Lev, "The secret protocols of 1939 as a problem in Soviet historiography," in G. Gorodetsky (ed.), *Soviet Foreign Policy*, pp. 75–85.

Bix, Herbert P., "Rethinking 'emperor-system fascism': ruptures and continuities in modern Japanese history," *Bulletin of Concerned Asian Scholars*, vol. 14, 1982, pp. 2–19.

Black, Naomi, "Decision making and the Munich crisis," *British Journal of International Studies*, vol. 6, 1980, pp. 278–303.

Boemeke, Manfred F., "Woodrow Wilson's image of Germany, the war-guilt question, and the Treaty of Versailles," in Manfred F. Boemeke *et al.* (eds), *The Treaty of Versailles: A Reassessment after Seventy-Five Years*, Cambridge, 1998, pp. 603–14.

Bosworth. R., "Italian foreign policy and its historiography," in R. J. B. Bosworth, and G. Rizzo (eds), *Altro Polo: Intellectuals and Their Ideas in Contemporary Italy*, Sydney, 1983, pp. 65–85.

Bouvier, Jean, and Robert Frank, "Sur la perception de la 'puissance' économique en France pendant les années 1930," in René Girault and Robert Frank (eds), *La Puissance en Europe*, Paris, 1984, pp. 169–86.

Breccia, Alfredo, "La politica estera italiana e l Ungheria, 1922–1933," *Rivista di studi politici internazionali*, vol. 47, 1980, pp. 93–112.

Carley, Michael J., "The shoe on the other foot," *Canadian Journal of History*, vol. 26, 1991, pp. 581–7.

—— "Five kopecks for five kopecks: Franco-Soviet trade negotiations, 1928–1939," *Cahiers du Monde Russe et Soviétique*, vol. 33, 1992, pp. 23–58.

—— "End of the 'low, dishonest decade': failure of the Anglo-Franco-Soviet Alliance in 1939," *Europe–Asia Studies*, vol. 45, 1993, pp. 303–41.

—— "Down a blind-alley: Anglo-Franco-Soviet relations, 1920–39," *Canadian Journal of History*, vol. 29, 1994, pp. 147–72.

—— "Prelude to defeat: Franco-Soviet relations, 1930–1939," *Historical Reflections / Réflexions Historiques*, vol. 22, 1996, pp.159–88.

—— and Richard K. Debo, "Always in need of credit: the USSR and Franco-German economic cooperation, 1926–1929," *French Historical Studies*, vol. 20, 1997, pp. 315–56.

Cassels, Alan, "Deux empires face à face: La chimère d'un rapprochement anglo-italien, 1936–1940," *Guerre mondiales et des conflits contemporains*, no. 161, Jan. 1991, pp. 67–96.

Childers, T., "The Kreisau circle and the twentieth of July," in D. C. Large (ed.), *Contending With Hitler: Varieties of Resistance in the Third Reich*, Washington, DC, 1991, pp. 99–118.

Chomsky, Noam, "The revolutionary pacifism of A. J. Muste," in Noam Chomsky, *American Power and the New Mandarins*, New York, 1969, pp. 159–220.

Cienciala, Anna. M., "Poland in British and French policy in 1939: determination to fight – or avoid war?," in P. Finney (ed.), *The Origins of the Second World War*, London, 1997, pp. 413–33.

Cohen, Barry M., "Moscow at Munich: did the Soviet Union offer unilateral aid to Czechoslovakia?," *East European Quarterly*, vol. 12, 1978, pp. 341–8.

Crowe, S. E., "Sir Eyre Crowe and the Locarno pact," *English Historical Review*, vol. 87, 1972, pp. 49–74.

Crowley, James B., "A new Asian order. Some notes on prewar Japanese nationalism," in Bernard Silberman and H. D. Harootunian (eds), *Japan in Crisis*, Princeton, NJ, 1974, pp. 270–98.

—— "Intellectuals as visionaries of the new Asian order," in James Morley (ed.), *Dilemmas of Growth in Prewar Japan*, Princeton, NJ, 1971, pp. 319–73.

Dülffer, Jost, "Des deutsch–englische Flottenabkommen vom 18. Juni 1935," in Wolfgang Michalka (ed.), *Nationalsozialistische Aussenpolitik*, Darmstadt, 1978, pp. 244–76.

Danielson, Elena S., "The Elusive Litvinov Memoirs," *Slavic Review*, vol. 48, 1989, pp. 477–83.

Dayer, R. A., "The British war debts to the United States and the Anglo-Japanese alliance, 1920–1923," *Pacific Historical Review*, vol. 45, 1976, pp. 569–95.

Delmas, Général J., "La perception de la puissance militaire française," in René Girault and Robert Frank (eds), *La Puissance en Europe*, Paris, 1984, pp. 127–40.

Di Nolfo, E., "Der zweideutige italienische Revisionismus," in K. Hildebrand, J. Schmädeke, and K. Zernack (eds), *1939: an der Schwelle zum Weltkrieg*, Berlin, 1990, pp. 94–114.

Dilks, D., "Appeasement revisited," *University of Leeds Review*, vol. 15, 1972, pp. 38–49.

—— "Appeasement and intelligence," in D. Dilks (ed.), *Retreat from Power*, 2 vols, London, 1981, vol. 1, pp. 139–69.

—— " 'We must hope for the best and prepare for the worst': the prime minister, the cabinet and Hitler's Germany, 1937–1939," in P. Finney (ed.), *The Origins of the Second World War*, London, 1997, pp. 43–61.

Dore, Ronald and Tsutomu Ôuchi, "Rural origins of Japanese fascism," in James Morley (ed.), *Dilemmas of Growth in Prewar Japan*, Princeton, NJ, 1971, pp. 181–209.

Doughty, Robert A., "The illusion of security: France, 1919–1940," in Williamson Murray *et al.* (eds), *The Making of Strategy: Rulers, States, and War*, New York, 1994.

Dreifort, John E., "The French Popular Front and the Franco-Soviet pact, 1936–37: a dilemma in foreign policy," *Journal of Contemporary History*, vol. 11, 1976, pp. 217–36.

Duus, Peter and Daniel I. Okimoto, "Fascism and the history of pre-war Japan: the failure of a concept," *Journal of Asian Studies*, vol. 39, 1979, pp. 65–76.

Duval, René, "Radio–Paris," in Olivier Barrot and Pascal Ory (eds), *Entre deux guerres. La création entre 1919 et 1939*, Paris, 1990, pp. 129–46.

Edwards, P. G., "The foreign office and fascism, 1924–1929," *Journal of Contemporary History*, vol. 5, no. 2, 1970, pp. 153–61.

—— "The Austen Chamberlain–Mussolini meetings," *Historical Journal*, vol. 14, 1971, pp. 153–64.

—— "Britain, Fascist Italy and Ethiopia, 1925–1928," *European Studies Review*, vol. 4, 1974, pp. 359–74.

—— "Britain, Mussolini and the 'Locarno–Geneva system,' " *European Studies Review*, vol. 10, 1980, pp. 1–16.

Ferguson, N., "Keynes and the German inflation," *English Historical Review*, vol. 110, 1995, pp. 368–91.

Ferrante, Ezio, "Un rischio calcolato? Mussolini e gli ammiragli nella gestione della crisi di Corfù," *Storia delle relazioni internazionali*, vol. 5, 1989, pp. 221–44.

Fest, J., "Hitlers Krieg," in N. Frei and H. Kling (eds), *Der nationalsozialistische Krieg*, Frankfurt am Main, 1990, pp. 103–21.

Fink, Carole, "The NEP in foreign policy: the Genoa conference and the Treaty of Rapallo," in Gabriel Gorodetsky (ed.), *Soviet Foreign Policy, 1917–1991: A Retrospective*, London, 1994, pp. 11–20.

—— "The protection of ethnic and religious minorities," in William Keylor (ed.), *The Legacy of the Great War: The Peace Settlement of 1919 and its Consequences*, Boston, MA, 1997, pp. 227–38.

—— "The minorities' question at the Paris peace conference," in Manfred Boemeke *et al.* (eds), *The Treaty of Versailles: A Reassessment after Seventy-Five Years*, Washington, DC, 1998, pp. 249–74.

Fletcher, Miles, "Intellectuals and fascism in early Shôwa Japan," *Journal of Asian Studies*, vol. 39, 1979, pp. 39–63.

Foster, A. J., "An unequivocal guarantee? Fleet Street and the British guarantee to poland, 31 March 1939," *Journal of Contemporary History*, vol. 26, 1991, pp. 33–48.

Frank, W. C., "The Spanish Civil War and the coming of the Second World War," *International History Review*, vol. 9, 1987, pp. 368–409.

Frankenstein, Robert, "The decline of France and French appeasement policies, 1936–1939," in Wolfgang J. Mommsen and Lothar Kettenacker (eds), *The Fascist Challenge and the Policy of Appeasement*, London 1983, pp. 236–45.

Geiss, Immanuel, "The Weimar Republic between the Second and Third Reich: continuity and discontinuity in the German question, 1919–33," in M. Laffan (ed.), *The Burden of German History, 1919–1945*, London, 1988.

Geyer, M., "Das Zweite Rüstungsprogramm, 1930–1934," *Militärgeschichtliche Mitteilungen* vol. 16, 1975, pp. 125–72.

—— "Rüstungsbeschleunigung und Inflation: zur Inflations Denkschrift des OKW von November 1938," *Militärgeschichtliche Mitteilungen*, vol. 30, 1981, pp. 121–86.

Girault, René, "The impact of the economic situation on the foreign policy of France, 1936–1939," in Wolfgang J. Mommsen and Lothar Kettenacker (eds), *The Fascist Challenge and the Policy of Appeasement*, London 1983, pp. 209–26.

—— "Les décideurs français et la puissance française en 1938–1939," René Girault and Robert Frank (eds), *La Puissance en Europe*, Paris, 1984, pp. 23–44.

Glaser, Elisabeth, "Von Versailles nach Berlin," in N. Finzsch *et al.* (eds), *Liberalitas*, Stuttgart, 1992, pp. 319–42.

—— "The Making of the Economic Peace," in Manfred F. Boemeke *et al.* (eds), *The Treaty of Versailles: A Reassessment after Seventy-Five Years*, Cambridge, 1998, pp. 371–400.

Goldman, A. L., "Sir Robert Vansittart's search for Italian cooperation against Hitler," *Journal of Contemporary History*, vol. 9, no. 3, 1974, pp. 93–130.

—— "Two views of Germany: Nevile Henderson *vs* Vansittart and the foreign office, 1937–39," *British Journal of International Studies*, vol. 6, 1980, pp. 247–77.

Goldstein, Erik, "The evolution of British diplomatic strategy for the Locarno Pact, 1924–1925," in Michael Dockrill and Brian McKercher (eds), *Diplomacy and World Power: Studies in British Foreign Policy, 1890–1950*, New York, 1996, pp. 115–35.

Gorodetsky, Gabriel, "The impact of the Ribbentrop–Molotov pact on the course of Soviet foreign policy," *Cahiers du Monde Russe et Soviétique*, vol. 31, 1990. pp. 27–42.

Greenwood, Sean, "Caligula's horse revisited: Sir Thomas Inskip as minister for the co-ordination of defence. 1936–39," *Journal of Strategic Studies*, vol. 17, 1994, pp. 17–38.

Gruner, Wolf D., "The British political, social and economic system and the decision for peace and war: reflections on Anglo-German relations 1800–1939," *British Journal of International Studies*, vol. 6, 1980, pp. 189–218.

Hahn, Erich C. J., "The German foreign ministry and the question of war guilt in 1918–1919," in Carole Fink *et al.* (eds) *German Nationalism and the European Response, 1890–1945*, Norman, OK, 1985.

Hatano Sumio, "Japan's foreign policy, 1931–1945: historiography," in Sadao Asada, *Japan and the World, 1853–1952: A Bibliographic Guide to Japanese Scholarship in Foreign Relations*, New York, 1989, pp. 218–33.

Hatheway, J., "The pre-1920s origin of the National Socialist German Workers' Party," *Journal of Contemporary History*, vol. 29, 1994, pp. 448–53.

Hauner, Milan, "Did Hitler want a world dominion?," *Journal of Contemporary History*, vol. 13, 1978, pp.15–32.

—— "Czechoslovakia as a military factor in British considerations of 1938," *Journal of Strategic Studies*, vol. 1, 1978, pp.194–222.

Heinrichs, Waldo H., Jr, "1931–1937," in Warren I. Cohen (ed.), *New Frontiers in American–East Asian Relations: Essays Presented to Dorothy Borg*, New York, 1983, pp. 243–59.

—— "The middle years, 1900–1945, and the question of a large US policy on east Asia," in Warren I. Cohen (ed.), *New Frontiers in American–East Asian Relations: Essays Presented to Dorothy Borg*, New York, 1983, pp. 77–106.

Herndon, James H., "British perceptions of Soviet military capability, 1935–9," in Wolfgang J. Mommsen and Lothar Kettenacker (eds), *The Fascist Challenge and the Policy of Appeasement*, London, 1983, pp. 297–319.

Hogenhuis-Seliverstoff, Anne, "French plans for the reconstruction of Russia: a history and evaluation," in Carole Fink *et al.* (eds), *Genoa, Rapallo, and European Reconstruction in 1922*, Washington, DC, 1991.

Holtfrerich, Karl-Ludwig, "Internationale Verteilungsfolgen der deutschen Inflation, 1918–1923," *Kyklos*, vol. 30, 1977/8, pp. 271–91.

Iriye Akira, "Americanization of east Asia: writings on cultural affairs since 1900," in Warren I. Cohen (ed.), *New Frontiers in American–East Asian Relations: Essays Presented to Dorothy Borg*, New York, 1983, pp. 45–76.

—— "The Asian factor," in Gordon Martel (ed.), *The Origins of the Second World War Reconsidered: The A. J. P. Taylor Debate After Twenty-five Years*, Boston, MA, 1986, pp. 227–43.

Irvine, William D., "Domestic politics and the fall of France in 1940," *Historical Reflections/Réflexions Historiques*, vol. 22, 1996, pp. 77–90.

Jackson, Peter, "France and the guarantee to Romania, April 1939," *Intelligence and National Security*, vol. 10, 1995, pp. 242–72.

Jacobson, Jon, "Is there a new international history of the 1920s?," *American Historical Review*, vol. 88, 1983, pp. 617–46.

—— "Strategies of French foreign policy after World War I," *Journal of Modern History*, vol. 55, 1983, pp. 78–95.

—— "The Soviet Union and Versailles," in Manfred F. Boemeke *et al.* (eds), *The Treaty of Versailles: A Reassessment after Seventy-Five Years*, Cambridge, 1998, pp. 451–68.

Jordan, Nicole, "Maurice Gamelin, Italy and the eastern alliances," *Journal of Strategic Studies*, vol. 14, 1991, pp. 428–41.

Jukes, G., "The Red Army and the Munich crisis," *Journal of Contemporary History*, vol. 26, 1991, pp. 195–214.

Kaiser, David, T. Mason, and R. J. Overy, "Debate: Germany, 'domestic crisis' and war in 1939," *Past & Present*, no. 122, 1989, pp. 205–40

—— "Hitler and the coming of war," in Gordon Martel (ed.), *Modern Germany Reconsidered, 1870–1945*, London, 1992, pp. 178–96.

Kasza, Gregory, "Fascism from below? A comparative perspective on the Japanese Right, 1931–1936," *Journal of Contemporary History*, vol. 19, 1984, pp. 607–30.

Keeton, Edward D., "Economics and politics in Briand's German policy, 1925–1931," in Carole Fink, *et al.* (eds), *German Nationalism and the European Response, 1890–1945*, London, 1985, pp. 157–80.

Kennedy, P., "Idealists and realists: British views of Germany, 1864–1939," *Transactions of the Royal Historical Society*, series 5, vol. 25, 1975, pp. 135–56.

—— "The tradition of appeasement in British foreign policy, 1865–1939," *British Journal of International Studies*, vol. 2, 1976, pp. 195–215.

—— "Appeasement and British defence policy in the inter-war years," *British Journal of International Studies*, vol. 4, 1978, pp. 161–77.

—— "Strategy versus diplomacy in twentieth-century Britain' *International History Review*, vol. 3, 1981, pp. 45–61.

Kettenacker, L., "Die Diplomatie der Ohnmacht," in Wolfgang Benz and H. Graml (eds), *Sommer 1939. Die Grossmachte und der Europaische Krieg*, Stuttgart, 1979, pp. 223–79.

Klein, Fritz, "Between Compiègne and Versailles: the Germans on the way from a misunderstood defeat to an unwanted peace," in Manfred F. Boemeke *et al.* (eds), *The Treaty of Versailles: A Reassessment after Seventy-Five Years*, Cambridge, 1998, pp. 203–20.

Knox, MacGregor, "Conquest, foreign and domestic, in Fascist Italy and Nazi Germany," *Journal of Modern History*, vol. 56, 1984, pp. 1–57.

—— "Il fascismo e la politica estera italiana," in R. J. B. Bosworth and Sergio Romano (eds), *La politica estera italiana (1860–1985)*, Bologna, 1991, pp. 287–330.

—— "The Fascist regime, its foreign policy and its wars: An anti-Fascist orthodoxy?', *Contemporary European History*, vol. 4, 1995, 347–65.

Koch, H., "Hitler's 'programme' and the genesis of Operation 'Barbarossa' ", *Historical Journal*, vol. 26, 1983, pp. 891–920.

Krüger, Peter, "A rainy day, April 16, 1922: the Rapallo Treaty and the cloudy perspective for German foreign policy," in Carole Fink *et al.* (eds), *Genoa, Rapallo, and European Reconstruction in 1922*, Washington, DC, 1991, pp. 49–64.

Laffan, M., "Weimar and Versailles," in M. Laffan (ed.), *The Burden of German History, 1919–1945*, London, 1988, pp. 91–9.

Lammers, Donald N., "The May crisis of 1938: The Soviet view considered," *South Atlantic Quarterly*, vol. 69, 1970, pp. 480–503.

Ledeen, M., "Renzo De Felice and the controversy over Italian Fascism," *Journal of Contemporary History*, vol. 11, 1976, pp. 269–82.

Leffler, Melvyn P., "The origins of Republican war debt policy, 1921–1923," *Journal of American History*, vol. 59, 1972, pp. 585–601.

Lukowitz, D., "British pacifists and appeasement," *Journal of Contemporary History*, vol. 9, 1974, pp. 115–28.

MacDonald, Callum A., "Britain, France and the April crisis of 1939," *European Studies Review*, vol. 2, 1972, pp. 151–69.

—— "Radio Bari and Italian propaganda in the middle east and British counter measures, 1934–1938," *Middle Eastern Studies*, vol. 13, 1977, pp. 195–207.

Manne, Robert, "The British decision for alliance with Russia, May 1939," *Journal of Contemporary History*, vol. 9, 1974, pp. 3–26.

—— "Some British light on the Nazi–Soviet pact," *European Studies Review*, vol. 11, 1981, pp. 83–102.

Marder, A. J., "The Royal Navy and the Ethiopian crisis of 1935–36," *American Historical Review*, vol. 75, 1970, pp. 1327–56.

Marks, Sally, "German–American relations, 1918–1921," *Mid-America*, vol. 53, 1971, pp. 211–26.

—— "Mussolini and Locarno: Fascist foreign policy in microcosm," *Journal of Contemporary History*, vol. 14, 1979, pp. 423–39.

—— "Ménage à trois: the negotiations for an Anglo-French-Belgian alliance in 1922," *International History Review*, vol. 4, 1982, pp. 524–52.

—— "Mésentente cordiale," in Marta Petricioli (ed.), *A Missed Opportunity? 1922: The Reconstruction of Europe*, Bern, 1995, pp. 33–45.

—— "Smoke and mirrors: in smoke-filled rooms and the Galerie des Glaces," in Manfred F. Boemeke *et al.* (eds), *The Treaty of Versailles: A Reassessment after Seventy-Five Years*, Cambridge, 1998, pp. 337–70.

Martel, Gordon, "The meaning of power: rethinking the decline and fall of Great Britain," *International History Review*, vol. 13, 1991, pp. 662–94.

—— "The prehistory of appeasement: Headlam-Morley, the peace settlement and revisionism," *Diplomacy and Statecraft*, vol. 9, 1998, pp. 242–65.

—— "Reflections on the war-guilt question and the settlement: A comment," in Manfred F. Boemeke *et al.* (eds), *The Treaty of Versailles: A Reassessment after Seventy-Five Years*, Cambridge, 1998, pp. 615–36.

—— "Military planning and the origins of the Second World War," in Brian McKercher and Michael Hennessy (eds), *Military Planning and the Origins of the Second World War*, Westport, CT, 1999, pp. 1–28.

Mason, T. M., "Some origins of the Second World War," *Past & Present*, no. 29, 1964, pp. 67–87.

May, Ernest R., "Military and naval affairs since 1900," Warren I. Cohen (ed.), *New Frontiers in American–East Asian Relations: Essays Presented to Dorothy Borg*, New York, 1983, pp. 107–28.

McCormack, Gavan, "Nineteen-thirties Japan: fascism?" *Bulletin of Concerned Asian Scholars*, vol. 14, 1982, pp. 20–33.

McKercher, Brian, "Reaching for the brass ring," *Diplomatic History*, vol. 15, 1991, pp. 565–98.

Meyers, R., "Britain, Europe and the dominions in the 1930s," *Australian Journal of Politics and History*, vol. 22, 1976, pp. 36–50.

Michaelis, M., "World power status or world dominion?" *Historical Journal*, vol. 15, 1972, pp. 345–59.

Mierzejewski, Alfred C., "Payments and profits: the German National Railway Company and reparations, 1924–1932," *German Studies Review*, vol. 18, 1995, pp. 65–86.

Minardi, Salvatore, "Mussolini, Laval e il désistement della Francia in Etiopia," *Clio*, vol. 22, 1986, pp. 77–107.

—— "L'accordo militare segreto Badoglio–Gamelin del 1935," *Clio*, vol. 23, 1987, pp. 271–300.

Minniti, Fortunato, "L'ipotesi più sfavorevole. Una pianificazione operativa italiana tra strategia militare e politica estera (1927–1933)," *Nuova Rivista Storica*, vol. 79, 1995, pp. 613–50.

Mori, Renato, "Delle cause dell impresa etiopica mussoliniana," *Storia e politica*, vol. 17, 1978, pp. 689–706.

Morton, Louis, "1937–1941," in Warren I. Cohen (ed.), *New Frontiers in American–East Asian Relations: Essays Presented to Dorothy Borg*, New York, 1983, pp. 260–90.

Murray, Williamson, "The collapse of empire: British strategy, 1919–1945," in Williamson Murray *et al.* (eds), *The Making of Strategy: Rulers, States, and War*, New York, 1994, pp. 393–427.

Neary, Ian, "Tenkô of an organization: the Suiheisha in the late 1930s," *Proceedings of the British Association for Japanese Studies*, vol. 2, 1977, pp. 64–76.

Niedhart, Gottfried, "British attitudes and policies towards the Soviet Union and International Communism, 1933–9," in Wolfgang J. Mommsen and Lothar Kettenacker (eds), *The Fascist Challenge and the Policy of Appeasement*, London, 1983, pp. 286–96.

—— "The problem of war in German politics in 1938," *War and Society*, vol. 2, 1984.

Ormos, Maria, "L'opinione del conte Stefano Bethlen sui rapporti italo–ungheresi, 1927–1931," *Storia contemporanea*, vol. 2, 1971, pp. 283–314.

Overy, R. J., "German air strength, 1933 to 1939," *Historical Journal*, vol. 27, 1984, pp. 465–71.

Palumbo, M., "Goering's Italian exile," *Journal of Modern History*, vol. 50, 1978, no. 1 D1035.

Parker, R. A. C., "The British government and the coming of war with Germany, 1939," in *War and Society*, M. R. D. Foot (ed.), London, 1973, pp. 3–15.

—— "Perceptions de la puissance par les décideurs britanniques, 1938–1939: le cabinet," in René Girault and Robert Frank (eds), *La Puissance en Europe, 1938–1940*, Paris, 1984, pp. 45–54.

—— "British rearmament, 1936–9: treasury, trades unions and skilled labour," *English Historical Review*, vol. 96, 1981, pp. 306–43.

Petrov, Vladimir, "A missing page in Soviet historiography: the Nazi–Soviet partnership," *Orbis*, vol. 11, 1968, pp. 1113–37.

Pithon, Rémy, "Opinions publiques et representations culturelles face aux problèmes de la puissance. Le témoignage du cinéma français, 1938–1939," *Relations Internationales*, no. 33, 1983, pp. 91–101.

Prazmowska, A. J., "Poland's foreign policy: September 1938–September 1939," *Historical Journal,*, vol. 29, 1986, pp. 853–74.

Preston, Paul, "The creation of the Popular Front in Spain," in Helen Graham and Paul Preston (eds), *The Popular Front in Europe*, London, 1987.

Quarteraro, Rosario, "Imperial defence in the Mediterranean on the eve of the Ethiopian crisis (July–October 1935)," *Historical Journal*, vol. 56, 1984, pp. 1–57.

Rader, Ronald R., "Anglo-French estimates of the Red Army, 1936–1937," *Soviet Armed Forces Annual*, vol. 3, 1979, pp. 265–80.

Répaci, Francesco A., "Le spese delle guerre condotte dall Italia nel ultimo quarantacinquennio, 1913/14–1957/58," *Rivista di politica economica*, vol. 50, 1960, pp. 695–713.

Rhodes, B. D., "Reassessing Uncle Shylock," *Journal of American History*, vol. 55, 1969, pp. 783–803.

Rice, Richard, "Economic mobilization in wartime Japan: business, bureaucracy, and military in conflict," *Journal of Asian Studies*, vol. 38, 1979, pp. 689–706.

Roberts, Geoffrey, "Infamous encounter? The Merekalov–Weizsäcker meeting of 17 April 1939," *Historical Journal*, vol. 35, 1992, pp. 921–6.

—— "The fall of Litvinov: a revisionist view," *Journal of Contemporary History*, vol. 27, 1992, pp. 639–57.

—— "A Soviet bid for coexistence with Nazi Germany, 1935–1937: the Kandelaki affair," *The International History Review*, vol. 16, 1994, pp. 94–101.

Roi, M. L., "From the Stresa Front to the Triple Entente: Sir Robert Vansittart, the Abyssinian crisis and the containment of Germany," *Diplomacy & Statecraft*, vol. 6, 1995, pp. 61–90.

Rollet, H., "Deux mythes des relations franco-polonaises entre les deux guerres," *Revue d'histoire diplomatique*, no. 96, 1982, pp. 225–48.

Ryan, Stephen, "Reflections on the psychohistory of France, 1919–1940," *Journal of Psychohistory*, vol. 2, 1983, pp. 225–41.

Salerno, Reynolds, "Multilateral strategy and diplomacy: the Anglo-German naval agreement and the Mediterranean crisis, 1935–1936," *Journal of Strategic Studies*, vol. 17, 1994, pp. 56–63.

Sauvée-Dauphin, N., "L'occupation prussienne à Versailles," in P. Levillain and R. Riemenschneider (eds), *La guerre de 1870/71 et ses conséquences*, Bonn, 1990.

Sbacchi, Alberto, "Italian mandate of protectorate over Ethiopia, 1935–36," *Rivista di studi politici internazionali*, vol. 42, 1975, pp. 559–92.

—— "The price of empire: toward an enumeration of of Italian casualties in Ethiopia, 1935–40," in Alberto Sbacchi (ed.), *Legacy of Bitterness. Ethiopia and Fascist Italy, 1935–1941*, Lawrenceville, NJ, 1997, pp. 87–101.

—— "Italian colonization in Ethiopia: promises, plans and projects, 1936–1940," in Alberto Sbacchi (ed.), *Legacy of Bitterness. Ethiopia and Fascist Italy, 1935–1941*, Lawrenceville, NJ, 1997, pp. 103–22.

Schroeder, P. W., "Munich and the British tradition," *Historical Journal*, vol. 19, 1976, pp. 223–44.

Schuker, Stephen A. "Frankreich und die Weimarer Republik," in M. Stürmer, (ed.), *Die Weimarer Republik*, Königstein, 1980, pp. 93–112.

—— "Origins of American stabilization policy in Europe, 1918–1924," in H.-J. Schröder (ed.), *Confrontation and Cooperation*, Providence, RI, 1993, pp. 377–407.

—— "Europe's banker: the American banking community and European reconstruction, 1918–1922," in Marta Petricioli (ed.), *A Missed Opportunity? 1922: The Reconstruction of Europe*, Bern, 1995, pp. 47–60.

—— "The Rhineland question: west European security at the Paris peace conference of 1919," in Manfred F. Boemeke *et al.* (eds), *The Treaty of Versailles: A Reassessment after Seventy-Five Years*, Cambridge, 1998, pp. 275–312.

Schwabe, Klaus, "Germany's peace aims and the domestic and international constraints," in Manfred F. Boemeke *et al.* (eds), *The Treaty of Versailles: A Reassessment after Seventy-Five Years*, Cambridge, 1998, pp. 37–68.

Sellin, Christine, "Les manuels scholaires et la puissance française," *Relations Internationales*, no. 33, 1983, pp. 103–11.

Semiriaga, M. I.," 'Kruglyi stol': vtoraia mirovaia voina–istoki i prichiny," *Voprosy istorii*, 1988, no. 12, pp. 3–46.

Senn, Alfred E., "Perestroika in Lithuanian historiography: the Molotov–Ribbentrop pact," *The Russian Review*, vol. 49, 1990, pp. 43–56.

Serra, Enrico, "La questione italo-etiopica alla conferenza di Stresa," *Affari Esteri*, vol. 9, 1977, pp. 313–39.

—— "Dalle trattive sul confine meridionale della Libia al baratto sull Ethiopia," *Nuova Antologia*, no. 542, 1980, pp. 164–74.

Seton Watson, Christopher, "The Anglo-Italian Gentleman's Agreement of January 1937," in Wolfgang J. Mommsen and Lothar Kettenacker (eds), *The Fascist Challenge and the Policy of Appeasement*, London, 1983, pp. 266–82.

Shillony, Ben-Ami, "Japanese intellectuals during the Pacific War," *Proceedings of the British Association for Japanese Studies*, vol. 2, 1977, pp. 90–9.

Sontag, John P., "The Soviet war scare of 1926–27," *Russian Review*, vol. 34, 1975, pp. 66–77.

Soutou, G., "Problèmes concernant le rétablissment des relations économiques franco-allemandes après la première guerre mondiale," *Francia*, vol. 2, 1974, pp. 580–96.

—— "Die deutschen Reparationen und das Seydoux-Projekt 1920–21," in *Vierteljahrshefte für Zeitgeschichte*, vol. 23, 1975, pp. 237–70.

Spaulding, Robert Mark, "The political economy of German frontiers, 1918, 1945, 1990," in Christian Baechler and Carole Fink (eds), *The Establishment of European Frontiers after the Two World Wars*, Bern, 1996, pp. 229–48.

Stafford, P. R., "The Chamberlain–Halifax visit to Rome: a reappraisal," *English Historical Review*, vol. 98, 1983, pp. 61–100.

—— "The French government and the Danzig crisis: The Italian dimension," *International History Review*, vol. 6, 1984, pp. 48–87.

Steinbach, P., "The conservative resistance," in D. C. Large (ed.), *Contending with Hitler: Varieties of Resistance in the Third Reich*, Washington, DC, 1991, pp. 89–98.

Steinhoff, Patricia G., "Tenkô and thought control," in Gail Lee Bernstein and Harahiro Fukui, (eds), *Japan and the World: Essays on Japanese History and Politics in Honour of Ishida Takeshi*, London, 1988, pp. 78–94.

Stern, W. M., "Wehrwirtschaft: a German contribution to economics," *Economic History Review*, series 2, vol. 13, 1960–1, pp. 270–81.

Stevenson, David, "The empty chair at the peace conference: Russia and the west," in William R. Keylor (ed.), *The Legacy of the Great War: The Peace Settlement of 1919 and its Consequences*, Boston, MA, 1997, pp. 56–61.

Strang, G. Bruce, "Once more unto the breach: Britain's guarantee to Poland, March 1939," *Journal of Contemporary History*, vol. 31, 1996, pp. 721–51.

Sullivan, Brian R., "The Italian armed forces, 1918–1940," in A. R. Millett and W. Murray (eds), *Military Effectiveness*, vol. 2: *The Interwar Period*, Boston, MA, 1988, pp. 169–217.

—— "The impatient cat: assessments of military power in Fascist Italy, 1936–1940," in W. Murray and A. R. Millett (eds), *Calculations. Net Assessment and the Coming of World War II*, New York, 1992, pp. 112–35.

—— "The Italian–Ethiopian War, October 1935–November 1941: causes, conduct, and consequences," in A. Hamish Ion and E. J. Errington (eds), *Great Powers and Little Wars. The Limits of Power*, Westport, CT, 1993, pp. 167–202.

—— "The strategy of the decisive weight: Italy, 1882–1922," in Williamson Murray, MacGregor Knox, and Alvin Bernstein (eds), *The Making of Strategy. Rulers, States, and War*, New York, 1994, pp. 343–51.

—— "Fascist Italian involvement in the Spanish Civil War," *The Journal of Military History*, vol. 59 1995, pp. 697–727.

——— "From little brother to senior partner: Fascist Italian perceptions of the Nazis and of Hitler's regime, 1930–1936," *Intelligence and National Security*, vol. 13, 1998, pp. 85–108.

Thimme, Annelise, "Stresemann and Locarno," in Hans W. Gatzke (ed.), *European Diplomacy Between Two Wars, 1919–1939*, Chicago, IL, 1972, pp. 77–93.

Toepfer, Marcia Lynn, "The Soviet role in the Munich crisis: A historiographical debate," *Diplomatic History*, vol. 1, 1977, pp. 341–57.

Tucker, Robert C., "Stalin, Bukharin and history as conspiracy," in Robert C. Tucker and Stephen F. Cohen (eds), *The Great Purge Trial*, New York, 1965, pp. ix–xlviii.

——— "The emergence of Stalin's foreign policy," *Slavic Review*, vol. 36, 1977, pp. 563–89.

Uldricks, Teddy J., "Stalin and Nazi Germany," *Slavic Review*, vol. 36, 1977, pp. 599–603.

——— "The impact of the great purges on the people's commissariat of foreign affairs," *Slavic Review*, vol. 36, 1977, pp. 187–204.

——— "Russia and Europe: diplomacy, revolution, and economic development in the 1920s," *International History Review*, vol. 1, 1979, pp. 55–83.

——— "Evolving Soviet views of the Nazi–Soviet pact," in Richard Frucht (ed.), *Labyrinth of Nationalism / Complexities of Diplomacy*, Columbus, OH, 1992, pp. 331–60.

——— "Soviet security policy in the 1930s," in G. Gorodetsky (ed.), *Soviet Foreign Policy*, London, 1994, pp. 65–74.

Vaïsse, Maurice, "Against appeasement: French advocates of firmness, 1933–1938," in Wolfgang J. Mommsen and Lothar Kettenacker (eds), *The Fascist Challenge and the Policy of Appeasement*, London, 1983, pp. 227–35.

——— "Le pacifisme français dans les années trente," *Relations Internationales*, no. 53, 1988, pp. 37–52.

Vincent, J., "Chamberlain, the Liberals and the outbreak of war, 1939," *English Historical Review*, vol. 113, 1998, pp. 367–83

Volkmann, H.-E., "Aspekte der nationalsozialistischen 'Wehrwirtschaft' 1933 bis 1936," *Francia*, vol. 5, 1977, pp. 513–38.

Volkogonov, D. A., "Drama reshenii 1939 goda," *Novaia i noveishaia istoriia*, no. 4, 1989, pp. 3–27.

Waddington, G. T., "Hitler, Von Ribbentrop, die NSDAP und der Niedergang des Britischen Empire 1935–1938," *Vierteljahrshefte für Zeitgeschichte*, vol. 40, 1992, pp. 273–306.

Walker, Stephen G., "Solving the appeasement puzzle: contending historical interpretations of British diplomacy during the 1930s," *British Journal of International Studies*, vol. 6, 1980, pp. 219–46.

Wark, W. K., "British military and economic intelligence: assessments of Nazi Germany before the Second World War," in C. M. Andrews and D. Dilks (eds), *The Missing Dimension: Governments and Intelligence Communities in the Twentieth Century*, London, 1984, pp. 78–100.

——— "Something very stern: British political intelligence, moralism and grand strategy in 1939," *Intelligence and National Security*, vol. 5, 1990, pp. 150–70.

Watt, D. Cameron, "The Anglo-German naval agreement of 1935," *Journal of Modern History*, vol. 28, 1956, pp. 155–75.

——— "The Secret Laval–Mussolini agreement of 1935 on Ethiopia," *The Middle East Journal*, vol. 15 1961, pp. 69–78.

——— "Appeasement, the rise of a revisionist school?," *Political Quarterly*, vol. 36, 1965, pp. 191–213.

——— "The historiography of appeasement," in A. Sked and C. Cook (eds), *Crisis and Controversy*, London, 1976, pp. 110–29.

—— "Misfortune, misconception, mistrust: episodes in British policy and the approach of war, 1938–1939," in M. Bentley and J. Stevenson (eds), *High and Low Politics in Modern Britain*, Oxford, 1983, pp. 214–54.

—— "British intelligence and the coming of the Second World War in Europe," in Ernest R. May (ed.), *Knowing One's Enemies: Intelligence Assessment Before the Two World Wars*, Princeton, NJ, 1984, pp. 237–70.

—— "Chamberlain's ambassadors," in Michael Dockrill and Brian McKercher (eds), *Diplomacy and World Power: Studies in British Foreign Policy, 1890–1950*, Cambridge, 1996, pp. 145–54.

Index